140°
150°
10°
20°
30°
160°
Cape York
63
Weipa
Groote Eylandt
31
GULF OF CARPENTARIA
47
CAPE YORK PENINSULA
Wellesley Islands
31
EAT BARRIER REEF
94
63
47
PACIFIC OCEAN
LY TABLELAND
Y
Mary Kathleen
Mount Isa
ow Creek
CENTRAL QUEENSLAND
GREAT DIVIDING RANGE
47
Springs
MPSON
ESERT
Mount Morgan
EASTERN GREAT ARTESIAN BASIN
GREY RANGE
47
Fraser Island
4
Cooper's Creek
Eyre
ow
evel)
Brisbane
24
31
STRALIA
LOWLANDS
16
63
Darling River
Lake Torrens
FLINDERS RANGES
63
Broken Hill
Whyalla
63
NEW SOUTH WALES
TASMAN SEA
Spencer Gulf
Murray R.
Lachlan River
47
Murrumbidgee River
Adelaide
Sydney
Gulf St. Vincent
Island
MURRAY BASIN
Murray River
Canberra
AUSTRALIAN CAPITAL TERRITORY
24
VICTORIA
Melbourne
AUSTRALIAN ALPS
31
31
31
Port Phillip Bay
BASS STRAIT
King Island
147°
Furneaux Group
41°
31
TASMANIA
63
24
47
31
Hobart

D0849212

INSIDE AUSTRALIA

A Cassell BOOK

Books by John Gunther

Public Affairs

Inside Europe
(First published 1936, repeatedly revised and republished)
Inside Asia
(First published 1939, revised 1942)
Inside Latin America
Inside U.S.A.
(First published 1947, revised 1951)
Inside Africa
Inside Russia Today
Inside Europe Today
(First published 1961, revised and republished 1962)
Inside South America

Biography

Death Be Not Proud
Roosevelt in Retrospect
The Riddle of MacArthur
Eisenhower: The Man and the Symbol
Taken at the Flood: The Story of Albert D. Lasker
Procession

Autobiography

A Fragment of Autobiography: The Fun of Writing the *Inside* Books

Novels

The Red Pavilion
Peter Lancelot
The Golden Fleece
The Bright Nemesis
The Troubled Midnight
The Lost City
The Indian Sign

Reporting

The High Cost of Hitler
D Day
Behind the Curtain

Miscellaneous

Days to Remember
(With Bernard Quint)
Chicago Revisited

Juveniles

Alexander the Great
Julius Caesar
The Golden Fleece
Meet North Africa
(With Sam and Beryl Epstein)
Meet South Africa
(With Sam and Beryl Epstein)
Meet the Congo and Its Neighbors
Meet Soviet Russia
(Two volumes)

Travel

Twelve Cities

JOHN GUNTHER'S

INSIDE AUSTRALIA

COMPLETED AND EDITED

BY

William H. Forbis

1817

HARPER & ROW, PUBLISHERS

NEW YORK, EVANSTON, SAN FRANCISCO
LONDON

Maps by Jean Paul Tremblay

JOHN GUNTHER'S INSIDE AUSTRALIA. Copyright © 1972 by Jane Perry Gunther. All rights reserved. Printed in the United States of America. No part of this book may be used or reproduced in any manner whatsoever without written permission except in the case of brief quotations embodied in critical articles and reviews. For information address Harper & Row, Publishers, Inc., 49 East 33rd Street, New York, N.Y. 10016. Published simultaneously in Canada by Fitzhenry & Whiteside Limited, Toronto.

FIRST EDITION

STANDARD BOOK NUMBER: 06-011661-7

LIBRARY OF CONGRESS CATALOG CARD NUMBER: 70-181625

Contents

A Note on How This Book Was Written ix

1. The Australasian Texture 1
2. The Continent That Nature Left Unfinished 6
3. From Convict Colony to Commonwealth 18
4. The Lucky Country 33
5. Australian Rules—And Other Arts 51
6. Aborigines I: Sophisticated Savages 66
7. Aborigines II: Their Role Today 79
8. Labor Versus Liberals 90
9. Who Owns Australia? 112
10. Sydney and New South Wales 127
11. Canberra 146
12. Melbourne and Victoria 157
13. Inside Tasmania 175
14. Adelaide and South Australia 186
15. El Dorado in Western Australia 203
16. Across the Blazing North 216
17. Darwin and Alice Springs 222

18. The Splendid Entity of Queensland 230
19. New Guinea: Men and Wigs, Women and Pigs 243
20. Niugini: The Future Nation 264
21. New Zealand: High Alps and Walking Birds 284
22. New Zealand: Pakeha and Maori 301
23. New Zealand: Politics, Grass, and Potters 320
24. How Australasia Fits with Asia 335
25. Some Thoughts in Conclusion 346

Acknowledgments and Bibliography 351
Index 359

MAPS

Australia and the South Pacific vii
Australia—Major Physical Features xii-xiii
Southeast Australia, New Zealand, and *New Guinea* 128-129

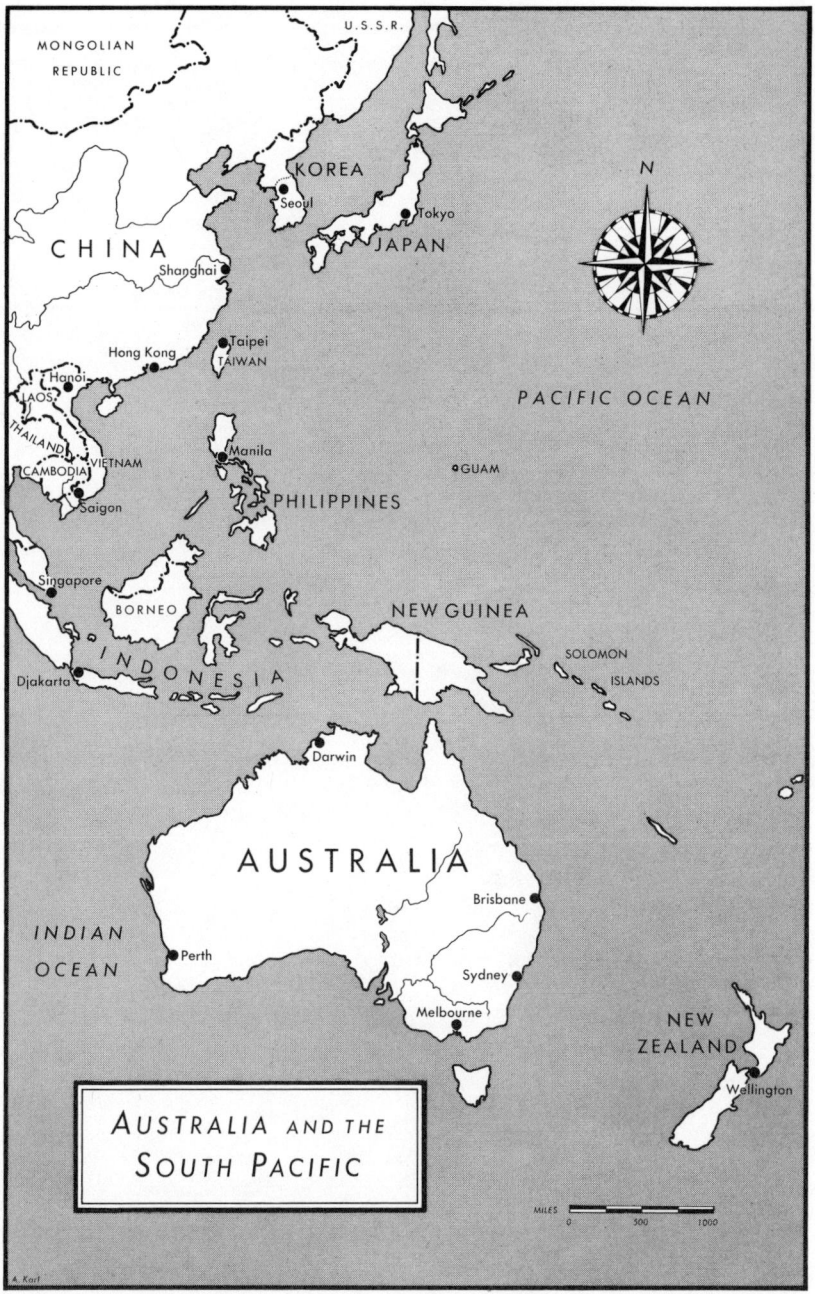

AUSTRALIA AND THE SOUTH PACIFIC

A Note on How This Book Was Written

DURING the five months he spent in and around Australia, John Gunther traveled everywhere, from a Sepik River village in New Guinea to the capital of each Australian state and to both the islands of New Zealand. This was in late 1969 and through January 1970, after which he returned to New York to start writing this book. As in the case of his other *Inside* books, he did not write straight through from beginning to end; it caught his fancy to commence the job by doing some of the middle passages. I never knew Gunther personally, but from what he had written it was obvious that he was attacking this project with the buoyancy and zest that characterized his other work. Suddenly, at the end of May 1970, Gunther became ill and went to the hospital. Within a week, he was dead, of a cancer that neither he nor anyone else knew he had.

His totally unexpected death left the book well begun but far from finished, and some decision had to be made about its fate. Could it, and should it, be completed at all? The assets of the project were ample: forty thick notebooks containing Gunther's interviews and observations, innumerable notes on scraps of paper (his repository for stray thoughts), documentation in the form of 150 books that Gunther had collected, mountains of clips from his well-stocked personal morgue—much of this sorted and marked—and curious memorabilia right down to the annual report of the New Zealand Cooperative Dairy Company Limited. In boxes filled with colored folders there were letters, Xeroxes, menus, photographs, briefing papers. And of course there were the chapters Gunther had written, his outline of the whole book, and, for guidance, his own book *A Fragment of Autobiography*, which describes how he put his books together. An indispensable further asset was John's wife Jane. She had been with him on the Australia–New Zealand trip, taking part in every interview, and sharing observations with him when they returned to their hotel rooms, just as she had during their trips through other continents. She had a very specific insight into what he intended to make of the book, and was anxious to work with someone on it.

It was decided to find a writer to undertake the task. One morning in July 1970, the telephone rang in my house in Missoula, Montana, where I was living a life of sportive idleness after twenty years of work as a writer, senior editor, and correspondent for *Time* magazine. The caller was Cass Canfield, Senior Editor of Harper & Row, who had heard of me from Richard Clurman, a vice president of Time Inc. and a long-time friend of mine. Acting on Canfield's suggestion, I went to Greensboro, Vermont, where Jane Gunther has a summer house. I was strongly attracted to the job of completing the book. I admired Gunther's earlier books, particularly the one on South America; I covered that continent for *Time* for several years, and found, upon starting the assignment, that Gunther's book offered useful studies of the nine countries I had to deal with. Moreover, the thought of learning and writing about Australia and New Zealand, places that have a strong hold on the American imagination, intrigued me. It seemed to me to be a worthwhile project, much needed by many thousands of readers. While Jane Gunther was deciding that I could satisfactorily finish the book, I was deciding that the arrangement was feasible.

Soon several hundred pounds of documentation for the book arrived at the Missoula airport, and I set about completing it on the Gunther outline, with a few modifications. I also then visited Australia and New Zealand for a period of time that would have been far too short had not the reporting and interviewing for the book already been done by Gunther. The purpose of my trip was simply to get a better feel for the subject, to acquire a framework for understanding Gunther's notes, and to hear the speech and sounds of the two countries.

While I was completing the book based on Gunther's original work, and my own impressions and research, I was frequently pleased to find that whenever I needed a specific example or fact or even transition, a Gunther note would turn up to supply it. Indeed, when Australia changed Prime Ministers halfway through the writing, Gunther's notes produced an interview that he had had with the man who became the new Prime Minister. I gradually evolved a form and style for this double-authored book. For example, I at first left untouched the passages that Gunther had written in the first person, and even sometimes added an "I"—meaning Gunther—when it seemed to flow naturally and directly out of his notes. But later I thought that this made the book sound sporadic and inconsistent, and on revision I expunged all the "I's" from the completed text. As to the book's exposition in general, I believe that I share Gunther's respect for facts, his yearning to tell them interestingly, his sense of curiosity and wonder, and his desire to be lucid. Gunther welcomed, and made use of, every fact of interest that he came across (even if the source was only a railroad timetable), though he used facts with discretion and only after rigorous checking. I tried to do the same. I made no effort to "write like Gunther," apart from adopting a few of his stylistic trademarks, using passages from his notes and relying on his methods. I like to think that the book has turned out somewhat as Gunther would have written it. Gunther was a generalist who, without apology, took the whole world as his subject, believing that specialists give too little of the spectrum to satisfy most of us; I tried to apply that principle to Australia and New Zealand. Like all the *Inside* books, this is for the reader who, knowing a little about those two countries, wants to know a thousand times more.

John Gunther's notes for this Preface observe that this is "the eighth *Inside* book (or is it the ninth?)." It is the ninth, but Gunther was in too much of a hurry to get into a new book to bother to sit down and count old ones. He wanted to bring out the "fascination and importance of Australia," and thought that "New Zealand should be of particular interest because no contemporary book exists covering it as I do." Let me add that both Gunther and I found the two countries highly agreeable, even though the reader may find some critical passages. Acknowledgments of the book's numerous debts will be found at the end, but here I wish to pay special tribute to the beautiful, discriminating, observant, cooperative, and sensitive Jane Gunther (who hates strings of adjectives). She gave me help and criticism from beginning to end, increasing the book's accuracy, clarity, relevance, and directness.

WILLIAM H. FORBIS

AUSTRALIA
Major Physical Features

J. P. TREMBLAY

140°
150°
10°
20°
30°
160°
Cape York
Weipa
Groote Eylandt
GULF OF CARPENTARIA
CAPE YORK PENINSULA
CORAL SEA
PACIFIC OCEAN
GREAT BARRIER REEF
Wellesley Islands
Mary Kathleen
Mount Isa
QUEENSLAND
EASTERN HIGHLANDS
GREAT ARTESTAN BASIN
LOWLANDS
Mount Morgan
Fraser Island
Brisbane
Cooper's Creek
Darling River
Lake Torrens
Broken Hill
Whyalla
Spencer Gulf
Gulf St Vincent
Adelaide
Murray R.
Lachlan River
Murrumbidgee River
Murray River
MURRAY BASIN
NEW SOUTH WALES
Sydney
TASMAN SEA
Canberra
AUSTRALIAN CAPITAL TERRITORY
VICTORIA
Melbourne
Port Phillip Bay
BASS STRAIT
King Island
Furneaux Group
TASMANIA
Hobart
63
47
31
94
24
16

CHAPTER 1

The Australasian Texture

Australian history . . . does not read like history, but like the most beautiful lies. And all of a fresh new sort, no moldy old stale ones. It is full of surprises, and adventures, and incongruities, and contradictions, and incredibilities; but they are all true, they all happened.

—MARK TWAIN IN Following the Equator

THE WAY to start thinking about Australia is in terms of its Wild Colonial Boys, who, as an old folk song says, "robbed the rich and helped the poor and never hurt a good man." And this bold image brings up the convicts sent out from England who sired the Wild Colonial Boys, and the subsequent descendants of those early settlers who fought, with the brims of their digger hats turned up, for England in two world wars. From these legendary figures the mind moves on to images of the inferno-like desert of the outback, and the millions of Merino sheep that have given the coats off their backs to keep Englishmen warm, and the kangaroo, the wallaby, and the duck-billed platypus. This is the traditional Australia, and it can still be sensed in the antiauthoritarian swagger of the Australians, and the exotic flora and fauna.

But then we must swerve around and face the Australia of today: a country that has suddenly turned out to be rich with minerals from one end to the other, an urban country with a pair of cities each equal in population to all but the very biggest in the United States, a country awash with recently landed Yugoslavs and Poles and Italians and Americans, and a country that has exchanged its former economic kinship with England for an apronstring relationship with Japan. New Zealand shares this remolded image in a paler form: this nation that once existed to satisfy the English appetite for butter and lamb chops is now becoming a workshop making harvesters and lumber and newsprint.

The image of the cosmopolitan, citified Australian, replacing that of the "fair dinkum digger," and of the industrial New Zealander, replacing that of the shepherd, suggests substantial changes in the last ten years. In the case of Australia, these changes are shaking the whole nation; in the case of New Zealand, they are pushing a complacent country to modernize and adapt. The more notable of the changes are these:

1. Australia and New Zealand, which for a century and a half preferred to be regarded as displaced parts of Europe, have been forced to acknowledge themselves to be parts of Asia, with urgent interests in the prosperity of their neighbors, with vital economic connections to Japan, with a crucial need to know the Oriental mind, and with a growing necessity to find a way to live with China. Militarily, Australasia,* abandoned by Britain, now finds the United States' commitment weakened by the American withdrawal from Indochina. In short, Australia and New Zealand feel that, for better or worse, they are going to wind up alone, white nations in a sea of brown.

2. The Australian economy, stimulated by fabulous discoveries of iron ore, bauxite, nickel, and other minerals, has been growing explosively, both requiring and facilitating a huge, society-changing immigration. New Zealand, without massive immigration, has managed to surpass even Australia in population increase, in proportion to size.

3. The money for Australia's growth, once derived almost solely from English investors, now comes mostly from the United States, with significant additions from Japan, which has become Australia's biggest customer. Thus many decisions vitally affecting Australia are being made in other countries; Australians are grateful for the incoming funds—and at the same time worried.

4. There has been a quantum jump in quality of life and sophistication, especially in Australia. The Australia of the beer-swilling, big-kneed man willing to "have a go" at anything is fading; an Australia of style, urbanity, education, and culture is flowering. Wellington, the wooden capital of New Zealand, is more and more becoming something of a South Seas San Francisco. In short, both countries have chucked away the dullness they once seemed not only to tolerate but to cherish.

Those are the recent changes; there remain some observations to be made about the more permanent qualities of life in these two countries.

* This somewhat flexible appellation is here construed to mean Australia, New Zealand, New Guinea, and the Bismarck Archipelago.

Australia and New Zealand are not known in familiar detail to most of the rest of the world, yet the world senses that they are worthy of greater interest. Very few Americans can name the six states of Australia—a shortcoming all the more embarrassing because millions of Australians can name most of the American states. How many Western Europeans, apart from Englishmen, can say instantly whether Auckland or Wellington is the capital of New Zealand? Yet, without being able to cite more than one or two facts about Australia or New Zealand, millions of Americans and Europeans have grasped that these antipodean countries do indeed offer a fair go, that life there might be, as one American immigrant put it, "healthier and less perplexed." A Gallup Poll says that more than *five million* Americans would like to move to Australia—enough to raise the population by 40 percent!

This hunger to be Australian comes at least in part from a strange sort of nostalgia, a yearning for the equivalent of an earlier America, less beset by intractable problems. Australia and New Zealand have the innocence of the United States in the 1950's, when mere growth seemed a good thing in itself. Australia, at least, still has a frontier feel about it—lots of land resources untapped (if perhaps untappable), and continuing mineral discoveries that make anything seem possible. There is, of course, genuine concern about the environment in Australia and New Zealand, but there are few pollution-killed rivers to despair over, and the people seem hopeful that they can keep Los Angeles' fate from becoming theirs. Worry about families with too many babies is diluted by the plain need for more population, more workers for the farms and factories. National problems trumpeted in the newspapers frequently have a made-up air when compared to the racking plights of countries elsewhere.

Yet Australia and New Zealand are not fresh-born countries, pacing along twenty years behind the United States. Melbourne was settled long before Denver, and Sydney earlier than Melbourne. The Midland Hunt in Tasmania has been going on every year since the 1820's. A full century ago, New Zealand fought its own equivalent of the American Indian Wars. In short, these nations *have tradition.* Well over one hundred years ago, Melbourne had a theater that seated four thousand, a university, a zoo, race tracks, gaslighted streets, and balloon ascents; and its people ate such civilized delicacies as roasted black swan with port wine sauce. Australia has for ages been dotted with Stately Homes.

Another point is the importance of water. Aridity conditions all life in Australia, for even city-dwellers are conscious that they live on the perimeter of an enormous "gibber plain" where rain may not fall for years on end and no rivers run. This is country so dry that the Aborigines survive by digging for "soaks" of wet sand that they put into their mouths to suck on and then spit out. A sign at Ceduna, on a southern stretch of the highway that rings the continent, says: "LAST RELIABLE WATER FOR 770 MILES WEST." The only sizable river, the Murray, is drawn down for irrigation water so frequently along its course that little remains to flow into the ocean—and the Australian ideal would be to conserve stream water so thoroughly that not a drop would ever reach the sea. Water could make millions of acres bloom, and vastly raise the continent's ability to support human life, and thus, perhaps, make it a target for military conquest if humanity overpopulated the rest of the earth beyond capacity. To paraphrase an old Texas joke, all that Australia needs to be a Garden of Eden is water—but that's all hell needs.

Along with dryness there is a sense of isolation and distance. A large advertising sign in Melbourne reads: "FLY QANTAS TO THE WORLD"—and the world indeed seems a far-off place. The quickest flight from New York to Sydney takes twenty-one hours and thirty-five minutes. This factor—"the tyranny of distance," as historian Geoffrey Blainey has defined it—affects all life. As an example: it was because of, not in spite of, distance that England first sent convicts to Australia. The painters of New Zealand have historically displayed a style of their own because distance kept them from tapping the trends of France or England. Isolation accounts for the fact that the flora and fauna of each nation—those kangaroos, eucalyptuses, kiwis, and tree ferns—are markedly unlike the plants and animals of the rest of the world. Similarly, distance within the country has shaped both history and modern life. A city like Perth, in Western Australia, two thousand miles from Sydney, is comparable to Honolulu in its isolation. Exploring this forbidding space took not one but many epic expeditions like that of Lewis and Clark in the United States.

Next, Australia and New Zealand are pronouncedly different from one another in half a dozen ways. Australia's climate ranges up to the hot tropical; New Zealand's ranges down to the sub-Antarctic. Australia is dry; New Zealand is plentifully watered. Australia lives in uneasy guilt with its Aborigines; New Zealand's whites and Maoris form the most successful plural society in the world. Australia, though it has supplied some of the world's best fighting men for battles abroad, has never suffered significant bloodshed on its own soil; New Zealand underwent the shattering trauma of war at home when the whites seized paramountcy from the Maoris. Australia, accepting millions of immigrants, is increasingly cosmopolitan; New Zealand, apart from its Polynesians, is quite stodgily British. Australia builds with masonry; New Zealand builds with wood. Even the birds and the trees of the two nations are quite distinct from one another. Finally, and quite simply, an Australian feels like an Australian and a New Zealander feels like a New Zealander—two different things.

But the two countries do have in common left-leaning political philosophies, though neither is by any means socialist, despite widespread public ownership of utilities and even a few industries. The left-wing parties in both countries are against further nationalization, and the right-wing parties that have governed each country most of the time since World War II accept the existing degree of state ownership while continuing to support free enterprise—capitalism remains potent and healthy.

Here, then, are two countries well known to be stable, prosperous, and wholesome. It is a pleasure to discover that they also possess rich layers of interest, color, even excitement. Let us proceed, discussing Australia for a number of chapters, then New Zealand, and then the two together again.

CHAPTER 2

The Continent That Nature Left Unfinished

Oh! there once was a swagman camped in a billabong,
Under the shade of a coolibah tree;
And he sang as he looked at his old billy boiling,
"Who'll come a-waltzing Matilda with me?"
—FROM "WALTZING MATILDA"

BILLABONGS AND COOLIBAHS. Barramundis and wallaroos. Bandicoots and bimbils. Here is a continent where all life, and the land itself, have evolved their own individual patterns. There is a bird in Australia that builds a house and plants a lawn, and a tree that grows as tall as the spires of St. Patrick's in Manhattan. It is the world's sixth largest nation—inhabited by fewer people than Peru. You often sense in Australia that great, weird, dawn-of-history movies could be made in the long reaches of unpopulated, unpopulatable back country. You remember old theories of continental drift, and wonder where this superisland may have floated in aeons past. You are told that its rocks are the earth's oldest, to be compared with those that astronauts bring back from the moon.

*

To convey Australia's size to an American is simple: it equals the old forty-eight states minus one average-size state—say, Alabama or North Carolina. To be precise, it measures 2,967,909 square miles. It is more than twice as big as India. A man standing on Ayers Rock, in the center of the continent, would have to walk at least a thousand miles in any direction to reach the sea.

This is the only continent in the world occupied by a single nation. The main subdivisions are six states: in order of population they are New South Wales, Victoria, Queensland, South Australia, Western Australia, and Tasmania. For the most part interminable straight borders (one of them a full twelve hundred miles long) define the states in a checkerboard pattern, following lines of latitude and longitude. Except for Victoria, which is only a little bigger than Kansas, and Tasmania, the Scotland-size island off the south coast, the states are huge. California, Oregon, Washington, Idaho, Utah, Nevada, Arizona, New Mexico, Colorado, and Wyoming could all fit into Western Australia alone.

In this book each of the states is discussed in a chapter. So are (1) the Northern Territory, the prodigious square on the checkerboard that is still administered by the federal government; (2) the Australian Capital Territory, site of Canberra; and (3) the Australian, or eastern, half of the big island of New Guinea, off Australia's north coast. A curiosity is that Australia has four more territories, some none too well known even to Australians, for reasons of smallness, remoteness, or forgettableness. An example is Christmas Island* (population: 3,700), fifty-two square miles of phosphate mine in the Indian Ocean south of Java. Similarly, Australia administers the Cocos or Keeling Islands farther west in the Indian Ocean, having acquired them in the 1950's (like Christmas Island) from Britain. They produce copra and house about 630 souls. To the east is Norfolk Island, a speck of territory (three by five miles) in the Pacific 1,035 miles from Sydney. Its fifteen hundred people grow cut flowers and bean seed and pay no taxes, except that once a year the Administrator is entitled to require every male between twenty-one and fifty-five to pay a sum anywhere between ten and twenty dollars, or work for between five and ten days. Despite having no beaches—indeed, no inlets or harbors—Norfolk draws seven to eight thousand tourists a year from the Australian mainland; the round-trip air fare from Sydney is $116.

The fourth territory measures 2.4 million square miles, not far short of Australia itself. This is the Australian Antarctic Territory, a wedge of the polar continent between 45 degrees and 160 degrees east longitude. Australia runs research stations at Mawson on the Antarctic coast, at Macquarie Island off that coast, and intermittently elsewhere. Neither the United States nor the Soviet Union recognizes Australia's (or anybody else's) ownership of any part of Antarctica.

* Not to be confused with an even less impressive atoll called Christmas Island in the Pacific south of Hawaii, claimed by the U.S. but actually held by Britain.

*

Some points about population: (1) It is small, a mere thirteen million people, averaging out at one person for each 160 acres, or four persons per square mile. If the population were evenly spread over the country, each Australian would be standing one-half mile from the next. This is a density 1/166th that of Europe. Only twelve hundred miles from Australia is Java, which has twelve hundred persons per square mile, for a total of 65 million. (2) It is growing fast, having doubled in forty years, although high immigration and natural increase together do not achieve a total growth rate as great as many underdeveloped countries reach by births alone. (3) It is urban. Almost one-half of the whole population lives in two cities, Sydney and Melbourne, and only 15 percent of Australians live in the countryside.

Let us now get an idea of the look of the land itself—the strange plants and animals and the eerie geological formations.

Fauna

For someone used to the flora and fauna of the rest of the world, exploring the plants and animals of Australia is startling and fascinating. The key fact in explaining this exotic life is Australia's isolation. All the other continents of the world are, or were at one time, linked so that species of life were able to spread quite easily. On this great "World Continent" more than sixty million years ago the forces of evolution were shaping two kinds of mammals. One was marsupial, in which the newborn infant, after a short period of gestation, crept into a pouch on its mother's abdomen, attached itself to a teat, and completed its development outside the mother's body. The other was placental, in which the fetus remained in the womb, fed through a placenta, until relatively well developed. The marsupial mode was efficient enough at that time to have produced a big and varied population; the placentals, though basically a better model, were not yet in full production.

At this point Australia may have been briefly linked to the World Continent, allowing animals to migrate. Probably the migration route was Asia–Indonesia–New Guinea–Australia, all presumably bridged together as the result of some geological upheaval. If a short sea passage was necessary, the migrating animal may have crossed in various ways. A delightful theory, advanced by the paleontologist George Gaylord Simpson, is that some dauntless, pregnant, tree-dwelling female animal rode a tree, possibly toppled by a storm into the sea, across the water gap between the World Continent and

Australia, and proceeded to found a race. Another possibility, less credible because it depends on the unlikely theory of continental drift, is that Australia was once part of Gondwanaland, a hypothetical continent joining South America, Africa, and Antarctica.

Probably because at that time marsupials were dominant in the World Continent, Australia got an infusion of them. Then the geographical link for some reason broke, and placentals in the World Continent proceeded to evolve all the way up to Man, displacing marsupials (except for the opossum) 25 million years ago. But in Australia, marsupials had a clear track. They evolved into forms fewer in number and variety than the placentals, while retaining certain resemblances to them. Thus numbats are like anteaters, wombats like marmots, cuscus like sloths, koalas like bears, and notorcytes like moles.

The most interesting marsupials, of course, are kangaroos. They come in forty-five species, ranging in size from one foot to nine, but the most common is the red or gray kangaroo about the height and weight of a boy or man. Some big ones weigh more than two hundred pounds. The baby kangaroo, called a "joey," is one inch long at birth, following six weeks of gestation. Using the powerful forelimbs characteristic of newborn marsupials, this tiny embryo finds his way to his mother's pouch. It is astonishing that he does not lose his way. Sometimes, if he does fetch up on some other part of her body, she may distractedly scratch him away as though he were a bothersome insect. In the pouch, he clamps his mouth to a nipple and nurses unremittingly for many weeks, not leaving the pouch until six to eight months later. Even when weaned, he still uses the pouch for shelter and transportation, and may jump out to graze at the same time that his mother does.

Kangaroos walk by planting their forepaws and tail on the ground while swinging their back legs forward into position for a step. At half-speed they hop, coming to the ground on back feet and tail. At full speed, forepaws are tucked in and tail is held up as the back legs, like steel springs, thrust the animal into the air. He can travel thirty miles an hour, yet veer abruptly. The forepaws are useful for boxing—joeys box at play, and older kangaroos, suitably gloved, box human beings in circuses, occasionally scoring clever knockouts. In a fight a kangaroo uses a forepaw to pin an enemy—dingo (wild dog) or man—by the neck while rearing up on his tail and ripping the victim's belly with a hind claw.

Astonishing numbers of kangaroos are hunted and killed every year—at least a million and a half in New South Wales and Queensland alone. One hunter shot 130 kangaroos in a single night. Shooting them is easy—they bound away from any source of alarm, then pause, stock-still, to see what the danger was. Licensed hunters get two dollars per animal. The kangaroo supplies meat for kangaroo-tail soup, pet food, and human consumption in Hong Kong and Japan.* It tastes like beef. The fur goes for coats, such toys as koala bears, and the leather is used for boots and baseball gloves. But much of the slaughter is simply to exterminate kangaroos as competitors for grass on Australian sheep runs. Nevertheless, this animal does not appear to be facing the fate of the American bison; perhaps as many as 100 million kangaroos of all kinds remain, owing to high birth rates. Graziers call them "noxious animals," and favor slaughtering them as the only method of control. (Somebody has said that the Australian formula for the treatment of wildlife and the environment in general is: "If it moves, shoot it. If it doesn't move, chop it down.")

Similarly plentiful are wallabies, essentially just small black scrubland kangaroos. One type of phalanger (something like a flying squirrel) is so tiny that it would fit into a slipper; its babies, the smallest form of mammal life, cannot be seen without a magnifying glass. There is a mean marsupial mouse which, if caged with a real mouse, quickly converts the real mouse into nothing but a pelt, peeled off and turned inside out. Another mean marsupial is the Tasmanian devil, raccoon-size and beady-eyed, a scavenger. Many marsupials eat meat—but the two-thumbed koala eats nothing but the tips of certain eucalyptus leaves. The pouches of all marsupials that walk on four legs open to the rear.

"Monotremes Oviparous, Ovum Meroblastic"

Even more primitive than the marsupials are the monotremes (from Greek roots that mean "one" and "hole"), the duck-billed platypus and the echidna (spiny anteater). One orifice (cloaca) serves as outlet for the intestine, kidneys, uterus and ovaries in the female, and sperm in the male. Sexual intercourse is apparently carried out cloaca to cloaca. Eggs hatch in a week or two, and a few days after that the mother's abdomen begins to sweat milk, which the babies avidly lap up. Verification of the fact that platypuses lay eggs, which had been rumored for decades, was made by a young British zoologist in 1884, who cabled the news as follows: "MONOTREMES OVIPAROUS, OVUM MEROBLASTIC."†

Australia has lizards ten feet long, which sometimes walk on their hind legs; worms ten feet long, at least when extended; dugongs, mammalian sea cows, ten feet long and half a ton in weight; and crocodiles that grow twenty feet long. There are 136 varieties of snakes, many venomous and about half

* Fifty-two percent of the carcass is edible, compared to 32 percent of a pig.
† Translation: "Monotremes egg-laying, egg of partial cleavage."

a dozen deadly. The most lethal is the taipan, which invariably kills its victim, and can produce enough venom at a single milking to kill two hundred sheep. The brown snake, also deadly, is noted for the wrestling matches staged by the males, who coil around one another like the strands of a rope and struggle until one is exhausted and falls away. Other killer snakes are the six-foot tiger, the black, and the death adder. But, as Alan Moorehead has pointed out, none of these snakes will attack unprovoked; instead, they run away, for the snake "is an intensely frightened and fragile creature; one blow on those delicate hairpin-thin bones will instantly break its back." Many snakes, besides being harmlessly nonvenomous, are positively beneficial; the carpet snakes and the children's python, both seven feet long, feed on rats and rabbits, and farmers hold them in esteem. Incidentally, Australia has a certain renown for its spiders. One of them measures eight inches across, and spins a web sturdy enough to catch small birds.

Bird evolution in Australia seems to have come to a dead halt for some species and reached world records of sophistication in others. The flightless, ostrich-like emu, five feet tall, can run forty miles per hour and is too stupid to stop for a paddock fence, hence crashes through. The bowerbird builds a wigwam-shaped playhouse from twigs, decorates it with colorful feathers, pebbles, shells, and broken glass, paints it with pigments of his own manufacture using a beak-held spongy brush, and plants a lawn of moss in front. The old theory was that this bower (it is not a nest) lured females for copulation. A newer idea is that the bowers, of which each male builds several, serve to stake out his territory against other birds.

Another sophisticate is the lyrebird, which improvises songs of its own, but also imitates sounds, such as a squeaky wheel or a violin or a piano chord or a baby's cry. In courting, the male climbs an earth mound of his own making, opens his fernlike tail to a lyre shape, flips it over his back so that the feather ends hang in a fringe in front of his eyes, and goes into a song-and-dance that is formidable and beautiful. In *Their Shining Eldorado* Elspeth Huxley says that the lyrebird does not sing for joy; his song warns other males away from the two to five acres that he considers his own, and is basically an instrument of hate, not pleasure.

The cassowary, another bird that does not fly, runs at express-train speed with head outstretched, armed against collision with trees by a sort of bone helmet. The male mallee fowl leads a life of desperate, panicky exhaustion keeping an even temperature in the hole-in-the-ground egg incubator that he and his wife maintain; he uses rotting compost to raise the temperature and night-cooled wet sand to lower it. Brolgas, which are cranes, dance together in groups of six to several hundred. There are also wedge-tailed eagles, a pageant of parrots, birds of paradise, pugnacious geese, black swans, the laughing, kingfishing kookaburra—among them, 431 species of birds *unique* to Australia.

Flora

The spectacular results achieved among fauna by isolating a few species for sixty million years in a sort of continental laboratory are matched among the flora (Australia has 100,000 species of plants and animals). The most remarkable plant is the eucalyptus. We know a few forms of this tree in the U.S., transplanted from Australia to Florida and California; Americans call it gumwood and use it for pews in churches and dunnage in ships. It has also been taken to Africa and South America—it is, for example, the most prominent feature of the Andean landscape around Bogotá. But only in Australia can one see the whole exultant spread of 603 species of this tree.

The eucalyptus called karri, which flourishes in the southwest corner of Australia, grows as much as 280 feet high and 24 feet around, with trunks that shoot up without branching for 160 feet; they are comparable to many redwoods. The karri produces a tough and beautifully grained lumber, and, like a similar eucalyptus, the jarrah, is often felled by explosives. An even bigger eucalyptus is the mountain ash. By contrast, the mallee, ten to thirty feet high, covers the enormous worthless scrubland to the north and south of the central desert. Finding names for every species of eucalyptus seems to have been an exercise in inspiration: moort, bloodwood, bastard box, coolibah, red tingle, ironbark, bimbil, wandoo, and scribbly gum (from its calligraphic bark design). Despite such immense variety, the eucalyptuses share many common characteristics, as they must being of the same family. They all shed bark—the manna gum sheds fifty tons per year per acre, creating a fire hazard. The eucalyptuses' feather-shaped leaves, colored a melancholy gray-green, hang straight down, receiving sunshine on both surfaces. They stay on the tree the year round, and, when crushed in the hand, give off a camphorous odor. The name "eucalyptus" derives from Greek for "well covered," a reference to the fact that the petals fuse to cover the bud before they drop off. The brushy-looking flower consists only of stamens.

The chief vegetation of the sandy deserts (apart from plants that germinate like ghosts after a rain and then disappear) is the spinifex, a tussocky grass. In the arid margins of the desert grows mulga, a sapling-like acacia. In fact, species of acacias, or wattles, number 630, more than the eucalyptuses. Their leaf appears in the national coat of arms. Also found in the desert are saltbushes and bluebushes, with succulent leaves that absorb night moisture and serve as sheep fodder. The semiarid savannas grow wallaby grass and kangaroo grass, making good pastoral property. In really wet places there are forests of beech, coachwood and bunya pine. The cypress pine in the mountains is thought to be the world's oldest species of conifer.

Arid Australia

> *One who would travel this country for pleasure would go to hell for a pastime.*
>
> —GEOGRAPHER R. T. MAURICE

Australia, which is shaped like a humped rhinoceros with its horn aimed at New Guinea, divides into three zones of differing characteristics. The *highlands* parallel the whole east coast, and although they are called the Great Dividing Range, they are actually only a series of plateaus thirty to a hundred miles wide, averaging twelve hundred feet in elevation. Next west are the *central eastern lowlands,* which traverse Australia north and south without ever rising to more than seven hundred feet above the sea. The *western plateau,* about three-quarters of the land mass, running fourteen hundred miles to the Indian Ocean, is the flat, arid, harsh, empty, and often grotesque stretch that typifies Australia in the world's imagination. Australia is mostly desert (though the word is unpopular there). More than three-quarters of the entire population live in a boomerang-shaped coastal area on the southeastern corner, where the climate is temperate and eminently habitable.

*

Alps in Australia? In the southern end of the Great Dividing Range, centered around Mount Kosciusko, there are (and the Australians drum it into you constantly) "more snowfields than in all of Switzerland." In subtropical terrain like this, the possibility of plentiful snow is difficult to grasp. But many mountains in the Australian Alps rise to six thousand feet or more, elevations sufficiently cold to guarantee skiing from June to October, and sometimes as late as Christmas. Kosciusko, Australia's highest mountain, reaches 7,310 feet. The area is within easy reach of both Sydney and Melbourne, because development of the Snowy Mountains Hydroelectric Scheme —more about that in a later chapter—has led to the construction of numerous roads. So skiers come in droves to well-equipped resorts, one of them, Thredbo, being also unashamedly expensive. The Kosciusko chalet has a chairlift three and one-half miles long; the architecture of the area is mostly Tyrolean.

The views can be both spectacular and quietly pretty—there is an awesome sense of distance. Driving through in the summer, you climb and descend and climb again, reaching alpine vegetation on the ridges and penetrating silent eucalyptus forests farther down. The inkblot waters of the lakes and ponds of the hydroelectric complex lie all around, and you are aware that inside the mountains, in blasted-out chambers, generators hum. A surprising number of parrots flap through these forests.

North of the Alps, the mountains of Australia are interesting chiefly as well-watered tablelands that support much of the country's crop farming.

The lowlands, bisecting the country along the 140th meridian of east longitude, have generally good soil but dreadfully insufficient rainfall. Oddly enough, however, it is easy to water cattle here, for the lowlands contain the world's largest artesian basin. It is necessary only to puncture the seven hundred feet of shale that seals the tops of the aquifers to get water suitable for animals (but too alkaline for irrigation). Nine thousand "bores" (as Australians call wells) make it possible for this area to support a large part of the Australian sheep-raising industry.

The southern part of the lowlands contain the Darling, Murrumbidgee, and Murray rivers, the only river *system* in the country. They are reluctant rivers. The Darling is shown on maps as a long stretch of dotted line, an indication that it ceases to flow when rain is insufficient in the headwaters. The Darling once stopped running for eighteen months, turning itself into a series of billabongs, or oxbow lakes. In short, this country, like most of Australia, is vulnerable to long and parching droughts. Lake Eyre, a feature of the lowlands, is shown as 150 miles of blue on some maps, but it is really a salt flat, 39 feet below sea level. Only a few times every century is it covered with a thin sheet of water. The rivers that flow into it are equally bogus, but technically Lake Eyre is one of the largest internal drainages in the world, more than twice as big as the Great Basin of Utah, Nevada, and California.

*

We reach now an area that seems less a geographical subdivision than an immense and forbidding Fact: the prodigious western plateau. This Fact stands stubbornly in the way of the theory that Australia can fill itself up to the brim with population. Australia's look of immensity on the map fails to show the impossibility of human life (at least with present technology) in much of the western plateau. An enormous area in the middle of it has no population at all, barring a handful of nomadic Aborigines. Almost as underpopulated is the area stretching from this "dead heart" to the north and out to the settled strips on the east and south, where most Australians live—only one person for every *eight* square miles. This is the "outback" that city-dwellers speak of, in Sydney or Melbourne or Brisbane; this is the "back-of-beyond"; this is the "never-never."

The plateau rises a thousand feet from the lowlands that we have been investigating, and in general maintains an average elevation of twelve hundred feet. In the geographical center of the country is a scattering of low mountains, chiefly the Macdonnell and Musgrave ranges. The Macdonnells run mile after mile in geometrically parallel ridges. Both the sand and the mountains are the color of terra cotta—this is the "red center" of Australia. These tones complement the unexpected verdure of the pure-white ghost gums, desert oaks, and kurrajongs that grow there in defiance of the aridity.

Australia is sometimes called the "fossil continent" because the pedestal of the western plateau is the pre-Cambrian shield, a vast rigid block of granite a billion and a half years old. The plateau gets only four to sixteen inches of rain a year, quickly evaporated. The result is deserts, or extremely arid plains, five hundred miles wide, that sever Australia north and south, from the Eighty Mile Beach on the northwest coast to the Great Australian Bight, the concavity on the south coast. A formidable oddity among these deserts is the sterile gibber plain, many thousands of square miles in which soil and sand are blown away, leaving only loose rocks, from pebble-size to one-foot boulders. The stones can be exquisite—wind-polished chalcedony, siliceous fragments, striped and translucent quartz. These lands are not only dry on the surface; they are dry beneath. A mine in the Kalgoorlie area went down four thousand feet without hitting any water.

More desolate yet is the Nullarbor (pronounced "NULL-a-bore") Plain, a crescent of limestone adjacent to the pre-Cambrian granite on the Great Australian Bight. Any water that falls here sinks instantly into the nine-hundred-foot-deep limestone that underlies the plain. The result, as the imitation Latin name suggests, is no trees. Such is the flatness of the surface that the transcontinental railroad crosses the Nullarbor Plain in an arrow-straight line for 330 miles. The shelf terminates on the south in spectacular high cliffs, saw-tooth-edged when seen from above, that run for 120 miles unbroken, dropping vertically into the milky-green ocean.

The western plateau ends sharply in a scarp along most of the west and northwest coast. A plain at the foot of the scarp provides space for the city of Perth and the lush, well-watered shoreline to the south of that city and around the bend of Australia. On the northern edge of the western plateau lie the impressive Hamersley Range and Kimberley Mountains. Large numbers of kangaroos, wild buffaloes, dingoes, crocodiles, and birds live here, and are all regarded as fair game for hunters.

By a road with a rather romantic conception, Australia's Highway One, a motorist can drive around the rim of the continent, barring only one gap in the north. The route is surely the world's longest: 7,664 miles. Driving it takes many weeks, because though most of it is easy going, parts are slow, rough, and even perilous. The trip starts in Cairns, on Cape York Peninsula in northeastern Australia, and sweeps around the country like the hand of a clock. Highway One goes clear to Darwin, about as far from Cairns, to stick with the clock image, as the distance from one to eleven.

It would be tidy if the road went clear around the face of the clock. But between Darwin and Cairns there are 1,150 straight-line miles, and a road would be much longer. Eventually it will be built, as a "beef road" to transport cattle that presently walk a couple of thousand miles from breeding stations in the northwest to fattening lots in the east. It could also link up with the new bauxite mines on the Gulf of Carpentaria. Otherwise it would traverse some of the world's mightiest nothingness.

*

Coolest Australia, in the south, is like warmest Europe, Spain, or southern Italy. Hottest Australia, in the north, is as torrid as equatorial Africa. The highest recorded temperature is 127.5 degrees at Cloncurry in western Queensland in 1889—which compares with the U.S. high of 134 degrees at Death Valley, California, in 1913. Except in high mountains in southeast Australia and in Tasmania, the only snow is a light freak dusting sometimes in the south. Temperature swings are not great as between day and night, and summer and winter. Sydney's mean temperatures are 71 degrees in summer (which, opposite to the Northern Hemisphere, runs from December to February) and 55 degrees in winter (from May to September).

The average annual rainfall is sixteen and one-half inches, as compared to twenty-six for the whole world. But the Australian average is compounded of coastlines in Tasmania that get one hundred inches a year weighed off against deserts that get as little as four inches a year. Even the statement that the deserts "average" four inches a year is misleading—the average is likely to be calculated from one torrential twelve-inch rainfall followed by three years of no precipitation at all. In the northwest below the monsoon belt, as much as twenty-seven inches of rain may fall in one day, to be followed by years of drought. On the other hand, the monsoons of the north and northeast are pretty reliable: during "The Wet," from November to April, twenty to fifty inches of rain fall. Perth and the big cities of the southeast have fairly even rainfall. Cyclones and anticyclones determine the weather of Australia as they migrate through the Indian and Pacific oceans.

*

The Australian Aborigines, as we shall presently see, have survived the arrival of the white man only with great loss of numbers and culture, but their place names prevail in abundance, and give Australia much of its flavor. For the visitor, collecting these melodious, many-syllabled, and tongue-tripping words can become a mania. Herewith a well-culled list, to suggest the feel of traveling this continent: Dulkaninna, Kopperamanna, Ooroowillanie, Gringegalgona, Koolynobbing, Bimbimbie, Derribong, Oodnadatta, Nindalyup, Goondiwindi, Collymongle, Bulla Bulling. All of them have translations. Grong Grong, for example, is "very hot," and Boolaroo is "many flies."

CHAPTER 3

From Convict Colony to Commonwealth

The jury says, "He's guilty,"
And says the judge, says he—
"For life, Jim Jones, I'm sending you
Across the stormy sea."

—OLD CONVICT BALLAD

As soon as men attempted to make world maps, they sensed that there had to be an Australia—an antipodes to Europe. Ptolemy called it Terra Australis Incognita on maps he made about A.D. 150, and a French cartographer in 1550, unable to contain his impatience for the actual discovery of the unknown southern world, sketched in an Australia connected to Antarctica and fitted out with camels, deer, men, and castellated fortresses. Of course, not every early authority believed the myth. St. Augustine, to whom several present-day Australian churches are forgivingly dedicated, hooted down the whole "fabulous hypothesis of men who walk a part of the earth opposite to our own, whose feet are in a position contrary to ours." But a Spanish explorer named Juan Arias, pleading with King Philip II for ships, argued that the then known land-to-sea ratio in the Northern Hemisphere had to be matched in the Southern, "according to what we are taught by sacred writ and philosophical reasoning." As late as 1769 (after many seafarers had actually touched the Australian coast) the myth-making continued. A one-time employee of the British East India Company deduced that Australia must be bigger than Asia and inhabited by fifty million people.

Considering the certainty of expectations that the "great southern continent" existed, the explorers who groped toward it, over many centuries, seem to have been the victims of some grim cosmic joker intent on keeping them from finding it. The Spaniard Luis Vaez de Torres, sailing from South America to look for Terra Australis Incognita, managed in 1606 to shoot right through the strait (which now bears his name) between Australia and New Guinea, hardly a hundred miles wide, and never realized that his goal was almost within sight. A few decades later Abel Tasman, a Dutch East India Company skipper, discovered Tasmania and New Zealand, and died without ever knowing that Australia lay within the twelve-thousand-mile south-swinging loop he had sailed. Later Dutch ships reached Australia's west coast many times; they named the coastline New Holland, and so it was known for two hundred years.

William Dampier was the first Englishman to touch on what was finally to become a patch of British red on the map of the world. Dampier was no valiant officer seeking colonies for the Crown; he was an enterprising buccaneer who had lately seized a ship and put its captain ashore in the Philippines. Discreetly retiring from the busy trade routes, he stood south in his stolen ship and on January 4, 1688, reached the north coast of Australia. Returning to London, this amazing con man persuaded the Admiralty not only to forget his piracy but to provide him with a ship for further exploration. He managed to reach Australia briefly again before his squabbling crew forced him to return to England. Jonathan Swift took Dampier's yarn as the basis for part of *Gulliver's Travels*.

The Dutiful, Tireless, and Honorable Captain Cook

Nearly a century went by with all the colonizing nations of Europe aware that some vast land must attach to the sketched-in coast of New Holland, but none pursuing the exploration. Finally Britain saw the urgency of preserving its South Pacific interests, and in 1769 sent off Captain James Cook on the ship *Endeavour*. His ostensible mission was to observe the transit of the planet Venus from Tahiti. Turning west from Tahiti, he circumnavigated New Zealand and defined it as two islands, then sailed west again and bumped into Australia. What a picture of duty, discipline, and happy industry we get of this Yorkshire laborer's son, who is said to have invented the proverb, "An apple a day keeps the doctor away." Up the coast he went, tirelessly naming every physical feature—Point Hicks, Cape Howe, Cape Dromedary, Point Upright—of what he took to be a land of "very agreeable and pleasant aspect, diversified with hills, ridges, plains and valleys, with some few small lawns . . . we saw the smoke of fire in several places, a certain sign that the country is inhabited."

Australia was—at last—really discovered. At length Cook came to a large bay, and explored its shores for eight days, in company with the botanist Joseph Banks, discovering, among other wonders, Aborigines, oysters, and gum trees. "The great quantity of this sort of fish found in this place occasioned my giving it the name of Stingrays Harbour," he wrote in his log. Then he drew a line through that sentence, and replaced it with: "The great quantity of plants Mr. Banks and Dr. Solander found in this place occasioned my giving it the name of Botany Bay." Thus the legendary name that for a while came to signify the whole of Australia. Cook thereafter sailed along the coast eighteen hundred miles to Australia's northernmost cape, and, stepping ashore on Possession Island, gave the coast the name of New South Wales. Cook lived on, still exploring the Pacific, until 1779, when he was murdered by natives of the Hawaiian Islands.

Convicts

We come now to a touchy, paradoxical event, the second landing at Botany Bay, eighteen years after Cook. To Stone Age Australia, the continent that somehow could not even be discovered until modern history was well advanced, came its first white settlers. And who were they? Convicts from the jails and prison hulks of England. What sorts of human beings were they? How does their heritage affect Australia today?

Any American prone to condemn Australia's convict origins might well recollect a bit of history. Early in the seventeenth century American colonists induced the British Crown to send—more precisely, sell, at ten pounds each—English convicts for labor in Maryland, Virginia, and Georgia. A statute in 1666 formalized this transportation of "lewd, disorderly and lawless" persons to the American colonies, and they came at a rate of about five hundred a year for more than a century, until the American Revolution. Thus there is a not inconsiderable leaven of descendance from convicts in our own nation.

The Revolution was the operative factor in the diversion of the flow of English prisoners from our shores to Australia's. Let us get a picture of the state of crime in England at that time. The industrial revolution and the enclosure acts were tearing society apart, creating hordes of hungry, jobless, crime-prone people. Law enforcement was sketchy and primitive; criminals frequently and literally got away with murder. "Pickpockets plied their trade in the crowds that watched pickpockets being hanged at Tyburn," wrote an English historian. The frightened Establishment tried to cope by prescribing heavy exemplary punishment for those criminals who did happen to be caught. About two hundred crimes were made punishable by death, including, incredibly, the crime of "impersonating an Egyptian." Generally the death sentence was remitted if the convict agreed to being sent out of the country. The term for this was "transportation."

Most convicts sent to Australia, or to America for that matter, were guilty of what would now be regarded as minor offenses. "The bulk of the prisoners, who comprised about one-fifth of those convicted of crime at the Assizes and Quarter Sessions of England, were the town thieves, pickpockets, and shoplifters that constituted such a serious menace to the badly policed English society of the early nineteenth century," says A. G. L. Shaw, professor of history at Monash University, Melbourne. In *The Crimes of the First Fleet Convicts,* published in 1970, historian John Cobley tracks down and describes the precise offenses of the first batch of convict colonists transported to Australia. Typically, someone stole "one sattin waistcoat, value 3s, and one corded dimity waistcoat, value 5s." To the antipodes for thefts amounting to eight shillings! But Dr. Cobley flatly denies that the convicts were "more sinned against than sinning." He also denies that any of the first convicts were transported for political crimes. What the book does not bring out is how many of the convicts were incorrigibles, transported because the specifically cited felony was only the last of many. This is probably the case with most of them. And in later shipments there were ruthless murderers and rapists, exact proportions unknown. Further as to the makeup of the convicts, of the 160,000 ultimately transported to Australia only 20,000 were women, many of them prostitutes. Of the males, a great many were boys—the Artful Dodgers and orphans and deserted children of London.

Of such components as these was the band that sailed into Botany Bay in January 1788: the First Fleet, as the Australians call it in an oddly prideful way. We cannot tarry long over their early years and hardships. The main point is that, though a raffish lot, by and large, they built a settlement just as surely and persistently as if they had landed from the *Mayflower.* The first Governor, Captain Arthur Phillip, decided at once that Botany Bay would not do as a town site.* He went up the coast in a small boat, and discovered the merits of what is now Sydney Harbor. Phillip chose for settlement a well-watered inlet that he called Sydney Cove, in honor of

* One of the strangest coincidences in the long hit-or-miss history of Australian exploration took place the day of the landing. Beginning in 1771, the French government interested itself for more than thirty years in South Pacific exploration. The ranking French explorer was Count Jean-François de La Pérouse, who sailed into Botany Bay just a few hours after the First Fleet arrived. Had he been first, de La Pérouse might have established a strong French claim to Australia. As it was, he and Captain Phillip greeted one another amiably, and a bit later de La Pérouse sailed off to death by shipwreck in the New Hebrides.

the Home Secretary of the time. On January 26, now Australia Day, the colonists—736 convicts and 294 marines, officers, and officials—landed there.

No Devil's Island, this. A strange aspect of the Australian penal colony was that relatively few convicts ever did time behind bars. From the first, they were more colonists than prisoners. The immediate task was to provide housing and food for themselves. Though a sorry and often drunken bunch, they—and the convicts landed by three subsequent fleets—managed in the end to build a viable community. Men once skilled only at picking pockets learned perforce how to farm. The difficulties were overwhelming —for instance, no one thought of sending the colony a plow for years. The convicts were assigned by the government as free labor to the military officers and other settlers, to work on farms or in small business enterprises. Obedience was enforced to a great extent by bribery, perquisites, or actual wages. The settlers could also get balky convicts flogged, and 42,000 of them were flogged in New South Wales between 1830 and 1837. "The way they floged them was theire armes pulled Round a large tree and their breasts squezed against the tree so the men had no power to cringe or stir," runs one vivid account of a three-hundred-lash flogging by a convict forced to witness it. "I was to leew'rd of the flogers and I protest, tho' I was two perches [rods] from them, the flesh and skin blew in my face as they shooke off the cats."

Liquidating the Convict Culture

How did Australia dissolve the convict culture, and become, in the end, a nation so much like our own? The convicts were on the whole a depraved lot. One observer called the colony "little less than an extensive Brothel." The convicts drank anything alcoholic that their betters would sell them; most of their children were bastards. But the children of the first convict settlers generally turned out to be upright and industrious. A hard-bitten lawyer sent out from London to investigate the condition of the colony in 1817 was flabbergasted to discover that "the class of inhabitants who have been born in the colony affords a remarkable exception to the moral and physical characters of their parents." There is a simple and credible explanation for the contrasting morality of the second generation. Australia provided the convicts' children with abundant opportunity; work offered better prospects than crime.

In 1813 three young explorers (of whom more later) scaled the Blue Mountain escarpment west of Sydney and changed the city from a sealed-off prison colony to a gateway to the interior. Settlers poured in from England —greengrocers, vicars' sons, sheep raisers—altering the character of the population. An enlightened Governor, Lachlan Macquarie (1810–1821), insisted against pressure from England and from the free settlers that "emancipists," convicts who had served their terms, were in every way the equals of other men.

New South Wales resisted the landing of more convicts, and got the Crown to send them to Van Diemen's Land (as Tasmania was then called in honor of the Dutch Governor who had sent Tasman to discover it), and to the northern coast, present-day Queensland. Transportation to New South Wales ended in 1840, and the gold rush of 1852 signaled the end of convict shipment to any part of eastern Australia. "There are few English criminals who would not regard a free passage to the gold fields . . . as a great boon," wrote a governor of Van Diemen's Land, commenting on the end of transportation. Western Australia still wanted English criminals for labor, and a model system of receiving and rehabilitating convicts continued there until 1868.

Exploration's Fascination

We turn now to an intriguing question: How was a continent known only as a shoreline on nautical charts opened up and laid bare to the white man's gaze? Even after Cook's discovery of New South Wales no man knew how this eastern coast was connected to west-coast New Holland. Captain Matthew Flinders settled the riddle by finding a continuous shoreline from New Holland to New South Wales along the south coast. It was his suggestion that the continent should be known as Australia (from Latin "*australis*"—"southern"). With the known parts of the continent hooked together, the problem to the people of Sydney became: what lay back of the thousand-foot scarp thirty miles west of Sydney? Going up the valleys led only to vertical gorges and impassable waterfalls. A clever young man named Gregory Blaxland overcame this obstacle in 1813; keeping to the top of a long highland spur he was able to look down to the other side.

Blaxland figuratively had the continent at his feet, but he could not know that. Subsequent invaders, following Blaxland's route, found languid rivers, the Murrumbidgee, the Murray, and the Darling, that flowed westward for a ways and then disappeared in seas of reeds. Charles Sturt, who discovered the Darling in 1829, wrote: "Its course is involved in mystery. Does it make its way to the south coast, or exhaust itself in feeding a succession of swamps in the center of the island?" The next year, he and his party carried a whaleboat by bullock cart to the Murrumbidgee, and then, cutting themselves off from any possibility of returning the way they had come, floated down that river, discovering its junction with the Murray and a bit later with the Darling. Proceeding downstream, he passed through terrain of which he wrote, "My eye never fell upon a country of more promising aspect or more favorable position"—words that inspired the founding and colonization of South Australia six years later. Sturt emerged at the mouth of the Murray on the south coast of Australia near present Adelaide, and thus in one bold stroke solved the riddle of the river drainage.

In the life of this Australian explorer, there remains another story touched with romance—and this time with failure. Taking note of bird-migration routes at two widely separated points in southern Australia, Sturt in 1844 triangulated a point on the empty map where the courses of the flyways theoretically had to cross. He concluded that some paradise, desirable at least to birds, had to exist there. His expedition to find it encountered brutal hardships and broke his health. He never found whatever it was the cockatoos and parakeets were flying toward. Sturt was left in despair at failing to be "the first to place my foot in the centre of this vast territory."

We can mention only two or three of the other explorers. Edward John Eyre *walked* the entire south coast along the Great Australian Bight in 1841 and found not a single watercourse in fifteen hundred miles. A Polish count named Strzelecki explored the heights of the mountains southwest of Sydney, and named Mount Kosciusko in honor of the Polish soldier-statesman who volunteered in the American Revolution and served under Washington at Yorktown. In 1860 John McDouall Stuart penetrated to the very center of Australia and planted a Union Jack as "a sign to the natives that the dawn of liberty, civilization, and Christianity is about to break upon them." A year later Robert O'Hara Burke and W. J. Wills explored Australia, south to north and back, starting from a base in New South Wales, using camels imported for the purpose. They suffered such torments and delays on the return trip that the staff at the base camp gave up hope of seeing them and pulled out just seven hours before they finally got back to the camp. Both men thereupon died of privation. Many of these explorers *navigated* their way through the trackless, empty outback; Burke and Wills, for example, followed the meridian of 140 degrees east longitude. By 1875 the exploration of Australia was basically finished, the continent known.

Australia Grows Up

The tapestry of nineteenth-century Australian history is woven of wool and touched with many colors, most excitingly gold. We see in it the extraordinary conversion of a convict colony into a rousing radical democracy, a nation put together with neither princes nor peasants.

The century divides, in the political sense, with the discovery of gold in 1851. During the first half, following the explorations we have traced, the geographical lines were drawn that defined what were then six colonies and are now six states. New South Wales was founded as a place to dump convicts. It sent out the first settlers to Tasmania to keep France from claiming that island. They in turn, after some years, sent settlers to Victoria because it seemed fertile and rich. South Australia was born of lengthy intellectual discussions on the founding of an ideal colony, spun out chiefly by an incredible theorizer, Edward Gibbon Wakefield, who was serving a term in a London jail at the time. Queensland was another convict colony resulting from New South Wales' wish to have no more prisoners. Western Australia was the consequence of British determination to colonize the west coast.

A Gallery of Scoundrels and/or Heroes

A half-dozen fabulous men gave the colonies their directions in the first half of the century. The most eccentric of them was John Macarthur, who arrived in Sydney in 1791 as a lieutenant in the New South Wales Corps. He set himself up as businessman, sheep raiser, and financier, attending to military duty in what little time he had left. When a Yankee trader sailed into Sydney Harbor with a cargo of general supplies and rum, Macarthur and some other officers bought the cargo, retailed it at monopoly prices, and even paid the troops in rum. Henceforward for years, amidst corruption and drunkenness, this "Rum Corps" peddled monopoly liquor and dominated commerce. One of Macarthur's many enemies, a man with a talent for balanced alliteration, called him "as sharp as a razor and as rapacious as a shark." Debt and rum paralyzed the community. Settlers sold out to officers.

Yet to this avaricious scoundrel belongs much of the credit for founding Australia's greatest industry, sheep raising. As early as 1797 he bred Spanish Merinos that turned out to thrive on Australian pastures and remain the top breed of Australian sheep to this day. When he was sent to England in 1801, to stand trial for dueling, Macarthur took along samples of his wool and persuaded the Privy Council to grant him five thousand acres of good pasture and thirty convicts to work it. In 1806 he and fellow officers confronted a Governor who tried to break up their rum dealing, and summarily deposed him from office.

The Governor whom Macarthur and Company deposed was none other than Captain William ("Breadfruit") Bligh, victim seventeen years earlier of the mutiny on the *Bounty*. Set adrift by the mutineers with a few loyal men, he had sailed an open boat four thousand miles west from Tahiti to Timor, not far off the northwestern coast of Australia. Despite his reputation for brutality, Bligh actually did have a heart, and as Governor he attempted to keep the Rum Corps from exploiting the poor. So Macarthur and other officers packed him off to Tasmania.

Bligh's successor, Lieutenant Colonel Lachlan Macquarie, was such a significant figure in Australian life that ultimately *two* rivers were named for him, the Lachlan and the Macquarie. He has been described by historian Ernest Scott as a man "of thoroughly dependable character, gentlemanly in his manners, kindly but firm, with the pride of a pedigreed Highland laird, the paternal authority of a Hebrew patriarch, the masterful self-sufficiency of a Norman baron, and the personal rectitude of an English squire." Macquarie succeeded in liquidating the Rum Corps. Having established the principle that an emancipated convict had repaid his debt to society and was worthy of general respect, he proved the point by occasionally inviting former convicts to dinner.

The end of the Napoleonic Wars in 1815 freed shipping to resume the transportation of convicts, and 18,500 of them were sent to Macquarie. However, New South Wales was transformed from a prison camp to a prosperous colony under Macquarie's long regime. His imprint on the face of Sydney is all-pervasive. He laid out the streets and, employing the exceptional talents of a convict-architect, Francis Greenway, gave the city many beautiful buildings; Macquarie Lighthouse, a colonnaded hospital, St. Andrew's Cathedral, and a tower-fronted stable now used as the State Conservatorium of Music are some of them. For his work Greenway, whose crime had been forgery, was duly pardoned. One sees his face today on the Australian five-dollar bill.

The first native-born Australian of note was the flamboyant William Charles Wentworth. A town in New South Wales is named for him as is a leading hotel in Sydney. He was the son of a convict mother and a gallant surgeon who, though not actually convicted on a charge of highway robbery in London's Old Bailey, had volunteered his services for the voyage of the First Fleet. As a youth Wentworth accompanied Blaxland on his exploration over the mountains west of Sydney. Wentworth's inauspicious parentage did not prevent him from going to Cambridge, and he came back to make himself, through politics and journalism, the most famous of all Australians at mid-century. At one point early in his political career he turned so angrily anti-British that he suggested Australia should tie its destiny to the United States. His great achievement was gaining a representative legislature for New South Wales, by lobbying in the British House of Commons. He also established the University of Sydney, the country's first, in 1852. Though the "exclusionists," free settlers and their descendants who wanted to bar anyone with convict associations from their society, snubbed Wentworth socially, by the time he died, in 1872, he was known as "the father of Australian democracy."

*

"Squatter" is a term of contempt or pity in the United States; in Australia it commands respect. The bountiful fleece of the Merino sheep, as we have noted, was seen to be Australia's salvation almost from the first. Before 1830 the government granted land free on the pastures west of Sydney; then, changing policy, it proposed to sell land for five shillings an acre, limiting purchases to areas in nineteen counties conveniently close to Sydney. Defying the policy, graziers headed west with their flocks to squat on land beyond the nineteen counties. Soon "not all the armies of England, not 100,000 soldiers scattered throughout the bush" (as one Governor put it) could have herded the squatters back. The government retreated and asked the graziers only that they pay a ten-pound-a-year license. Courts began to uphold the squatters' land claims. This successful "land grabbing" gave the squatters some status; their success in raising sheep completed the work of making the word respectable. Not that the life—generally in a fly-specked, verminous one-room hut—was in the least gratifying. "There is no romance in monotony and mutton fat," wrote S. H. Roberts in *The Squatting Age in Australia.* In only three decades Australia became the main foreign supplier of high-quality wool for the mills of England.

To go ahead a bit: by the 1850's, '60's, and '70's Australian graziers had almost universally adopted the fence, at first post-and-rail and later wire, and abandoned the European principle that flocks had to be brought to shelter each night; these two measures vastly reduced the labor needed to run sheep and gave them thicker fleeces. They also found how to get water for their sheep from artesian wells. In 1880 the sailing of the refrigerator ship *Strathleven* to London with forty tons of meat signaled the big-scale use of sheep for mutton. At the close of the century Australia was grazing 100 million sheep—shepherd to the world.

*

Now: gold. It was incredibly, joyfully, easy to find. Huge nuggets, most notably the $50,000 Welcome Stranger, which weighed 141 pounds, lay in clay only a foot or so beneath the surface. Around Bendigo and Ballarat, both within one hundred miles of Melbourne, gold was found not in placers or in solid rock as in the U.S., but in alluvial deposits, carried there in ages past by streams. To find it, at first, took scarcely any more effort than leaning down.

The first big gold strike was made by Edward Hargraves, who had been a California forty-niner. He found gold in a creek near Bathurst, a hundred miles from Sydney. Then came the discoveries at Bendigo and Ballarat. The news went round the world. Gold-seekers rushed to the fields, at first from Adelaide and Tasmania, then from abroad. Laborers left factories; graziers deserted their sheep runs; sailors quit ships. Sydney ran out of soap and candles, for lack of anyone to make them. In 1852 in the month of September alone, nineteen thousand immigrants landed in Melbourne, plus some thousands in Sydney, and trudged to the goldfields afoot. By nationality they were mostly English, Scottish, Welsh, or Irish—followed in numbers by Americans and Germans. Then the Chinese began to arrive, forty thousand of them by 1857, most of them meekly mining the tailings from earlier diggings. The population of Australia grew from 405,000 in 1851 to 1,146,000 in 1861. In the same period Victoria grew from 87,000 to 540,000, to surpass New South Wales as Australia's largest colony.

The Australian gold rush brought none of the lynching, vigilantism, and killing that characterized the much smaller California gold rush (where a thousand men were murdered in the early 1850's, and only one killer punished). But it did foment the only battle ever fought on Australian soil. To dig, miners paid licenses of thirty shillings a month, and mounted policemen were unleashed on "license hunts" to collect the fees. The very concept of police in Australia triggers a hostility that apparently goes clear back to convict days (and continues until now). Miners found it particularly onerous to climb a mine shaft at the peremptory call of a cop. The police grew ever more arrogant and brutal. By a familiar escalation—a murder, a riot, prosecution of the rioters—feeling heightened until the miners felt obliged to build themselves a stockade at a town named Eureka. Some of the miners, increasing their list of demands from abolition of licenses to universal manhood suffrage, called for the formation of a Republic of Victoria. Police and the military charged the stockade. In the brief skirmish twenty-two miners and six policemen were killed. This fight was the bloodiest ever fought on Australian soil.

Australians have always seemed to sense that the gold rush, climaxed by the Eureka battle, has deep national meaning. As early as 1851 W. C. Wentworth foresaw that the gold era "must in a few years precipitate us from a colony into a nation."

The Second Half of the Nineteenth Century

After the gold rush, the population tripled. The proportion of unemancipated convicts dwindled to virtually zero. The rebellion at Eureka helped inspire reforms that ultimately included male suffrage, the secret ballot, and land reform. The seeds of Australian racism—the so-called White Australia policy—were planted; miners were prejudiced against and envious of the Chinese, who "were hard-working and had the usual good fortune attending those who work hard."

Finally, the Australians came to call themselves "diggers," a word then adopted by the rest of the world.

*

When did Australia become independent from Great Britain? That is a question often asked by Americans who have our own Revolution somewhat obsessively in mind, and who in certain cases of ignorance may not concede that Australia (or Canada either) has independence even yet. Australia (as well as Canada) does, of course. But independence came imperceptibly, and vestiges of English control remain to this day.

New South Wales was the mother colony, from which were later severed Tasmania, Victoria, and Queensland. As early as 1825 it had a Legislative Council named by the Governor, consisting entirely of government officials, and empowered only to approve measures submitted by the Governor. It was impotent, but it contained the possibility of change. Three years later, the British Parliament enlarged the size of the Council and gave it the right to have "opinions." By 1842 Parliament provided for a thirty-six member Council, two-thirds of whom were locally elected. By 1853 the Council was able to change the Constitution, a prerogative now traditional in Australia (but to this day regarded as unthinkable in the United States—as though our Congress could amend the Constitution as easily as it passes a law). The new Constitution created a powerful elected Legislative Assembly. In the ensuing process of widening the electorate and increasing democracy, the Governor gave up powers gradually and gracefully, moving from virtual dictator to a mere symbol of the Crown. One Governor of New South Wales found at a certain point that he was "powerless to do good, or to prevent it."

The exact steps by which the states became independent of colonial rule varied in curious ways. Victoria, breaking off from New South Wales in 1851, gave itself self-government two years later with an Executive Council collateral to its Legislative Council. South Australia, created a Crown Colony in 1841, had a partly elected Legislative Council by 1851 and a constitution and self-government by 1856. Tasmania, held back in the democratic process by its heavy proportion of convicts, got independence from New South Wales in 1825 but no "representative institutions" until 1853, and responsible government came only in 1856. Western Australia, first colonized in 1825, waited until 1893, the date of big gold strikes in Coolgardie and Kalgoorlie, to attempt government by an *appointed* Legislative Council and Assembly. It did not move on to elected legislatures until 1911, well after the founding of the federal government. That part of Australia which to this day does not govern itself, the Northern Territory, was originally part of South Australia. In 1911 it became a territory under the jurisdiction of Canberra.

*

The influence of the country's social complexion on politics throughout this period is fairly clear. The convict heritage dedicated the nation to the ordinary man, and squatters and free settlers who tried to imitate the English landed gentry succeeded only in being slightly ridiculous. Australian agriculture, built around the ratio of one sheep to forty acres of dry land, prohibited the formation of a European-style peasantry. By 1885, wrote Shaw, Australia had "a society with a high standard of living, and a strongly egalitarian outlook lacking that respect for birth, wealth, and intellect which was usual in nineteenth-century England. In this sense, the Australian colonies were in the van of progress, and had successfully pioneered a radical political system, part cause and part result of the high status in the community of the 'common man.' "

A part of this political system, more radical than we now remember, is the Australian ballot. In the U.S. in the middle of the nineteenth century, ballots were generally printed by political parties on differing colors of paper, making secrecy dubious. Australian states, as soon as they began to elect representatives to their councils and assemblies, specified a uniform ballot printed by the government. This simple guarantee of secrecy struck Americans as most desirable, and it came into general use in the U.S. in the 1890's.

A quite natural concomitant to the thrust for democracy was the growth of unions. Craft unions started in the 1830's, and miners were pretty thoroughly organized by 1878. The Australian sheep shearers were organized into a powerful union in 1886. Trade unionism in Australia was stronger than in any other country at the time. However, a Great Maritime Strike in 1891, involving many unions, failed. William Lane, a labor journalist and strike leader, who had soaked up his philosophy from the Americans Henry George and Edward Bellamy, quit Australia in disillusionment and tried to found an Australian Utopia in Paraguay. By the end of the century, labor had regained its power, pioneering effective compulsory arbitration with a success not yet achieved in the U.S.

In 1893 a severe depression exposed the weakness of six separate colonies on one continent with no machinery for joint concerns. Federation, apathetically discussed for a decade, took on urgency, if for no other reason than to gain respect for Australia in the eyes of world bankers, who found the states poor risks taken one by one. The hampering separation of the states grew painful and ludicrous, notably in the customs duties that they charged one another on goods in interstate commerce.

One Tasmanian politician told his people, in urging support of federation: "If you vote for the bill you will found a great and glorious nation under the bright Southern Cross, and meat will be cheaper, and you will live to see the Australian race dominate the South Seas . . . and you will have a market for potatoes and apples." On January 1, 1901, the first day of the new century, the Commonwealth of Australia came into being.

An Epilogue on the Convict Heritage

The problem of coming to grips with the convict heritage "gave most Australian historians megrim and threatened not a few with schizophrenia," says historian Russell Ward. Some theorized that the convicts, painted as simple rabbit poachers, were basically more innocent than the harsh judges in England; this was what was taught in schools. Others skated through the topic in a hasty and gingerly way—some still do. Still others took the nobody's-perfect line, quoting Daniel Defoe on Englishmen: "The most scoundrel race that ever lived; a horrid crowd of rambling thieves and drones." There was a poignant need for rationalizations. Melbourne and Adelaide took pride in not having been settled by convicts. Descendants of convicts burned papers that connected them to their ancestors. An English clergyman wrote, "There is no word in the English language of which one requires to make a more studied use in Australia than the word 'convict.' "

Now, seen in the light of Australia's success as a country, this national skeleton in the closet has mostly become a matter for jokes and indifference. How should a book like this one touch on the convict derivation? "Exploit it to the utmost!" bellowed one leading Australian editor. People boast that they are among the one in twenty Australians descended from . . . well, not so much convicts as colonizers. One is urged to look at the results, a great functioning nation, and to judge people by what they are, not by what their ancestors may have been. The subject is out in the open. If there is shame, it is for the wretched treatment of many of the convicts after they reached Australia.

But apparently Australia is doomed never to escape completely from having had felons for founding fathers. A year or so ago a Manila columnist, inveighing against the White Australia policy, charged that Australians "still cling to the habits they inherited from their forefathers—the convicts from England's prisons." One converses with a noted author in Adelaide, and the phrase "lousy convicts dumped on us" slips out in his speech. At dinner, there may be a half a dozen Australians boisterously putting down the whole concept of any shame in convict colonization. But there are likely to be one or two who are not making jokes, but sitting strangely silent.

CHAPTER 4

The Lucky Country

Then live Australia! Matron young and mild,
Bear still bright Mercy's banner high unfurled!
Pardon and peace for Britain's fallen child,
Refuge for all the oppress'd of all the world.

—FROM A PROPOSED AUSTRALIAN NATIONAL ANTHEM

AUSTRALIA HAS no national anthem of its own, and in fact one does not sense much nationalism here. What one notices more are symptoms of pragmatism, hedonism, and philistinism. In a moment of irritation, former Prime Minister Harold Holt once called Australia a "lotus land." There's some truth in that. But it would be fatuous to portray all of Australia as a lazy nation; prodigies of work have been accomplished in building the nation and its industries. The country functions—the plumbing works, the trains run, the mail gets delivered, the schools educate.

Still, where many Germans or Americans, for example, tend to make a cult of work, going on and on, obsessively, the bulk of Australians seem to keep in mind a certain moment every day and every week when work stops and the enjoyment of life begins. This state of mind implies a number of corollaries. For one, money loses priority as the all-powerful incentive. Constance Lee Butler, an American woman who went to Australia many years ago and married an Australian, observes that the Australian "often would prefer to earn less in order to have more free time to go to his weekender and swim and sail or paint his house and grow roses." Through some legality, the forty-hour week here officially works out at exactly thirty-five hours and fifty-one minutes. An American corporation officer says, "The

Australian working man has a nice setup here. He likes things pretty much as they are. It's difficult to tempt him with higher wages."

Australia offers vast possibilities for pleasure—and not only the simple pleasures of sport and the outdoors, but the larger tranquillities of freedom, prosperity, stability, and very little responsibility for the plight of the far-off, troubled rest of the world. Australians like to think that Australia exists for the good of Australians, not the other way around. This is not a lack of patriotism —more about that in a minute—but rather what Australians regard as the right order of priorities.

This pleasure principle works a couple of other ways, too. A girl journalist in Sydney argues that "Australians are happy because they consciously set aside religion and philosophy and take pleasure in what they have: prosperity, indifference to the world's problems, plenty of sunshine." In cab-driver language this comes out as: "Why worry about things you can't control?" A consequence is a kind of easy optimism. "She'll be right" is an all-purpose reassurance used whenever disaster impends. Strangely, she often is right; the gods seem to be on the side of the users of this jaunty Australianism. A parallel attitude is "It's good enough," said, perhaps, of a slapdash repair job—rarely do Australians take a tough, meticulous, Teutonic stand that something has damn well *got* to be right.

Is Australia, then, an earthly paradise? Not quite. People suffer diseases, fight, hate, work at unpleasant jobs, get bored. Books pour from the presses to tell Australians that they really don't have it so good. Nevertheless, the undercurrent of stubborn optimism flows strong. In 1964 Donald Horne, editor of the weekly newsmagazine the *Bulletin*, wrote a book criticizing every aspect of Australian society, and for a final flourish of irony called it *The Lucky Country*. To his astonishment, everyone took the title in its straightforward meaning, and it has been repeated so much in speech and print as to become an Australian byword, expressive of the country's euphoria.

Things the way they are are quite good enough to keep the majority of the people from wanting to rock the boat. Some force from the outer world —the pressure to accept Asian immigration, perhaps—may eventually muss up Australian complacency. Until then, a national characteristic is what New Left critic Dennis Altman calls "extraordinarily pronounced squareness." One is told that university students routinely undergo a period of derivative rebellion, "but they get square in two years."

To many people, elsewhere in the world, the sources of Australian contentment might appear to be rather slender. It's a boring, petty kind of life where ex-servicemen have an absolute right to a government job, and, worse yet, want it. Broadly speaking, the country seems quite satisfied to be badly dressed—the pedestrians make the streets look like Brighton on a dim Sunday. The country is solid with people who have a low threshold of contentment—unambitious, middle-class people who are indifferent about getting on. "Outside the intellectual pockets, a bare-minded philistinism prevails . . . a bronzed, back-slapping, amiable mass, for whom foreign affairs and the world of ideas might as well not exist," says Ross Terrill, an Australian political scientist.

When Pope Paul VI visited Sydney in December 1970, he chided the Australians for their materialism and isolation. He warned of the temptations of "self-centeredness, hedonism, eroticism," and he implored Australians not to "close your limited circle for the sake of selfish satisfaction." Hedonism is indeed widespread in Australia, and the "closed circle" charge apparently referred to racial immigration bars.

*

An enduring source of Australian pride is its military tradition. There is a genuine and permanent awe at how the Aussies twice went out and threw away their lives and blood for England. The country is cluttered with monuments to World Wars I and II, and Anzac Day, April 25, the anniversary of the attack on Gallipoli (of which more later), is taken far more seriously than Australia Day, January 26, anniversary of the landing of the first convicts.* In the background are other struggles where Australians served—the Boer War, the Sudan, the siege of Peking. Australians contend that their soldiers, though prone to refuse to salute their officers, are the world's toughest fighting men, the winners of the country's international reputation. Sometimes the country seems to be symbolized by the rugged bare knees of the troops. Nowadays, it must be added, one senses that the older generation of Australians trades on the martial tradition—the young hate it, and joke about it.

The convict heritage interacts with patriotism in both pride and shame. A verse from the nineteenth century says:

> *Small honor have we for the mother's name,*
> *Who stained our birth with the brand of shame.*
> *We* were *flesh of her flesh, and bone of her bone,*
> *We* are *lords of ourselves, and our land is our own.*

A spillover from convict ancestry is a healthy distrust of authority. The historian Clive Turnbull notes "an impulse to snatch from the judicial system anyone who may fall foul of it. This is manifest on the most respectable

* Prime Minister Menzies always played down Australia Day.

level in distrust of politicians of all kinds. . . . The police, in the Australian race memory, bear the brand of 'the system.' . . . Australians hate seeing people put in jail." Yet the convict heritage carries with it, inevitably, a distinct note of inferiority complex. "We are the most insecure people in the world," says one Melbourne editor.

Little touches bear this out. A boast heard again and again is "best (or biggest, or tallest) in the Southern Hemisphere." This is a safe and fairly meaningless comparison, since the chief competition in that hemisphere comes only from Brazil, Argentina, or South Africa. Defensive pride also shows through in claims like "This book was printed on Australian paper." Sugar packets honor the memory of Captain Cook with pictures of his sextant, compass, portrait, cottage.

The national inferiority complex comes, one is told, from that convict background (despite all attempts to make it a virtue), from domination by Britain in the beginnings of the country, from being looked down upon by the world as "too rough," from the slow development of Australian culture, and even from the blatant Australian accent. Self-criticism is a national hobby. A government booklet for immigrants confesses that the "ugly Australian" can be a "blusterer, often loud-mouthed and ignorant"; a leading educator says that the average Australian "would rather run half a mile than sit and think deeply for five minutes." Jack's as good as his master, Australians endlessly repeat—but Jack seems to lack the confidence to go on to be anything but Jack.

*

> *Good will devoid of grace, a down-to-earth pragmatism that can be aesthetically offensive, a culture that is deliberately, almost defiantly suburban.*
>
> —THE AUSTRALIAN CHARACTER ACCORDING TO ARTHUR KOESTLER

For most of the world, the Australian myth of the outback obscures the fact that this is one of the most urban countries in the world. Moreover, it has been citified for a century; way back in the 1860's the proportion of urban to rural population in Australia surpassed that of the United States and most of Europe. Four out of five Australians live in the cities, and most of these in the six state capitals plus Canberra and Darwin—these two are growing at the rate of 10 percent a year.

In addition, between 70 and 80 percent of all Australians own their own houses. The consequence is that the cities spread over land areas as big as any in the world. "Suburban sprawl" really takes on meaning when you fly over the major cities of Australia. And undoubtedly this makes for an existence that is more conformist than anything found in the spreading "developments" around U.S. cities. Polls show that 98 percent of Australian suburbanites never go out in the evening except Saturdays, and television sets are on for an average of four hours a day.

Yet the Australian goes at suburban life with such a zest that he half-redeems it. Gardens are important, and whole streets bloom prettily. Men conserve energy on the job in order to slave zealously in their workshops over house repair and improvement. The trying relations of landlord and tenant are evaded by ownership. "You buy a home, engage in sports, you're on your own," says one contented householder. Moreover, a bit of sophistication is creeping into suburban life—your host may serve you a very good chicken in white wine sauce. For many an Australian, life on his own 7,500 square feet of the surface of the earth is paradise enow. Australians are indeed defiantly suburban, enthusiastically, overwhelmingly, unchangeably suburban.

*

Once the first-time visitor leaves Sydney airport and heads for his hotel, the game begins: is this country a transplanted England or a transplanted America? The expressway has the familiar engineering of the U.S. freeway system: America. But traffic keeps to the left: England. The highway signs have the interstate white-on-green colors and typography: America. But they may have a note of Old World courtesy ("DRIVE SLOWLY PLEASE"): England.* On a nearby railroad track, big double-truck freight cars (American) are interspersed with little four-wheel goods wagons (English). In the city, the newer glass-and-aluminum architecture speaks of America, the older Victorian architecture speaks of England. The commercial television derives from America, the sports from England. The excitement seems American, the manners are English. Brand names everywhere are American; the style of the newspapers is English.

"Australians combine the best and worst of California and Texas," says Sheila Scotter, former editor of the Australian *Vogue*, a magazine that is published in America, England, *and* Australia. But those two states certainly have no reverence for a queen, and Australia decidedly does. Queen Elizabeth visited Australia in 1970, strolled the streets with engaging informality, and cut prorepublican sentiment in the Gallup Poll from 40 percent to 25 percent. The Gallup Poll also shows that 65 percent of Australians want to

* There are even signs that say "PLEASE READ THE NEXT SIGN."

recognize Prince Charles as King when Elizabeth dies.* A Londoner reports that in general Englishmen feel very much at home in Australia, and a cynical Australian says that his countrymen will accept a bogus Englishman over an honest Australian. There are still people in Australia who have never forgiven the Duke of Windsor for abdicating.

All these comparisons grate on Australian nerves. Some say that they do not like what they had, Anglicization, and do not like what they are heading for, Americanization. Many Australians find identity by being anti-British, while laughing at Americans as naïve and immature. They say that they want an authentic independence, not to be compared with Canada's, which is flawed by the proximity and power of the United States. But Australia has not bothered to cut its ties to the British Crown with the same thoroughness as Canada. The upshot of all these tugs and pulls seems to be that Australia wants to be independent—with close ties to both Britain and the U.S.

*

Something between a pal, a friend, and a fellow worker—this is the Australian "mate," pronounced "mite." Mateship is an outgrowth of the taming of the bush in the last century, an egalitarian experience. The Australians, wrote a startled English observer in the middle of the century, "present a marked contrast to the population of England and Europe generally. As a rule, every man there is, may be, or expects soon to be, his own master. Here are no conventionalities, no touching of hats." But pioneering in the sometimes terrifying outback required more dependence of one man on another than, say, breaking sod in Nebraska. Thus a man was always pleased to find a mate, someone he could trust, and mateship took on a semi-mystical construction as an Australian quality.

Mateship produces a goodly measure of trust and candor; a man is taken at face value until proved otherwise. This makes for a generally cooperative community. Every man in a pub is the next man's mate, and the cab driver opens the door with a cheery "Hop in, mate." All this leads to a certain all-male complacency, a pub-and-club society that excludes women. Whether there is any relationship between mateship and homosexuality awaits the attention of a good sociologist.

* Which was not the case in a similar occasion in the past. In 1896 John Norton, editor of the Sydney *Truth*, raised a toast to Queen Victoria's health and long life, "if only to keep her rascal of a turf-swindling, cardsharping, wife-debauching, boozing rowdy of a son, Albert Edward, Prince of Wales, off the throne."

The Japanese, dependent on Australia in many business relationships, have made a careful study of mateship. Purchasing missions are given instructions in the intricacies of the Australian national character, as to wit:

> To understand the Australian better the Japanese must appreciate that although Australia is not a socialistic country, there are deep rooted elements of "mateship" and a genuine, "Jack is as good as his master" attitude outside the place of employment. Australians in authority tend to work closer with their immediate seniors or with their executive employees as colleagues and much more is done by discussion and conference than by authoritative direction. Any action of an overseas country which affects Australia and which in any way can be interpreted as an expression of superiority will incur an automatic antagonism from most Australians and this of course would not be in the best interests of international relationships.

The Australian Language

Sidney Baker, who has labored for more than twenty years in doing for the Australian language what H. L. Mencken did for the American, has accumulated more than five thousand words or phrases that are purely Australian, or have an Australian twist, or are greatly favored by Australians. With origins in England, the convict experience, the outback, the Australian expeditionary armies, and Pidgin English, this private language has extraordinary humor and expressiveness.

"Bloody" is the Great Australian Adjective—English too, of course. "Kangabloodyroo," they say. "Bloke" similarly survived the passage from England. Everybody is a bloke. Some odd verbs are: "winge," to complain; "yabber," to chat; "barrack," to root for; "bludge," to cadge; and "bugger," to wreck. If you want to speak this language, you must know the meaning of these nouns: "wowser," bluenose; "tucker," food; "jackeroo," apprentice on a sheep or cattle station; "poofter," male homosexual; "blue," a fight; "kip," a bed. An all-purpose exclamation is "Strewth!" To praise someone, the Australian says "Goodonyer!" "Digger" has largely gone out of style, but "dinkum," meaning true and admirable, and "fair dinkum," meaning even more so, still prevail. Some Australianisms are unbloodybelievable: the expression for "to attempt to deceive" is "to come the raw prawn." Or too vivid: the word for "vomit" is "chunder."

About the Australian accent, only a few points can be made with certainty and without giving offense. The great bulk of Australians, from one end of the country to the other, speak in a distinctive twang, employing the vocabulary suggested above. At least one other large group, generally better educated, speaks an English that sounds to Americans and Britons much less accented, closer to the universal English of radio announcers.

The catchiest tongue, of course, is that of the first group, the accent of the pubs and sports stadiums, of tradesmen and miners and football players. London Cockney formed this accent in the beginnings of the colony, but Australians grow rather inflamed if you call it Cockney now. "Lady" becomes "lydy"; "mate" becomes "mite"; "mailing" becomes "myling"; this is "Austrylian." Accents land in strange places, and pronunciations get odd twists. A dispute is a "contrOHversy"—accent on the second *o*. A little reminder is a "meemo." A bookstore clerk in Sydney says that she frequently gets requests for "poultry," and learned only by hard experience that the customers really wanted poetry. Inevitably the day came when a man asked for a book of "poultry" and confusion reigned until he could at last make clear that he needed instructions on how to raise chickens.

A few years ago, a professor identified as Afferbeck Lauder defined a genial new language called "Strine," which is the word "Australian" telescoped. Strine utilizes the numerous elisions of Australian speech and the way its vowels veer unpredictably into diphthongs. The results can be hilarious. "*Hazzy gairt non wither mare thorgon?*" turns out to be "How is he getting on with the mouth organ?" Professor Lauder isolated many useful phrases, such as "*egg nishner,*" a machine to cool a room, and "*noker parison,*" incomparable. "Strine" came to be a household word; an English lady, complaining of the difficulties of train travel in Australia, said recently, "Try following an announcement comprising an Aboriginal place name read by a Greek whose halting English is complicated by a Strine accent." The merry professor turned out to be a commercial artist named Alistair Morrison. You may want to decode Afferbeck Lauder, his *nom de Strine*. Clue: the dictionary is arranged in . . .

Beer, Bountiful Beer

Wanted, a beautiful barmaid,
To shine in a drinking den;
To entrap the youth of a nation,
And ruin the City men.

Australia does *not* lead the world in beer-drinking—Czechoslovakia does, with 227 pints per capita per year. Australia is fourth (after West Germany and Belgium), with 201 pints (Britain averages 164, and the U.S. 111). But Australia talks a great game of beer-drinking; indubitably beer is the national beverage; and individual prodigies of consumption are achieved.

One Melbourne guzzler, for example, reportedly downed six pints of beer while the post office clock was striking six, which used to be the closing time in the pubs. *The Australian* solemnly reports that the country consumes 4,899,056,000 middies of beer a year, but this statistic is none too enlightening, since a middy measures ten ounces in New South Wales, seven ounces in Western Australia, and is not used as a measure elsewhere. Lore is so plentiful that author Cyril Pearl managed, a couple of years ago, to do a whole delightful book called *Beer, Glorious Beer!*

The circumstances of Australian beer-drinking are quaint and sometimes doleful. The beer itself, as anyone disgusted with the dry, thin, pale, light Pilsners of the United States can testify, is strong and hearty. This seems to be the consequence of using sugar, as well as malt and hops, in the brewing. The strength, depending on the state, runs from 3.5 percent of alcohol by weight to 4.5 percent—not too strong.* New South Wales law requires that beer contain *not less* than 3.3 percent of alcohol by weight. The ubiquitous pubs of Australia are only now beginning to turn themselves into amenable places along the lines of English pubs or American bars. Traditionally they have been (and often still are) grubby rooms lined in white tile like lavatories. This is traceable, at least in part, to the days when the six-o'clock closing hour meant that the pub existed not for sociability, games, or human warmth, but solely for grim, rapid drinking, which of course was bound to cause a lot of vomiting—and tile is easy to clean. The publicans, who encourage the singleminded boozing because it makes for profits, are not admired, by and large, in Australia. Connected to the public bar there is often also a saloon, where the drink may be Scotch and the customers professional men, and a lounge, where women are allowed. Pubs close on Sundays, except in Queensland, Western Australia, and Canberra.

Barmaids (sympathetically dealt with in the verse above by a last-century bluenose who wished to get the girls out of the pubs) are collectively a precious Australian tradition—cheery women who josh the customers as they fill a glass, let the head subside, top it off with more beer, and serve it: "Seventeen cents, thank you, love." Their expression for a repeat is "something similar," on the indisputable grounds that you can't have the "same" drink that you just drank. Treating in Australianese is "shouting"—"I'll shout you a beer"; the best guess about the origin of the expression is that rich, expansive gold miners used to shout for everyone in the neighborhood to come to the pub and have a beer. Taxes on beer produced $338,614,000 in government revenue in a recent year. There is much learned

* U.S. beers range from 2.89 to 4.95 percent. New Zealand's Kings Brew measures 5.64 percent.

controversy over whether each new serving of beer requires a freshly washed glass. Superstition holds that refilling makes the beer taste better. "Most men in bars, I think about seven out of ten, prefer to keep their old glass," says the president of the Australian Hotels Association.

Clubs as well as pubs serve beer, but the implications can be misleading. An American in Brisbane wangled membership in exclusive Tattersalls, and presented himself at the bar for a beer. The bar, the barmaid, the beer, and the customers all turned out to be precise replicas of those to be found in any Brisbane pub.

Assorted Manners and Morals

A brand of matches called Federal is widely preferred because the wooden box slivers nicely to provide toothpicks and fingernail cleaners.

Women's liberation in Australia centers on a group that publishes a monthly magazine called *Mejane*, a switch on the famous line in the Tarzan movies. Germaine Greer, author of *The Female Eunuch* and a leading feminist on the London–New York axis, is an Australian. Women often have to resign their jobs when they marry. But not all women feel oppressed. "Women's liberation? What for? I can even go to a prize fight alone if I want to," argues strong-minded Sheila Scotter.

Sex among the Australian middle classes, it would seem, still suffers from Victorian attitudes; to have intercourse is to "have a naughty." Contraceptives are taxed at 27.5 percent as luxuries, and cannot be advertised.

The suicide rate for women in Australia is twice as high as the rate for men; no one knows why. The total suicide rate, 15.2 per hundred thousand of population, is considerably higher than that of, for example, the U.S., which is 10.9.

Sideburns are called "sidelevers" or "sideboards." A haircut costs $1.40. Long hair on men is every bit as common as in the United States or Europe, but the wearers give the impression that they are just being conventionally unconventional.

Vacationing abroad from this remote continent is expensive and exhausting —although one young businesswoman recently managed to make two trips to both New York and London in less than eight weeks.* Singapore and Tahiti are places that draw many better-off Australians. Fiji is the foreign

* These flights expose the traveler to maximum risk of suffering circadian dysrhythmia, the up-to-twelve-hour wrench of the human system's internal clock away from sun time. The disturbance seems to be worse when the flight goes from west to east, such as Sydney to London.

country (it became independent from Britain in 1970) that average Australians find near enough, exciting enough, and cheap enough to visit in large numbers—they form the islands' most numerous tourists. The shops there sell duty-free goods; one can pop over from Sydney, spend a few days at the Suva TraveLodge or the Fijian, and make purchases that save enough to pay for the trip.

Radio station call letters start with a figure: 5AD in Adelaide, 2CN and 2CY in Canberra, for example.

Americans, spending Australian dollars, tend to forget after a while that they cost $1.19 in U.S. money, and that therefore goods are not as cheap as they may seem. Thus the forty-five-cent shot of Scotch served at the Canberra Rex Hotel actually costs around fifty-one cents in American cash—still a bargain.

*

Australia used to be a world leader in cushioning its citizens from life's pitfalls by social security, but years of prosperity and antisocialist government have caused the system to fall behind. Health care is provided almost entirely by private insurance companies, which are subsidized by the government. Sick people pick their own doctors, pay the bills, and collect an average of 90 percent from the insurance companies. This self-help system works well enough to prevent the kind of medical disaster that bankrupts a family, but one is told that it helps the insurance companies more than the patients. Old-age pensions, introduced in 1908, have not kept pace with world standards, and now rank with those of Saudi Arabia and Trinidad. The full pension for a man over sixty-five (or a woman over sixty) is only $17.25 a week, and this sum is reduced, through a complicated "means test," in proportion to the pensioner's private income or wealth. For example, the pension is cut by an amount equal to about one-half of any private income over $10, and therefore drops to zero when private income reaches $41. Similarly the pension goes down in proportion to the value of a person's savings or property (apart from his house, car, furniture, personal effects, and a certain amount of life insurance), cutting out when these assets reach $21,200. People have to squander saved money to qualify for pensions. The Liberal Party wants to patch up the machinery by eliminating the means test, which would cost the government $370 million a year; the Labor Party wants a new, full-fledged National Superannuation Scheme.

With virtually full employment and evenly spread prosperity, Australia does not suffer the scabs of poverty that afflict big U.S. cities and the countryside of the poorer states, but nevertheless nearly a million Australians live on the edge, with incomes of less than thirty-seven dollars a week for families of four. The poor include most Aborigines, the chronically sick, semiskilled workers with large families, and students.

*

Australia's auto-accident death rate, per mile traveled, is the worst in the world (though the rate per 100,000 population just about equals that of the U.S.). Upwards of 3,500 people are killed each year, and about 80,000 injured. Probably one reason is the lack of expressways with divided lanes—there are only 1,325 miles of them. Most of the 560 miles between Sydney and Melbourne are merely adequate two-lane highways; Brazil, with its Rio–São Paulo superhighway, far outclasses Australia in connecting major cities. The slaughter is carried out in a rather small arena. Australia has only 105,000 miles of concrete or asphalt highway and 143,000 miles of gravel; the rest of the 560,000-mile (versus 3,152,000 in the U.S.) network is described as "formed only" or "cleared only." Road maps show dotted-line tracks bleakly labeled "natural formation." The *Sunday Australian* carries a prominent report on "Roads to Avoid." Bumpy surfaces, lack of lighting, and fast driving at night by car-crazy kids are also blamed for the death toll, although Australian drivers in general are notoriously inept and careless. The state of Victoria in 1970 became the first jurisdiction in the world to make wearing seat-belts compulsory, as part of an effort to cut down on the killing. The move met some opposition on the grounds that civil liberty includes the right to risk death, but most people cheered the new law, and New South Wales soon passed a similar law.

The White Australia Policy

Australia has encouraged the immigration of literally millions of new settlers in recent decades, and the overwhelming majority of them have white skin. Australians are not very proud of excluding the black, brown, and yellow people of the surrounding nations and of Africa. They know that this discrimination seriously undermines their moral position in world councils. But among the vast bulk of Australians, shame is easily overbalanced, not by racism per se so much as relief at avoiding a problem. Historian A. G. L. Shaw speaks for millions when he writes: "Nor can any observer of South Africa or the Southern States of the U.S.A. now fail to rejoice that the color problem at least is one which Australia has never had to face."

Surely this is the ostrich hiding its head. Preserving a continent for thirteen million whites in a world of two and a half billion people of other colors does not sound much more viable over the long run than South African apartheid. Enforcing the immigration restrictions raises many poignant problems. Australia has to insist on visas on passports* in order that consular officers can get a look at the skin color of the prospective visitor. The exhaustive visa application requires the names of close relatives who are *not* accompanying the traveler, and the names of foreign countries where the applicant may have lived in recent years. A British technician can move to Australia quite readily unless—as in the recent case of Jan Allen, British subject, electronics engineer, and Jamaican—he happens to be black. Exclusion is a highly subjective, nothing-in-writing process, going back ultimately to the discretion of the Minister of Immigration himself. Desirable white immigrants get travel subsidies; blacks and Asians, unless superlatively qualified, get bland refusals.

Late in the last century, the *Bulletin,* then as now an important Australian periodical, carried a shamelessly racist motto: "Australia for the Australians —the cheap Chinaman, the cheap nigger, and the cheap European pauper to be absolutely excluded." The operative word then was "cheap": these races would work for less than the white man, and take his job. The second Prime Minister, Alfred Deakin, was thought to be most decently tolerant when he said in a speech that the Japanese were not inferior to white men, but simply different, and perhaps superior in some respects. One Immigration Minister, speaking more bluntly, said: "Two Wongs don't make a white."

The *Bulletin,* let it quickly be said, is now the country's leading advocate of a truly open immigration policy. "All that saves Australia from being a tenth-rate outthrow of European colonialism has been the constantly enlivening effect of immigrants," says this magazine. "If it makes sense to bring Turks to Australia to do some of the heavy work, why does it not make sense to try to get a few Japanese technologists to help think up some things for the Turks to do?" In point of fact, about 35,000 nonwhites and persons of "mixed descent" have immigrated since 1966. By and large Australians of the current generation know as well as any civilized men that skin pigmentation has nothing to do with a person's character and ability, and they accept individuals on a personal basis without much regard for

* The United States, of course, also insists on visas, and restricts immigration to 176,000 a year, less, in certain years, than Australia. But priorities other than color (such as having close relatives in the U.S.) determine who gets in, and in 1969, for example, 73,621 Asians and 5,876 Africans were admitted to the U.S.

color. But here a vicious circle comes into play: Australia is underpopulated, and therefore a sizable immigration of people with black and yellow skins would change Australian society more radically than it would if the country were more populous; and yet the mere fact of underpopulation makes excluding blacks and Asians from overcrowded places all the more disgraceful. A second consideration is that Australia is a Southeast Asian country, and must get along with its neighbors; it cannot pretend to be distant and isolated. Thus the White Australia policy has been steadily modified from the time it was first made law in the Immigration Restriction Act of 1901. Now the idea is to admit some, but not too many, nonwhites, with a preference for Asians, under the terms of the 1958 Migration Act, which set up a system of temporary and permanent entry permits.

The people who get in through these cracks in the wall are scientists, engineers, university lecturers, businessmen, teachers, nurses, and some other professionals. About forty thousand people of these categories, mostly Asian, now live in Australia. An Asian trader who can prove a business turnover of $20,000 a year or more can gain admission to Australia, and even bring an assistant. In addition, fifteen thousand Asian students go to Australian universities, but they are obliged to leave Australia when their education is complete. An ironic upshot is that they often emigrate to Canada or the United States, putting Australia in the position of subsidizing the training of talented people for the benefit of those two countries, while simultaneously frustrating Australia's desire to aid its Far Eastern neighbors by providing them with education.

Thus white Australia has a little leavening of nonwhites, surprisingly visible on the streets of the cities. The dark-skinned immigrants report generally good relations. A journalist from India says that his daughter was teased by white kids who jeered that she looked like she needed a bath. But his summation was: "Once Australians get to know you and like you, they accept you totally." An American Negro, supposedly the first, was accepted for Australian citizenship late in 1970. He was Bernard Byers, who had served for four years as a teacher of French at Melbourne's posh Trinity Grammar School, after first visiting Australia in 1959 as choreographer for a Brazilian government dance company. "I haven't found the racial bit here," he says. "Once you get a job and a circle of friends, you fit in."

An area where Australian exclusion hurts badly is the lesser Pacific islands. Many have populations much too big for their coconut economies, and need to export people. Perhaps more pointedly, not even the people of New Guinea, who are legally Australian citizens, are permitted to move to the continent.

"Britain got itself into a cleft stick in years past by having to admit Jamaicans and Pakistanis and so on or be kicked out of their lovely colonies," muses Bill Russell, a Sydney journalist. The temper of Australia in matters racial is the desire to go on being a white Asian nation. The descendants of the original English, Scottish, Welsh, and Irish settlers have found it traumatic enough to absorb the great white immigration of recent years. To aspire to the unity-in-diversity of a massive nonwhite immigration is just too unsettling. An undefined "gradualist" approach is the closest thing that anyone offers as an ultimate solution to the dilemma.

The New Australians

An awareness that Australia was in painful need of more population pervaded most of the country's history, but in this century immigration ran low until 1945 because of labor's fear of job competition and because of the Depression. Such immigrants as came were almost all British, pulling out of the dismal England of the 1920's. Attempts were made in the 1930's to send Australia's few Italians back, because of the shortage of jobs. At the Evian Conference on refugees in 1937 Australia refused to accept German Jews: "As we have no real racial problem, we are not desirous of importing one."

The war convinced many Australians that they had no more than twenty years to build a bigger industrial base founded on a bigger population. Minister of Information Arthur Calwell coined a catchy slogan, "Populate or perish." Britons were still first choice, but the snotty attitude toward troubled Europeans was dropped, and 218,000 displaced persons admitted. With a cheerful disregard for the niceties of Old World geography, the Aussies lumped all these immigrants together as "Balts and Letts." Then Australia reached out to get Europeans of every kind, with the goal of raising the population to thirty million in fifty years. The device for bringing them, apart from the propaganda that attracts their attention,* is the "assisted passage" payment of most of the ship or plane fare to Australia—or all of it, in the case of immigrants younger than nineteen. An adult Englishman, for example, need contribute only twenty pounds toward his passage.

This vigorous program brought 1,850,000 immigrants to Australia between 1947 and the end of 1971. Along with them came an equal number of unassisted "intending" settlers and persons who came on their own and

* An advertisement in the Manchester *Guardian*, for example, stresses Australia's easier living, economic boom, stable democracy, and snowless climate. It urges readers to send for a booklet called *Living in Australia*, which reprints ads from Australian periodicals showing prices, land values, and so on.

stayed in Australia for a year or more; but most of these two groups, plus some of the assisted settlers, did not stay. The net gain to the population since 1947 is something like two and one-half million, or one-fifth of all Australians. Britons comprised more than half of the immigrants, followed by Italians, Greeks, and Yugoslavs. In lesser numbers, but decidedly visible among the New Australians, are Spaniards, Scandinavians, Americans, Hungarians, South Americans, Czechs, Turks, Poles, Icelanders, and Arabs.

The swallowing of this horde of humanity has gone astonishingly well. The immigrants stirred up a latent tolerance among the natives, who learned to stop saying "dago" or "Polack" and start using the rather egregious but certainly friendly term "New Australian." An Englishman, however, remains a "pom" or "pommy,"* a word more jocular than pejorative. Integration into Australian society went so well for one Englishman, Bernard Hesling, that he wrote a genial book called *The Dinkumization and Depommification of an Artful English Immigrant*. Language problems seem more comic than troublesome. Women, staying home, are sometimes slow to learn English, but men on a job pick it up fast enough, though the result may be a jolting Hungarian-Australian accent. Some areas of the cities fill up so completely with immigrants that English is hardly to be heard. A third-generation Australian living near Prahan, a Greek-dominated suburb of Melbourne, went to the infant welfare center there and for starters was asked, in loud, carefully enunciated syllables, "D-o y-o-u s-p-e-a-k E-n-g-l-i-s-h?"

Fifteen newspapers are published in languages other than English. The government-run Overseas Telecommunications Commission advertises three-minute telephone calls for eleven dollars to "talk to someone in Europe you love," and the picture shows an Italian woman saying presumably, "*Mamma mía*!" An Italian contribution to Melbourne is a branch of the Mafia.

More broadly, the immigrants shook up the self-satisfied Old Australians by working hard and releasing new energy into the system. A story is told of a Yugoslav lens-grinder whose work was so good that his employers readily agreed to sponsor the immigration of his brother, also a lens-grinder. The brother was put on the night shift, turned out to be just as skilled, and in the end, of course, was revealed to be the same man working two shifts.

A case of particular improvement in Australia that everyone notes is culi-

* The origin of this word cited by Sidney Baker is so extravagant that it is herewith reprinted *in toto*: "There has been a popular theory that *pommy* came from *jimmy-grant* (1845), as a rhyme on 'immigrant,' which was shortened to *jimmy*, the word then being merged by rhyme into *pomegranate* (it is suggested that the rosy-cheeked English may have given some association with the ruddy fruit) and subsequently clipped back to *pommy*."

nary standards.* There are hardly any really native dishes, except kangaroo-tail soup. Good cheese is rare; the best is cheddar. Oddly, restaurants don't serve lamb or mutton very often. It is still impossible to find truly Australian food, but you can get anything else from dolmades or a fettucini to a knish or a piroshki. No less than 40 percent of university staffs in Australia are people from other countries—also one-third of hospital staffs.

Australia's economy has run so well in the past twenty years that immigrants have had no trouble getting work. But there are plenty of cases of mutual disillusionment between Australia and the immigrants. In 1966, for example, eighteen thousand of them went back to their native countries. Immigrants are received, upon arrival, in hostels made largely of Nissen huts from old army camps, and some of them have to stay there for as much as four years before finding housing. Social tensions arise; the bluer-blooded Old Australians resist contact with the newcomers. Professional men are often disappointed to find their degrees unacceptable, forcing them to sit for new exams or take menial jobs. A few fainthearted Australians express second thoughts about expansion-by-immigration, which requires, for example, so many new schools—forgetting that the immigrants are providing Australia with talents acquired at the expense of the nations whence they came. The immigration program is criticized more soundly for its execution. A pertinent case in point, mentioned earlier, is that the government accepts unskilled Turks and Arabs but still bars skilled Japanese and Southeast Asians.

Americans moving to Australia have lately reached six thousand a year, the motive for many being disillusionment with the troubled, violent United States, and for a few stark fear of the blacks, curable only by settling in white Australia. The Australian government even subsidizes air fare for them, up to $360. Almost all of the 5,500 letters of inquiry received by a U.S. firm that gives advice on moving to Australia mentioned social unrest and violence. Inquiries to the Australian consulates in Manhattan and San Francisco shot to record numbers after the Chicago riots of 1968. Stuffy comments abound in the explanations offered by American immigrants in Australia: "We didn't like the idea of subjecting our young son and daughter to the kind of future we saw taking shape in the cities." "We knew that in Australia there was

*Until the food-conscious immigrants came, Australian food was confined, pretty much everyone agrees, to steak and eggs. Cyril Pearl offers a tongue-in-cheek recipe: "Take a piece of old bullock, cut as thin as possible, throw into a frying-pan with a spoonful of sump-oil (winter grade is preferable) and burn to the ground. Fry an egg in same oil. When both are cold, toss on to a soapy plate and cover with tomato sauce."

nothing to be frightened of racially." An Australian official says, "The largest number, very frankly, are attracted by the stable social climate."

The Gallup Poll reported a while back that one out of every twenty-five American adults would like to emigrate to Australia. Many of the American New Australians, of course, have motives more admirable than flight from U.S. troubles. They sense a frontier spirit, an opportunity for business success, a chance for a sunnier, easier life. With nice irony, many go for a motive best expressed in a famous document of the land they leave: "the pursuit of happiness."

Many return to the U.S., too, let down by Australia. The chief reason is the lower standard of living. Australia is prosperous, but its per capita GNP is half that of the U.S. Prices are lower, but wages much lower. A business executive who may have been getting twenty-five thousand American dollars a year in the United States will get ten thousand Australian dollars* in Australia—and is less likely to yearn for more because high-bracket income taxes are so steep. The bulk of the immigrants accept these setbacks in return for a less competitive life. They become plumbers, journalists, schoolteachers, businessmen; they run mines, ranches, garages, small industries. Some are professors, earning from $6,000 to $15,000 a year. One American became a maker of boomerangs for tourists. The Americans blend quickly into Australian society, do not stick together in "ghettos" and soon cannot be told from old Australians except at meals: they hold their forks in their right hands. Quite often they find what a New York woman, who moved to Sydney at the age of thirty-six, calls simply "a more satisfying brand of happiness."

Just as Britons have always been favored in Australia, Australians have historically been able to migrate freely to Great Britain—but no longer. The new British immigration law makes an Australian an "alien" unless he has at least one parent or grandparent born in Britain. This makes England foreign territory to some of Australia's bluest-blooded families. One victim of this law is the son of the Queen's own Governor in New South Wales, Roden Cutler.

* Throughout this book, money figures are expressed in Australian or New Zealand dollars, which in terms of U.S. money rose from $1.12 to $1.19 when President Nixon devalued the American dollar. The U.S. reader should remember, when he encounters a money figure in this book, that the same figure expressed in American currency would be about one-fifth higher.

CHAPTER 5

Australian Rules—And Other Arts

Australians of my generation grew up in a world apart. Until we went abroad we had never seen a beautiful building, hardly ever heard a foreign language spoken or been to a well-acted play, or eaten a reasonably sophisticated meal, or listened to a good orchestra; and outside two or three art galleries in Melbourne and Sydney, there was scarcely a house that contained a collection of worthwhile paintings.

—ALAN MOOREHEAD

TODAY, Moorehead finds his native country improved and even transformed. The way the Australians live, what *interests* them, is made of many parts—sports, arts, books, music, the press. On the scene are eccentric painters, genteel women playing at bowls, kinetic newspapers, football stars, book-bannings, opera singers, and twelve-tone composers. A country that was placid and even stodgy ten or twenty years ago is lively, active, and interesting now. Another quality is a certain lightheartedness: Australians are spared the frustrations of Britain and the great social and military-oriented schisms of the United States. The previous chapter attempted to say something about what Australians *are*—in this one let us try to examine what they *do*, at leisure, in the arts, and on television, with a look, too, at the press.

*

"Sport to many Australians is life and the rest a shadow. . . . To many it is considered a sign of degeneracy not to be interested in it," writes Donald Horne.

And of the sports, football is king. Australians play four kinds. Rugby

Union is for amateurs; Rugby League is the main winter spectator sport in New South Wales and Queensland. Soccer is mostly played by immigrants —Italians and Yugoslavs nostalgic for the game so popular in the old countries. Australian Rules, played in Western Australia, South Australia, and Tasmania, but most fervently in Victoria, is the authentic native game. It is basically a game of flowing movement, like Rugby or soccer, rather than of formation and downs, like American football. The field is enormous—190 yards long and 120 yards wide—and oval-shaped, like the ball which is used. In the end zones are four goal posts, standing in a line at intervals of seven yards. Each side has eighteen men, who aim to advance the ball to the neighborhood of the goal posts, and kick or punch it through for six points (if it goes between the two center posts) or one point (if it goes between a center post and an outer post). To move it forward, the ball can be kicked, punched, or carried (provided that it is dribbled once every ten yards). The most spectacular play is the "mark," a successful ten-foot-high catch of a kicked ball; the marker gets a free kick to the goal posts. A ball-carrier grabbed by an opponent must get rid of the ball by kicking or punching.

More than 100,000 fans turn out regularly in Melbourne to "barrack" for their teams, of which there are a couple of dozen. The tackles are not as rough as in American football, but since the players wear no protective gear, the mayhem—black eyes, cuts, bruises, and broken bones—is considerable.

*

Australians love horse racing. There is a track in every city. TAB shops, with windows for betting on horse and greyhound races, are all over the place. The initials mean Totalisator Agency Board, the state-controlled betting organization, comparable to New York State's off-track betting system. The totalizator (U.S. spelling), or pari-mutuel machine, was invented in racing-crazy Australia, as was the photo-finish camera.

The great annual madness in Melbourne is the Melbourne Cup, run every year for 111 years on the first Tuesday of November. For a few minutes the streets are deserted, as all of Australia glues itself to the radio or television broadcast. At Flemington Racecourse, a vast arena, crowds of more than 100,000 watch. Australian troops fighting in New Guinea during World War II are supposed to have declared an unofficial cease-fire so that they could listen to the running of the Cup.

One of the most memorable figures in Australian sports history is not a man but a horse. He was Phar Lap, a "mountain of a horse," over seventeen hands high, with a stride in gallop of more than twenty-five feet. He won the Melbourne Cup in 1930. Two years later, right after winning the Aqua

Caliente Handicap in California, he died. His body was disposed of in an equitable way: the skeleton went to New Zealand, where he was born; the heart went to the Institute of Anatomy in Canberra; and the hide was duly stuffed and placed in the National Museum in Melbourne, where Phar Lap may be seen to this day.

The great summer sport is cricket; it is also much more a participatory sport. Australians are so good at sports that merely reading about their skill and energy makes one want to lie down and rest for a while. Of 178 Test Matches in cricket played with England since 1882, Australia has won 73 to England's 67, with 43 drawn. Australians won the Davis Cup in tennis fifteen times in the eighteen years between 1950 and 1967. In football, golf, swimming, and Olympic sports Australia's winning record is all out of proportion to the country's small population. Undoubtedly part of this good show derives from the stress on sport instilled in every Australian child from infancy. Another reason is that Australians generally are big, strong, physically fit people. A third might be the long evenings, year round; while the people of northern nations are forced indoors in the winter, Australians are still outside doing something strenuous.

Innumerable golf courses spangle the suburbs of the big cities, and tennis courts are everywhere. Even old ladies have a sport: bowls, although, to be exact, the game is also played by old men, plus the middle-aged of both sexes. Bowling greens, impeccably level with crew-cut grass, are to be found all over the cities, the players uniformed in white except for colored hatbands; the women look a bit like nurses. The point of the game is to roll the bowl (the bowling ball) as close as possible to the jack, a small ball resting at the other end of the green. This apparently simple endeavor is complicated by a bias cut into the bowl, which makes one hemisphere more convex than the other and causes the ball to take a curved path.

The ultimate Australian madness is surfing, done in many ways: with a surfboat (four oarsmen and a man to steer), with a sort of canoe, with inflated rubber mats, with plastic-foam floats, with ordinary surfboards, with small hand boards, and, finally, with nothing at all—a trick called "body shooting." Great green waves rolling in from the Pacific and the Indian oceans make this sport the main test of skill and virility all around the continent.

The Art Scene

Art in Australia? The average American strains his brain, and eventually the names of the painters Sidney Nolan and Sir William Dobell may float to the surface. The Englishman may recall a few others, because many Australian artists have lived, or live, in London. Yet when seen close up, art—particularly painting—in Australia turns out to possess surprising sophistication and prosperity.

In the National Art Gallery in Melbourne, a building massively elegant, there hangs (together with a good representative selection of classical painting from Europe) the work of great Australian landscapists dating back to 1837. The effect is a sense of deeper and denser tradition than the country's short Westernization and historically thin population would seem to justify. The search for comparisons brings to mind the American experience—the paintings of the Hudson River School in the Metropolitan, perhaps—and it would seem that the Australian masters equal the Americans man for man.

Australian artists today are suddenly finding considerable confidence in themselves. No longer isolated from the great trends in art in France and New York, they now want to measure themselves on international standards rather than striving to be "the best Australian."

Art is booming, which is evident from the number and prosperity of the painters and the presence of their works on every wall. The boom may be tainted by status-seeking and speculation, but it is certainly a boom in terms of energy, awareness, and the high quality of the best work.

*

Australian painting got off to a bad start, with a European academic tradition so strong that the painters could not see what was right before their eyes, and depicted Australian eucalyptuses as though they were English oaks, leaves extended instead of hanging. At length a painter named Tom Roberts visited Europe in the early 1880's, and returned full of the liberating principles of Impressionism. He and a fellow painter, Arthur Streeton, became the country's first masters. Yet isolation continued to afflict both painters and the public. A show of modern art by French and British painters, put on by the Melbourne *Herald* in 1938, produced the same jeers that similar art had earned from philistine New Yorkers at the Armory Show a full twenty-five years before. But as with the Armory Show, the Melbourne exhibit also opened eyes, especially among artists. A couple of decades of rich creativity followed, in work by the men who are now Australia's most noted. Let us see who they are.

A Gallery of Australian Painters

SIDNEY NOLAN, Melbourne-born in 1917, kept in touch with Europe in the 1930's and learned the concepts of Picasso and Klee. Drafted in 1942, he betook his urban eye to an army camp at Dimboola, in the wheatlands of western Victoria, and painted powerful landscapes, his personal vision stirring the Australians to recognize the beauty of their stark land. The landscape is quintessentially Australian. These pictures, and Nolan himself, were at first largely unappreciated in Australia until it was learned that London admired them. Nolan then turned from landscapes to scenes from the lives of Australian legendary heroes. Among them was Mrs. Frazer, a Scottish woman who was shipwrecked on the Queensland coast in 1836 and compelled to live among the Aborigines. Meeting an escaped convict, she promised to have him pardoned if he would guide her—she was by then naked and distraught—back to white civilization. She did not keep her word, and the convict, having saved her, had to flee back to the bush. A subsequent theme has been the gibber-strewn outback (crazy birds flying upside-down over pubs with names like Dog & Duck). Nolan now lives in London, though he goes frequently to Australia and his pictures remain Australian.

*

FREDERICK WILLIAMS lives in a converted winery, with vast vinous tubs like secret rooms beneath it. This Melbourne man, born in 1927, trained at the National Gallery Schools and in London, says he "doesn't much care for the bush." This is an extraordinary statement, because for the past four years he has painted little but the bush, at first in closeups of vertical sapling country on busy canvases about five by seven feet in dimensions, now in even bigger sizes that show, typically, a gray surface sparsely dotted with candy-cane-shaped squeezings of oil colors which stand for scrub trees. To see the landscape itself after looking at a Williams painting is to see it as limitless and desolate—compelling and perhaps fear-inspiring. He makes his canvases huge as a way of suggesting that the vast Australian countryside cannot be framed. Of his present painting style, he says, "If it's good figurative it's abstraction, and if it's good abstraction it's figurative." James Mollison, the government's Director of the National Art Gallery in Canberra, thinks very highly of Williams: "Each new work is better than the last. He could compete with the top artists in New York and London."

*

WILLIAM DOBELL, who died in 1970, was called the "reincarnated Hogarth." In his thirties, which corresponded to the 1930's, he studied and traveled in Europe. Returning to Australia, he developed a personal style of portraiture, of elongated limbs and turbulent motion. In 1943 he painted an attenuated, Greco-esque picture of a friend that won a prominent prize.

Two losers sued the judges, contending that Dobell's work was a caricature, not a proper academic portrait. In a sensational trial, a court of law decided for Dobell. The artist, who did not think of himself as a modern, found the experience traumatic. It brought him a frightening overload of commissions, and he became the country's favorite portraitist and "best painter." Art historians have pigeonholed Sir Williams as a "minor twentieth-century mannerist," but of course time will tell about that.

*

RUSSELL DRYSDALE, like Dobell a Sydney artist, started painting for the paradoxical reason that his eyes were bad—it was something to do in the hospital after a corrective operation. Trained in modern art in Europe, he returned to Australia in 1939, at twenty-seven, and began painting iron-roofed buildings on the main streets of the country towns of the outback where he grew up. A newspaper sent him to make paintings of the effects of a bad drought, and these pictures made him famous as a regionalist painter. Drysdale's work has given Australia a more precise picture of itself. He was the first major Australian painter to use the Aborigines as subjects.

*

ALBERT TUCKER is an angry painter who fought his native environment until he stormed off to Japan, London, and Paris, "a refugee from Australian culture." Preoccupied with morality and evil, he became convinced that art could produce social change. Slowly a strange image took form in his work in a series of paintings: the Antipodean Head—a Buster Keatonish physiognomy painted as though cast in bronze, angular, ax-nosed, jut-jawed—an Australian! "Psycho-landscapes" he called these paintings—reflections of "the human involvement with the Australian landscape." Tucker had returned spiritually to his origins, and thereafter went back to Australia.

*

Australian art, says Mollison, is "in the situation of American art at the close of World War II." It is moving away from the nationalism represented by Nolan, Drysdale, and Tucker. Young Australian artists now go not to London but to New York and Japan. Fred Williams hopes that the internationalization of Australian art will also inspire an immigration of foreign painters. BRETT WHITELEY, the most visible of the internationalists, detects a "will for a new definition—not nationalism or antipodeanism, with the old soft sunny blink, but something fiercer and more delicate."

One Australian dealer, Max Hutchinson, who founded galleries in Melbourne and Sydney, now operates a Manhattan branch for "high-caliber artists of all nations but most of all Australian." A Hutchinson favorite is sculptor CLEMENT MEADMORE, a Melbourne man. His basic shape is a long, massive, iron quadrilateral, twisted like the parts of a wire puzzle, and reposing in odd balance. Many New Yorkers, including Nelson Rockefeller, own Meadmores, and a fine big example rests in the plaza of the Australian Mutual Provident Society's skyscraper in Melbourne.

*

The most spectacular museum in Australia is the National Art Gallery in Melbourne. Sydney's Art Gallery of New South Wales has lately been closed for the construction of a new wing, to be named for Captain Cook. There are many charming private galleries. Bonython's, in a terrace house on the winding streets of Paddington, Sydney's Soho, sells works by Nolan, Whiteley, and Tucker, among others. Rudy Koman, in nearby Woollahra, represents Fred Williams, Jan Senbergs, John Olsen, Clifton Pugh, and David Aspden, all prominent artists. Koman sold a painting by Leonard French to the government of New South Wales, which presented it to Pope Paul VI when the Pope visited Australia in December 1970. Patrick Sharpe, a small and delicate man with a flourishing Van Gogh beard, chooses art for the Strawberry Hill Gallery, among Greek stores and Lebanese restaurants on Elizabeth Street. This also is a terrace house, 104 years old. The artists are relatively unknown moderns, and the prices are set for beginner collectors: nothing more than $70.

The market thrives. Art students twenty years old grumble if they do not make $20,000 a year on the gallery circuits. Works by big-name painters go for $8,000 and up—way up. A good Drysdale recently brought $26,000, and one of his works sold for $45,000. In part, this is a *nouveau riche* spending spree resulting from the country's minerals boom. And what is bought must be Australian; the country is proud of its parochialism.

General affluence lets everybody buy art. Buyers of contemporary art can be adventurous young businessmen, intellectuals, and architects, or well-established old families who have been buying for so long that they are sure of their taste. The Australians' house-owning complex creates a pride that needs to be complemented with paintings on the walls—and it is.

The Performing Arts

The theaters of Brisbane, Sydney, Melbourne, Adelaide, and Perth content themselves mostly with the plays of London and New York, plus interesting classics; one week late in 1971 the main productions on the boards were *Hair, Jesus Christ Revolution, Move Over Mrs. Markham, Next* and *The Guerrilla,* and *The Au Pair Man.* Smaller houses—converted cinemas, church halls, boat sheds, comparable to Off-Broadway—get into more radical theater, sometimes tough and exciting, student works, explorations into Australian history. But new Australian plays of authentic power appear so rarely that almost everyone cites Ray Lawler's 1955 *Summer of the Seventeenth Doll,* a drama of Queensland sugar-cane cutters much produced in England and the United States, as the most recent major work. Moreover, the Elizabethan Theatre Trust, a foundation for the promotion of the performing arts, subsidizes Australian plays thought to be of value, such as *The Legend of King O'Malley* (of which we will hear more later). *Oh! Calcutta!,* incidentally, opened in Melbourne despite attempts to censor it, and ran for weeks.

Many of the talented theater people have left Australia, or wish that they could. "There are more Australian actors, writers, producers, and designers working and succeeding in England than there are in Australia," says Lance Peters, president of the Australian Writers Guild. Some well-known expatriate Australian actors are Peter Finch, Leo McKern, Diane Cilento, Judith Anderson, Zoë Caldwell, and Coral Browne.

As to film, the world's first feature, *Early Christian Martyrs,* was made in Australia by the Salvation Army in 1899–1900, and subsequently two hundred silent movies were filmed there. The talking picture decimated this industry, and now the theaters cannot fulfill their legal obligation to show Australian films at least 3 percent of the time. Still, some refreshingly different movies have come out of Australia in the last couple of years. One little noticed but original film was *Ned Kelly,* directed by Tony Richardson and starring Mick Jagger as the famous Australian outlaw (more about him later). Another was *Walkabout* set in the outback and featuring a sensitive Aboriginal actor named David Gumpilil. The rate of film production is one or two a year. A big production of Patrick White's popular novel, *Voss,* is presently under way.

In ballet the situation is bright. The Australian Ballet, a young, state-aided company, toured the United States with Rudolf Nureyev in 1971 and earned from the *New York Times* the praise of being "a promising and enjoyable company in its own right." It is co-directed by the choreographer

Sir Robert Helpmann, who is Australian though often mistaken for British because of his long career in the Royal Ballet of London. Indeed, nearly one-fourth of the dancers in the Royal Ballet are reportedly Australian.

*

Australian concern with music runs broad and deep. The country that gave the world Nellie Melba and Joan Sutherland is prolifically involved in opera, ballet, symphony, composition, and its own old folk songs.

Composers are numerous. The more interesting, possibly, are:

PERCY GRAINGER (1882-1961). Born in Melbourne and buried in Adelaide, Grainger spent most of his life studying in Germany or working in the U.S. But his themes, as he said many times, were Australian, and a lifelong project of his was the Grainger Museum that now stands in the University of Melbourne.

JOHN ANTILL. Now around sixty-seven, and an incipient grand old man, Antill wrote the first symphony based on Aboriginal music, a Stravinsky-like composition called *Corroboree*. Played by a large orchestra, augmented by clunking Aboriginal thora sticks and whirring bull-roarers, and accented by shrieking flutes and piccolos, it can make the hair stand on end.

PETER SCULTHORPE. A composer who began writing music in 1937, when he was eight years old, Sculthorpe conveys the loneliness and sadness of the Australian landscape. His *Sun Music*, which comes in a four-part suite, uses gongs and cymbals and a choir that grunts, wails, and shouts. Sculthorpe has been influenced by Balinese music.

RICHARD MEALE. A story told of Meale is that he flushed an early piano composition down a toilet, for fear that if anyone played it he would be deemed mad. Born in 1932, Meale is—or was—the rebel of Australian music. His *Homage to García Lorca* is played, in tumult sufficient to shatter glass, by *two* orchestras, using twelve-note chords. Meale sometimes uses themes from the music of Japan.

Opera is practically an Australian sport; there is a theory that a dazzling high note in singing is akin to a dazzling high catch in football, and that healthy, sunny Australia produces people good at both. Historically opera has flourished, and as theater for everyone rather than something for the rich only. Yet lately it has faltered, and the Elizabethan Trust divides its boons uncertainly between theater and opera. So the performers are apt to emigrate.

Symphony concerts, eight hundred a year, are hungrily attended in Australia. When the Australian Broadcasting Commission was founded in 1932, to give the government a role in the improvement of radio, the charter vaguely suggested that it could form studio orchestras. Energetically accepting the hint, ABC formed orchestras in all six state capitals, and turned their performances into public concerts. Soon ABC began selling seats by subscription, and now boasts of being the largest concert-giving organization in the world. The Sydney and Melbourne symphonies, subsidized by ABC and the states, have high standards, equal to American or European orchestras. Smaller orchestras are conscientiously professional; performances are almost always sold out. The ABC network takes its musical obligations seriously. One ABC programmer, asked for extra news time on the night of the Kennedy assassination, is supposed to have replied, "Oh, no, we can't interrupt the Sibelius." The drawbacks are that ABC is fusty about programing modern music, and that it has never gotten around to frequency-modulation (FM) broadcasting.

Television's pattern is a recognizable variation of the British system. Government-owned ABC (often called "Auntie") provides, on thirty-nine stations, good drama (much of it from the British Broadcasting Corporation), news, lectures and current affairs, and absolutely no advertising. The main current-affairs program, *This Day Tonight*, holds between 20 and 25 percent of the viewing audience. ABC tries to appear independent, but it is actually sensitive to government pressure. Over all ABC-TV holds only 16 percent of the audience, because it is up against the attractions of commercial television broadcast on forty-five stations mostly owned by the four big newspaper chains. These stations show *Mod Squad, The Dick Van Dyke Show, Family Affair, Here's Lucy, Flip Wilson*, etc.—eight out of ten top shows are American. The rest of the time—Australian TV offers four hundred hours of viewing a week—is given to films and sports. The number of Australian families watching television at peak hours has dropped from an astonishing (or even appalling) 80 percent in 1960 to 70 percent now. There will be no color TV in Australia until 1974.

Books and Publishing

At the busy Robertson & Mullens bookstore in Melbourne just before Christmas in 1970, one noticeable offering was a catalogue 1,037 pages long. This turned out to be a bibliography of Australian children's books, thousands and thousands of them. The point is that this underpopulated land publishes books in extraordinary volume.

Bookstores sell—with exceptions resulting from an absurd censorship—the major works of all the world, but what is most striking is the concentration, almost obsessive, on Australian themes. The stores display titles like these: *The Early Australian Architects, A Yankee Merchant in Goldrush Australia, The Story of the Flinders Ranges, A Pictorial History of Australia at War, Aboriginal Mission Stations in Australia, The Effluent Society: Pollution in Australia.* There are books on Australian spiders, marsupials, high-country birds, lizards, venomous wildlife, wild flowers, seashells, and gem stones.

Australians claim to read more books per capita than anyone else except New Zealanders—a tradition, supposedly, that comes from days gone by when reading was almost the only entertainment on the sheep stations. An average novel can quite easily sell five thousand copies, which is thought to be good in England, a country with more than four times as many people.

With all that, literature is not as exciting in Australia as painting. The outstanding novelist is Patrick White, author of *Voss*, a psychological investigation of the life of the explorer Ludwig Leichhardt (who traveled to the west coast of the Gulf of Carpentaria and then disappeared), and *The Vivisector*, a narrative of the life of a Sydney painter who—figuratively, in his pictures—cut up his friends and relatives alive. White, born in 1912, endured a long obscurity before Australians could accept his bleak, tragic themes. Other good novelists, also accused of too close preoccupation with Australian society, are Thomas Keneally and Hal Porter.

Australia, like Ireland, does have a way with words—perhaps because a lot of Australian writers are Irish by descent. Education and a dry, irreverent wit add to the natural talent. However, experimental novels seem to be missing, and many good writers are drawn to journalism or television.

A talented Australian writer of nonfiction is Alan Moorehead, who after covering World War II in books, and going on to write extensively about Africa, returned to Australian themes in books about Captain Cook (*The Fatal Impact*) and the exploration of the interior (*Cooper's Creek*). Poetry, too, is alive and healthy. The *New York Times* calls A. D. Hope, Australia's leading poet, "one of the master conservative poets in English in this century."

*

Australian book-banning could be called comic if censorship were not always pregnant with dangers to free speech and thought. Certainly the authorities have made themselves fools time after time, banning, in the past, such books as *Ulysses, Brave New World, Farewell to Arms, God's Little Acre, Catcher in the Rye, Appointment in Samarra, The Women of Rome, The Kama Sutra, The Postman Always Rings Twice, Forever Amber, Peyton Place,* and *Lady Chatterley's Lover.* More recent examples are *The*

Ginger Man, Last Exit to Brooklyn, Naked Lunch, Borstal Boy, Another Country, The Group, and *The Carpetbaggers*; *Naked Lunch,* at least, remains banned still. A wryly comic case was that of *The Trial of Lady Chatterley,* banned for import in 1965; somebody simply set it into type and printed it in Australia, a process which turned out to be perfectly legal.

The book-banners are the Ministry for Customs and Excise, and the vice squads of the various state governments. Politicians solemnly support censorship, for the most part, in deference to the bluenoses. In the public consciousness, the Minister of Customs is best known as the chief censor, but Don Chipps, the Minister appointed in 1970, a man with a rugged, deep-lined, good-humored face, has been trying to steer his customs agents away from the more ludicrous kinds of censorship. He ruled in favor of admitting a book of essays by Timothy Leary that had been kept out of Australia for four years. He also stripped away secrecy concerning precisely what books the customs men had seized, and got the list down from 136 to 80. But one still meets mature, intellectual Australians who until lately suffered the humiliation of being protected by their government from reading *Tropic of Cancer* or *Tropic of Capricorn*—and are doubly resentful at having to wait so long to discover what unimportant books they are.

Portnoy's Complaint was banned by all state governments except South Australia, whose modern-minded Premier, Don Dunstan, approved its sale while professing, for the benefit of the bluenoses, that it nauseated him. Censorship in Australia is typically quite leaky—no one really determined to get a copy of a book fails to do so. In the case of *Portnoy,* the 75,000-copy edition that the police banned was actually mostly sold before the crackdown. The vice squad raiders managed to get only the last few copies, snatching one from the hands of novelist Patrick White as he was about to pay for it. At the trial over *Portnoy,* humorist Cyril Pearl testified with a straight face that the book was in a class with Rabelais and Chaucer.

Newspapers

> *To learn what great things God has done in the past, read your Bible. But to learn what he permits to be done today, read your* Herald.
>
> —JOHN FAIRFAX

Ownership—that is the key word in understanding the Australian press. The British press has its lords—Lord Rothermere, Lord Thomson, the late Lord Beaverbrook. The Australian press has its knights—Sir Frank Packer, Sir Warwick Fairfax and his cousin Sir Vincent, Sir John Williams, and the late Sir Keith Murdoch. Out they went a-jousting, and when the dust settled,

Australia's press had been cut up into three empires. Unlike the lords, who still break a lance against one another from time to time, the knights provided themselves with near-monopolies. Sometimes they look quite fierce, charging out to buy some stray newspaper property that may be up for grabs. Actually they are in collusion in a number of ways, most notably in joint ownership of the commercial television industry. But in recent years, as we shall see in a moment, a young publisher has got loose among the knights and stirred up much excitement.

The major agglomerations and their flagship newspapers are:

The Melbourne *Herald* group, which has the *Herald* (circulation 500,000), the Melbourne *Sun News-Pictorial* (circulation 635,000—the nation's biggest daily), big chunks of Brisbane's *Courier-Mail*, *Telegraph*, and *Sunday Mail*, the Adelaide *Advertiser*, the Hobart *Mercury*, and Perth's *West Australian* and *Daily News*. Sir Keith Murdoch put this fiefdom together, and it is bigger by far than the others. Sir John Williams ran the company shrewdly for fourteen years, before retiring in 1970.

The Fairfax group, which has the Sydney *Morning Herald*, the Sydney *Sun*, the Sydney *Sunday Sun-Herald*, the *Financial Review*, Canberra's *Times* and *News*, and Newcastle's *Morning Herald* and *Sun*. John Fairfax, quoted above, founded this empire with the Sydney *Herald* in 1831. The Fairfax family turned it into a public company some years back, but Sir Warwick (a leading art collector) and Sir Vincent still dominate.

The Packer group (Consolidated Press), which publishes Sydney's daily and Sunday *Telegraph*, the newsmagazine the *Bulletin*, and *Women's Weekly*. Sir Frank Packer is the fabled yachtsman whose *Gretels* regularly, but so far unsuccessfully, make a challenge for the America's Cup.

In the whole country, only one leading paper stands by itself. That is the venerable Melbourne *Age*, which was long dominated by the Symes family, who started it 118 years ago. Now the Fairfax group has been buying into it, and apparently controls it. The *Age* company also runs a flock of country weeklies.

A decade ago Sir Keith Murdoch's son, Rupert, got as an inheritance the unimpressive Adelaide *News*, and set out to see what he could do by way of surpassing his father's empire. He had a flair, and before long managed to acquire a couple of sex-and-crime tabloids in Sydney, the *Mirror* and the *Sunday Mirror*. Then Murdoch got the Brisbane *Sunday Truth*, the Melbourne *Sunday Truth*, the Perth *Sunday Times*, and the Adelaide *Sunday Mail*.* Murdoch has never been embarrassed at publishing gossipy, trivial, sometimes sensational papers, as all of these are, but in 1964 he took on the

* Which has to get off the presses by Saturday midnight because of a South Australian blue law.

nervy task of starting a new, serious, national paper, *The Australian*. Published first in Canberra, it met rough competition on its own intellectual level from the Canberra *Times*, and finally had to move to Sydney, where it pushed circulation up to 150,000. Next Murdoch stormed into London, winning control of the Sunday *News of the World* in exchange for the Melbourne *Sunday Truth;* a bit later he acquired the London *Sun* (which was Hugh Cudlipp's moribund attempt to make a new paper out of the remnants of the equally moribund old *Daily Herald*). Murdoch turned it around, got circulation up from 850,000 to 1,800,000, and now lives in London, running the Australian papers by phone and frequent trips. He found breaking into London tough. "In Australia and America, you know who your friends are more quickly. There's a lot more subtlety here."

The fight of the knights to get and keep papers implies that they are highly profitable, and for most of them this is indisputably true. The circulation of all the Sydney dailies runs around 300,000 each; the Sunday papers run up as high as the 750,000 of the Sydney *Sun-Herald* ("the paper you can take into your home"). In short, Australians are avid newspaper readers; there are 50 dailies in all, plus 550 others, and total circulations equal one-half of the population. Advertising runs heavy—65 percent of the Sydney *Morning Herald*, for example. The papers do not have to fight television for advertising dollars, for publishers own the bulk of the commercial stations, and own them in interesting patterns. BTQ in Brisbane is owned by the Melbourne *Herald* group *and* Packer. NWS in Adelaide is owned by Fairfax *and* Murdoch. WIN in Wollongong and NBN in Newcastle are owned by Fairfax *and* Packer *and* Murdoch. What more could a publisher ask?

If all this sounds as though profit dominated the press to the exclusion of competence in news—not so. Most of the papers, true enough, pander to the taste for animal stories, a bit of sex, disasters, local squabbles, police-court news, comics, betting odds, and sports, sports, sports. Quite shockingly, there is not a single major paper in the country that supports Labor, the party of almost half of all Australians. A pervasive establishmentarianism enervates the press. Foreign news coverage depends to a large extent on the Reuters news service, which works in conjunction with the Australian Associated Press. On the other hand, the journalists are by and large sufficiently trained and talented, and a lot of intelligence and hard thinking shows through. The Sydney *Morning Herald* and the Melbourne *Age* are responsible papers that tackle trends and problems, and occasionally take some interest in the rest of the world. And *The Australian*, amplified in 1971 with a Sunday edition summarizing the week, is serious, well written, and comprehensive, with careful attention to the arts, books, science, plus a heavy dose of business. Circulation is 150,000. The *Bulletin,* Packer's *Time*-like magazine, heir to a fine nineteenth-century reputation for publishing Australia's best writers of the time, is now a sprightly reporter and critic of the national life. Donald Horne, the editor, is prolific, witty, observant, meditative, and a most engaging luncheon companion. Typical *Bulletin* headline (upon the downfall of Prime Minister Gorton): "WHAT WAS A NICE COUNTRY LIKE US DOING IN A POLITICAL MESS LIKE THAT?"

Reading the press can be diverting. Headline abbreviations are occasionally cryptic: "AUST" for "Australian," "MELB" for "Melbourne," "UNI" for "university," "QLD" for "Queensland," "C'TTEE" for "committee." The typography is mostly English style, which assumes that nobody will read anything unless the type is made to perform gymnastics. One paper, the Brisbane *Courier-Mail,* may not be the best in the world but it certainly must be the widest—17½ inches (compared to the *New York Times'* 14½), *eleven* columns of type. The sum impression of the Australian press is that it writes down too much, takes itself a little too seriously, and could exchange some of its circusy qualities for more depth. Nevertheless, it is certainly as informative as all but the best in England and the United States.

CHAPTER 6

Aborigines I: Sophisticated Savages

Why change our sacred myths for your sacred myths?
—ABORIGINAL POET KATH WALKER

SHARING THE CONTINENT with the white-skinned millions, whose works and ways we have been describing, is a minority race of blacks who are troubled, downtrodden, and fascinating: the Aborigines. Including persons with 50 percent or more Aboriginal blood, this race numbers 80,000, according to the 1966 census. Other authorities, by including less-than-half-bloods and allowing for increase, estimate that there are as many as 130,000 Aborigines now. This would be one Aboriginal for every one hundred whites, which compares with one American Indian for every three hundred whites. Aborigines are increasing at a rate faster than the general population—but they are still fewer than one-half of the 300,000 who, in the estimate of Professor A. R. Radcliffe-Brown, inhabited Australia in 1788. At that time there were some 500 tribes, ranging in size from 100 to 1,500 members.

The Aborigines are most visible in the sparsely populated north. Arnhem Land, the torrid, bird-ornamented protuberance on the north-central coast, is a reserve for Aborigines. Other Aborigines live in Roman Catholic, Methodist, or Anglican missions in the Northern Territory, or work on pastoral properties there. By the census, there are 21,000 Aborigines in the Northern Territory, 19,000 in Queensland, 18,500 in Western Australia, and 14,000 in New South Wales.

These are the remnants of a destroyed civilization. Before the white man arrived, the Aborigines had a beautifully elaborated culture, one that fitted the people to the land rather than the land to the people and was pre-eminently gratifying to human emotions. Like white Americans with regard to Red Indian culture, white Australians have historically accorded the Aboriginal heritage little or no value. The memorable first comment by a white man on the Aborigines, made by explorer William Dampier in 1688, was that "The Inhabitants of this Country are the miserablest People in the World. . . . They are long-visaged and of very unpleasing Aspect, having no one graceful Feature in their Faces."

It perhaps took Sir James Frazer's publication of *The Golden Bough* in 1890 to explode upon the white world the notion that "primitive" cultures could be qualitatively comparable to those of the whites. The astounding corollary that even the "miserablest People in the World" had worthwhile traditions had to await the work of some brilliant Australian anthropologists —chiefly Professor A. P. Elkin of Sydney University—in the 1920's and 1930's. Even today most white Australians have only an indifferent glimmering as to Aboriginal* cultures, and the American writer must tackle the subject with great circumspection.

Religion, Magic, and Sex

We are talking now of the beliefs held by Aborigines in the past and to some degree even now by all but a few thousand completely integrated city-dwellers. Two main points here: (1) Aboriginal thought is inductive, not deductive; that is, cause and effect are not ineluctably related, and this is partly because (2) the religion is totemic; that is, persons have *blood relationships* with natural spirits, and these are the main determinants of life. It is thus a culture that most satisfyingly fuses man, nature, art, belief, life and death—past, present, and future. The sacred outweighs the profane. As Professor Elkin explains it, a man begins as the spirit-child of an animal or a rock or a pool, that is incarnated by his mother (sexual intercourse, in Aboriginal belief, having only a collateral role). Raised in a profane world until puberty, he is reintroduced to the sacred life by initiation ceremonies, sustained in that life by ritual until he dies, and by the rite of death returned to the totemic center for recycling into another round of life. This spiritual life is reserved chiefly for men. The Aboriginal woman, spiritually and otherwise, is considered inferior.

This belief is built on the concept of a Dream Time that goes back long

* The Australians often use the word "abos" for "Aborigines." It has an offensive and disparaging connotation and has therefore been avoided in this book.

before the arrival of the first Europeans, to a vague and indefinite period in the past. "In Dream Time there were no blackfellow; but kangaroo, iguana, bird," one Aboriginal explained to anthropologist Phyllis M. Kaberry, in Pidgin English. "All bin walk like blackfellow. Him all the same blackfellow. After he bin turn into kangaroo, iguana, bird." In other words, the animal spirits of the men of the Dream Time eventually turned into present-day animals, and the spirits of men remained totemically related to them.

These ancestral spirits have abodes—trees or pools or caves or heaps of stone—where rituals must be performed by painting, chanting, or shedding blood. Along with all this go many myths and legends. Mythology says that a giant marsupial carved the hills, and a giant rainbow snake scored out the rivers. A typical legend explains death: the moon-man Alinda had two sons who went fishing and returned claiming that they had caught nothing. Alinda, seeing grease on their hands, took them to the sea and drowned them as liars. When his two wives inquired, Alinda in turn lied that the sons had merely gone hunting. The wives discovered that he had murdered them, and burned him to death. Alinda thereupon pronounced that henceforth death would be the fate of everyone but he himself, the man in the moon—"Except for three days every month, I will live forever." Yet to tribal Aborigines, death is not natural; the blame has to be placed. Often someone in another tribe is chosen, and revenge or compensation (a woman, sometimes) is exacted.

Magic, pure black magic, was until very recently a good way of causing death. Among the Dieri tribe, a magician had merely to point a human fibula at a victim, thus "giving him the bone," to cause him to pine away and die. In another kind of magic, kidney fat, taken from a freshly garroted hostile tribesman, was used to anoint bodies and thus increase prowess and virtue. Writer Eugene Burdick reported only a decade ago that rain makers performed their magic task by prying off a chosen victim's thumbnail with an opossum tooth while chanting, "Blood flows like a river/Rushes along like a river."

The basic concept of profane and sacred life (which in itself is perfectly comprehensible to any member of a Masonic lodge) requires elaborate manhood initiation ceremonies, including circumcision. A particular horror in these rites among many Aborigines has been the practice of subincision: some time after circumcision, a young man, perhaps out hunting, is suddenly pinioned by his elders and thrown to the ground, and the underside of his penis slit from end to end through to the urethra. The purpose of this mutilation, which in Australian slang is called "whistlecock," is as vague as the purpose of ritual circumcision. The operation does not affect the man's sexual powers.* A much-repeated story about the Aborigines is that they do not connect copulation with conception, and apparently in the past they did not, but nowadays they are mostly a bit wiser than that. They seem to think that intercourse is necessary for conception, some holding that it takes five or six ejaculations on successive days, but sex is less a prerequisite to procreation than the entry into the fetus of its spirit. Women associate awareness of pregnancy with an animal, rock, tree, whirlwind, or whatever. This spirit, entering the mother through foot, flank, navel, or mouth (but never vagina), becomes the totem of the child. In the Kimberley district of northwestern Australia, the spirit-children are thought to inhabit pools as fish or birds, waiting to infiltrate the womb of the mother-to-be. The totem determines all the child's future relationships and behavior—much as the sign of the zodiac is believed to do in some other parts of the world.

Aborigines always marry spouses who bear some degree of consanguinity. Among some tribes, a man must marry a woman who is his mother's brother's daughter; among others, the prescribed relationship is mother's mother's brother's daughter's daughter.

The Aborigines have seven hundred tongues, apparently dialects of a common original language, and none of them written. The "dialect chain" is such that an Aboriginal who talks language A can talk to one speaking language B, who in turn can talk to one speaking language C, who in turn can talk to one speaking language D. But one who speaks D cannot talk with one who speaks A. The languages have as many as forty thousand words, including four genders of nouns declinable into eight cases. A sample of one language, taken from anthropologist A. W. Howitt's early research, looks like this, when the sounds are set down in the Roman alphabet:

Yakai! yai!	Ngata	wata	tanana	ngantyai,	tananana	turu-etya.
OH DEAR!	I	NOT	HER	LOVE,	SHE	FIRE-PERSON.

How to Kill and Cook a Kangaroo

Utilize the animal's curiosity. Send part of your hunting party on ahead; the kangaroo will follow, and the rest of the party can sneak up behind him and kill him with a boomerang. To cook: dig a kangaroo-size hole and build a roaring wood fire until the hole and surrounding edges are covered six inches deep with live coals. Heave the kangaroo

* In an even bloodier initiation ceremony, a number of old men successively tie off their upper arms and lance veins at the elbow, directing the stream of blood over the head and body of the young man being initiated until he becomes stiff with encrusted gore. The purpose of the ritual is to infuse courage, by showing that the sight of blood is nothing and that wounds are not to be feared.

into the hole, feet protruding upward, cover with coals from the fire's edges, then shovel sand over the coals. Roast until rare.*

How, indeed, have the Aborigines survived in their hostile environment? Few foreigners, not to mention Australians, have ever seen them living primitively, but Eugene Burdick went to the outback some years ago, and produced a vivid report. In the middle of a burning desert, crouched in the shade of a boulder, were an extremely thin six-foot man, his *lubra* (woman) and their two sons. Flies crawled across the *surface* of the man's eyeballs. All were naked, though covered, in effect, by a second skin of dirt and ashes glued on with sweat. The odor was an overwhelming smell of sex. Their entire possessions consisted of: two rubbing sticks for fire, two knife-shaped stones, a container of dried worms, a dead rodent, a boomerang, spear and woomera (spear-thrower), and a dingo dog. (By contrast, anthropologist John Greenway of the University of Colorado lists the following items as essential equipment for a white man in the same terrain: a four-wheel-drive vehicle, extra fuel and water tanks, food for twice the expected stay, two spare wheels and tires, extra battery, tools, medicine, cooking gear, fly and mosquito nets, blankets, aero maps, compass and radio to call for help.)

Burdick's guide pressed the Aboriginal for a show of skill. The sons led off, hanging the rodent in a bush and peppering it with stones flung with flat trajectories and deadly accuracy. The father announced that he would throw his boomerang at the rodent and deliberately miss it. His body coiled, snapped. The boomerang started out far to the left, grazing the ground, then rose to fifteen or twenty feet. Turning, it seemed to stop. Then continuing its return, it shot down to knee height and swooped back up to miss the rodent by an inch. The Aboriginal had to move only one step sidewise to pluck the boomerang out of the air. In a third demonstration, the man disappeared toward the horizon with spear and dingo. Burdick waited briefly; the hunter trotted back with a small dead kangaroo, already half-skinned. As Burdick left, forty bloody fingers were stuffing four bloody faces. The Aboriginal's adieu was to crunch a bone between his teeth.

In a sweep of the nearby desert, barren to a white man's eyes, the Aboriginal and his family, employing uncanny powers of observation, could quickly collect ten or twelve pounds of food. The boys, throwing rocks,

* "On the Lower River Murray emu was cooked in this way, with its head left out, so that when steam came from its beak it was judged to be properly done." *The World of the First Australians*, R. M. and C. H. Berndt. Another Australian (though not Aboriginal) recipe tells how to cook a galah (parrot): boil with a stone until stone is tender; throw away galah and eat stone.

would kill birds, toads, snakes, and rabbits; the woman would gather insects and edible plants; the man would kill big game. As for water, Burdick watched another group of Aborigines spot a cloud on the horizon and lope over the ground for *three hours* (while he followed in a Land Rover) to get a few swallows from the puddles they finally found. Greenway notes a case in which a group of Aborigines traced a rain cloud two days, and when it failed to provide water, they calmly dug graves and lay down to die. As it happened, a patrol officer came by with water before they expired. They casually got out of their graves and asked him for a *kapati* (cup of tea).

The Aborigines do without metals, the bow, money, pottery, the wheel, politics, arithmetic,* and writing. Most importantly, they never learned to farm. They harvest and eat grass seed, but—perhaps because of the generally inhospitable terrain, perhaps because they never hit upon a suitable crop, perhaps because they were so isolated from the example of societies that did develop agriculture—they never discovered how to plant and tend and reap. Thus the consequences of agriculture—settled life and communities—eluded them, and they have always been nomads. To travel light, families may limit their possessions to about twenty pounds. The tools they prize are stone knives, ax-chisels, clubs, spears, boomerangs, hair-string bags, pandanus-palm baskets, long wooden bowls. The tools are simple but cunningly constructed of fastidiously selected materials: greenstone for axes, sandstone for grinding them, mallee wood for spears, and *keti*, an epoxy-like powdered resin from spinifex, for fastening axheads to hafts. These materials were so vital that they were long the commodities of long-distance, intertribal commerce. Pearl shell from the east coast of Cape York Peninsula, valued for ceremonial gifts, was delivered all over Australia by Aboriginal trading. Of course the most interesting weapon is the boomerang, which so impressed the first explorers of Australia. "The boomerang is a very formidable weapon," wrote the British seaman Philip Parker King (1762–1828), giving the world one of the first accounts. "It is a short curved piece of heavy wood, and is propelled through the air by the hand in so skilful a manner, that the thrower alone knows where it will fall. . . . It is used by the natives with success in killing the kangaroo, and is, I believe, more a hunting than a warlike weapon." Incidentally, the best boomerangs nowadays are made of plastic, either in Australia or by an American firm that exports to Australia. They are used for sport, and the record throw, by the late Frank Donnellan, an Irish-Australian, was 125 yards, out and back to the thrower's hand.

* Their languages have no word for numbers beyond three, although Aborigines can express higher numbers by finger signs.

The diet of the Aboriginal is as varied as a smörgåsbord. Witchetty grubs, the cigar-size larvae of a certain huge moth, are favored. "Lightly toasted, it has quite a pleasant flavor," reports anthropologist Andrew Abbie. Ants are eaten, particularly one kind that stores a sweet liquid in its abdomen in a hard ball the size of a marble. Aborigines eat wild honey, yams and tubers, pandanus and baobab nuts, grass seeds, roots and berries. From rivers they get fish and platypuses, and from the sea shellfish* and the dugong, the extraordinary thousand-pound sea mammal.

Some Aborigines make houses, "wurlies," by planting a circle of flexible sticks, bending and tying the tops together, and covering the frame thus formed with leafy branches. More commonly, families sleep in depressions of the ground, curling up into "family balls" of human flesh for warmth if necessary, or lying between two fires and rolling into the warm ashes in the cold predawn. There is a theory, which is supposed to explain the Aborigines' nakedness, that human beings can often stay warmer without clothes, covered only with dust or ashes, and that white men do not know this because they have never given the practice a fair go. Be that as it may, Aborigines often do wear some clothes, and in the south possum-skin rugs.

In appearance, Aborigines in general share several characteristics. The skin is chocolate brown, the stature somewhat less than that of white men. The hair is straight or wavy, not fuzzy; most hair is black; the men have strong black beards and mustaches. Aboriginals have broad but not Negroid noses, and deep-set eyes usually topped by a pronounced ridge. Yet there are wide divergences among them. Some Aborigines are only four and one-half feet high; some are strongly muscled and some shockingly thin-shanked and thin-armed. Many children are blond until adolescence. Skin color, according to Abbie, comes in a range from "sienna and umber through light and medium to dark vandyke." In manner the Aborigines are said to be cautious and secretive at first meeting, then gentle and quick-spoken but still rather withdrawn, and often crafty.

Some tidbits: Aborigines are rarely shortsighted or color-blind, and tooth decay is not one of their problems. Neither was alcohol, until the white man appeared; they never invented the stuff. The Aboriginal's blood pressure tends to be lower than that of the white man, but his brain size is just the same. Aboriginal women sometimes suckle dingo pups, since these dogs are much needed in indigenous life.

* Earlier Aborigines left huge shell mounds, which served to mark the sites of small settlements, at Weipa on Cape York Peninsula and in Arnhem Land. Carbon dating places the origin of one mound in the fifth century B.C.

Antiquity of the Aborigines

The popular theory of the origin of the Aborigines is that they crossed from New Guinea during the last Ice Age, somewhere between 10,000 and 25,000 years ago, when so much of the ocean was bound up as ice that the sea level dropped and the strait between Australia and the island was exposed as a land bridge (even now it is a mere one hundred feet deep). This has a plausibility that fades upon examination, chiefly because it presupposes that these colonists had sailed from Southeast Asia to New Guinea, since there was no continuous land bridge along that route. Once at sea, they might just as well have sailed to Australia. Indeed, in the more likely event that they drifted uncontrollably along the course of the regular northwest monsoon, they would have more probably landed in Australia than in New Guinea. Furthermore, there are no Australoid* people in present-day New Guinea, which suggests that it was not a steppingstone.

If the land-bridge theory can be dispensed with, so can the time it fixes for the arrival of the Aborigines, usually put at 25,000 years ago. The tendency now is to estimate the arrival at a bit upwards of eight thousand years ago, based on (1) guesses as to the age of the oldest skull found in Australia, and (2) the homogeneity of the Australoid stock. Had the Aborigines arrived as long as 25,000 years ago, surely greater variations in their tribal characteristics would have developed. Professor Abbie suggests that the early ancestors of the Aborigines were "Proto-Caucasoids" who lived in Central Asia twenty thousand years ago and sent out migrations that became the genetically related Ainus of Japan, Veddas of India and Ceylon, and the "Aryan" Europeans.

The land-bridge theory assumed that the Tasmanian Aborigines, a fuzzy-haired group now extinct, came from a wave of immigration even earlier than that of the first Australian Aborigines. Abbie and others now believe that they probably drifted to Tasmania from some island in Melanesia, which is largely inhabited by similarly fuzzy-haired people.

The early Aborigines may have had to deal with some weird animals now extinct—three huge marsupials, including the rhinoceros-size diprotodon, two kinds of giant flightless birds, and some lesser marsupial carnivores, one the size of a leopard and the other the size of a wolf. Archaeological diggings provide some interesting key dates, all B.C.: 4850, linear engravings; 2820, spearhead points in use; 1800, tulas (flake-edge knives) in use; 1470,

* By blood group typing it is possible to define the Aborigines as Australoids, a stock distinct from Caucasoids, Negroids, and Mongoloids.

specialized bone industry active. D. J. Mulvaney, an anthropologist at the Australian Institute of Aboriginal Studies, delineates a period of prolific invention signaled by the adoption of tools with hafts (handles) about 5,500 years ago.

The arrival of the white man led to such horrendous decimation of the Aborigines that Australian historians still look upon it as a subject to be got through very quickly. At first, the Englishmen were kindly. The Sydney suburb of Manly got its name from the behavior of the Aborigines there, as observed by the admiring Captain Phillip. But in the early settlements the Aborigines were quickly reduced to paupers who did odd jobs, caught measles, scarlet fever and dysentery,* and died out. When the whites first pressured the Aborigines for land, the tribes moved closer together and fell murderously upon one another. Then, greedy for yet more land, the whites started the "dispersal," a bland euphemism for massacre. They went out to "shoot abos" for fun—a gay sport on Saturdays. The police participated, to make examples of Aborigines who stole sheep or produce from land recently theirs. At its worst, the "vermin" were given food poisoned with arsenic, or killed for their tattooed skins, Ilsa Koch–style. "I am told it is no uncommon thing for these rascals to sleep all night with a Lubra (Native Female) and if she poxes him or in any way offends him perhaps shoot her before twelve the next day," says a passage from the journal of the chronicler Niel Black. In Tasmania occurred the world's only complete genocide of an entire ethnic group. The two or three thousand Aborigines there were hunted down until only some two hundred remained, and they were deported to nearby Flinders Island. By 1847 only forty were left; the last sixteen were returned to Tasmania, and the last of them, named Trucanini, died in 1876.

Ironically, even as the slaughter continued, Aborigines were giving succor to such nearly helpless white men as the Burke-Wills expedition, the "first" men to traverse Australia north and south—provided one does not count the innumerable journeys by Aborigines over that route. English humanitarians finally blew the whistle on the killing of Aborigines, and Australian states started "protection" policies in the 1870's. In 1877 a Lutheran mission penetrated to a point in the interior seven hundred miles from the nearest railhead, made contact with the nomadic blackfellows, and planted a hospital, a school, and the Gospel. By the turn of the century many

* But not much syphilis. The prevalence among Aborigines of yaws, a milder form of syphilis spread by lack of hygiene, seems to have provided a cross-immunity, according to Dr. Abbie.

Aborigines were beggars, pleading for gifts of clothes, without which they were not allowed in the white man's towns.

The unlovely hypothesis that the Aborigines were a self-solving problem—that is, that they would die out—dominated official policy until 1939. Even such a sober work as the *Modern Reference Encyclopedia,* published in Melbourne that year, could blandly say, "The Aborigines, of many tribes, of primitive habits, and a low order of intelligence, are disappearing." It was the realization that they were not dying out that forced the shift of policy from protection to assimilation, which meant that they would be "civilized" and given citizenship. In 1951 Paul Hasluck, then the Minister of Territories, set up a Department of Native Welfare to prepare assimilation by training Aborigines in Western ways and educating their children.

But it took until 1964 for Parliament to replace the act that made Aborigines wards of the state with one that put them under the Social Welfare Act that applies to all citizens. A peculiar referendum in 1967 completed the legal process of equality for Aborigines: census-takers were ordered to count them along with the rest of the members of the genus Homo sapiens in Australia. Much special and presumably beneficial legislation has been passed since then. "We didn't do a bad job of killing them off, but now we are trying to build them up again," says one rueful Australian government official.

A Flowering of Art and Music

> *Only through art can we get outside of ourselves and know another's view of the universe which is not the same as ours.*
>
> —MARCEL PROUST

If there is one aspect of Aboriginal life that stirs empathy and understanding among average white Australians, it is Aborigine art. Here we get, in fairly communicable form, another view of the universe, with diversity, humor, tradition, and an aesthetic pleasing to any eye. Art seems to have come so naturally to the Aborigines that they had no need to invent a word for it, though they have words for the individual acts of painting, carving, singing, and dancing.

The majority of Aboriginal men can paint, carve, and incise—some artists, of course, being better than others, and only a few are entitled by age, status, or prestige to create certain sacred emblems. Their motivations are never purely the artist's own satisfaction; art is for communication to others. It teaches the laws of the tribe, explains creation, endows weapons with visible potency, keeps alive religious beliefs. The most sacred secret objects, churungas, oval-shaped slabs of painted wood or stone, contain such powerful symbolic messages among their abstract dots, meanders, spirals, and animal tracks that in some tribes women who catch a glimpse of them are put to death.

The flourishing art is produced with distinctly primitive tools and materials, at least until recent times. The historic engraving tool is an incisor tooth from a possum, with the jawbone in which it is rooted as a handle. Brushes are twigs or human hair. Sharkskin serves for sandpaper. The common painting surfaces are rock facings, in caves or outcrops, and the insides of sheets of bark, often from the stringybark eucalyptus. Wood, beeswax, and clay are used for modeling and carving. Pigments are made of charcoal, or of red and yellow ocher (both forms of hematite, iron ore), ground in water. But some of the more sophisticated artists nowadays, with the assistance of missionaries, order paints and sable brushes from Winsor & Newton, the celebrated London dealer in art supplies.

The most extraordinary works of Aboriginal art are cave paintings, found by the thousands across northern Australia, often inaccessibly high on walls and ceilings. In the northwest are the Wandjinas, spooky, looming, gigantic physiognomies of dead white, with long-lashed black eyes and black coblike noses—but no mouths. They represent the mythical creators of the surrounding land, who supposedly painted the pictures themselves. In fact, most sacred cave paintings are thought by the Aborigines to be of "nonhuman" origin, dating back to the Dream Time. They depict mythical beings who "became a painting." Other motives for cave paintings were: hunting and fishing magic, the illustration of stories and legends, and love magic, accomplished by paintings depicting copulation. The shallow caves of Ayers Rock, the big tourist attraction of central Australia, portray mythical lizard-men and other anthropoid figures.

A fascinating branch of cave art, found in western Arnhem Land and nowhere else in the world, is X-ray painting, depictions of animals, birds, fish, and reptiles showing both the external form and the internal organs—skeleton, stomach, heart, lungs, and intestines. Another variation in the same area, and a charming one, is the Mimi painting, the work of some now extinct Aboriginal people. Mimi paintings, just a couple of inches high and done only in red ocher, show stick-figure humans running, fighting, and throwing spears with a ballet-like suggestion of movement. Near Delamere, in the Northern Territory, are the mythical Lightning Brothers painted sixty feet up on a sheer rock face. These are a pair of male figures nine feet tall, each with a penis as long as his legs, tipped in red, indicating subincision.

Bark paintings apparently originated as decorations for the interior of wet-weather shelters made of this material. A typical bark painting, done in a semiabstract style with dots and patterned lines, shows men in canoes, dolphins, and nesting seagulls—the story of an expedition to collect seagull eggs. Bark paintings are so popular nowadays among fanciers of Aboriginal art that they are turned out in the thousands by a somewhat synthetic native-art industry. The National Gallery in Melbourne displays authentic examples.

The Pukamuni burial ceremony (more on that in the next chapter) on Melville Island off the north coast of Australia requires decorated poles that constitute a minor branch of Aboriginal art. Similar poles in Arnhem Land, exhibiting skillfully carved figures, are objects as sacred as the churunga. Recent anthropological discoveries among the Aborigines are figures in the round, wood sculptures of fierce faces and so on. Aborigines also expend much artistic effort on bull-roarers, slabs of wood attached to a string so that they can be whirled in the air to make a noise supposed to be the voice of a great spirit.

Three curious forms of Aboriginal plastic art remain to be mentioned. One is ground drawing, on earth smoothed and hardened with water or blood, then painted abstractly in ocher or perhaps incised in channels lined with down. Another is body painting, almost exclusively by and for men, in designs drawn in ocher or in down, cotton, or kapok glued on with blood. The last is petroglyphs, outlines of animal figures sometimes sixty feet long cut ages ago on sandstone surfaces in the neighborhood of Sydney.

*

Up and up soars the Evening Star, hanging there
in the sky.
Men watch it, at the Place of the Dugong, the Place
of the Clouds, the Place of the Evening Star.
Far off, at the Place of the Mist, the Place of the
Lilies, the Place of the Dugong.
The lotus, Evening Star, hangs there on its long
stalk held by the Spirits.

So goes an Aboriginal song, part of a long legend about the moon. The Aborigines see to it that their lives have plenty of entertainment, in song, dance, drama, and storytelling.

The songs are short and repetitious verses that go together in long cycles and tell stories. A song about a journey will touch on the traveler's thirst, the sharp stones that hurt his feet, the wild honey he found, the water he thirsted for, the trees and spirit people he encountered. The verses are full of vivid imagery—a sunset is "like circumcision blood."

The main musical instrument is the *didjeridu*, a stopless, end-blown wood or bamboo drone pipe four to seven feet long. Elspeth Huxley describes the sound as "*gibba-yerra, gibba-yerra, gibba-yerra*"—"something between a grunting and the far-off bellow of a bull." With it go various combinations of clapping sticks, pillow drums (possum skins stuffed with feathers), bull-roarers, rattles made of baobab nuts or shells, and rasps.

Music plus dancing equals the corroboree, an Aboriginal word long since taken into Australian English to signify a big festivity. Aborigines divided their song-dance-dramas into religious cult ceremonies celebrating the adventures of Dream Time heroes, totemic ceremonies to secure the increase and prosperity of individual totems, and "playabouts," purely for fun. They often involve the miming of a totemic animal: a man may wriggle like a crocodile between the spread legs of a row of standing men; or the troupe may stamp like a herd of buffalo. The drama may recount a dream or convey a parody. A group of anthropologists attending a corroboree at Barrow Creek a few years ago watched in puzzlement as a dancer approached the other dancers one by one, scrutinized them carefully, then went through the motions of writing in a notebook. Suddenly the anthropologists realized, red-faced, that the drama was a spoof of their own interviews of members of the same tribe some time earlier. Men dance much more than women, but in some areas women have a graceful dance performed while making cat's cradles with string. Big poofs of flame from bundles of dried grass often illuminate corroborees. The ceremonies arouse strong sexual emotions, and generally end in a copulative free-for-all.

CHAPTER 7

Aborigines II: Their Role Today

The abo pleads nolo contendere, *I do not wish to contend, every time his eyes meet those of a white man.*

—EUGENE BURDICK

JIM HAMILTON was born in an Aboriginal settlement named Cherbourg—nobody knows how it got this Gallic name—150 miles north of Brisbane, the capital of the state of Queensland. His native language, one of 150 different Aboriginal languages in the area, representing 150 different tribes, is known as Gorang Gorang. His daily language nowadays, however, is English, for he lives in Brisbane and works as a civil servant (a status few Aborigines have achieved), employed by the Queensland government's Department of Aboriginal and Island Affairs. His career is that of service to his fellows, and he is well versed in the life of the Aborigines in this state.

Most Aborigines here, according to Jim Hamilton, are what are colloquially called "no-hopers," because they have no sense of "now, past, or future." Townsmen get equal pay for equal work at industrial and other urban jobs, but they do not understand the time clock and are apt to be undisciplined. Out in the bush they have a happier environment, but they constitute a big "problem" in the country towns because they seldom become fully integrated into the community. They have a good deal of pride in their "national" position; for instance, much resentment was expressed about reports—which proved to be false—that Aboriginal graves had been bulldozed on Melville Island to make room for cypress plantings. The Aborigines in Queensland are somewhat distrustful of education; a young boy starts school at five for a ten-year course, whereupon he may matriculate into the local university. There are only *two* Aboriginal students at the local university, however, out of some seventeen thousand. An Aboriginal boy will say, "All that schoolwork won't get me a sharper pick."

There are no rich Aborigines, and they do not even benefit from the discovery of mineral rights on their land. Aborigines are free to accept or reject military service on the same terms as whites in the Australian armed forces. They have the vote, and most vote Labor. Many still live as nomads, getting seasonal work "mustering" (rounding up) cattle on the stations. Except socially, there is no color bar or segregation of any kind; any Aboriginal can go to the best hotel (if he can afford it) or shop. On the other hand, invisible and mysteriously exerted pressure may make it difficult for him to buy or rent a dwelling in a location of his own choosing. More often than not the Aboriginal lives on the fringes of the towns, where water, sewage, and other public amenities are deficient, and where seasonal unemployment can be severe. Every Aboriginal shares money and all other possessions with other members of the tribe. It does not seem important to him to keep them for himself, even to improve his own housing or clothing.

*

In Darwin, modern Aborigines do not in general have a fruitful life. They live mostly in huts in outlying parts of the town, and when working often get less than the official minimum wage. However, most full Aborigines manage to look proud, and stride the streets like cowboys. A basic problem is that the Aborigines themselves are in such different and rapidly shifting stages of education, assimilation, and integration. But they lack drive (or so the whites say); they drink too much (or so the whites say); they desperately need more schooling, better housing, fuller amenities. Entering Darwin from the bush, most begin at once to deteriorate.

Social mixing with whites is at the minimum, but mixed football teams play in vigorous games of Australian Rules. At some of the new mines, like Gove, on the Gulf of Carpentaria, Aborigines complain that white workers molest their women. Occasionally marriages occur between the Aborigines and the Chinese; the local legend has it that "the genes click," and that most such unions are happy. Intermarriage between Aboriginal and white is rare; usually a white man marries an Aboriginal girl, not vice versa. There has been at least one case of the reverse in recent years, a marriage between an Aboriginal athlete and a Dutch nurse, which broke up after eighteen months.

Aborigines on Melville Island

Half an hour away by air on the northern coast off Darwin are two small islands, Melville and Bathurst, closely linked and inhabited by a curious Aboriginal people, the Tiwis. From the air, Melville, which marks off the Timor Sea from the Arafura Sea, gives the impression of searing, stinging jungle. This is a wet green madhouse. The plane puts down on a crude airstrip marked by oil drums painted white; a black ibis may sometimes be seen strolling among them.

Traveling by Toyota land cruiser—rough ground here—one passes the metal carcass, intertwined with decrepit foliage, of a Japanese aircraft shot down during the war, near Snake Bay settlement. Here, local folklore has it, the first European settlement was established in the 1820's by a Belgian bishop named Gsell, who wrote an autobiography, *The Bishop with One Hundred Wives*. The story is that, determined to wipe out polygamy, he picked a hundred youthful maidens and married them all himself, so that they could not become partners in polygamous marriages with the local natives.

The chief industry of the island is the production of wood chips exported to Japan. There are long transverse rows of cypress, and at the end of each row is the name of the cutter responsible for the logs—Black Joe, Tractor Joe, Big David. Between bouts of work the Aborigines amuse themselves by shooting crocodiles. The patriarch of the community, King Larry, about sixty-five, has a splendid white beard, thirty wives (apparently the Belgian bishop's injunctions have not been carried forward), and several hundred children; he wears intricate finery for ceremonies, and is proud of the fact that, singlehanded, he "murdered," as he puts it, an entire Japanese pearling crew in 1932.

Snake Bay is an official welfare station, operated by the Commonwealth government to give sustenance to these forlorn but stubborn islanders. The natives call it Millikapiti. The population is about 250 Tiwi and a handful of whites. The Tiwis are a complicated people. They do not throw the boomerang, or play the *didjeridu*, but they speak *seventy* different languages; to master the easiest, one is told, takes ten years. The traditional Tiwi costume includes a fiber ball, called a biting bag, swung below the neck; men and women chew on this, as Arabs fondle amber beads. In Snake Bay there is a store with retail sales running to $8,000 a month, as well as a museum containing wooden totem figures and other artifacts, and a canteen, where the residents are permitted three cans of beer per day—no hard liquor. They must drink their three beers on the spot, under supervision. There is a hospital of sorts—twelve beds under an iron roof, and so hot that if a patient did not have a temperature going in, he would surely have one coming out.

Superintendent of the Snake Bay settlement is Ian Rodgers, an impeccably civilized Briton who served many years in Kenya as a district commissioner there. According to Rodgers, the Aborigines are good carpenters, good craftsmen, and they have little temptation to leave the station (anybody is free to go) because family ties tend to hold them there. Comparing the local Tiwis with the Kikuyu in Africa, he said first that he did not think that he really knew or understood the Tiwi mind deep down, as he had come to understand the Kikuyu, but he went on to say the Tiwi are more explosive and give quicker expression to resentment or other emotions in passionate outbursts, whereas the Kikuyu always seek to hold everything in. Yet Kenya had the Mau Mau revolt, which would be unthinkable in Australia.

The Pukamuni burial ritual is unusual and ornate among the Tiwi. On the death of a person the family assembles, and an artist in the group cuts and paints a batch of wooden poles, which are placed around the grave. These poles have a special arcane significance, each symbolizing a particular member of a family, living or dead. The corpse is hung overhead. Even if it starts to decay (which as a matter of fact it does almost at once), it is not cut down till the next full moon. Then an elaborate recital takes place describing the dead man's life and qualities; after this, the family goes through a purification ceremony, and at last the actual funeral occurs. Members of the family are not allowed, as a rule, to return to their homes until rain has fallen; hence, they may be obliged to sleep out of doors for days or even weeks. Only rain can produce the necessary purification. Moreover, a tribal taboo has it that the ceremonial poles must *not* be cut, carved, or painted by any close kin of the dead; this work is assigned to outsiders, and the cost, believe it or not, can be $500.

The Tiwis are renowned for their dancing, which may be seen at their corroborees. The celebrated dancers Ted Shawn and Ruth St. Denis came here to study it on one occasion, and a group of Tiwi dancers performed at the 1970 Osaka Fair.

Aborigines and Whites—An Uneasy Relationship

White Australians, one is told, do not ever really *see* the Aborigines, not only because they live in distant places but because they are "psychologically invisible"—though perhaps this last is not so true as it used to be.

The Aborigines fit in closest to the white economy as hired hands in stock raising. Mustering cattle through the scrub, they can wear out four horses a day, and they are willing to ride boundaries on the enormous stations for as long as three months away from the homestead. And they have been willing to work for one-fifth of the pay of a unionized pastoralist, taking pay, moreover, in food and goods, thus sparing the station manager the inconvenience that stems from giving Aborigines money—the theory being that they will spend cash on liquor and tobacco and neglect their families. Aborigines on the stations live in fly-specked huts of corrugated iron, called "humpies." Often the station manager's wife does the cooking for the "gins," the Aboriginal women, who themselves do nothing at all. Unfortunately, Aboriginal horsemen are now being replaced on a large scale by helicopters and motorcycles. Though these stockmen are reasonably Westernized, they may still disappear for months at a time on "walkabouts." There they resume, to some extent, the life of killing kangaroos, of trapping goannas (lizards), of sleeping by fires, or heeding the animal spirits. It is typical to see Aborigines hovering timidly, namelessly, at the edge of a sheep shearing; but they may also be seen relaxed and chatting on the street in front of a handsome new bank in Alice Springs. For every Aboriginal standing one-legged in the desert, in the traditional posture of one foot tucked against a knee, there is another digging Grand Funk Railroad on a transistor radio.*

Whites and Aborigines do not mix much in homes. Even on the far reaches of the stations, alone in the night around a campfire, white stockmen won't always "doss down" next to Aborigines. (Contrariwise, a civilized Aboriginal lately moved out of the West End of Adelaide because of "too bloody many Italians coming in.") In fact, some whites still profess to have lynch rights over the Aborigines; the *Bulletin* quotes a cattle station manager as boasting that "if they bothered one of my girls they would be dead men, just like that, and you would get away with it here, too."

Some ten thousand Aborigines live in Sydney; others in towns like Moree and Walgett in New South Wales mix a culture of humpies, drink-scrounging, movies, and cars. In Sydney's Greenwich Village-like King's Cross, you can find bars that cater mostly to beery, staggering Aborigines and their blowzy women. Formerly, various laws forbade the Aborigines to drink, but such bans have been repealed throughout the country. Favored drinks

* Greenway gives this picture of a partly detribalized Aboriginal. "I had an experience with one such fellow; he emerged from the Adelaide prison with jailhouse English, the winsome habit of breaking his wife's forearm across his knee whenever she became too 'cheeky,' and a hand-cranked phonograph with one record, *Adeste Fideles*, which he played over and over again as he squatted in the red sand with the temperature 106 degrees in the waterbag."

among them are cheap wine and methylated spirits. Black prostitution is commonplace in Australia; in such a mining boom town as Roebourne, on the northwest coast, Aboriginal girls get $40 to $50 a night.

Only one percent of Aborigines get through secondary school—but in the bauxite fields Aboriginals are making $112 a week. Aborigines have suffered depressing discrimination at swimming pools, hotels, and restaurants —which spurs protests among idealistic university students in Sydney. On the other hand, welfare officers are now required to address an Aboriginal man as "mister," not "Jackie" or "Billie," as they used to. Last year the Aborigines of Arnhem Land sued to establish ownership of the bauxite there, just as Nabalco Proprietary Ltd. (a Swiss-Australian firm) prepared to mine it; the tribesmen said that mining would damage sacred places, and that they have secret tribal documents (which unfortunately, by the terms of their beliefs, cannot be shown to the public) proving ownership of the land. They lost the suit.

Assimilation Versus *Integration*

What is to become of these people, who are partially adapted to white culture and growing in numbers? The debate in Australia, which often rings of the American dilemma over white-Indian relations, centers on those two code words, assimilation and integration.

Government policy toward the Aborigines in Australia has gone, historically, from (1) complicity with attempted genocide to (2) belated application of English humanity and justice to (3) welfare and protection. The fourth and present official policy goes like this: "All Aborigines and part-Aborigines will attain the same manner of living as other Australians and will live as members of a single Australian community, enjoying the same rights and privileges, accepting the same responsibilities, observing the same customs, and influenced by the same beliefs, hopes and loyalties as other Australians." This is assimilation; it conjures up a picture of a proper Aboriginal wearing shorts, drinking beer, playing at bowls or golf, watching television, and raising roses in a suburban garden. Many well-intentioned whites approve of the government policy. They want the "natives" to have better housing, but there are inevitable qualms about accepting them as neighbors. All the squirming evasions of U.S. racial strife are here, though in pallid imitation.

The concept of integration, on the other hand, aims at the coexistence of white and Aboriginal cultures, with the bulk of the Aboriginal values surviving. It assumes that Aboriginal art and music must continue to exist, that Aboriginal language and religion can exist side by side with English and Christianity. "Integrationists" concede that naked-nomadic Aboriginal life is finished. But their point is that Aborigines have something to give, to teach, to the whites.

Mr. Wentworth's Theory

The Australian Minister for Social Services, W. C. Wentworth, has been in a lesser incarnation also the Minister-in-Charge of Aboriginal Affairs, and the latter job seemed to be his special enthusiasm.* It would be scientifically fascinating, he believes, to know what man's society was like before farming led to storage of food, division of labor, settled cities, and today's technological civilization. And, he argues, the study can be made, if tackled by anthropologists right now. The Australian Aborigines are the only people left in the world "not contaminated with agriculture." The focus, he thinks, would be on the cohesiveness of small groups, and on their language differences, which maintain tribal unity and distinguish friends from strangers. It would reveal an ancient psychology that may have planted patterns in the race memories of us all. In Australia such a study could be "pulled out of the memories of men still alive." But the opportunity is slipping away: "A language dies every month" among the rapidly detribalizing Aborigines, says Mr. Wentworth.

A similar note was struck in an interview in Canberra with Frederick D. McCarthy, the distinguished anthropologist who heads the Australian Institute for Aboriginal Studies. "In some cases, there are only two or three survivors of a tribe left," he said. "We have to act quickly. The 'wild' Aborigines are very tense. Not many left, just the few on the eastern side of Western Australia." Typically, in South Australia, construction of the space-age Woomera rocket range uprooted a lot of Stone Age Aborigines, who moved to white settlements. A drought a decade ago forced hundreds of Aborigines into missions and settlements.

One great hope for getting Aboriginal culture down on film, tape, and paper before it disappears is the Institute itself. It has fifty projects under way. Enough languages have been recorded to guarantee considerable enlightenment about Aboriginal linguistics. Similarly, hundreds of songs have been recorded, and much work done in social anthropology. The hitch, according to Wentworth, is a shortage not of money or goodwill, but of

* Prime Minister William McMahon, after taking office in March 1971, created a new ministry. Mr. Peter Howson is the first Minister for the Environment, Aborigines, and the Arts.

interest by the anthropologists of the rest of the world in a rapidly fading opportunity.

Recognition of this situation tends to modify the official policy of forcing Aborigines to attain "the same manner of living as other Australians." The government concedes the Aborigines' right to their languages and their customs, just as it gives that right to other religious or immigrant groups. But it still proposes to promote assimilation and to discourage "any kind of compulsory and permanent apartheid."

The various forms of government aid run around $30 million a year, which averages $1,500 each for the approximately twenty thousand Aboriginal families. Federal funds are pouring into the Aboriginal reserves in the Northern Territory, where housing, food, and work are offered to any Aboriginal who asks for them. Houses are concrete platforms on which rest one-room aluminum buildings with verandas. Schools are staffed at twenty students per teacher. Aboriginal children in remote spots are taught at a particularly ingenious mobile school that can be wheeled in over roadless terrain. The teachers find the mental equipment of the Aboriginal children equal to that of white ones, but question whether at adolescence the old sex and initiation ceremonies will dominate the children's energies.

Despite these efforts, the majority of Aborigines still face a discouraging future, well described by that eminent Australian, Dr. H. C. Coombs, who is among other things chairman of the Australian Council of Aboriginal Affairs. His prognosis:

> If an aboriginal baby is born today it has a much better than average chance of being dead within two years.
>
> If it does survive it has a much better than average chance of suffering from substandard nutrition to a degree likely permanently to handicap it (a) in its physical and mental potential, (b) in its resistance to disease.
>
> It is likely in its childhood to suffer from a wide range of diseases but particularly ear, nose and throat and respiratory infections, from gastro-enteritis, from trachoma and other eye infections.
>
> If it reaches the teen ages it is likely to be ignorant of and lacking in sound hygienic habits, without vocational training, unemployed, maladjusted and hostile to society.
>
> If it reaches adult age it is likely to be lethargic, irresponsible and, above all, poverty-stricken—unable to break out of the iron cycle of poverty, ignorance, malnutrition, ill health, social isolation, and antagonism: if it lives in the north it has a good chance of being maimed by leprosy and, wherever, its search for affection and companionship may well end only in the misery of venereal disease.
>
> If it happens to be a girl it is likely to conceive a baby at an age

when her white contemporary is screaming innocent adulation at some pop star and she will continue to bear babies every twelve or eighteen months until she reaches double figures or dies of exhaustion. And so the wheel will turn.

The Aborigines' Point of View

It would obviously be interesting to know what the Aborigines want in the way of integration, but apparently no well-researched study exists. A couple of factors seem clear, however. After nearly two centuries of losing life and land to the white man, the Aboriginal is distrustful of belated attempts to square things up. Yet when offered houses, schools, and jobs in the white world, the remaining primitive nomads slowly but surely shuck off their old culture and join this new one. Beyond these elementary observations, there are, of course, some worthwhile opinions about the problem from various articulate Aborigines. A typical voice is that of Bob Maza, the president of the Victorian Aborigines Association, one of about sixty-five groups defending Aboriginal interests. He calls government policy "cultural obliteration," and says, sardonically: "Let us not be too hasty about rushing into a society that is at present foundering." The closest thing to a Black Power group in Australia is the National Tribal Council. Its leader is Bruce McGuinness, who is just past thirty years of age and would appear to take his style from American black militants. "We want our land and the wealth that Honky dug out of it," he wrote last year. "We are sick and fed up with being told that we are being helped by the Man and that the Man is being very generous in giving us this and giving us that. We know that this is a whole lot of Toro Excretia. All the Man is doing is appeasing his conscience. . . . us Black Boys ain't buying any of his con."

The National Tribal Council makes ten demands in its official platform. They include better health, better education, a law against discrimination, black administration of government programs of aid for Aborigines, and legal aid and protection—Aborigines "need more lawyers than welfare officers." They also want "reacculturation. . . . Governments must abandon the failed policy of assimilation which amounts to cultural genocide." Finally, they want recognition of their ownership of "traditional" land, and compensation for the whites' seizure of it, plus royalties from mining or other exploitation of it.

Aboriginal militance in general, however, is disorganized and weak—nothing to perturb the government or anyone else. There are only one-tenth as many Aborigines in Australia, in proportion to the total population, as there are Negroes in the United States, and no effective rebellion can be expected from these people.

Kath Walker, a best-seller poet and Queensland State Secretary of the Federal Council for the Advancement of Aborigines and Torres Strait Islanders, contends that the real pinch in Aboriginal-white relations is land. The government, she charges, flatly refuses to listen to Aboriginal demands for the return of land, while on the other hand leasing it in Kentucky-size chunks to American and British absentee landlords at fifty cents a square mile. Kath Walker, herself a vigorous and effective Aboriginal, was born in 1920, worked as a servant, joined the Australian Army, learned shorthand, and went on to write poetry. Her totem is the carpet snake. Another Aboriginal poet is Jack Davis, who some time back picketed the United Nations building in Manhattan to call attention to the Aborigines' plight. His lament:

The tribes are all gone,
The spears are all broken.

*

A number of other Aborigines, though painfully few all told, have been able to come from the Stone Age to eminence in the white culture. Harold Blair turned his resonant tenor into a career in opera and in teaching at the Melbourne Conservatorium of Music. Albert Namatjira made himself one of the country's best-known landscapists, in bone-and-ocher paintings that catch the desert's torrid, barren beauty—the heat that chills. Evonne Goolagong, nineteen, won the Wimbledon Women's Singles Championship in mid-1971, upsetting Margaret Court. Sister Jeanne Marie, of the Murinbadda tribe, a few years ago became the first full-blooded Aboriginal nun, and the Rev. James Noble is one of several who are Anglican clergymen. Lionel Rose, who grew up in a humpy near Melbourne and wrapped his hands in rags in order to learn how to fight, became world champion bantamweight by beating a Japanese boxer in 1968. He is said to be the first of his race to be best in the world at anything. The Australia Day Council made Rose Man of the Year in 1969. "A hundred and eighty years ago one of my mob would have been a dead cert for this," he remarked dryly.

The first Aboriginal to get a seat in any Australian Parliament, state or federal, is Neville Bonner, who was endorsed in mid-1971 by the Queensland Parliament to be a Liberal federal Senator from that state. He had been a boomerang-maker and carpenter, earning $75 a week as compared to the $263 paid to a Senator. Other Aborigines have become authors, inventors, cricketers, actors. A number of them served with distinction in World War II and the Korean War.

*

Only faintly bruited about in Australia today is the thought that white society might not only let the Aborigine keep his values but even adopt some of them. The possibilities, though probably remote, are tantalizing. Valuable insights might be gained by studying the Aborigines' animistic religion in the light of Jungian psychology. We might also benefit by examining the Aboriginal trait of sharing and his distrust of competition. Nowadays white men everywhere suffer doubts about the ultimate value of their computerized, war-prone, often philistine civilization, and they impose it upon other and differing societies with less confidence than in the past. Perhaps Australia will be the nation that finds a way toward a more comfortable give-and-take between Western culture and the cultures that we perhaps quite wrongly call primitive.

CHAPTER 8

Labor Versus Liberals

They call no biped lord or sir,
And touch their hat to no-man.
—HENRY LAWSON

THE TREND of Australian politics in the nineteenth century was populist, collectivist, and democratic, which should have led to an advanced experiment in socialism. Instead, the political system today is a curious preservation of some old radical values (such as every man's absolute right to a job) combined with deep caution and conservatism. A social-minded person concerned with the individual's economic rights can be reasonably happy in this system, while big business and the banks are eminently comfortable. The system has bumbled along for years on basically managerial governments, and indeed managerial governments appear to be good enough for the present. We now proceed to examine Australia's modern politics, starting with a brief look at how the government works.

*

The Australian Constitution has been called "an extraordinarily uninteresting document that does not hold any great truths to be self-evident." It has no bill of rights. But it does have some curious wrinkles. For example, any Member of Parliament can introduce legislation to *reduce* expenditure or taxation, but only ministers of state can do so to *increase* expenditure or taxation.

Australia adopted from the U.S. the constitutional concept of listing federal powers and giving all others to the states. The federal powers, in brief, are control over defense, post and telegraph, customs, trade and commerce, marriage and divorce, banking, naturalization, and external (foreign) affairs. Also roughly patterned on the U.S. model are the Senate and House of Representatives. Each of the six states elects ten Senators, an arrangement which, as in the U.S., gives the less populous states leverage against the others. The House has "as nearly as practicable" twice as many members as the Senate (or 120). To create their constituencies, the population is divided by 120 (which currently yields a quotient of somewhat more than 100,000), and the states map out electoral districts containing about this many voters. In practice this leads to much gerrymandering, usually favoring the countryside. The Senators are elected for six-year terms, with one-half retiring every three years to make it a "continuing body." Representatives are elected for a maximum of three years, but as in England the Prime Minister, if defeated on a vote of confidence, must call for an election. Thus House and Senate elections are generally out of step, which, plus the same situation in each of the states, gives Australians *lots* of elections to vote in—and they must vote, under penalty of a fine.

But because of Australia's British heritage, the Constitution does not separate the executive and the legislative powers (as the U.S. Constitution does); it gives both functions to Parliament. The leader of a political party stands for election in his own constituency, and if he and his party win a plurality, he becomes Prime Minister. He then picks a cabinet from Representatives and Senators, chiefly the former. Most decisions are taken by the cabinet sitting in secrecy, and enacted rather docilely by the House and Senate. Australian Representatives are called Members of Parliament—M.P.s, as in England or Canada. The Labor Party has pledged itself since 1919 to abolish the Senate, partly because anti-labor forces have dominated that body throughout most of Australian federal history, but is not working very hard at it. On paper, the Senate does not seem powerful; for example, it can only "request" changes in money bills sent up from the House. But it can veto House bills by simply failing to pass them, and if in practice it is less powerful than the U.S. Senate, it is vastly more powerful than the Canadian Senate.

The federal government as a whole is stronger than the federal government of the United States, for three reasons. It has the sole power to borrow money—that is, the states cannot borrow. It controls all social and welfare services. And, most important, it has the sole power to levy income taxes. The federal government shares this revenue, on its own terms, with the states, much as President Nixon was in 1971 proposing to share U.S. federal government revenue with the fifty states. The central government can thus dictate much policy to the states, even though 70 percent of the money is disbursed to them without specifying how it should be used.

The High Court of Australia, with a chief justice and six other justices, is the court of appeals from state courts, since Parliament has not created any lower federal courts. It has original jurisdiction in a few matters, chiefly issues between the Commonwealth and the states, and review of legislation. Here we come to one of the few tenuous remaining governmental links between Australia and Britain. For there is a court higher than Australia's High Court, to which appeals can be made on certain questions. It is Britain's Privy Council. But the High Court itself must certify, that is, permit, any such appeals. It has done so only once. And that was in 1912.

A typical case of High Court action was its invalidation of a law to dissolve the Communist Party in 1951. Until a suitable building can be put up in Canberra, the capital, the seat of the High Court remains in Melbourne.

The Political System

The play of modern politics in Australia is not as simple as Democrat versus Republican, but it can be comprehended quickly. The Labor Party would control the majority of votes except for a festering schism created by some of its more conservative members, the Democratic Labor Party. This weakness lets a minority rightist party, the Liberals, in coalition with the Country Party, rule Australia. Some consequences are: (1) that Labor, the biggest single group even though it is stymied for the moment, remains potent and likely to regain control of the government at some point; and (2) that the Country Party, vital to the Liberals, swings more weight than its small constituency merits.

The last twenty-two years have been years of gratification and self-satisfaction for the Liberals, but the more active shapers of Australia, since it became a nation, have been the politicians of the Labor Party. This country is where the concept of a Labor Party germinated. And Labor, in the phrase of Australia's great interpretive historian, Sir Keith Hancock, has usually been the "party of initiative," working against the Liberals and their predecessors as the "parties of resistance." The political story of Australia since federation shows how this has come about.

The Labor Years

The secret ballot and universal manhood suffrage came to Australia well before Disraeli introduced them in England. Thus long before federation the idea that the vote could really be made to work for change had been planted. So when the unions lost the great strikes of 1891, aimed at better hours, better pay, accident compensation, and so on, they turned grimly but confidently to politics for redress. Labor parties in the states soon developed a discipline that required Labor politicians to vote as a bloc on major issues. The first federal parliaments were split three ways, but Labor's bloc-vote solidarity gave it decisive control in the first decade of federal government.

It was a decade that fixed some of the main lines of Australian life. A navy was begun, old-age and invalid pensions established. Tariffs were raised, with the significant condition that protected industry must pay "fair and reasonable wages"; that is, the tariffs were enacted less in the interests of the manufacturer than in those of his employees. In a test case this led an influential judge to set a firm minimum wage, a social concept that did not come into effect in the U.S. until the New Deal. With no guidelines as to what might be fair and reasonable, Justice Henry Bourne Higgins took a deep breath and ruled that the minimum wage must meet "the normal needs of the average employee regarded as a human being living in a civilized community." This definition has prevailed in Australia ever since.

*

Labor got an absolute majority in Parliament in 1910 and put through further measures that the opposition denounced as socialism, chiefly the establishment of the government-run Commonwealth Bank as a "people's bank" in competition with private banks. It was a Labor Prime Minister, Andrew Fisher, who took Australia into World War I, vowing to support Britain "to the last man and the last shilling." The first fate of the "Anzacs" (Australia and New Zealand Army Corps) was to be sacrificed in Winston Churchill's ill-executed plan to take the Dardanelles. Under shattering fire, the Australians stormed the steep hill at Gallipoli, dug in and held their position for eight months, until withdrawn. To no purpose, ten thousand Anzacs died there. The date of the landing, April 25, is now Australia's most fervently celebrated national holiday, marking the most poignant episode of a war that ultimately cost Australia 59,258 dead and 166,819 wounded.

Enlistments *increased* after the Gallipoli disaster, such was Australia's patriotic fervor, but the succeeding Labor Prime Minister, William Morris Hughes, a man of furious invective,* decided under British pressure that only conscription would ultimately raise enough troops for Australia to do her share of the fighting in France. He thereupon forced the nation through

* He once compared a political enemy unfavorably to Judas Iscariot, on the grounds that Judas "did not gag the man he betrayed, nor did he fail to hang himself afterward."

two wrenching referendums designed to authorize conscription. The draft was sulphurously opposed by Melbourne's Roman Catholic Archbishop, Daniel Mannix, and by thousands of Irish Catholics in the Labor Party, who were furious at British suppression of the Easter (1916) Rebellion in Dublin. The referendums failed to pass, splitting Labor and destroying its power for years. Hughes, expelled from the party, teamed up with the Liberals to form a party labeled Nationalists. They ruled, partly in coalition with the Country Party, until the Depression made the country yearn for Labor's humane touch again.

Labor's sway this time lasted only a few years, until a new split. John Thomas ("The Big Fella") Lang, Labor Premier of New South Wales, semidesperate over the suffering caused by the Depression, moved wildly against the banks, alarming conservatives, including those in his own party. They defected to join the Nationalists and form a United Australia Party. This group ruled until World War II. Fighting the slump in the 1930's with the conventional economic wisdom of the time (deflation, wage cuts, government economy), the United Australia Party managed to provide Australia with a particularly miserable Depression. The birth rate dropped, immigration stopped, development ceased, and *one-third* of all workers were jobless.

By World War II the United Australia Party was weak and squabbling, and shortly before Pearl Harbor the voters put Labor back into power. High-voltage shocks went through the nation as the Japanese sank the British warships *Prince of Wales* and *Repulse* in the Gulf of Siam, overran Singapore, the Dutch East Indies and Timor, and invaded first New Britain, off New Guinea's north coast, and then New Guinea itself. Bombs fell on Australian soil at Darwin, killing 243. Here Mr. Churchill, deviser of Gallipoli, entered the picture again. He had already won sour criticism from Australia earlier in the war by opposing the withdrawal of exhausted Australian troops who had resisted eight months of siege at Tobruk in North Africa. Now, while Australians clamored to get a couple of Aussie divisions transferred home from the Middle East for defense, Churchill coolly proposed that it was more important to send them to Burma. Churchill is, to put it dryly, not quite the hero in Australia that he is elsewhere.

This is a crucial moment in Australian history. John Curtin, the new Labor Prime Minister, made a famous speech in which he said: "Without inhibitions of any kind, I make it quite clear that Australia looks to America, free of any pangs as to our traditional links or kinship with the United Kingdom." Defying Churchill, Curtin brought the Australian divisions home to fight in the Pacific theater. Events moved swiftly. General Douglas Mac-

Arthur went to Melbourne and then Brisbane as Supreme Commander of the Allied Forces in the Southwest Pacific. By May 1942, only five months after Pearl Harbor, American and Australian ships and planes shot the Japanese out of the Coral Sea, off Australia's northeast coast. For the rest of the year, and through 1943, Americans and Aussies struggled with Japanese troops on New Guinea, winning the eastern end so that MacArthur could begin the island-hopping that led to victory in the Pacific.

The war period was a time of solid success for Labor. The party put over conscription for overseas service with hardly a murmur. Essington Lewis, brilliant manager of Broken Hill Proprietary Ltd., the country's biggest mining and steelmaking firm, took charge of the wartime economy, and Australia learned to make machine tools, sulfanilamide, optical goods, and airplanes. To finance the war effort, the federal government took from the states the power to levy income taxes, a much needed advance toward stronger federalism.

This good record inspired voters to keep Labor in power after the war ended. Curtin died in 1945, and his successor Joseph Benedict ("Ben") Chifley, a former locomotive engineer: (1) brought off a carefully planned transition to peace, establishing many veterans on farms; (2) launched Australia's car industry; (3) started the huge Snowy Mountains Scheme for irrigation and hydroelectric power; (4) opened new universities in Sydney and Canberra; and (5) began the immigration policy that has recast Australia.

Suddenly and disastrously, Labor's idyl fell apart. Chifley had tried to nationalize all banks, jangling conservative nerves. Churchill's Iron Curtain speech at Fulton, Missouri, reminded Australians that Communist influence was dangerously strong in many unions. A coal miners' strike caused power shortages. And a refurbished opposition party, operating again under the Liberal label, was waiting in the wings with an eloquent if arrogant leader, Robert Gordon Menzies, lusting to take over the government. At elections in 1949, Labor toppled, and Menzies' Liberal-Country coalition took power.

Labor has never returned to power.* To understand why, we must now peer a little more closely at Labor's membership and ideology. Obviously, Labor's main constituency is the membership of trade unions—53 percent of the entire work force of 5,535,000—but the party is large enough and disparate enough to include a large left-right spectrum. The party's traditional

* This account, showing that Labor ruled the federal government only three times between 1910 and the present, may not seem to bear out the party's critical importance. But it was under Labor governments that the world wars were fought and the Depression was faced. And over the whole period Labor overwhelmingly dominated all state governments except those of Victoria and South Australia.

philosophy is heavily qualified socialism. Its "objective," announced in 1921, goes like this: "The democratic socialization of industry, production, distribution and exchange—to the extent necessary to eliminate exploitation and other anti-social features in those fields." But another declaration issued simultaneously, states that the party does not seek to abolish private ownership. The party is generally pacifist, holding that wars are started by capitalists, not workers.

Not many Roman Catholics in the early part of this century cared for this leftish program. But the prelate who dominated Catholicism in Australia from 1884 until his death in 1911, Francis Patrick Cardinal Moran, was an enlightened and foresighted man, who gave his imprimatur to the Labor movement, despite the predominance in it of Protestants and freethinkers. The net of this was to attach the great mass of Irish-descended Catholics in Australia firmly to the Labor Party, whether or not their ideologies quite jibed. Historically Catholics, though only a fourth of the electorate, have provided Labor with one-third of its vote. Two-thirds of all Catholics vote Labor. Any state or federal cabinet controlled by Labor is likely to contain a *majority* of Catholics.

The issue of Communism in the Labor Party provided the divisive factor. The Communist Party is tiny, but it has managed to appeal to militant Laborites who have not forgotten the days of strikes and lockouts, and the Depression. Solidly supporting the war effort from 1940 until 1945, the Communists proceeded to win great influence in many unions: ironworkers, sheet metal workers, engineers, sailors, clerks, railwaymen, dockworkers.

To a devout young Catholic lawyer in Melbourne, B. A. Santamaria, this infiltration was profoundly alarming. Using the same discipline and persistence as the Communists themselves, he initiated a movement, operating through secret union cells, to pry loose the Communist hold on union after union. Santamaria and his cohorts became a conservative force in the Labor Party.

The inevitable effect was to split the party, and the split was then greatly aggravated by the celebrated Petrov case. The leader of the party in 1954 was Herbert Vere Evatt, intellectual, lawyer, and radical thinker, whom the world had come to know well as an influential Foreign Minister at the founding of the United Nations. Now he was contesting elections with Prime Minister Menzies and the Liberal-Country coalition. With fifteen days to go before the voting, Menzies sprung on the nation the fact that Vladimir Petrov, third secretary of the Russian Embassy, had defected and turned over to the government documents reflecting on Labor, and particularly on two associates of Evatt. The well-timed blow may have cost Evatt the election, since Australia was in a state of anti-Communist hysteria comparable to the McCarthy era in the U.S.

Anyway, Evatt thought that it did. Evatt was by no means a Communist, but in his fury at losing he rashly decided that *all* anti-Communists were his enemies, including Santamaria and his movement. Until then the movement had remained virtually unknown to the public because it had been felt that to expose it would stir up anti-Catholicism, always a potentially explosive political issue. Evatt stripped open the story of the movement and its cells. Labor split, and fell from power in several states. At length the anti-Communist, Catholic elements of the party cut out completely, and formed the far-right Democratic Labor Party. The 10 to 20 percent of votes that the DLP removed from the Australian Labor Party (to use the full name of the traditional party) account for two decades of losing to Liberal-Country coalitions.*

Menzies and the Liberals

Thus the rest of Australia's political story belongs to the Liberals, and largely to the urbane, royalist, fear-inspiring grandson of a gold-rusher who led them, Robert Gordon Menzies.

The Liberal Party represents order, respectability, the Establishment.

* The mechanism that the DLP employs to deprive the ALP of votes is the excruciatingly complicated Australian preferential voting system. Suppose five candidates are running for Representative. The voter does not mark "X" in the square opposite his choice; rather, he writes numbers, from one to five, opposite all the candidates' names in the order of his preference. In practice, the count may show that no one of the five has an absolute majority of first-preference votes. In that case, the candidate with the fewest first-preference votes is eliminated, and the second-preference votes on those ballots are distributed among the remaining four candidates. If, after the second-preference votes are added to the first, there is still no candidate with a majority of the total ballots cast, the process is repeated: the ballots of the candidate trailing at this stage of the computation are divided up on the basis of second preference. If he inherited some second-preference votes from the first man eliminated, these are now redistributed on the basis of third preference. And so on. Ultimately one of the five gets an absolute majority, even if his votes are composed of first, second, third, fourth, and even fifth preferences.

Senate elections, involving the choice of not one but perhaps five candidates from a list of, say, fifteen, are, God help us, *much* more complicated, using the principle of proportional representation. Australian elections can take days to count. Voting machines cannot be used. Most Australians, especially newly arrived immigrants, do not understand the system in full detail.

The DLP operates by ordering its members to vote for DLP candidates on first preference, and for Liberal candidates on second and other preferences. Few DLP candidates ever win, but the party's votes count anyway, through second preferences that work against the Australian Labor Party.

Large business firms rely upon it and finance it. It is a private-enterprise party that may regulate, but will not nationalize, business; it fosters trade and the stock market. Conservative as it is, the Liberal Party differs only by a few degrees from the Labor Party on many of the crucial issues. They stand close to one another on anti-Communism and White Australianism, and both support large-scale immigration and social welfare. Australian voters prefer choices of emphasis rather than diametrical opposites.

Menzies—born in 1894 in the Victorian countryside, educated at the University of Melbourne, a rich barrister before entering Victoria state politics—was Prime Minister as Australia entered World War II, and he was tottering. The House of Representatives was so closely divided that a mere smidgen of rebellion in Menzies' party was enough to knock the pins from under him. He fell, rather ignominiously. "It was a terrible thing to be told that your services were no longer required, at a crucial time in the world's history," he recalled later. During Labor's wartime rule, Menzies pondered deeply and formulated a proposal for a "true revival of Liberal thought which would work for social justice and security, for national power and national progress and for the full development of the individual citizen though not through the dull and deadening process of socialism."

In 1949, amidst waning confidence in the Labor Party, Menzies came to power again. Eighteen years later, the Washington *Post* called Menzies "probably the most completely successful public man of his time." Britain's Harold Wilson compared Menzies to Churchill. Sufficient facts exist to argue this case. Between the beginning and the end of Menzies' term: (1) national income grew from $4.4 billion to $20.8 billion; (2) the population grew from 7.9 million to 11.5 million, because of well-promoted encouragement to immigration; (3) university enrollment grew from 32,000 to 80,000; (4) the percentage of homeowners increased from 60 to 76; and (5) car ownership rose from one car for every twelve persons to one car for every four. Menzies and his Liberal Party started out their long regime operating under the hard-nosed theory that a bit of unemployment, say 3 or 4 percent, was salubrious. The uproar when the jobless rate reached merely 2 percent* forced Menzies to a policy of full employment through measures that others might have called socialist but in any case worked to keep the populace contented. Great foreign investments in auto-making, petroleum, cattle, farming, mines, and chemicals poured in, contributing to euphoria (while raising worries about the pinch of foreign control). Menzies turned Canberra from country town to flourishing capital. He devised federal help for universities, and saved them from going to ruin. He developed a much-needed Insti-

* In 1971 joblessness in the U.S. hit 6 percent.

tute for Aboriginal Studies. And he gave the country good management.

He failed, in 1951, to get a majority in a national referendum for a bill designed to hobble the Communist Party by forcing anyone charged with being a Communist to prove that he was not; the fair-minded Australians refused to swallow this guilty-until-proved-innocent approach. He ardently supported the 1956 British–French–Israeli invasion of Egypt to keep the Suez Canal open, and shared with those three nations the ignominy of being denounced and repudiated by the United States and the United Nations. (Menzies remained "unrepentant.") He took a "legalistic" view of South African apartheid that amounted to approving it.

Menzies retired January 20, 1966, winding up a cabinet meeting by casually saying, "Well, gentlemen, this is the last time I shall be with you." In an oddly candid chat with one of his more contrary opponents, James Ford Cairns, a left-wing Labor M.P., he explained why. "He told me," said Cairns, "that he was very worried about what had happened to Winston by staying in politics too long. He thought it was sad to see Winston decline before the public eye."

*

Menzies as politician and statesman was a man of cautious innovation and no bad mistakes. He remained in power for more than twice as long as any other Australian Prime Minister, helped by the postwar boom and the split among his opponents. This tough, secretive, canny, and self-centered politician is more interesting as a presence than as a shaker and mover. He did not serve in World War I at least partly because he declared himself "too valuable to be used for cannon fodder."* In his school years he rejected sports—which is heresy in Australia—and spent the time he might have wasted on cricket or football in intensive study of Shakespeare. In consequence he developed stunning powers of articulation. In Parliament he could think briefly, set down three or four topic headings, and then speak at length with compelling logic, eloquence, and—not least—perfect syntax. He was tremendously cutting. To an opponent in the House: "The conducted tour of the honorable member's mind would have been more instructive had it not taken place in gathering darkness." To hecklers during a rally in Tasmania: "I am not directing my speech tonight to the descendants of convicts, but to free Australian citizens." In the Parliament building in Canberra, Menzies would sometimes theatrically open the door to the office of Harold Holt, the Deputy Prime Minister, draw himself up to full height,

* And partly because tradition exempted third sons from volunteering if the older two had.

and inquire, "Is the young master in?" Menzies could be nettlesome to newsmen. To one reporter he asked, "Is the Sydney *Sun* still being edited by fourteen-year-olds?"

Another reporter started an interview by saying: "I'm from the *Daily Mirror*, Mr. Menzies."

"You have my deepest sympathy."

Such arrogant intelligence gave Mr. Menzies almost tyrannical power. His ministers feared—and respected—him. A long-time collaborator, Arthur Fadden, always called Menzies "the big bastard," though never within Menzies' hearing. Gathering for a meeting of the House during a crisis, his ministers would say confidently, "We'll get some pretty good ham from Bob tonight." One effect of his towering control of men was what has been called "cabinet dictatorship." Policies and courses of action were decided in secret cabinet meetings, with Menzies dominating the discourse, and presented to Parliament for rubber-stamping—typically, the little-debated entry of Australia into the Vietnam war.

This man had a prudish side, too. He upheld the tendency of lesser authorities toward excessive censorship, specifically approving the banning of *Ulysses* and *Lolita*. On the other hand, he is reputed to have been able to put together the most potent martini in Australia.

With all Menzies' autocracy in Australia went a reverence for the monarchy in England. When Australia switched from pounds to decimal currency, Menzies wanted to name the new unit of money the "royal." Without a blush, he saluted Queen Elizabeth, at a state occasion in Parliament House, by quoting some lines from the sixteenth-century English poet Barnabe Googe: "I did but see her passing by / And yet I love her till I die." His loyalty even survived a Buckingham Palace banquet during which the soup ran out and Dame Pattie, Menzies' wife, could not be served. England repaid Menzies' fealty by making him Privy Councilor, Companion of Honor, Queen's Counsel, Fellow of the Royal Society, Lord Warden of the Cinque Ports, and, to top it off, *Sir* Robert Menzies, Knight of the Thistle. Nowadays he lives a quiet life in Melbourne.

It should be remembered, incidentally, that Menzies' long career would not have been possible without the aid of the Country Party. During his years in office, this party managed to elect an average of eighteen Members of Parliament, and when they were added to the Liberals' average of fifty-two, the coalition could outvote Labor, which averaged fifty-nine. The Country Party arose after World War I to speak for sheep graziers, cattlemen, wheat raisers, and farmers, who always darkly suspect that the city-oriented parties will sabotage them. By balance-of-power tactics, this lean and efficient party extracts concessions for its members—for example, loopholes that let agriculturalists dodge most income taxes. The leader of the party from 1958 until 1971 was John ("Black Jack") McEwen, horny-handed and histrionic, who had been in the House of Representatives since 1934, often serving as a minister and latterly as Deputy Prime Minister. He amplified the party, appealing to industrialists by urging tariff protection for them. His successor is a tanned and hawk-eyed farmer (fruit, dairying, pigs), forty-two years old, whose name is Douglas Anthony.

The Short Regime of Harold Holt

The succession went easily to Menzies' choice, Harold Holt, then fifty-eight, an associate of Menzies for more than thirty years, who had been standing on tiptoe for the No. 1 job for eight years. He served not quite two years, and then one day he went swimming and was never seen again.

Holt was born in Sydney, son of a theatrical impresario who upon divorcing his wife sent the boy at the age of ten to a tough private school in Melbourne. He was barely out of law school at the University of Melbourne when he joined Menzies and others in a rightist organization called Young Nationalists, and he won a seat in the House of Representatives at the age of twenty-seven. Menzies put Holt in the cabinet in 1939, but Holt resigned in a few months to enlist in the artillery. One afternoon he was performing the lowliest of army chores, cleaning latrines, when a message came from Menzies that, like it or not, Holt had to return to one of the country's highest jobs, a cabinet post. Ironically, Holt then concluded that Menzies was not good enough to be Prime Minister, and helped to shaft him on that famous day in 1941 when Menzies was forced out. Usually an unforgiving man, Menzies in this case overlooked the slight, and on return to office brought Holt to the top by giving him important assignments.

Holt proved loyal and patient, and based his political stance on the Gallup Poll. "Vacillation can be part of the technique of achievement," he said. As Minister of Immigration, he humanized some of the more egregious aspects of the White Australia policy. Australians liked him because he had "no complexes."

In office he turned out to be as pro-American as Menzies was pro-British. He stood on the White House lawn and said that he would go "all the way with LBJ." He took a hard line on Vietnam, putting over conscription to keep the army big, and sending a couple of extra battalions to fight in the war. "It's bad luck for the Vietnamese that the world power conflict is being waged on their territory," he said. This proved a popular formula. Holt won the 1966 election easily by pinning an anti-American label on Labor (which opposed the war and the draft), getting a boost from a tour of Australia by President Johnson. But, surprisingly, Holt reversed Menzies' attitude of indifference to Australia's Asian neighbors, and toured them as far as Cambodia; he also lowered immigration bars a bit. Possessed of a very Australian respect for a man's right to leisure, he would sometimes disappear for two days at a time; once his aides could not find him to deliver an "eyes only" message from President Johnson. Holt did not run the cabinet very firmly; quasi conspiracies to bring him down got started; the Liberals lost two by-elections and a Senate election.

Holt was an athletic man, a surfer and swimmer, and one Sunday morning in December 1967, after a tiring cabinet session, he went to the beach near his seaside house fifty-nine miles from Melbourne. The waves were ten feet high, and only one of the four neighbors who were with him even dared dip into the water. Holt, perhaps out of bravado, dived in and swam strongly out, just as the tide turned. He disappeared about five hundred yards from the shore, and his body was never found. Rumors may still be heard that this was suicide, but Canberra newsmen don't believe them—he was not by any means the type, they say. They guess that he was caught in a riptide and swam out with it, as surfers often do, intending to turn and get carried back; instead, handicapped by a recently injured shoulder, he was swept away. President Johnson made the long trip to Australia again to attend the funeral of his admirer, and in Djakarta, President Suharto went to a mosque to pray for the man who had made Australia a bit more neighborly toward Indonesia. Later the American Navy christened a new destroyer escort the U.S.S. *Harold E. Holt.*

John Gorton's Rise and Fall

The rise of John Grey Gorton, the next Prime Minister, was an intricate political gavotte. Holt's sudden death left no one neatly groomed for the job, as Holt had been. William McMahon, a longtime M.P. from New South Wales raised at this juncture to treasurer and deputy leader of the Liberal Party, stood out as the ranking Liberal; and Paul Hasluck, a prominent cabinet minister since 1951, had ambitions for the job and a strong following in New South Wales. Unbeknownst to them, a coalition of forces based in Victoria decided to attempt the nomination of the Victorian Gorton, then a Senator. The first step was to eliminate McMahon, which was tidily accomplished by John McEwen, the leader of the Country Party. McEwen, serving as caretaker Prime Minister after Holt, announced, giving no reasons, that he would not serve in a government with McMahon, who then had no choice but to withdraw. It is said that McEwen was grateful to Gorton for not running against him some years previously in a local election in Victoria. Gorton was now in a position to compete for Liberal Party leadership. He defeated Hasluck, stepped up to the prime ministership, and then elevated Hasluck to Governor-General (by the customary process of recommending him to the Queen). This was patronage on a grand scale, and full of irony, for in effect Gorton made his defeated opponent into head of state, toothless as that job is in the British-Australian system. Not every Australian liked the move—the appointment of the Governor-General is supposed to be above politics. Since the Prime Minister is expected to be a member of the House of Representatives because legislation mostly originates there, Gorton resigned from the Senate, ran for the seat left vacant by Holt, and was duly elected.

The leader that Australians were so surprised to find in power turned out to be a bull in a china shop. In manner he combines the homespun and the patrician. His father and mother—he a prosperous orange grower, she a poor Irish girl—were not married; Gorton recently demolished a critic by saying that he had "achieved a status by his own efforts which I hold through action not by me but by my parents." His caved-in countenance, the result of being shot down by the Japanese off Singapore when he was a Royal Australian Air Force pilot ("My face got rather mixed up with the instrument panel"), is a political asset both as common-man homeliness and as evidence of bravery.* His patrician component comes from the schools his father sent him to: Geelong Grammar in Victoria and Brasenose College at Oxford, where, favoring Etonians as friends, he replaced his Australian twang with a cultivated British accent. In private, incidentally, the homespun side of Mr. Gorton gives way completely to the patrician. He is alert, graceful, aware, attentive, and humorous. He is married to the former Bettina Brown, of Bangor, Maine, whom he met while she was a student at the Sorbonne and he was touring Europe with her brother, an Oxford classmate. During World War II she ran the family orchards in Victoria, packing oranges, driving a tractor, irrigating, and keeping books. Since then, at Australian National University, she has intensively studied Indonesian language and literature, and once made a broadcast in Indonesian to the women of that country.

Despite his elitist English education, Gorton says he is "Australian to the bootheels," thus distinguishing himself from Sir Robert ("I'm British to

* Later Mr. Gorton crashed again, on Melville Island off the north coast of Australia, and lived there for ten days, like Robinson Crusoe, on turtle eggs and swordfish.

the bootheels") Menzies. A tentative Australianism was the trademark of his term of office. He proposed to change the national anthem from "God Save the Queen" to "Waltzing Matilda." He aimed at a little less subservience to the U.S. and Britain. He tried to make foreign investment profit Australia more, by letting local investors have a share of the action, and by discouraging foreign takeovers of prosperous existing industries. He doubted that Australia's minerals should be dug up and exported as rapidly as possible, and called himself an "economic nationalist." Domestically, he tried some changes, diverting some of the country's new wealth to the betterment of health and education; he faced up to the fact that Australia has some poverty, among Aborigines and New Australians and others, and proposed to fight it. He battled the Australian Medical Association, attempting to head off a raise in doctors' fees. He started a government-run Australian Industrial Development Corporation. He proposed to make the cities more aesthetically attractive and amenable, with particular concern for the monotonous suburbs.

Australians have a saying that all their Prime Ministers are either prima donnas or larrikins—and Gorton played the role like a larrikin, roughshod and impetuous, stressing his homespun side. At the first, this served to get him votes, but then he began to appear uncertain, gawky, weak and bullying at the same time, slow to think through issues, unable to accept discipline and work. Speaking on television, "a mixture of four parts nitrogen, one part carbon dioxide would pass out of his lungs, through his vocal cords, but the result lacked meaning," said the *Bulletin*.

The Americans found that they did not like Mr. Gorton nearly so well as Mr. Holt. New Zealand found him confusing and difficult. Mr. Gorton began to pressure the Arbitration Commission, chief tribunal for wage settlements since the times of Justice Higgins. The Prime Minister's goal was to keep down inflation, running at 4 percent a year, but it is bad form for the federal government to strong-arm the Commission. He fought state governments over control of offshore sea-bed resources, and turned them down cold when they asked for more revenue-sharing. Gorton's private life excited gossip. He took a nineteen-year-old girl, daughter of an opposition Senator, to a midnight party at the U.S. Embassy and stayed until three o'clock talking to her and no one else. He also visited Judy Garland's daughter, Liza Minnelli, in her dressing room at a Sydney night club, which was enough to set Australian tongues wagging.

In the November 1970 Senate elections, Gorton's Liberals lost eight percentage points, fetching up with only 35 percent of the total—quite a feat considering that the Liberals had unprecedented prosperity going for them.

Party backbenchers, especially those of the right, grumbled that they not only had a "socialist" for a Prime Minister, but also a vote-loser. It took only a minor blunder, in March 1971, for Gorton's enemies, some of them in his own cabinet, to get him.

Responding to a scandal in the army (of no importance to us here), Gorton telephoned the army chief of staff, saying, "I think you'd better come over here and see me." In the rigidly hierarchical Australian cabinet system, this summons bypassed the Defense Minister, Malcolm Fraser, and Mr. Fraser became furious. Gorton's going directly to the general, Fraser felt, made him look a fool and seriously damaged his career. After steaming for a few days, and after a hostile session with Gorton, he resigned, charging that Gorton had been "disloyal" to him. The Prime Minister was staggered, and set about heading off the resignation, which would certainly bring a ballot among Liberal M.P.s and Senators on whether he should continue to lead the party.

Through all this William McMahon, the Foreign Minister, stayed quiet, sensing that his ambitions were about to be fulfilled. Gorton summoned Fraser for a final appeal, but Fraser held firm. That night the party gathered for a vote, McMahon sitting just back of Gorton. The division was 33 to 33. It fell to Gorton, presiding, to cast the deciding vote. He voted, of course, against himself. On a second ballot, McMahon was elected leader and Prime Minister, and Gorton (running against his nemesis, Malcolm Fraser) was chosen deputy leader. "Which portfolio do you want?" McMahon asked the defeated Prime Minister. "Defense," Gorton replied, and thereby Mr. Fraser lost his job. But five months later Mr. McMahon fired Mr. Gorton from the Ministry of Defense, charging that he had "breached cabinet solidarity" by writing some newspaper articles; and the next week the Prime Minister put Mr. Fraser back into the cabinet as Minister for Education and Science.

William McMahon and the Established Values

Billy McMahon, a tough little sparrow, proposes to keep Australia going, and his party running it, not by innovation but by managerial competence. He has high dedication, energy, and technical proficiency in the politician's trade. Australia, in his opinion, has gone exceedingly well under two decades of conservative government, and the way to improve is to move it further to the right. In an interview, he specifically and pointedly refused to talk about John Gorton's administration, but it is easy to surmise that Gorton was too disheveled and radical for him. Years ago Mr. McMahon defined Liberalism rather negatively as "avoiding the socialist threat," and when he became Prime Minister, he announced that he was still "very anti-Communist and very anti-socialist."

Mr. McMahon is (1) a Sydney man, succeeding three Liberal Prime Ministers from Victoria, and (2) sixty-three years old, an advanced age for a Prime Minister to take office in Australia. He comes from a family with business connections and money, which enabled him to go to Sydney Grammar, a famous 114-year-old private school. After a law degree at the University of Sydney, and a few years of practice, he enlisted in the army in 1939 and rose to major. Next he toured England, France, the United States, and Canada, and returned to study economics at the university, reading Marx, Keynes, and Schumpeter. Thus prepared, he turned himself single-mindedly to politics. He won election from a New South Wales constituency in 1949, and got ministerial rank in only two years. He was widely disliked by other ministers—but for the right reasons: he would go to cabinet meetings not only fully informed about his own department, but quite often much better briefed on other departments than their respective ministers were. Brash, ambitious, pushy, tactless—these were the adjectives applied to him then. But his talent and intelligence were undeniable, and he rose to deputy leadership of his party.

Defeated by Gorton for the prime ministership in 1968, McMahon accepted a senior-minister job as Treasurer, and proceeded to do what he does best: apply himself to mastery of the job. He ran the Treasury so well, and seemed to be taking such satisfaction in it, that Gorton waspishly moved him over to be Minister for External Affairs—to see if Billy might break his head on that one. Instead, McMahon turned in another performance of high competence, and in the process got the colonial-sounding title of the job changed to Foreign Minister. His party picked him to replace Gorton because he was the most experienced man around.

In office, William McMahon has seemed far right and uptight. Businessmen regarded him as "better than a new nickel mine." The Labor opposition labels McMahon a "big business" Prime Minister, "the most reactionary since the 1920's." He seemed obsessed with affirming Australia's support for Chiang Kai-shek and Taiwan, leaving himself off-base for dealing with such events as President Nixon's announcement that he would visit Peking, and the subsequent inevitable admission of the People's Republic of China to the United Nations. Belatedly and grudgingly, Mr. McMahon agreed to "explore the possibilities of establishing a dialogue with the government of the People's Republic." Even farmland conservatives deplore such recalcitrance; they want to sell wheat to China.

For the *Sunday Australian*, in May of 1971, Mr. McMahon wrote out his views on Australia's future. It will be a place where per-man output is higher and where strikes are less frequent: "Inside our community some reject the ethic of work and the established values." Traffic jams, traffic deaths, and "pockets of poverty" will be attacked and reduced. The government deplores South African apartheid, but it also deplores demonstrators who use tours of South African Rugby teams as occasions to protest apartheid—as they did so violently in mid-1971 that a tour of South African cricket players was canceled. A committee of seven ministers will tackle the problem of bringing the Aborigines into the Australian society without wrecking their culture. Immigration policy will stress fewer numbers and higher quality. McMahon's curious statement omitted any mention of education, health, Vietnam, or foreign investment policy; it bore out strikingly charges that he lacks vision.

The Prime Minister is a man who appoints committees and works through channels. One of his first acts was to raise the number of ministries from an already inflated twenty-six to twenty-seven. He believes in lengthy cabinet meetings in which every member gets his say; unlike Menzies, he also holds that backbenchers have a right to know the facts and reasons behind cabinet decisions that they are asked (or, perhaps more exactly, ordered) to approve. He is rough on subordinates, phoning them at any hour with assorted requests or demands, all expressed in a cultivated and well-modulated voice, and terminated with a half-humorous "R-r-r-r-ight." Many of his aides resent his constant prodding, but it results in a high quality of work, and McMahon seems genuinely pleased with them. T. M. Fitzgerald, a political writer, suggests that this may be a case of the irritation that produces the pearl in the oyster.

Six years ago, when he was fifty-seven, McMahon, until then a bachelor, married a stunning girl named Sonia Hopkins, then thirty-three, who at five feet nine is two inches taller than he. He has let his sideburns grow long, and the McMahons make a dashing pair. They have a daughter, Melinda, and a son, Julian, who have between them reduced this steel-minded, urbane bantam of a man to the customary dimensions of a proud father. He phoned them just after winning his country's highest office. "Guess what Daddy is?" he said.

Labor's Blueblood Leader

If Mr. McMahon chooses to run a mere holding operation and the Liberals can produce no one better, the government of Australia might return in one way or another to Labor. This party has gradually moved from lunch-bucket laborism to college-level liberalism. Among Laborites, foreign affairs now compete for attention with the acts of the Arbitration Commission. This new attitude is expressed and effected by Edward Gough Whitlam, leader of the party since 1967.

Gough (pronounced "Goff") Whitlam, who was born in 1916, is a bit blue of blood for a Labor man, but of course he has his job precisely because the party wanted a leader of cultivation and broad interests. He is very tall, always a commanding asset in an aspiring statesman, and his aristocratic grooming complements an arciform nose and George III lips. He studied law at the University of Sydney and "took silk" (joined the bar). His father-in-law, a New South Wales Supreme Court Justice, had close links with the Labor governments before 1949, which led Whitlam to contest and win a seat in Parliament in 1952, whence he rose to the leadership. Old-style Labor politicians, used to invective in the Billy Hughes style, questioned Whitlam's unimpassioned, lucid approach to issues. Still, Whitlam once lost his temper sufficiently to apply a gross epithet to William McMahon on the floor of the House, and to toss a glass of water at the Liberal Minister for External Affairs of the time, Paul Hasluck.

Up against Gorton in the 1969 Parliamentary elections, Whitlam managed to gain an impressive seventeen seats, and he similarly scored in the 1970 Senate election. Whitlam and his Laborites favored withdrawal from Vietnam, an end to the draft, and recognition of Communist China. Playing on a commonplace public apprehension, Whitlam charged that the Liberals were letting foreign investors turn Australia into "one vast quarry."

When McMahon took office, Whitlam tried an immediate no-confidence motion, losing 62 to 58. Then he stung McMahon by responding fast when Premier Chou En-lai showed, by inviting American and Australian Ping-Pong players to China, that he favored Chinese contact with the West. A delegation of Labor Party bigwigs, including Whitlam, went to Peking while the Prime Minister, caught in the "China lobby" thinking of the early 1950's, continued to fulminate about Australia's immutable obligations to Taiwan.

Mr. Whitlam's most mountainous task has been to weld Labor into a unified party of the left, specifically by reform of the weak Victoria branch, and he has done it effectively—barring the fact that the rightist Democratic Labor Party remains outside the mother party's folds. Labor, after being completely out of state government leadership, came to power in South Australia and Western Australia early in 1971. Unluckily for Mr.

Whitlam, he may not reap the rewards of his work. A rival has risen. He is Robert James Lee Hawke, forty-one, president of the Australian Council of Trade Unions.

Bob Hawke is an electric-minded man with a mop of wavy black hair—wavy sideburns too, a Teddy Kennedy look. He comes from the outback, Bordertown, Western Australia, where his father was a Congregational minister. He was a Rhodes scholar, and while at Oxford (arts, law, *and* economics) made the *Guinness Book of Records* by drinking two and one-half pints of beer in twelve seconds. His thesis was a study of the Australian wage arbitration system, which made him just the man, in 1958, to join the staff of lawyers that the Council of Trade Unions keeps for arguments before the Arbitration Commission. He rose to leadership of the unions in 1970.

Hawke has acted on the principle that union goals should be social change, and that the unions have the numbers and power to bring about such change without working through Parliament. He showed how this might work by a spectacular coup in 1971. The Liberals in Parliament had long blocked Labor's efforts to outlaw price-fixing by manufacturers, which keeps prices up and kills competition. So Hawke put the Council of Trade Unions into the retailing business by buying a share of a department store, which then began to demand the right to sell at discount prices, familiar enough to Americans. Specifically, Hawke zeroed in on British-based Dunlop's, maker of tennis rackets, sneakers, mattresses, and swimming-pool equipment. When Dunlop's refused to allow its products' retail prices to be lowered, the unions struck, refusing to move Dunlop's cargo and freight. In less than twenty-four hours, the limousine of the Dunlop's chairman appeared at Hawke's office, and the firm capitulated, allowing the union store to price Dunlop's products at any discount it chose. The Liberals in Parliament, seeing how the wind was blowing, hastily enacted a bill against price-fixing. All over Australia, competition increased, prices dropped, and consumers benefited.

Hawke would like to carry union initiative much further—at least into cheaper time-payment deals, building societies, perhaps banking and insurance. He may move into politics and shake up the Labor Party the way he has shaken labor itself. Australia is quite generally disenchanted with its gray, cautious, game-playing politicians; Hawke would be a fresh and youthful face. His mother recalls that when she was pregnant with Robert, her Bible fell open one day to Isaiah 9:6, which reads, "For unto us a child is born, unto us a son is given: and the government shall be upon his shoulder."

A Pair of Governors-General

A wise and cosmopolitan Australian is Richard Gardiner Casey, who aspired to be Prime Minister and became Governor-General. Casey, grandson of a pioneer Australian doctor, was at Gallipoli and France in World War I and after the war became liaison officer for Australia at the British Foreign Office. He served a decade in Parliament with the equivalent of the Liberals, losing out in the end to Menzies for Prime Minister. Menzies then sent Casey to Washington as first Australian Minister to the U.S. When the Labor government, in mid-war, seemed cool to Casey's staying in that job, he consulted with Winston Churchill and got a place in the British Cabinet as Minister to the Middle East, living in Cairo. That led him to the governorship of Bengal, certainly one up on Menzies, then the obscure leader of the opposition. But by the time Casey returned to Australia, Menzies was leading a Liberal Party that looked a sure winner, and Casey had to settle, in subsequent years, for lesser cabinet posts. He left Parliament in 1960, and Menzies saw to it that Casey got a peerage, and then appointment as Governor-General, the third native-born Australian to hold that post. His term expired in 1968; Lord Casey is a patrician, worldly in the best sense of the word, and surprisingly enough both he and his wife can pilot a plane.

*

Paul Meerna Caedwalla Hasluck, the present Governor-General, was born in Perth in 1905, and his parents were members of the Salvation Army. In his early career he was a newsman, university teacher, and civil servant in the External Affairs Department. As head of the Australian Mission to the United Nations after World War II, he clashed with the Minister, Herbert Evatt. Hasluck thereupon ran for Parliament on the Liberal ticket, and was a minister for most of the next twenty years.

Sir Paul (he is a Knight of the Grand Cross of the Order of St. Michael and St. George) is a meticulous, cautious, intellectual man, a poet moreover, with a reputation for coolness that he resents. "Just because I don't giggle or dig people in the ribs all the time, outsiders say I haven't got a sense of humor," he growls. "You go around my electorate and you'll find out what a warmhearted old fellow I am." As Governor-General, and therefore the Queen's surrogate in Australia, he has all the nonpowers of the Queen herself. As a scholar, he is finishing two volumes of a history of Australia during World War II. He gets $20,000 a year, plus a noble residence in Canberra with twenty servants and three cars.

What Lies Ahead in Australian Politics?

- In the next few years, Labor will return to power.
- More distantly, Australia will become a republic.
- And some time after that, the republic will elect a non-British European, the son of immigrants, as President.

CHAPTER 9

Who Owns Australia?

I was out with my two sons rounding up cattle when the big bay I was riding stumbled and fell. I was there rubbing my leg when I picked up a rock. I thought to myself, "Strewth, that's heavy." And no wonder. The flaming thing was all copper.

—KIMBERLEY RANGE STOCKMAN TOM WILSON, IN 1970

FOR A MOMENT we will bypass 175 million Australian sheep and talk about Australia as the land of mines. This is the continent whose very seashores provide riches—sands that yield titanium and other rare metals. Minerals have taken over from wool as principal foreign money-earners for Australia. Mining production last year exceeded $1.5 billion. In ten years Australia has jumped from a hoarder of iron ore to one of the leading suppliers of minerals to the world.

Some points about the boom:

• Minerals occur in old rocks, and Australia has very old rocks. The great western shield is pre-Cambrian granite, a billion and a half years old, and many rocks to the east are Cambrian, not much younger. A cover of dunes and soils keeps the riches lightly hidden in most places, but where the rocks lie bare many a mineral find has been made casually. The extent of Australia's mineral riches was unknown until the last decade owing to insufficient prospecting in desolate country. "By the mid-seventies Australia is likely to be the world's largest exporter of a whole range of industrial raw material—iron ore, alumina, bauxite and black coal, lead and zinc—and to be a major exporter of copper, nickel and beach sand metals," says the *Times* of London.

• The vital market that makes the mining possible is Japan, which on few resources of its own has risen to become the third-largest industrial power in the world and possessor of the world's biggest iron and steel firm. The two booms are complementary.

• Most of the giant international mining companies of the world are pouring capital into Australia. American companies mine and export Australian iron to Japanese smelters for conversion into steel that is then manufactured into products sent to America. Australians get taxes, royalties, and wages—and warn that they would like more of the profits and a bigger role in the whole process.

How the Boom Began

Australia has known rich mineral finds for more than a century. The gold rush of the mid-nineteenth century was followed by the conquest in 1883–1885 of Broken Hill, New South Wales (silver, lead, and zinc), the 1891 gold strike at Kalgoorlie, four hundred miles east of Perth, and the 1923 discovery at Mount Isa and Mount Morgan in Queensland (lead, zinc, silver, and copper)—as well as allied finds of iron ore and coal. Australia had an Institute of Mining Engineers as early as 1893, and a few years later was a recognized world leader in metallurgical skills. But all this was only a prelude. Between 1946 and 1966 various companies, prospecting in the west, found forty-two significant lodes of one metal or another. The predominance of iron ore among these discoveries relieved fears expressed in a 1938 law banning exports of the material. Landmarks of the boom were:

• The 1955 discovery of bauxite at Weipa in Queensland
• The discovery of iron ore at Mount Newman in 1957
• The 1960 discovery of Mount Tom Price, in the Hamersley Range 750 miles north of Perth
• The repeal in 1961 of the law banning the export of iron ore
• The discovery of nickel at Kambalda in 1966

*

Going with all this have been some breath-taking speculation and stock market scandals—we will say more about the market in a moment. But the boom is basically deep and solid. Iron is the hard core of it, and the geographical site of most of the mining is "The Pilbara," which encompasses the Hamersley Range in Western Australia, and nearby points. Two major companies get iron ore out. One is Hamersley Holdings, which mines Mount Tom Price. Conzinc Riotinto of Australia Ltd. owns 54 percent of this operation, and Kaiser Steel Corporation 34.5 percent. They spent $300 million developing the mine, building towns, a railroad, a pelletizing plant, and a port—Port Dampier, on the "cyclone coast"—that can take 150,000-ton ships. The mine produced 13 million tons of ore in 1969, and will produce 37.5 million tons in 1974. It all goes to Japan.

The other giant is Mount Newman Mining Company Pty. Ltd., which we report upon in detail later. Among lesser firms is Mount Goldsworthy Mining Company (owned by Cyprus Mines Corporation, Utah Construction & Mining Company, and Consolidated Gold Fields Australia Ltd.), which ships through Mount Newman's port at Hedland, a bit up the coast from Dampier. Another major Pilbara project, still being built, is the mine, railroad, and brand-new port of Cliffs Robe River Iron Associates, which has Australian, American, and Japanese money behind it. Japanese steel mills have contracted to buy $1.2 billion worth of Robe River ore.

The iron boom adds up to glittering totals. The ore reserves may be 100 trillion tons, four hundred times as much as the known North American reserves. Japanese contracts call for the export of 510 million tons in twenty years, at a price of $4.5 billion.

Aluminum and Other Metals

On Cape York Peninsula, in Queensland, is a port called Weipa, a town of pink brick houses under tall eucalyptuses. All around it for miles, one has only to dig through three feet of overburden to reach rich red bauxite, an oceanic layer of it eight feet thick, 2.5 billion tons in all, said to be the largest patch of the stuff on earth. This mining town is feverishly felling the trees, scraping away the soil, and scooping out the bauxite to make Australia the world's largest exporter. Comalco, the corporation in charge, stores the topsoil and puts it back after mining the bauxite, preserving the environment to raise cattle and grow mahogany and teak.

At the port, a half-mile moving belt conveys the warty-looking bauxite to fifty-thousand-ton ships which take it, at a rate growing toward fifteen million tons a year in 1975, to Japan, Sardinia, and the refinery at Gladstone, three hundred miles north of Brisbane. This refinery, a pretty thing in pink, green, and silver, put up at a painful cost in terms of strikes and balky labor, turns out 1,275,000 tons a year of the white powder concentrate called alumina (aluminum oxide). Alumina is exported, or smelted to aluminum in plants at Bluff, New Zealand, and Bell Bay, Tasmania, for use in Australia. Further huge deposits of bauxite at Gove, westward across the Gulf of Carpentaria from Weipa, are being mined at the rate of 700,000 tons a year, and a large alumina plant will go into production there in 1973.

Way out west, bauxite is also big. The Darling Range behind Perth contains big deposits, and the alumina plant at Kwinana, the industrial city near Perth, produces 1,040,000 tons a year.

*

Western Mining Corporation Ltd. was formed in 1933 to mine gold in Western Australia, but as its lodes ran out it began prospecting widely. Some ironstone outcrops near Kambalda, south of Kalgoorlie, caught the attention of company geologists, and they carefully sited a test bore. In 1966, first crack out of the box they struck nickel, a metal never before found in Australia in quantities profitable for mining.

Now Western Mining produces more than 600,000 tons of ore (4 percent nickel) a year from an underground mine of shafts and drifts. Since this sort of mining leaves supporting pillars of valuable ore, the company has developed an ingenious method of pumping sand and cement back into the mined areas, which provides sufficient support for the miners to return and remove the pillars. Side effects of Western Mining's exciting mine are these: (1) nearby Kalgoorlie, the wide-open Virginia City of Australia, slowly dying as its gold gave out, is booming again, complete with whorehouses; (2) Western Mining has built a $30-million nickel refinery at Kwinana and plans to build a smelter at Kalgoorlie; and (3) other big mining combines have arrived in the area to find and mine more nickel. Australia makes its coins out of its own nickel, but most of this metal is exported.

Main buyer? Japan.

Other minerals: *copper*, already an Australian staple, will begin to come in 1972 from the 900 million tons of ore on a mountaintop in Bougainville, in the territory of New Guinea, where $350 million is going into development; Queensland *coal* flows through Gladstone to Japan at the rate of three million tons a year; *uranium*, long produced at Mary Kathleen in Queensland and Rum Jangle in the Northern Territory, was found in considerable quantities in 1970 at Nabarlek, Ranger, and Jim Jim in the Northern Territory; Consolidated Murchison produces one-third of the world's *antimony;* the beach sands of New South Wales and Western Australia provide rutile to turn into *titanium* for toughening steel and pigmenting paint; *gold* still comes from Kalgoorlie's Golden Mile, source since 1891 of $400 million worth; *phosphate* underlies a 358-square-mile concession in Queensland; *manganese* is mined on Groote Eylandt, an island in the Gulf of Carpentaria; there is a new "rush" for *opals* at Glengarry, New South Wales (Australia produces almost 95 percent of the world's opal).

Sober opinion is that industrious exploration in the future will find minerals worth many times more than those so far discovered.

*

The involutions of corporate ownership in the Australian mining industry are too complex to concern us, but there is one giant that cannot escape attention, because it spreads over iron, aluminum, copper, lead, and zinc. This is Conzinc Riotinto of Australia Ltd. (CRA), which is 85 percent owned by Rio Tinto–Zinc Corporation Ltd. of London. CRA owns more than half of the aforementioned Hamersley Holdings, and 45 percent of Comalco Ltd., which gives CRA a strong interest in Weipa bauxite, the Gladstone refinery, and the smelters at Bluff and Bell Bay. CRA mines lead and zinc through Australian Mining and Smelting at Broken Hill, and it mines copper through a majority interest in Bougainville Mining Ltd. Sir Maurice Mawby, who was born in Broken Hill, is chairman of this octopus, and he is a shaping force in Australia.

Broken Hill Proprietary Ltd.

Moving from mining toward manufacturing, we come to Australia's biggest corporation, surpassing CRA, and No. 31 on *Fortune* magazine's list of the world's largest companies outside the U.S. Its name is a paradox, for it owns no mines at Broken Hill. The explanation is that BHP (letters as common in Australia as GM in the United States, or ICI in Britain) was the corporate vehicle in 1885 of the fortunate finders of the bonanza at Broken Hill. But slowly lead-zinc mining went sour for BHP, partly through ill-managed conflicts with labor, and partly because the company found iron ore, intending at first to use it only as flux for smelting lead. In 1915 BHP turned from lead-zinc miner to steel manufacturer, running Australia's first blast furnace near the coalfields of Newcastle, New South Wales. Under the great engineer Essington Lewis, BHP then moved into coal, shipbuilding, shipping, heavy transport, and integrated iron and steel, and came to loom in the

Australian industrial landscape like Krupp or I. G. Farben in prewar Germany, or the Du Pont or Rockefeller empires in the U.S. Its steel, more than six million tons of it a year lately and the cheapest in the world, became the base of Australian industrial advance. Additional blast furnaces and mills were built at Kwinana, near Perth, at Whyalla, in South Australia, and at Port Kembla, just south of Sydney. Port Kembla will produce 5.4 million tons a year when a $300-million expansion program is finished in 1973. BHP also clings to its old lead smelter at Port Pirie in South Australia, which is the world's largest. The company is, furthermore, a major holder of Mount Newman Mining Company Pty. Ltd. in the Pilbara.

Strangely, this far-flung activity only partially explains BHP's current immense profitability—$69 million in the 1970–1971 financial year, $160 million projected for 1975. In fact, at the end of 1971, the company was cutting back the production of lead, because of low world prices, and of steel, because of reduced local demand. The money mostly comes from a new, rich, and lucky venture: oil.

Historically, petroleum has been an embarrassing absentee from the roster of Australian minerals. Diligent exploration had produced commercial wells only at tiny Barrow Island, off the Pilbara coast, and at Moonie in Queensland. Australian production was about one-ninetieth as much as Venezuela's. In 1968 refineries had to import $246 million worth of foreign petroleum, and pay another $90 million in freight to bring it in. The first glimmer of relief came in 1968 with natural-gas strikes from offshore drilling by BHP and Jersey Standard in Bass Strait, the ocean passage between Tasmania and the continent. Oil soon followed, in quantity. By mid-1971 Australia was producing 70 percent of its refinery input, mostly from BHP's subsidiary, Hematite Petroleum. The price was a modest $2.05 per barrel.

Oil has thus already surpassed steel in BHP's profits, but the company is expanding in other minerals, too. It has prospects in bauxite near Perth, nickel at Kalgoorlie, lateritic nickel in Queensland, more iron ore at Marillana near Mount Newman, and more coal in Queensland. BHP employs 54,000 people and is capitalized at $2 billion. The company is putting up a forty-one-story head-office building in Melbourne that will generate its own electricity from natural-gas-fired engines, the exhaust heat of which will provide the structure with heating and air-conditioning.

Oil refining, incidentally, is big business in Australia and a vexed one. All the refineries and distribution networks are dominated by foreigners except one, Ampol. In advertisements, Ampol makes the purchase of gasoline a question of patriotism. "How big a slice of Australia will Australians own when your kids grow up? In the excitement of our vast new-found natural wealth aren't we inclined to give too much away? . . . In the oil marketing industry so vital to Australia's growth and development, Ampol is *the* Australian company. So *think* before you buy your next gallon. PUT YOUR MONEY WHERE YOUR COUNTRY IS."

A Word About the Stock Market

The Sydney Stock Exchange (Melbourne's is much soberer) has been described as "a casino where undisciplined and renegade gamblers run amok—and then weep on the croupier's shoulder when the chips are against them." Scandal after scandal hits it. Figures have sometimes been forged on the "scrip" ownership certificates issued by the exchange's computers. The exchange trades heavily in penny stocks, which skate up and down. Cores from test drilling of dubious mines are regularly produced to kite stock prices—although the "punters" (speculators) in the Exchange's galleries have a saying that the best way to kill a prospect is to drill it. The Geological Society of Australia charges that many of the drill-core assays that shoot stock prices up are made by nongeologists.

A typical case was that of Leopold Minerals—"leaping Leopold," they called it. Leopold had a "good address" among the big mines of the Pilbara region, and drilling produced a test core supposedly high in nickel. Leopold leaped. Then one of the company's directors demanded to see the core. From the management came a brief silence and finally a confession that the core had been lost. The trucker who brought it from Nullagine to Perth, it was explained, arrived when the company's offices were closed, so he left the core on the doorstep, and it disappeared. Leopold's credibility, and its stock prices, plummeted, dragging down, as usual, the rest of the market. Eight brokerages collapsed.

But no one in Sydney much cares about such scandals; the punters are looking for a "runner"—a stock that is rising, and they are indifferent as to whether by manipulation or real worth. Sometimes the volume on the Sydney Exchange is double that of Wall Street. On the other hand, the market sometimes goes into a bad slump, and such has been the case lately. A significant factor in this hurly-burly is that the government does not tax capital gains.

There is, to be sure, a reasonable justification for the highly speculative market. It brings out the hundred-to-one money, the real risk capital, that pays for all that give-it-a-try prospecting which occasionally strikes it rich. The search would go much slower otherwise. And thus the market can claim that it is doing just what it is supposed to do.

Sheep Raising

Camels are snobbish
And sheep, unintelligent.
—MARIANNE MOORE

Sheep certainly do not produce a meat that the world likes as much as beef, and their fleece must meet competition from synthetic fabrics. Fewer than 5 percent of the Australian people are pastoralists, stockmen, or farmers; the price of wool is low; government subsidies are supplanting what used to be an admirably free market. But Australia, to use the standard cliché, has "ridden the sheep's back" through all of its history until now, and relies on wool to earn foreign exchange vital to the country's balance of trade. The sheep still counts a lot. Let us go out on a big sheep run and examine the life style of this stupid, panicky, disease-prone, exploitable, submissive animal.

The scene is the property called South Burra, near Canberra, managed by Allen Sutton and owned by F. M. Diarmid. South Burra has 6,000 sheep on 2,500 acres, about two to an acre. The sheep weigh from 130 to 140 pounds, although rams go up to 220.

The critical time of the year is the shearing season. Four or five shearers, who go from property to property in groups, come to South Burra to work for a couple of weeks in the property's shearing shed, using power-driven shears. The shearer, dressed in blue undershirt and checked shorts, uses his elbows to clamp the sheep's forelegs for control, and shears it belly first, in such a way that the fleece comes in one piece, weighing an average of twelve or thirteen pounds. The sheep makes no objection. An expert shearer can shear 160 sheep a day, but the average is 125, one every three or four minutes for eight hours—from 7:30 to 5:30 P.M., broken up by an hour for lunch and half-hour rest breaks at 9:30 and 3:30. The pay is twenty dollars per hundred sheep. The number of these nomadic workmen—twelve thousand-plus in all of Australia—is declining, and sheep raisers worry about this.

Once shorn off, the fleece is graded into one of eight categories—graders travel with the shearers and have the most important and specialized jobs. The wool is pressed down in boxes, forming 320-pound bales, wrapped in jute from India and neatly stenciled.

"Do the sheep catch cold after shearing?"

"Yes, you can lose a lot of sheep if the weather is bad after shearing," says Mr. Sutton. "A sheep has an awful life." Indeed, sheep die with indecent frequency. If pushed hard while being herded, many will drop dead.

A perennial threat is foot rot, a virus that causes lameness and loss of appetite. The treatment has been to pare away the infected area and force the sheep to walk through a formalin bath. The highly contagious virus can be spread by the tires of a car, the soles of shoes, and even by waddling ducks. Sheep also have to be dosed three times a year for worms, and several times more for liver flukes. Sheep suffer from blackleg and pulpy kidney, and tend to get caught in brush fires.

Specialized breeding is by artificial insemination, the semen being captured in an artificial vagina skillfully held by a station hand while the ram mounts a ewe in expectation of normal copulation. At correct temperatures, the semen, kept in little labeled egg cups, lasts up to a week, and if frozen it can be kept six months and easily transported. The heat period for the ewes is seventeen to twenty-one days long, and it can be artificially induced by hormones. Good rams, which have their pedigree numbers tattooed in their ears, cost plenty—one brought $29,000 lately in Sydney—though the price for the average ram is more like $80 to $100. Most males are castrated, which makes them wethers. A breeding ewe costs only $14, and a good young sheep just $9. At about the age of seven sheep tend to grind their teeth down to the point where they cannot feed, and are then sold to slaughterhouses for $4.

Three-fourths of the sheep are Merinos, a breed which originated in Spain and spread to France, Germany, the U.S.S.R., the U.S., Argentina, and, most successfully of all, Australia. The first Merinos reached Australia in 1797, via the Netherlands and the Cape of Good Hope. Even the sheep not classified as Merinos usually have Merino blood, including the "comebacks," which are finer than the half-breeds. The rest are English breeds, used for fat lamb production. Merinos have fine wool, beautifully crimped, so that the fleece appears curly rather than rug-like.

*

Numerous as they are, Australia's sheep constitute only one-sixth of the world's wooled-sheep population. Yet they are so productive that they supply as much as two billion pounds of wool a year, 30 percent of the world's supply, and it is of such high quality that it constitutes 38 percent of the wool used in clothing. Fighting prices that stayed level or went down* while everything else rose, and competing against synthetics, Australian wool growers managed to *double* production between 1949 and 1969, through better breeding, disease control, use of trace elements in raising pasturage and

* The price in 1968 was 42 cents a pound, and in 1971, 28 cents.

feed, much government assistance, and high efficiency (the use of motorcycles in herding is an example). The wool, 95 percent exported, mostly to Japan, earns around $800 million a year. In a sense, every city-bred Australian is counting on fifteen sheep busily growing wool in the outback to provide him with what he needs from abroad: industrial raw materials, munitions of war, capital goods, consumer items.

Grain and Cattle

Two notes about the other main products of the Australian land:

Beef is doing well. Traditionally, cattle raising has been an activity that went on untouched by human hands in northern Queensland. Now better cows are bred; they are transported by truck instead of being moved by weight-losing drives; they are getting grain for feed as well as grass. With the future of wool in doubt, many sheep raisers are going into cattle as a hedge. A U.S. beef-import quota provides a market for beef for hamburgers, TV dinners, and the like. Moreover, Australians themselves consume 204 pounds of beef per person every year. Incidental intelligence: a "poddy" is an unbranded calf, and a "poddy-dodger" is a rustler who steals unbranded animals.

Wheat is problematical. Exports in 1971 set a new record, because the Australian Wheat Board happened to find a good market in Egypt and other important customers in Britain, Japan, Iraq, and Iran. In past years, heavy buyers have been the U.S.S.R., the People's Republic of China, India, Indonesia, and the Philippines. But there is no one dependable market or set of markets. And the whole crop tends to fluctuate widely with the weather.

Other crops worth a mention are cotton, the production of which grew from 8,000 bales in 1959 to 145,000 in 1968; apples and dried vine fruits, of which Australia produces 7 and 11 percent, respectively, of the world's supply; and forestry, not only for lumber but for paper and pulp, in which a new technology for using short-fibered wood like eucalyptus permits the country to supply 70 percent of its paper needs.

Land devoted to agriculture in Australia exceeds a billion acres, three-fifths of the whole country—a figure misleadingly high, since more than 90 percent of it is not cropped or plowed or watered but used in its natural state. This untended land is "pastoral" country, which gets less than fifteen inches of rain a year but does support almost a third of the nation's sheep. The part of Australia that gets enough water to cultivate or graze intensively amounts to only a twentieth of the country's surface.

Other Industries

> *We export stainless steel products to Sheffield, tulip bulbs to Holland, spaghetti to Italy, ball bearings to the Ruhr, waffle-making machinery to America, safari suits to Zambia, and Irish stew to Scotland.*
>
> —FORMER PRIME MINISTER JOHN GORTON

Australia is as intensively industrialized as any nation in the world. Twenty-seven percent of the work force is in manufacturing—the same as the United States. The auto industry, employing one-eighth of all factory workers, turns out 425,000 cars a year. The commonest car is the Holden, a compact made by General Motors–Holden; others are adaptations of European models put out by GM (34 percent of the market), Ford* (19 percent), and Chrysler (12 percent), plus Volkswagens and Japanese cars. There is one motor vehicle for every 2.7 Australians. Large oligopolies dominate industry: one, two, or three producers account for all sales in steel, soap, sugar, newsprint, tinplate, wire, glass, industrial gases, and matches.

As Mr. Gorton points out, Australia exports a surprising amount and variety of manufactured goods. An interesting specific case comes from Favelle Mort Ltd. of Sydney, builders of construction machinery. This firm supplied the eight 170-ton "Kangaroo" cranes used in building the twin 110-story skyscrapers of the new World Trade Center in New York. The company plans to start a U.S. subsidiary. A similar case of Australian enterprise abroad is the chain of TraveLodge motels in the Western U.S. which are controlled by the TraveLodge firm in Australia. Ford Motor Company of Australia exported 23,500 cars last year.

Labor constitutes the most influential pressure on Australian industry. Wage disputes are supposed to be settled, and in fact largely are settled, by the Commonwealth Arbitration Commission, which is usually under heavy pressure from the Australian Council of Trade Unions to raise wages, and by the government and employers to hold them steady. The Commission's across-the-board award at the end of 1970 was 6 percent. The machinery for arbitration, it must be pointed out, does not stop Australian labor from striking often and capriciously, in the awareness that there is always another job somewhere else.

Such aggressive labor, it would seem, might price itself too high and bring on mass unemployment. Three factors keep this from happening: (1) the

* Which early in the century built Australia's first car, a Model T, in an old wool store in Geelong.

long-term strength and depth of the Australian boom; (2) a reliable 2.5-3 percent per annum rise in productivity per man-hour; and (3) the still-modest levels of wages, which average $4,370 a year.

Thus Australia is generally a country of full employment, or even hyper-employment—although an exception must be made for late 1971, when uncertainty over world trade brought a downturn to the economy and pushed unemployment up to 1.57 percent. (By comparison, unemployment in the U.S. was running around 6 percent.) Almost anybody can get a job. More men and women are needed every year. Immigrants can flood in and be put to work at once. The proportion of married women in the work force rose from one-fourth in 1965 to one-third in 1970. Ten thousand *children* are employed in industry. *The Australian* for November 30, 1970, carried *four hundred* detailed, pleading display advertisements seeking employees. Inflation, like unemployment, has not been a serious problem in Australia. It ran around 3 percent a year during the 1960's. Unfortunately, however, it began to creep up, and in 1971 reached 6.5 percent—approximately the same rate as that of the United States.

Economic Oddities

The entire areas of power, railroads, water supply, telecommunications, ports, and a substantial part of airlines, banking, radio and television, and coastal shipping, are left in Australia to the state and federal governments. The railroads have an absurd impediment: the colonial governments that built them copied gauges variously from Ireland (5 feet 3 inches), from England (4 feet 8½ inches), and from remoter places that used the cheap narrow gauge (3 feet 6 inches). For years this meant that goods sent from Brisbane to Perth had to be transshipped five times; now, slowly, tracks are being standardized at 4 feet 8½ inches. Ocean shipping is also a weakness: Australian ships carry only 1.3 percent of the country's trade with the world.

The post office's telephone division still charges only five cents for a local call, and offers an STD (subscriber trunk dialing) service equivalent to the American DDD (direct distance dialing). All mail in standard envelopes goes to any part of Australia by air if air service is available. For a little extra postage, the post office guarantees to deliver mail overnight between major cities. The insurance business is dominated by London, and criticized as monopolistic and restrictive. The biggest operator of retail stores in Australia is Woolworth's Ltd., with annual sales of half a billion dollars.

Aviation is prosperous—the number of air trips per capita is the second highest in the world. Fares average 6.4 cents per mile in first class and 5.4

cents in tourist. Government-owned Qantas (pronounced Quantas—the name is an acronym for the parental Queensland and Northern Territory Aerial Services) flies ninety thousand miles of routes to thirty countries with safety, brusque virile courtesy, and sausages for breakfast. It is the second oldest airline in the world, after KLM. The main internal airlines are the government-owned Trans-Australia Airlines and the privately owned Ansett-ANA. One is told that "this is the best country in the world for flying—low mountains, hardly any bad weather."

*

There is a palpable intelligence back of Australia's industrial and agricultural progress, and a little inquiry reveals that this intelligence is called CSIRO, for Commonwealth Scientific and Industrial Research Organization. It was founded way back in 1926, when some genius realized that small amounts invested in brainwork would return large dividends in farm and factory efficiency. CSIRO's scientists have come through spectacularly. A favored example of their work is the fight against rabbits. This pest was imported to Australia in 1859 by a Geelong farmer who thought rabbits would be good for food and sport. As rabbits will, they multiplied. In sixteen years, they occupied most of the continent. A fence was built clear across Australia in an effort to stop them. Ravenously, they consumed the grass intended for sheep; they became a classic example of the dangers of tampering with an ecology. CSIRO got wind of a highly infectious rabbit disease called myxomatosis, discovered earlier by a Brazilian doctor named H. B. Aragão, and in 1950 learned how to spread it, via host mosquitoes, in Australia. In the next decade the rabbit population plummeted—but not to zero, and those that survived became immune to the disease and must be fought in other ways, chiefly poison.

Probably CSIRO's most useful work has been in agriculture. It perfected a kind of alfalfa called Townsend lucerne which is Australia's main hay. It found ways to fight erosion, noxious weeds, animal diseases. Lately it has discovered a chemical that can be introduced into the fourth stomach of a sheep to make it grow half again as much wool, and another chemical that can be introduced into the first stomach of a cow to prevent bloat. CSIRO has also devised an effective vaccine against sheep foot rot, which has been costing pastoralists $16 million a year in treatment and production loss.

CSIRO years ago pioneered in the development of radar, and lately has been into such work as making diffraction gratings, extremely flat metal-coated glass plates with fine parallel grooves, as many as 32,000 to the inch, cut into them. They are used in assorted optical instruments to break light into component colors. Some more typical recent projects are: the production of whiter wool and machine-washable woollen slacks, taking radio pictures of the sun, mapping bush fires from the air at night, measuring shadows. CSIRO's staff numbers about 6,500, and its budget is $60 million a year.

Who Owns Australia?

About one-fourth of Australian corporate assets are owned outright from abroad, a share that rises to two-fifths in the case of manufacturing. The degree of control, through partial ownership, goes well beyond these fractions. More than half of all mineral production is controlled by non-Australian interests. Twenty percent of the cattle land in the northern sector of Western Australia is owned by Americans. A billion dollars, more or less, from abroad pour annually into the economy, which runs to about $30 billion in Gross National Product. The British share of this investment is typically about one-third, the U.S. share about one-half. Total U.S. investment, in five hundred companies, is $3.5 billion. Japan is an increasingly massive investor in Australia.

The overwhelming benefit that all this investment has conferred on Australia is, quite simply, the boom—the very prosperity of the country, the key to its full employment and enriching immigration. "Without this stimulation there would have been no mineral boom—only at best a miserable little pop. . . . I can assure you that we are only at the beginning of a program of Cecil B. De Mille proportions," says Professor R. L. Whitmore. "We will be the top mining nation in the world in thirty years." Real growth in GNP is more than 5 percent a year and increasing. Moreover, the foreign investors bring with them essential technology, provide enormous payrolls, and pay taxes averaging 43 percent of profits plus an extra 15 percent on dividends taken out of the country. An unmeasurable but doubtless huge benefit of foreign investment to the Australian economy is efficient competition that keeps local industry on its toes. In return for these rewards, official policy is to allow almost unrestricted entry of foreign capital.

Nevertheless, Australians voice a great number of complaints about their foreign friends. Many have an uneasy feeling of being dominated, or of having had the country bought out from underneath them. Some specific worries are these: (1) It is pleasant to have a billion dollars pour in every year now, but it will be painful to the balance of payments when the investment stops arriving and the profits start going out. (2) Foreigners dominate the areas of greatest growth potential—autos, pharmaceuticals, oil refining and marketing, minerals. And their profits are higher than they expect or get elsewhere. Sir Alan Westerman, chairman of the government-backed Australian Industrial Development Corporation, a bank that is supposed to be a counterweight to foreign investment, contends that the profits after taxes of three hundred U.S. firms have been 28 percent higher than the same firms earned in any other country. (3) Foreigners restrict Australian participation, both in investment and dividends, and in management. General Motors–Holden is wholly owned by the U.S. parent* and takes the position that the Australian who wants to invest can buy GM on Wall Street. Speaking for the incoming Japanese investors, the chairman of Mitsubishi Bank says that the Japanese, by contrast, prefer joint ventures that give Australians some of the action. Ford, British Petroleum, and even GM in 1970 named Australians as the chief executives of their Australian subsidiaries, but much of the ranking management still comes from abroad. (4) Many foreigners are not true developers, bringing capital, but merely entrepreneurs who take over existing concerns, raise money on the Australian market—and then send the profits abroad.

*

Is the Australian economy socialistic? Most decidedly not. It is a mixed economy in a country run for the past two decades by conservative governments prone to give business every possible break.

Does it work? Most decidedly yes. It is hard to quibble with a full-employment economy that provides one of the world's highest standards of living. But much of this is luck—finding mineral riches.

Will it continue to work? Not without a hitch. Wool faces a declining market just as the costs of producing it go up. The discovery of ore may outrun the discovery of markets.

Should Australians be worried? Not yet.

* For assorted reasons. Ownership gives GM all the profits, avoids antitrust problems, and gains the rewards due the company from taking the risks of starting the foreign operation—risks Australians (who in former days were timid investors) did not share. It also preserves quality control, secrecy, and techniques.

CHAPTER 10

Sydney and New South Wales

My first feeling was to congratulate myself that I was born an Englishman.

—CHARLES DARWIN, UPON VIEWING SYDNEY

SYDNEY HAS the capacity to stir loyalty, to arouse emotions, to make people endlessly question its identity. The place is less a city, say its admirers, than an experience. It is a mixture of history, seaside beauty, metropolitan bustle, carefree energy, and confidence. Sydney commands a position of pre-eminence not only in Australia but in the whole South Pacific. With one set of mental spectacles, you see in Sydney a reflection of England; with another, you see a New York of the Southern Hemisphere. Numbering three million in population, this city by itself contains almost one-fourth of all Australians. Sydney is Australia's oldest, biggest, busiest, and most effervescent city. It also has an awful lot of flies.

The city proper occupies only 11 square miles out of the 670 square miles of the metropolitan area, which is equal to Greater London. This gives room for 368 separate suburbs (as locally defined), which crowd in upon the city so closely that one can walk from central Sydney to the suburb of Woolloomooloo, for example, in hardly more time than it takes to spell the name. The city, capital of the state of New South Wales, sits on the east coast of Australia. Inland, numerous small towns and highways run for 150 miles west of Sydney. Sydney residents tend to dismiss the less urbanized areas of New South Wales beyond that as the "Far West." This state, even if one of the dinkier Australian states, covers an area of 309,433 square miles, which is 50 percent bigger than Spain.

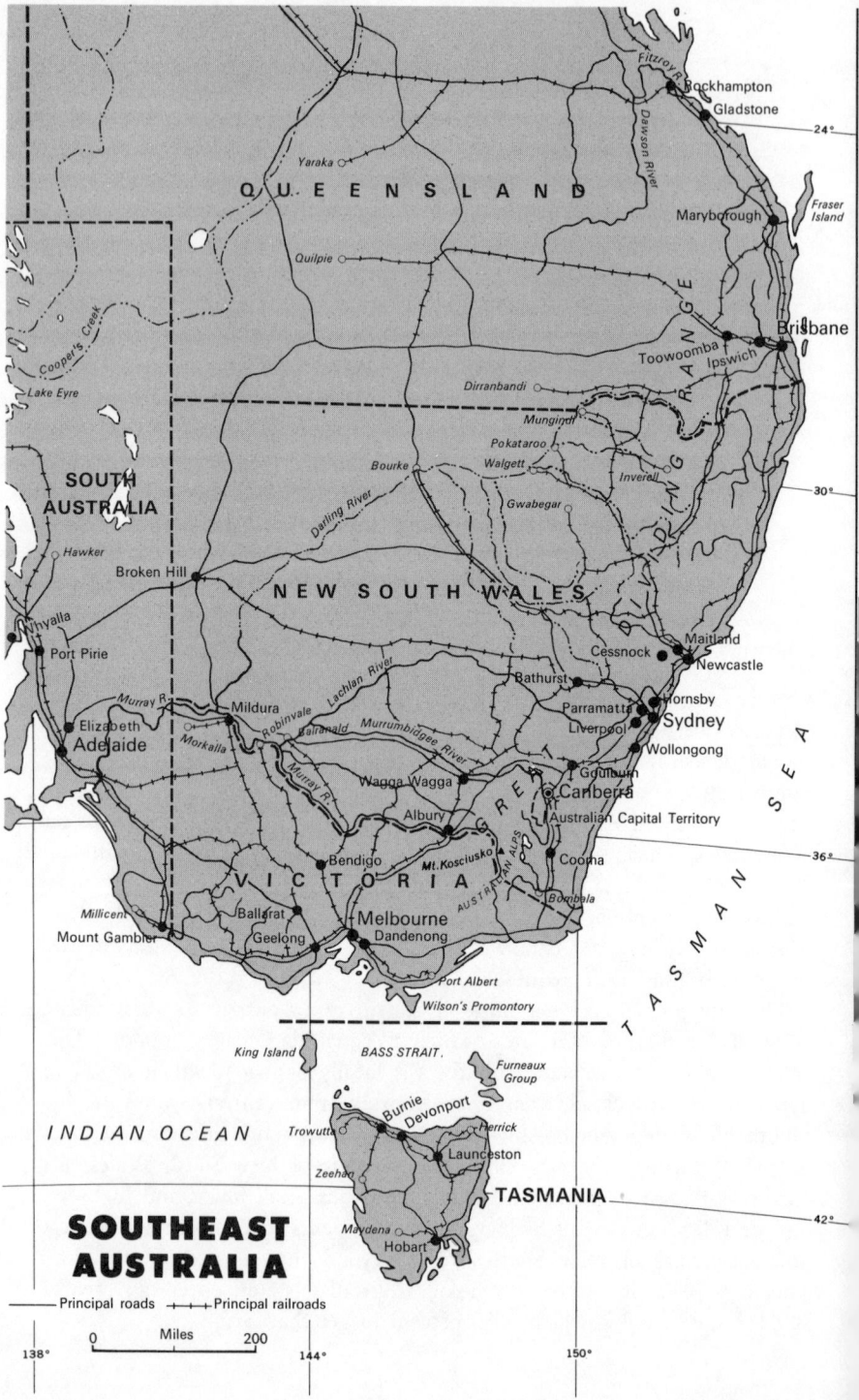
SOUTHEAST AUSTRALIA
QUEENSLAND
SOUTH AUSTRALIA
NEW SOUTH WALES
VICTORIA
TASMANIA
TASMAN SEA
INDIAN OCEAN
BASS STRAIT
Rockhampton
Gladstone
Fitzroy R.
Dawson River
Yaraka
Maryborough
Fraser Island
Quilpie
Brisbane
Toowoomba
Ipswich
Cooper's Creek
Lake Eyre
Dirranbandi
Mungindi
Pokataroo
Walgett
Inverell
Bourke
Darling River
Gwabegar
Hawker
Broken Hill
Port Pirie
Maitland
Cessnock
Newcastle
Bathurst
Murray R.
Mildura
Lachlan River
Robinvale
Balranald
Murrumbidgee River
Parramatta
Hornsby
Sydney
Liverpool
Elizabeth
Adelaide
Morkalla
Wollongong
Goulburn
Wagga Wagga
Canberra
Australian Capital Territory
Albury
Bendigo
Mt. Kosciusko
Cooma
Bombala
Millicent
Ballarat
Melbourne
Mount Gambier
Geelong
Dandenong
Port Albert
Wilson's Promontory
King Island
Furneaux Group
Burnie
Devonport
Trowutta
Penrick
Launceston
Zeehan
Maydena
Hobart
Principal roads
Principal railroads
Miles
0
200
138°
144°
150°
24°
30°
36°
42°

130°
140°
150°
160°
0°
10°
PACIFIC OCEAN
TERRITORY OF NEW GUINEA
(AUSTRALIA)
EQUATOR
ADMIRALTY ISLANDS
New Hanover
BISMARCK ARCHIPELAGO
New Ireland
Rabaul
Digiapura
Wewak
Sepik R.
INDONESIA
Madang
New Britain
Mount Hagen
Buka
SOLOMON ISLANDS
Bougainville
Choiseul
Lae
SOLOMON SEA
ARAFURA SEA
New Georgia Group
Gulf of Papua
Guadalcanal
NEW GUINEA
Port Moresby
D'ENTRECASTEAUX ISLANDS
Torres Strait
LOUISIADE ARCHIPELAGO
0 Miles 300
Cape York Peninsula
CORAL SEA
Whangarei
Dargaville
36°
Auckland
Hamilton
TASMAN SEA
NORTH ISLAND
Rotorua
Lake Taupo
Gisborne
New Plymouth
Napier
Wanganui
Hastings
40°
Palmerston North
Upper Hutt
Nelson
Lower Hutt
Wellington
Cook Strait
Westport
Greymouth
SOUTH ISLAND
PACIFIC OCEAN
Christchurch
Mount Cook
Franz Josef Glacier
Hermitage
Akaroa
44°
Timaru
Queenstown
Oamaru
NEW ZEALAND
Gore
Dunedin
0 Miles 200
Invercargill
Bluff
164°
STEWART ISLAND
170°
176
J. P. TREMBLAY

*

The function of Sydney is really that of a port, exporting wool, wheat, flour, and meat. The city also manufactures aircraft, ships, earth-moving equipment, paper, electrical and communications equipment, agricultural implements, and railway rolling stock.

The harbor is spectacular. One tiresome routine in Sydney is listening to the citizens boast about the incomparable beauty of the natural setting. Let us settle the issue with dispatch. Naples is more picturesque, because of its volcanoes and islands and grottoes. Rio is more breath-taking, because of its sugarloaf mountains plunging into the sea. Hong Kong is more exciting. San Francisco outclasses Sydney in the size and daring of its bridges. Yet if all these ports outrank Sydney for the given reasons, Sydney outranks all of them in sheer length and crenelation of shoreline, in its thirty-six bays and coves around a deep, safe harbor. Sydney is an enchanting minglement of spits of land and tongues of water, of islets and wooded peninsulas, of crescents and canals.

The site of Sydney is a drowned river mouth. Aeons ago the Parramatta River was just a narrow stream flowing east to the Tasman Sea. Then the coast tilted down and the sea backed into the river and its tributaries, forming coves and bays and fingers. The entrance to this immense harbor is a narrow passage called the Heads, so narrow in fact that Captain Cook sailed right past it without seeing it. Once inside, one can travel thirteen miles inland on the water, and the shoreline is 152 miles long. The harbor is deep and safe, if something of a bottleneck. The lighthouse which stands on the sandstone cliff of the south "head" (point) was designed in 1816 by Francis Greenway.

The best way to see the harbor is, of course, from a boat—the ferry to Manly will do. Marinas, Mediterranean houses, ships, buildings on stilts, yachts, overwater houses, and a surprising amount of brushy uninhabited foreshore—all these mix together with much allure. Twenty miles north of downtown Sydney, the Hawkesbury River and three tributaries juxtapose wild bush and superb yachting grounds, with the white-bellied sea eagle soaring in the skies.

From any of the lookouts around downtown Sydney you can spot in the harbor an island, barely more than a rock, that is officially known as Fort Denison but invariably called Pinchgut Island. There, a century and a half ago, incorrigible convicts did time on bread and water, and were occasionally hanged. Sydney residents find this poignant reminder of the injustice of

Australia's past so compelling a place to visit that a family tour on Saturday, the most popular day, must be arranged three and a half months in advance.

Of course, the dominating feature of the whole harbor scene is the Harbor Bridge, 1,650 feet in span and, despite competition from new skyscrapers, just about the highest structure on the Sydney skyline. This bridge was designed to be the world's longest single-arch span, something for Sydney to boast about. But after construction began in 1923, the American planners of the Bayonne Bridge over the Kill Van Kull in New York designed a span just twenty-five inches longer than Sydney's, and managed to finish it four months ahead of Harbor Bridge, which finally opened in early 1932. In those Depression days, New South Wales was ruled by the flamboyant Premier John Thomas Lang, regarded by conservatives as a dangerous and demagogic leftist who should not be given the honor of opening the bridge. Just as Lang was about to cut the ribbon, a young blueblood from the wealthy suburbs spurred forward on horseback and slashed the ribbon with a sword, yelling that he acted "in the name of His Majesty the King and all decent people."

Logically enough, Sydney uses its waterways for urban transport, antiquated green ferries bustling to various beaches and suburbs. Only three hydrofoils ply the harbor, crossing to the suburb of Manly from the Circular Quay at the foot of Sydney Cove. The harbor's great possibilities as a flexible commutation system seem to be far from sufficiently exploited. Still, at commuting hours the quay is lively, with the homebound girl office workers buying a concoction of fresh fruit cored, crushed, and served in a glass in the quayside shops.

But if you can fault the ferry system, you certainly cannot fault the passion of Sydney's addiction to yachting. Thousands of boats are out on Sydney Harbor and connecting waterways each weekend in the main sailing season, September through April. They range in size from eight-foot Sabots to mighty eight-meter (twenty-six-foot) racing machines. Most spectacular of all are the eighteen-footers, whose races are so exciting that yachting clubs hire ferries to follow the action, and lots of informal (and illegal) betting is the order of the day. Racing is controlled by the Yachting Association of New South Wales, which coordinates courses so that traffic around the buoys won't be impossibly dense. Despite this planning, sailors have to race right through ferries, ocean liners, and freighters. Any day one can see a fleet of small boats in the harbor. Sydney is also home port for the America's Cup challengers *Gretel I*, *Dame Pattie*, and *Gretel II*.

To ship captains, all the lovely water reached by steaming through Sydney Heads is merely the commercial Port of Sydney, also called Port Jackson.

Four to five miles in from the Heads, by way of two deep channels, are the wharves—120 general-cargo berths with a total length of more than eleven miles of wharfage, all close to the business center of the city. For ship repairs, the port has the Captain Cook Graving Dock, 1,139 feet long and 148 feet wide, one of the biggest in the world.

Sydney has grown to such an extent that Botany Bay, ten miles south of the city center, discarded as the original site for the penal colony, is now part of metropolitan Sydney. This bay is the expanse of water one sees from the plane landing at Kingsford Smith Airport.

Twenty-seven miles of beaches bracket Sydney Heads to the north and south. The names are melodious—Cronulla, Clovelly, Narrabeen, Curl Curl, Dee Why. Surfing is a national sport that has been growing ever since Duke Kanahamoku introduced the surfboard to Sydney from Hawaii in 1915. Surfies wear sun-bleached hair, dress California style, and expertly ride the great green waves. They drive the roads with surfboards on cars, like skis in the U.S. in the winter. A surfie cuts such a romantic figure that boys too timid to ride the big waves have been known to bleach their hair with Ajax to fake the surfie image.

Sunbathing is a mania. Above all, swimming, in this land where the Australian crawl was invented in the 1920's, is close to the universal sport. Any resident of Sydney who cannot swim is an object of pity or contempt. Perhaps that is as it should be in a city blessed with so much sand and 342 days a year when the sun shines at least seven hours, but there are perils. "BUSY DAY FOR RESCUERS," said a casual newspaper headline one day a year or so ago, and the story went on to tell how no less than two hundred swimmers had been rescued the previous day from "rips," currents that sweep out to sea.

The beaches are beset by sharks as well, so that every beach must be guarded by expert lifesavers. In practice these men are organized in voluntary lifesaving associations. There is intense *esprit de corps*, and, according to Craig McGregor in *Profile of Australia*, "many of the characteristics of pre-war Australian society are to be found there; the masculinity; the mateship; the emphasis on physical prowess, keg parties and grog-ups; the uncertainty of relationships with women; and throughout a certain homespun philosophy of life." Inevitably, however, the lifesaving clubs and surfies clash. The Surf Life Saving Association, for example, summarily refused to recognize the short-finned Malibu surfboard as lifesaving equipment, and barred those who rode them from the club.

Usually a life guard swims out tied to a light line and holds up the drowning person while other members of the lifesaving club on shore pull both in. But the clubs are equally adept at going out in surfboats to pick up swimmers who may yell for help from two hundred yards out or more. In 1938 three freak waves in succession carried thousands of bathers out to sea all at once; the lifesavers rescued all but five. Throughout New South Wales, in 1970, lifeguards rescued 7,318 swimmers in distress. Guarded parts of the beach are marked off by flags, and only the foolhardy swim outside the flags. Helicopters drop markers to indicate sharks.

Sydney provides the definitive answer to a question one still hears debated by supposedly informed people; do sharks really kill human beings? They do—right on the Sydney beaches. Some beaches are protected by nets, and some swimmers stick to beachside swimming pools. To protect the rest of the beaches, planes and boats patrol outside the surf line, with particular vigilance during the December-February summer season, when sharks weighing 500 to 750 pounds, "nasty brutes," come to shore. When an airplane spotter sees a shark, the boats close in and pursue him with spears. Bells or other alarms send swimmers to the shore, and only half a dozen lives have been lost in the last twenty years. To have a leg clipped off by a shark causes a hemorrhage that is usually fatal.

*

Except for the members of the Iceberg Club, and a few other similar groups, who go into the water every day, people do not swim in Sydney in the winter season, which is May to September. The city does not get quite chilly enough to require central heating, or even heaters in cars, but movie theaters often post banners announcing "IT'S WARM INSIDE." In sum, Sydney has an agreeably equable climate. Humidity can be miserably high on hot summer days, but the spell is often broken in late afternoons by the arrival of a "southerly buster." This sudden gale, hitting as much as sixty knots, bowls over yachts in the harbor, but it also instantly air-conditions the city. Another wind, dry and searing, comes from the western deserts to burn up lawns and gardens; still a third is the salty northeasterly, laden with humidity. Indian summers are gentle and enduring—and sometimes end with a bang, a storm that heaves up the seas, sends down torrents of rain, and blows away everything not bolted down.

Glancing Around Central Sydney

Downtown Sydney draws much of its architecture from Victorian-Edwardian England and Mies van der Rohe's Chicago style, and then throws in on its own behalf a generous portion of colonial classics, together with green parks and marquee-shaded sidewalks. The streets are crowded, bustling with people. Dress is varied; men wear conservative business suits or shorts with long socks. It all comes out looking uniquely Australian.

The city center begins where the great Harbor Bridge debouches onto an expressway that curves on stilts over the Circular Quay and then dives underground. Here are half a dozen glassy skyscrapers intermingled with many low buildings that go back as much as a century. Right near the foot of the bridge is a small quiet promontory, the Rocks, redolent of olden-days crime and present-day charm. The city's chief planner would like to remodel it along the lines of San Francisco's Ghirardelli Square; it possesses the requisite old warehouses and smell of history.

On the streets the endless marquees—a Sydney idiosyncrasy—form the sidewalks into open-sided tunnels, with uniform, plank-size signs hanging from above to indicate the wares and services offered in the adjacent stores. The window displays are by and large as jumbled and dusty as those of stores in country towns. A hardware store may have punches from Spain and electrical supplies from Adelaide and drills from England chockablock with vises and hammers and screwdrivers, all dangling scrawled tags. Store windows in general have a country-bumpkin look, and you have to remind yourself that you are in a big metropolis.

The main streets run broad, but not always straight or parallel: Elizabeth, Castlereagh, George; Macquarie, where the doctors' offices are; Pitt, once a row of convict huts, then the city's brothel district, and now the address of many insurance companies. There are intriguing, angled, short streets, too. On meandering Phillip Street, barristers in tight-curled white wigs, short dapper ties, and black gowns stride out among the crowds. Five-block Martin Place has been turned into a pedestrian mall by paving it with pink granite, banishing cars, and setting out fiberglass "street furniture," trees, and flower stalls—all to give Sydney what it has long needed, a central focus.

The streets are pictures of animation; vitality infuses the center of the city. The girls who descend from the high-rise office buildings wear the world's shortest skirts—anything briefer would hardly cover the navel. Australian girls more than women anywhere simply repulsed the maxi-midi fad, and adopted the mini as a permanent choice, which of course befits the climate, their exuberant personalities, and their slim, strong legs. There is much construction in the central city, surrounded by clamor, confusion, and a particularly sturdy kind of timber scaffolding. The men in shorts are businessmen—that is perfectly acceptable attire in Sydney in the summer. One also sees a surprising number of unshaven men in dirty work clothes, sometimes with packs on their backs. They do not look as if they belonged in a city, yet there they are, even in the bookstores.

The tallest building is a forty-seven-story cylinder called Australia Square, higher than the more famous spire of the eighty-four-year-old Renaissance-style General Post Office Building. The Post Office clock tower is lighter in color than the rest of the building, and for an interesting reason: it was dismantled stone by stone and stored during World War II, for fear that Japanese bombers might use it as a landmark, and thoroughly cleaned before its restoration was completed in 1964. A major hotel is the Wentworth, a high concave pile built by Qantas Airways a few years ago for $12,320,000; advice from wide-ranging Qantas pilots went into the planning, and the result was very much like a Hilton. The State Office Building, remindful of the fact that this city is New South Wales' capital, is a darkish glass edifice nicknamed "the black stump." Town Hall, the seat of city government, has an auditorium that can hold 2,500 people for concerts on its pipe organ. Immigrants completing naturalization come here to swear allegiance to the Crown and get a cup of tea and a cake. The New South Wales Parliament is housed in a building, lovely with age and classic in architecture, on Macquarie Street. The central part of it, with the wide column-supported verandas that characterize Australian colonial buildings, was constructed in 1811–1816 as the Rum Corps hospital.

Sydney has a nice little toy underground that connects with the suburban surface railway routes. The central railway station is a gloomy cavern, with people waiting to depart for the innumerable suburbs. One train, for example, goes to places with such names as Emu Plains, Blaxland, Warrimoo, Faulconbridge, Bullaburra, Katoomba, Medlow Bath, and Mt. Victoria. As for Sydney's buses, all that needs to be said is that ten cents will take you quite a distance, and the system continues to operate double-deckers that are, as they always were elsewhere, agreeable for sightseeing.

An Innocuous Center of Sin

King's Cross, not far from Hyde Park, houses the liveliest night life in Australia. It is likened to Soho, Chelsea, and Greenwich Village. It also emanates a whiff of Forty-second Street in New York, and North Beach in San Francisco. But it is really only a smidgen of these bawdier places. There is a bit of pathos in Sydney's pride that it at last has the strip-tease. The strip-tease?

The net effect of King's Cross—balancing off the queers, the strip-shows (including male strip-shows), the whores, and female impersonators (to titillate suburbanites) against the architectural and geographical charm, the pretty plane trees, the espresso coffee bars, the fine delicatessens, the excellent gastronomy, and the peculiar innocence of the place—is far less tawdry than that of sin centers elsewhere. Though cheek-by-jowl with poverty-ridden Woolloomooloo and other scruffy neighborhoods on one side, King's Cross melds with genteel Elizabeth Bay on the other. One feels that this is a rather innocuous place for American soldiers to come on "R and R" (rest and recuperation), which they have done lately from Vietnam, 4,500 miles away, and during World War II from all over the Pacific. Two hundred and eighty thousand of them visited Sydney and "the Cross" between 1967 and the end of 1971, to the tune of much mutual back-patting: "I wouldn't go anywhere else for R and R." "The Americans are the most courteous and polite boys we have known."

A century ago King's Cross was a Jewish neighborhood, a circle centered on the Elizabeth Street synagogue with a radius roughly determined by the two thousand cubits that constituted the maximum Sabbath journey for the Orthodox Jew. Later it became a stronghold of artists and writers; William Dobell lived and worked there. King's Cross area has several good hotels—the Chevron, the Kingsgate, the Gazebo—and the perfectly fascinating El Alamein fountain, a huge sphere like a dandelion gone to seed, filled with sparkling spray.

An Opera House with Sails

Cities everywhere yearn for the cachet of a lavish opera house. The opera house has become the cathedral of an era no longer much interested in building impressive churches. Manhattan, West Berlin, Los Angeles, Brasília, Santa Fe, and scores of other cities have built opera houses or concert halls in the past decade or two. But beyond a doubt the famed though unfinished opera house in Sydney is the most inspired and folly-ridden adventure of them all. "We've had first to look after basic things," explained Harry F. Jensen, who was Lord Mayor of Sydney when the project started in 1957. "Now we can expand and use some of our wealth in a major cultural endeavor."

The site *is* inspired. The highly visible structure is set on the eastern promontory of Sydney Cove, Benelong Point, named for an Aboriginal. Yachts with striped spinnakers cruise the blue harbor close at hand. The great bony arch of Harbor Bridge looms several hundred yards away. Landward are Government House and the Botanic Gardens.

The plan was bold, unique, brilliantly chosen—and trouble—from its inception. The Sydney Opera House Committee offered a prize of $10,600 for the best design, and the next year a jury of local critics met to judge 222 entries. The noted Finnish-American architect Eero Saarinen was invited to Sydney to advise the jury. He looked through the designs they had already rejected and chose a sketch by an unknown Dane, Jørn Utzon.

Utzon's design is essentially an extravagant sculpture: a building of soaring white concrete shells suggesting breeze-filled sails. The basic repeated element of the design is a three-sided pyramid, two sides formed of ballooning, white-tiled concrete shell that partly enclose the third, which is a bronze-mullioned, curving curtain of panes of glass. There are ten such shells, some embracing others and some back-to-back, some nearly vertical and some leaning sharply, and two of them off by themselves to house a restaurant.

But Utzon's imaginative concept was not matched by engineering foresight. A London consulting firm set six hundred men to work with computers on calculations of the stresses in his projected shells. Three years later, with the foundation well along, the consultants reported that casting the shells would be technologically impossible. Then Utzon, "after three years of search for a basic geometry for the shell complex," modified his design so that the shells could be prefabricated in blocks, each curve skinned off the surface of a single sphere having a radius of 246 feet, using the same molds over and over. The blocks were raised by hammerhead cranes and assembled with steel hawsers. It was then realized that the partly built platform could not be adapted to the prefabricated shells; so Utzon ordered the dynamiting of $300,000 worth of concrete piles already set into place.*

By 1966 Sydney's patience was beginning to wear thin. The newspapers discovered that Utzon had not planned parking fields for the opera house. He answered testily that there were no parking fields at the Parthenon either. He demanded $2.8 million to "build a full-scale wooden mockup of the main hall, and see whether it falls down." The government balked; he threatened to resign; the government quickly and gratefully accepted the resignation.

Peter Hall, a highly regarded Sydney architect, took over from Utzon and found shocking new obstacles. He did not believe that the main hall could be used successfully for two different purposes; "Concerts and operas do not happen in the same sort of rooms," he said. So the main hall (seating 2,750) was redesigned for symphonies only (Sydney has an excellent orchestra with a big following). If Australia produces any more opera singers like Nellie Melba or Joan Sutherland, they will have to perform in the smaller

* The earth, billed as firm sandstone before the project got started, turned out to be fill, "nothing but old boots and bedsteads," and ultimately 550 three-foot-thick concrete piles had to be driven to a depth of 70 feet below sea level, to reach a solid foundation.

adjacent theater (seating 1,500), which will be used for opera and ballets. Halls on other levels under the shells will seat 600, 450, and 150 people, and handle plays, films, rehearsals, and recitals. After all the energy and expenditure, Sydney will not have a structure that is primarily an opera house.

Meanwhile, the costs have mounted astronomically and the end is not in sight. What began as a projected figure of $10 million is now estimated to be $93 million (New York's new Metropolitan Opera House cost $45 million). Most of the fund-raising has been painless; it comes from the New South Wales Opera House Lotteries, which pay out a $224,000 first prize every two weeks. Ultimately the building will account for at least $200 million worth of gambling, or an average of $15 for every Australian.

No one really knows when the Sydney Opera House will be finished. It has been under construction since 1959, and the opening was first scheduled for 1963; the current target date for completion is November 1972, to be followed by a period of getting rid of bugs, and a grand opening in March 1973. But one thing is certain: it will be—indeed, it already is—an unforgettable building, absolutely original in concept, and a landmark oddly visible from many parts of the city, not because it is so tall but because it rivets the eye. A leading architect in the rival city of Melbourne may have summed up the whole project, when, confessing admiration, he called it "ridiculous, something you would expect of Latin America but not Sydney—and altogether wonderful."

A Sea of Suburbs

Neighborhoods around Sydney divide in class and aspect as sharply as though cut with a cleaver. The shores close to the center of town, where it may cost $150,000 to buy an apartment, are elegant indeed; the old rich and the high-fee professional classes live among fine views of the harbor, good architecture, chic shops, and sidewalk cafés in Potts Point, Double Bay, Bellevue Hill, Rose Bay, and Vaucluse. One sumptuous address is Elizabeth Bay House, a colonial mansion owned by the state and divided into sixteen apartments reached by a winding staircase.

Plunked among near-slums and near-ghettos is a region once decaying and now attractively restored, like Washington's Georgetown. This is Paddington—"Paddo," they call it. Its merit was its terrace houses, one fortunate legacy from the otherwise tasteless Victorian era. The houses are narrow, two-storied, with a door and a window on the street level, and above them a balcony with a lacework cast-iron railing, made of metal brought from England as ballast. Sharing common walls, painted in pastels, these houses march up and down the hills to form long repetitive rooflines embellished with chimney pots and finials. To buy one of these houses, which, renovated, may cost as much as $50,000, is the fashionable thing for artists, writers, and young professional people.

South of the city is industry and yawning tattiness, although the expressway from the airport manages to dodge the drab, and winds through golf courses and parkland. Botany Bay, though historically distinguished, is presently an eyesore of power poles, blatant signs, litter, and tourist-trap "museums."

The real suburbs are places like Waverley, which package people in at the rate of nineteen thousand to the square mile. Tumbledown Redfern gives over a couple of streets to city-living Aborigines. Taylor Square is a center for Greeks, Pendle Hill is Little Malta.

Across the harbor, to the north, is a huge domain of small suburban houses for the middle and upper classes, young business executives with two children and two cars. Some clean-lined new "Australian contemporary" houses can be seen here, and their occupants lead wholesome lives. Lights go out at ten o'clock on the north shore.

To the west of Sydney proper stretch twenty miles of bungalows, broken only by the Gothic architecture of the University of Sydney, industrial sites, and the remnants of a once-ambitious green belt that got trampled down in the rush to construct. Here is where the bulk of Sydney lives, happy in the face of monotony, often glued to the telly, and pleased with the crimson rosellas, gorgeous parakeets, that inhabit the back yards.

A Certifiably Gallant Governor

Through someone's splendid foresight, the downtown section of Sydney is provided with a vast grassy area, the Botanic Gardens and the Domain, where on Sunday soapbox orators, often in weird dress, advocate or denounce this and that. The only buildings here are the Conservatorium of Music, the Art Gallery of New South Wales, and Government House. The last of these is a crenelated, turreted castle, set among gardens, tennis courts, and a swimming pool, and against a huge rubber tree with roots that must be regularly hacked away to keep them from undermining and toppling the castle. The resplendence of the place is a reminder of the past glory of the British Empire. The Governor represents the Queen, and is today only a symbolic head of state. His power is slight—in reality, empty authority.

Sir Arthur Roden Cutler, V.C., K.C.M.G., C.B.E., K.St.J., the twenty-first occupant of the castle in the Botanic Gardens, is a tall and lanky man. On July 6, 1941, Cutler, then an artillery lieutenant in the Australian Army fighting in Syria, was carrying a phone line under heavy machine-gun fire to a forward outpost of his troops, and suffered serious wounds. He could not be rescued for twenty-six hours, by which time one leg was so infected that surgeons had to amputate it. It was for this and a number of earlier acts of similar bravery that Cutler won the Victoria Cross. His career was mostly in diplomacy—Australian High Commissioner in New Zealand, Ceylon, and Pakistan; Minister to Egypt; Consul-General in New York. As Her Majesty's Australian Ambassador to the Netherlands, he was dining one night at The Hague when the phone rang—Buckingham Palace on the line. The Queen had made him Governor of New South Wales, and he took up the position in January 1966.

Sir Roden talks with pride and affection about New South Wales, pointing out that the state has more industry than any other, with tremendous energy concentrated in Sydney. New South Wales has no unemployment—a labor shortage, rather. The Governor contends that Sydney is in fact the money center of Australia, though Melbourne claims the title.

The Governor cannot effectively attack the state's problems, because his powers are limited to "assenting in the Queen's name to bills passed by the Parliament of the State." But he can exert a bit of pressure here and there—perhaps "government by nudge" is a good way to put it—and he is deeply concerned about New South Wales' problems. He mentioned in particular the rebate system by which the Commonwealth government shares with the states the revenues it takes in as sole recipient of income taxes. Naturally, there is much controversy on this issue, since the richer states feel that they are contributing to the poorer states funds which they would like to have for their own improvement.

Sir Roden gets a tax-free salary of $20,000, but the whole cost of running Government House, including the wages of its carpenter-caretaker, is $105,000. At the end of a great hall in Government House are spaces for the coats of arms of each Governor and Sir Roden's was new and fresh there. What happens if a Governor does not have a private coat of arms? Sir Roden suspects, he says, that in times long past several of the Governors invented their own.

Epicurean Sydney

Here are the three main points to make, gastronomically speaking, about Sydney. First, it has shot in ten years from culinary dowdiness to authentic gourmet levels, solely because big-scale immigration finally brought international standards and every kind of cuisine. Second, Sydney rock oysters are the best, cheapest, and most plentiful in the world. Third, the possibilities for using the waterfront for restaurant sites have been scandalously neglected; there are only one or two restaurants built over water.

One of these is the Caprice, set on the shoreline among the tall luxury-apartment buildings that line Rose Bay. The cooking is French, and people say that it is the best place to dine in Australia. Short of being on the water, you can get a superlative view of Sydney, plus tolerable fare, from the Summit, a revolving restaurant (the world's biggest, of course—this is a land of superlatives) on top of the Australia Square building. An underground place called Weinkeller has smörgåsbord and a choice of seventy-two Australian wines, which one picks from rack after rack right in the middle of the floor. The Argyle Tavern bills itself as "137 years behind the times and proud of it." The Chelsea in King's Cross has a sensible idea, a menu in booklet form, the size of a postcard, with eight pages of offerings. The Newcastle Pub, unluckily soon to be torn down, provides not food, but rather lots of strenuous drinking among the many Sydney writers who find it congenial and the many Sydney artists who use it as a gallery to sell their paintings. It was the first pub in Sydney to serve women.

Sydney's rock oysters are grown in the Hawkesbury River. The system is to submerge long narrow wooden slats over the breeding grounds, and the young oysters, the "splat," quickly fasten themselves to the wood. After six months the oystermen transplant the sticks to less salty water upstream, and let them grow for three or four years. It seems to be a felicitous proceeding. One Australian dollar buys a huge plate of them at Victor's, an unpretentious place on King Street; and not long ago, at the annual convention of the Oyster Farmers of New South Wales, two thousand men sat down and consumed *ten thousand dozen* oysters.

In Sydney one can see, better than anywhere else, how this hearty egalitarian nation has expanded what might be the typical American country club into a remarkable phenomenon of mass eating and drinking, entertainment, and sport. An example is the St. George Leagues Club, which has 33,000 owner-members paying about $10 a year in dues in order to enjoy $2,250,000 worth of clubrooms, cabarets, gardens, squash courts, bars, movies, fashion shows, gymnasiums, and saunas—plus hockey, cricket, golf, swimming, bowling, football, and boxing. In the main dining room, three dozen Sydney rocks, plus Prawns Thermidor, Veal Normandie, wine, *and* a smörgåsbord can be had for about $2.40. The clubs are subsidized by slot machines—called poker machines because the spinning symbols form poker hands. One smaller club in Sydney nets a profit of almost $600,000 a year, while returning to the beer-drinking gamblers an average of $3,600 in winnings per day. It is said that the clubs "make gents out of workers," and "give every man his own Las Vegas." Perhaps this kind of thing simply reflects the indigenous uncomplicated contentment with suburbia, beaches, sports, and what are accepted as the good things of life—the attitude that it is, after all, a fine thing to be alive in Sydney, Australia.

*

Alcohol is the subject of much debate in Sydney, and the object of much moralizing and lawmaking. In short, the men there drink a lot, flying in the face of numerous (but diminishing) restrictions. The chief absurdity, inherited from England, is that by and large bars must pretend to be merely a licensed ancillary convenience attached to a hotel, the "public room." Thus what everyone knows to be nothing but bars must be substantial buildings that will actually rent rooms. In Sydney they are mostly built to the same plan, three stories of tan masonry, with swinging doors leading to the tile-lined pub with its U-shaped bar, and the name of the publican duly posted outside. It is commonplace to see these hotels planted on three of the four corners at an intersection. The names are jaunty: Captain Cook, Bat and Ball, Royal Oak, the Hero of Waterloo.

*

Sydney tidbits: pack rape, in which groups of young men assault a young girl by turn, is such a serious problem that a select committee of the state Parliament conducted an investigation. The investigators were shocked at the indifference shown by the rapists: most of them thought mass intercourse a reasonable thing to do, and they seemed sure that the girls did not object.

The great postwar migration to Australia is strikingly evident on the streets of Sydney. So many languages can be heard among the throngs that English will sometimes hit the ear as slightly bizarre, the way it does in Paris or Rome.

The telephone book has pink pages instead of yellow, and in the directory first names are listed by initials only. In fact, Australians prefer the use of initials for first names in general.

The American Club, atop a small skyscraper, has a unique men's room—a row of urinals with a view, being fitted with a fine large window. It is said that one visiting American was so impressed that he had the view, which is of the whole spectacular harbor, photographed, enlarged to mural size, and installed in his bathroom at home.

Outside of Sydney in New South Wales

Eucalyptus trees, as perhaps not everyone knows, give off an oil that floats in tiny droplets in the air. These droplets refract light, in accordance with the principle of Rayleigh scattering, which has the effect of making distant objects appear blue. And blue indeed, cobalt blue, are the eucalyptus-clad Blue Mountains west of Sydney.

These mountains are part of the Great Dividing Range, which, as we have seen, separates the narrow coast of New South Wales from its immense outback. The coast, of course, has the people—in Sydney; in Newcastle, population 360,000, a hundred miles north; and in Wollongong–Port Kembla, population 200,000, fifty miles south. There are no other towns in New South Wales with more than 40,000 people. Both Newcastle and Wollongong exist by virtue of immense fields of high-grade coal. North on the coast, near the Queensland border, most of Australia's bananas are grown.

In the mountains in the north, a set of plateaus, called New England, has rich soil and fast, clear streams. The western slopes here grow as much as eighty bushels of wheat per acre when it rains—and nothing when it doesn't.

Beyond the Dividing Range is a monotony of plains all the way to South Australia. Two million sheep are the weary inhabitants. The only town of interest is Broken Hill, great lode of many metals, described in the chapter on Adelaide because its links are all with that city. Toward the south of this region is Riverina, good productive land—even rice grows here, because it can be irrigated from the Murrumbidgee and Murray rivers, which, with the Lachlan, give the area its name.

Southwest of Sydney is high country discovered in convict times by escaping prisoners who had a curiously unswervable conviction that China lay off that way about 150 miles. If they had turned south, they would have come to purlieus equally exotic, the high Australian Alps.

The Snowy Mountains Scheme

At the most spectacular stretch of the Great Dividing Range, only a hundred miles from the sea and precisely in the southeast corner of the continent, a great hydroelectric scheme is being developed. Here within the space of a hundred miles rise six rivers: the Murrumbidgee, Murray, Tumut, Tooma, Snowy, and Eucumbene. Engineers have been tantalized for eighty years by the prospect of manhandling these rivers to generate power and irrigate land. An Act of Parliament started the Snowy Mountains Scheme in 1949. It is now better than three-quarters finished and will be done in 1974.

The project will produce 3,770,000 kilowatts, more than any existing plant except Russia's Bratsk, although, of course, the Snowy Mountains Scheme is a system of powerhouses rather than a single large hydrogenerator. Yet hydroelectric power, to be sold for $50 million a year, is only half the purpose. Diverting the course of one river—the Snowy—from the eastern to the western slopes of the Great Dividing Range will add two million acre-feet of water to the irrigation of the Riverina country. Farm produce is to rise $60 million a year in value as a result. The cost of the scheme is $800 million, $80 million from the World Bank and the rest provided by the Commonwealth government out of revenue. How's that for solvency? A doughty New Zealander, Sir William Hudson, is the engineer who headed the Snowy Mountains Authority for most of its existence, and of every ten construction workers seven are Australian immigrants. To honor them, the flags of thirty countries fly in Cooma, the project headquarters.

The scheme requires sixteen large dams and many smaller ones, seven power stations, and eighty miles of aqueducts as well as one hundred miles of tunnels.

The waters of the Snowy River were wasted in the past, flowing southward down the mountains to end up in the Tasman Sea. Modern engineering, by capturing its waters, has been able to reverse their course, causing them to flow westward, adding water to the Murray, Australia's principal river. Let us hypothesize a drop of water in the upper Murrumbidgee. Once it would have coursed down the mountains and ultimately to the southern ocean near Adelaide; now, still high in the mountains, a dam diverts it and shoots it eleven and a half miles through a tunnel to join the headwaters of the Eucumbene. There, stopped by a dam 381 feet high, this drop is sent *back* under the Dividing Range in another tunnel and rushed through power generators a thousand feet underground into the Tumut River. The Eucumbene reservoir, however, has *two* outlet tunnels; another drop of water can bob nearly fifteen miles underground to join the dammed-off Snowy River, be carried with it through a nine-mile tunnel, through generators, into the Murray. There are unbelievable complexities, the point being to collect the greatest amount of water at the greatest altitude and put it to the greatest use. Two towns, Adiminby and Jindabyne, were demolished in the process, but two new ones have been built to replace them.

All of this depends on plenty of snow, and this little corner of arid Australia has it. Easterly winds bring heavy precipitation, and the mountain elevations, though not arctic-frigid, are cold enough to keep snow flying for five months. Much of the project lies within Kosciusko State Park, both a summer and winter resort. Residents of New South Wales are proud of the good long ski tows, and vacationing Australians have their own Gstaad to go to.

*

> *. . . a huge, sprawling, turbulent city, full of bustle and a zestful materialism.*
>
> —CRAIG MC GREGOR

But now, back to Sydney. The sun has risen from the Tasman Sea, on any pleasant day in December, by 6 A.M. The city does not want to awaken, does not want to go to work, but the light floods into every room. The warmth, the rising humidity, put their mark on the kind of day it is going to be in the offices and factories. Out of it all percolates a peculiar blend of inertia and energy. This may be a place that is bland, unspiritual, hedonistic, far from God—but it is not violent, doubt-torn, or vicious. Here is a city with some dazzle and fun. Skyscraper roofs look down on sparkling sights. Sophistication is not yet something to be avoided. Perhaps it could have been more romantically named Botany Bay—but in the end Sydney has become a name with its own measure of romance. "No great city in the history of the world was born under so cruel a star," John Pringle, former editor of the Sydney *Morning Herald*, points out. Yet now those wretched beginnings seem transmuted into colonial tradition, and this blends with the sea and the beneficent sun and the extrovert population to make a city of character and individuality. There are those who love it, and no wonder.

CHAPTER 11

Canberra

In Western Australia they distrust "the East." In South Australia they also distrust "the East." . . . In Victoria they distrust New South Wales. In New South Wales they distrust Sydney. In Canberra, in the Australian Capital Territory, they distrust Australia.

—DONALD HORNE IN The Next Australia

A MUSICAL PLAY, put on lately in Melbourne by Australia's Elizabethan Theatre Trust, bore the title *The Legend of King O'Malley*. By no means pure legend, O'Malley was a real figure of obscure American origins, who moved in the 1880's to Australia, where he ran for elective office from Adelaide, Tasmania, and Darwin. He won his first election on a platform of: (1) legitimizing bastards if the parents later married; (2) lavatories on every train; and (3) the abolition of barmaids. A newsman of the time wrote that O'Malley looked like "a threefold compromise between a wild-west romantic hero from the cattle ranches, a spruiker [Australian for spieler] from Barnum's Circus, and a Western American statesman." His beard was Mosaic and his hair a shock of red—though he frequently described himself as "the baldheaded eagle of the Rocky Mountains." He was marvelously effective, and eventually became a cabinet minister during the early decades of this century. He fought for the populist cause of a Commonwealth Bank, and that government bank is now a great Australian power center. O'Malley's other major cause was even more noteworthy: the establishment of the Australian capital at Canberra.

*

To begin with, Canberra is a real capital. The balky job of actually getting the government to move from Melbourne has been brought nearly to completion with the leisurely transfer of the defense departments to Canberra in recent years. The filling up of its centrally located artificial lake has given Canberra, after half a century of waiting, a comprehensible aesthetic unity. Canberra has reached world pre-eminence as a garden city. And it has grown with more control than most master-planned cities. Some 130,000 people now live in Canberra. The city took shape through years of drumfire disapproval as a "capital village" and a waste of money; but now Canberra is there, and it functions, and it beguiles the eye.

Somehow, though, Canberra has never lost the pastoral feeling of a country town. Lively crowds fill the half-dozen good restaurants (there are no night clubs) in the evenings, but the customers are not cosmopolites—just plain Australians, civil servants mostly, informally enjoying a meal. Youngsters find the capital a sleepy place—"nothing to do at night." Traffic lights are few—a blessing, but still a small-town touch. Even to play slot machines, that beloved Australian amusement, people must go to the neighboring town of Queanbeyan. A report commissioned by Parliament found that the loneliness characteristic of cities was more serious in Canberra than elsewhere, and recommended a "European-type" Sunday, with bars left open and horse and dog racing allowed.

Only a few politicians actually have flats or houses in Canberra, most of them living in hotels or motels. The center of politico-social life, however, is the Hotel Canberra, which dates back to the origins of Canberra as the capital, and throngs with Senators and Members, lobbyists seeking their favors, and figures from the business world. Bars in this hotel buzz with what is presumably talk of important affairs. The newer Canberra Rex also attracts some of this life, and other modern hotels are springing up. But weekends, and other free times, the Members of Parliament fly off to home towns or bigger cities, and much of the politicking and electioneering that precedes legislation goes on outside the capital. Even Prime Minister McMahon, who has a comfortable official residence in Canberra called the Lodge, is frequently to be found in his Sydney home.

The insistent flavor of Canberra is that of a strong bureaucracy; one-third of the working population is in public service, and the high officials of the government either live there or spend time there. The real power of Australia is here, including all the departmental secretaries who advise the ministers, and frequently know more about a department than the minister himself. A Parliamentary press gallery, mostly seasoned and serious men, operates in Canberra, of course, and the capital has one of the country's more important and responsible newspapers, the Canberra *Times*.

Canberra itself is ruled, incidentally, by the Department of Interior of the federal government. If it is to continue evolving according to the plans of the National Capital Development Commission, this probably must be so. As a sop, the citizenry gets to elect to the House of Representatives one member, who may speak but cannot vote. To sum up, Canberra is essentially a civil servants' city, wholesome if somewhat sterile, ornamental if somewhat artificial, functional if rather remote.

The ACT and How It Grew

The state-by-state ratification of Australia's federal Constitution in 1899 required a two-thirds vote of approval by the people at large. The voters in New South Wales withheld approval until they were given a constitutional guarantee that the capital would lie within their state. The other states agreed to this, but only if the capital were established far away from sinister Sydney. Victoria made the stipulation that Melbourne should be the seat of government until the time when the new capital would be built. So the Constitution decreed that the capital "shall be in the State of New South Wales, and be distant not less than one hundred miles from Sydney."

That turned the site selection over to individual legislators from New South Wales, who battled for years, advocating existing towns. The ultimate brilliant compromise was a nearly empty valley, averaging 1,900 feet in elevation, in the Great Dividing Range, 148 air miles southwest of Sydney and about 70 miles from the Tasman Sea. As early as 1823 graziers had settled in the area, known then as Canberry, and around 1900 it had eleven big sheep properties but no sizable habitation. The only impressive structure was St. John's Church, built in 1841 by a devout sheep raiser; it stands to this day in the middle of Canberra. Though the planners of Washington, D.C., thought a mere 69 square miles sufficient, the federal government of Australia demanded and got free from the state of New South Wales a tract of 911 square miles, to include a watershed big enough to guarantee a water supply for Canberra. Later New South Wales threw in another 28 square miles on the coast at Jervis Bay, to give the capital a seaport.

King O'Malley, as Minister for Home Affairs, rammed through the legislation for the Australian Capital Territory (ACT) and, in 1909, chose the precise location of the capital town site. He then pressed forward with a grand international competition for the design of the city. The prize was modest, $3,500, but it attracted 137 entries—all from abroad, because of a sulky boycott by Australians. The winner, partly because O'Malley identified with his nationality, was an American, thirty-six-year-old Walter Burley Griffin, trained in architecture at the University of Illinois and M.I.T., a Chicago disciple of Louis Sullivan and an associate of Frank Lloyd Wright.

Dozens of names were suggested for the new capital, the most delicious, no doubt, being Sydmeladperbrisho, an amalgam of the first syllables of the names of the six state capitals.* Others much favored were Myola, Wheatwoolgold, and Shakespeare. The official choice was simply the area's traditional name, given to it by the Aborigines, and this time spelled as Canberra. It is supposed to mean either: (1) meeting place; or (2) bend in the Molonglo, the river that traverses the city; or (3) woman's breasts, from two cone-shaped hills on the site. At the ceremony to mark the beginning of construction, on March 13, 1913, King O'Malley laid the foundation stone, and the wife of the Governor-General, Thomas Baron Denman, officially christened the city. Seemingly unsure how to accent the word, she pronounced it "Can-bra." And so it remains—though there are still Australians who say "CanBEARa."

Griffin worked seven years as Federal Capital Director, getting in the main streets and a railroad link in spite of every kind of bureaucratic obstruction. Finally he resigned in frustration. This gentle vegetarian was reduced for a while to designing incinerators in Sydney. He went on, however, to bigger projects—the Capital Theatre in Melbourne, Newman College of the University of Melbourne, the Castlecrag suburb of Sydney. Moving to India, he built a library for the university in Lucknow, and there, in 1937, he fell from a scaffold and died.

A spurt of construction in Canberra in the twenties produced five hundred residences and a Parliament House built for the ages out of heavy stone, but considered to be temporary because a bigger and more stately one will eventually be put up. The impermanence of Parliament House is somehow supposed to explain its blocky ugliness, the product of a committee of pedestrian government architects. It is modeled on the U.S. Capitol in providing chambers for the Senate and the House of Representatives, but the colors for the decor of these halls, red for the Senate and green for the House, are derived from the British House of Lords and House of Commons. The arms of the Speaker's chair in the House are made of oak from Nelson's flagship, *Victory*, and one of the sights in the building is a copy of the Magna Carta dating from 1297. In front of this building on May 9, 1927, as Nellie Melba sang and Avro 504Ks droned overhead, the Duke of York (later George VI) formally installed the Australian capital in Canberra. The wives of the newly arriving civil servants complained stridently over the wood-fire stoves in their kitchens, so primitive compared to the gas flames they had left behind in Melbourne.

The Depression and World War II stunted Canberra's growth. The

* That is, Sydney, Melbourne, Adelaide, Perth, Brisbane, and Hobart.

population was a mere 5,000 in 1927, and twenty years later it was still only 16,000. During the war Australia's government was a snarl of confusion, divided among Melbourne, Canberra, and Sydney. The transformation of Canberra came in the decade of 1957–1967, when Prime Minister Menzies put his government and its pocketbook behind the National Capital Development Commission, and the population grew to 100,000. The estimated total cost, so far, is $800 million. Of course, the spending goes on, at $100 million a year, and the population is scheduled to reach 250,000 by the early 1980's. The growth rate is 8 percent a year, probably the highest in the world for major cities.

*

To Burley Griffin, the site of Canberra was a natural amphitheater. On the north, three hills, Mount Ainslie, Black Mountain, and Mount Pleasant, formed the "top galleries," and their slopes the "auditorium." The Molonglo River, running from east to west at the foot of the slopes, was, together with its flood basin, the "arena." The river's southern banks formed the "terraced stage and setting of monumental Government structures sharply defined rising tier on tier to the culminating highest internal forested hill of the Capital." Further to the south lie the Australian Alps—to an American eye more like the mountains of Vermont than anything in Switzerland, but in any case a pleasing blue backdrop. Three mountains in the ACT exceed six thousand feet.

Canberra's mountain setting is high enough to make it a rather cool place on the whole. The average temperature in the summer is only 67 degrees (though once the thermometer reached 109), and in the winter it runs around 45. A snow that lies on the ground is rare. Most houses do not have central heating, relying on oil space heaters and good insulation. On an average, only twenty-three inches of rain fall each year, and lawns turn brown if not watered.

The natural elements determined Burley Griffin's plan. In his imagination the river, dammed, became a meandering lake to give Canberra recreation, space, and definition. So it does. It is named Lake Burley Griffin, and it is seven miles long. Griffin picked a small elevation near it to be Capitol Hill, where he envisioned a building for "housing archives and commemorating Australian Achievements." Although a "Capitol" has never been built, the city is laid out, roughly, in concentric circles of drives around this focal point, with spokelike boulevards radiating from it. One spoke shoots off north across a bridge over the lake to a complex of stores, banks, office buildings, and the main hotels.* Between this spoke and another lies the temporary Parliament House and an ample lakefront area intended as the site for the future permanent Parliament House (actually, some Members of Parliament, including Prime Minister McMahon, now favor Capitol Hill for this structure).

The glory of Canberra is its trees, *eight million* of them. Many native eucalyptuses are here, because Griffin thought that species to be the "poet's tree," worth planting in large numbers. And, partly owing to a prelate at St. John's in the last century, who planted seeds wherever he went, Canberra also has most of the more colorful trees of the rest of the world. Spring is a blast of peach and cherry blossoms, fall an explosion of scarlet and orange oaks and maples. In Canberra's ten thousand acres of parks,† one can find box elders, silver birches, cedars, Indian deodars, hawthorns, cypresses, plane trees, Lombardy poplars, weeping willows, American, Chinese, and English elms, ashes, olives, walnuts, firs, spruces, and even pepper trees from Peru. An appealing custom is the government's gift, from its enormous nurseries, of forty shrubs and ten trees to any new household. Until a few years ago, the government even clipped your hedges for you. Trees stand in parking lots, shading cars and hiding their cumulative ugliness. Trees attract birds and butterflies in great numbers—one butterfly was to be seen fluttering around the office of a government official being interviewed for this book. Trees and the lake make Canberra a pleasant place for outdoor life. The numerous picnic spots have coin-in-the-slot, gas-fired barbecue hearths. You do have to slap away flies, though; the gesture is known as the "Canberra salute." The lake is splendid for sailing and fishing—but, incredibly for a new lake, too full of sewage to swim in. A powerful fountain—the Captain Cook Bicentennial Water Jet—under the surface of the lake shoots a stream as high as a forty-five-story building. Gardens in Canberra grow roses ten inches in diameter. Also engaging is the occasional sight of a kangaroo on the Canberra golf course.

The Public Buildings of Canberra

It is the capital's public buildings, unfortunately for a much-architected town, that disappoint the visitor. None seem very monumental, as Griffin

* When President Johnson visited Canberra, the Secret Service, for security and flexibility, booked him into several hotels, and installed hot lines to the White House in all of them. An Australian sheep raiser, visiting Canberra, was by mistake put into one of the rooms reserved for but not occupied by Johnson. The sheepman picked up the phone, and the White House, responding, was astonished to hear him bellow, "Send up a couple of beers!"

† By comparison, Manhattan's Central Park measures 840 acres.

would have had them; Parliament House, in the words of writer Colin MacInnes, is a "meaningless box"; the Treasury, the tiny-windowed Ministry of Defense, and other new edifices are neat and unmemorable. The higher buildings seem to know they are out of place, and try to hide their height by stressing horizontal lines; yet at around ten stories they are not high enough nor numerous enough, and too scattered, to make a skyline, which might be an asset. The War Memorial, on the slope of Mount Ainslie, is a ponderous fortress containing the "world's most comprehensive display of contemporary war relics"; it seems to celebrate war rather than lament the dead. The Memorial has already rushed to put up a diorama showing Aussies fighting in Vietnam. Australians take much pride in this building, reflecting their pride in the world recognition that they won by bold fighting in two world wars.

But the Parthenon-like National Library of Australia, designed by Sydney architect Walter Banning, is rectilinearly spare and proportionate, lovely as reflected in the lake, and set off by a garden of orange poppies. Inside is stained glass by the noted Australian artist Leonard French. A particularly exciting building is the Academy of Science: simply a shallow dome with the bottom scalloped so that it appears to sit lightly on a dozen delicate feet. Just inside the scallops is a moat whose water reflects light into the building. The Melbourne architect chiefly responsible, Sir Roy Grounds, says that he ranks it among his best. Canberra also has a business center, built years ago, that employs block after block of graceful arcades, almost in the Italian manner. A number of office buildings privately owned by banks and insurance companies rent space to house entire departments of the government, which thereby avoids the cost of constructing offices.

Three fascinating places to visit in and around Canberra are the mint, which is fitted with a visitors' gallery where you can watch coins being made; the Honeysuckle Creek tracking station, thirty-five miles southwest of Canberra and used in Apollo shots (it looms high and golden and seems to be worshiping outer space); and the Australian-American Memorial, an aluminum spire 258 feet high with an eagle on top—a commemoration of Australia's gratitude to the United States for helping to fight back the Japanese in World War II. It is one more sign of the uncomplicated Australian feeling of friendship for America. One curiosity is an elaborate carillon (Canberrans use the British pronunciation, and rhyme it with "million"), played for forty minutes once a fortnight by a carilloneur who comes from Sydney; no one in Canberra knows how to play it.

Establishing a new capital naturally compels the world's nations to build new embassies, in this case with decidedly mixed results, for many of them have attempted to bring a bit of homeland architecture to Canberra. South Africa displays Cape architecture on the curve of a prominent avenue. The Japanese Embassy looks Japanese, the French French. The American Embassy carries this notion to the ultimate with two buildings that would certainly make the DAR applaud. The chancellery could be set down anywhere in Williamsburg, Virginia, and be at home; the Ambassador's residence, grander and higher up the hill, could pass for a colonial capitol. The detailing of both buildings is meticulous, down to the red bricks imported from the States and the walnut paneling of the Ambassador's office, but the people who work there seem to yearn for at least one modern touch, air-conditioning. Whether these native-style buildings are fitting or not is a matter of much controversy in Canberra. Elspeth Huxley feels that to the general hodgepodge of Canberra architecture "foreign missions have added a musical-comedy touch with embassies in national costume, like peasants posed to dress for tourists."

The American Ambassador, by the way, is Walter Rice, a government trust-buster in the 1930's and more recently a member of the board of directors of Reynolds Metals and its subsidiaries. President Nixon appointed him in 1969. He is the father, by his charming young Danish wife, of two small children.

Residential buildings, it must be added, do not add much to Canberra's architecture. The government-built houses, though mostly of brick and roofed in red tile, are small, commonplace in look, and not very modern. As in other big Australian cities, the residential areas stretch endlessly, thousands of small suburban houses, each with its garden. Some glassy new apartment buildings are clean-cut and up-to-date, though it must be depressing to live in a place labeled "Block 17, Flats 1 to 9." Housing, as might be expected, is perennially short. Single people may have to stay in government hostels for as long as ten years.

The Australian National University

Canberra is the seat of the nation's major effort in postgraduate research, the Australian National University. Its Institute for Advanced Studies, comparable to Princeton's, is devoted to medicine, biological sciences, chemistry, physical sciences, social sciences, and Pacific studies. The undergraduate School of General Studies deals in the arts, economics, law, science, and Oriental studies. The teaching staff numbers close to three hundred, the students nearly four thousand. Attached to the university are a couple of Roman Catholic schools, Ursula College and John XXIII College. ANU is only adequately housed, having also missed the chance for architectural distinction. But the university is magnificently equipped with laboratories and a huge observatory, and it offers teachers high incentives in pay and freedom. The students, who include a couple of hundred Asians, express their antiestablishmentarianism in routine ways, such as reading lists of Vietnam war casualties.* Apparently they also smoke a lot of pot. Three of the dormitories house both men and women.

The National Library of Australia, equivalent to the Library of Congress, is run by Harold L. White, who upon being interviewed turned out to be a specialist in Americana and an admirer of things American. He spoke of his difficulties in getting across to Australians, even in the academic world, that the United States has authentic civilization and culture. "The British never encouraged the Australians to think that the U.S. is great. In any evaluation of any aspect of U.S. life, like films, the temptation is to say that they are no good." Mr. White also admires the "unparalleled" physical beauty of the U.S., and deplores the way Hollywood films fail to convey it. Like the Library of Congress, the Canberra library gets every book published in the country. It also has a collection on Byzantium in thirty languages, and in the last ten years has acquired 100,000 volumes in Japanese and Chinese. The U.S. collection totals 100,000 books. The library recently bought 12,000 books on Brazil from a Portuguese collector. Mr. White, a short, alert man with gray hair and mustache, was born on the land in Victoria, in the same house as his father and grandfather. He has been national librarian for twenty-two years.

*

What of the rest of the Australian Capital Territory, outside Canberra? It is rich agricultural country, home of 600 horses, 14,000 cattle, and 290,000 sheep. It also grows wheat. But no private person, except on one or two remote freeholds, owns any of the land. The government, in a prudent move in the years after the ACT was laid out, bought the land and lets it out only on lease, even in the case of city lots. The benefits were minimization of speculation, rental profits that helped build the capital, and, most significantly, control over the growth of Canberra. Thus, in contrast to Washington, which swelled to the northwest and left its planned center in

* When students protested the visit of Vice President Spiro Agnew in Canberra early in 1970, the police responded in novel fashion. Two cops would pinion a protestor, a third would hold up a clipboard giving his name and alleged offense, and a fourth would photograph the whole scene.

a corner, Canberra has grown symmetrically out to the planned green belt that surrounds it.

The detached part of the ACT, Jervis Bay, never did become a port. It is now the site of the Royal Australian Naval College and a navy airfield, plus some summer houses and holiday camps.

Standing beside the television tower on Black Mountain in Canberra, one can see what will become of a substantial part of the ACT nearby. Growing up six miles to the southwest, outside the green belt, is the first of Canberra's satellite cities, aimed at accommodating the capital area's eventual growth to perhaps 400,000 people. This is Woden, which presently has a population of 40,000 and will grow, by plan, to 120,000. Six miles to the northwest is the second satellite, Belconnen, which has 12,000 people and will have 120,000. The third, still in the planning stage, will lie south of Woden and be called Tuggeranong. The satellites will contain the government offices in which the residents work; thus are the principles of decentralization being carried out in the Australian Capital Territory. "Canberra is just beginning to receive world recognition for its form of planned development . . . in decentralizing by the use of satellite towns," boasts Roger Johnson, chief architect for the National Capital Development Commission. "It may, in the end, be the one Australian city that will contribute to the solution of those vast problems now faced by every city in the world."

Another striking project for the next few years was described by James Mollison, Director of the National Art Gallery, a long-haired young man on the order of Gregory Peck, with an office in the same building in Canberra as the Prime Minister. This is the Australian National Gallery, to be built by 1975 on the same stretch of lakefront that already holds the library. Mr. Mollison says that Canberra has a large collection of Australian and European painting rarely on view for lack of display space. The new gallery, designed to emphasize huge, flowing internal spaces, will provide eleven exhibition rooms connected by ramps. "Nobody really likes living here, so that the government must provide some of the attractions of the more cosmopolitan centers," said Mr. Mollison. "The National Gallery will be one of them, I hope."

*

Is Canberra a success? There would seem to be three or four ways to measure it. We can guess that it would have been better if Burley Griffin's original plan had been followed to a T. Bureaucrats in the early years forced many modifications on him, but then neither he nor anyone else provided for harmonious and aesthetic public buildings. Brasília is a better job in that respect, and has more flair (indeed, too much flair). Perhaps the comparison is worth pursuing: Canberra took far longer to build and came out smaller (Brasília went up in ten years, and now has 400,000 people). But Brasília is quite shoddy in construction and inhuman in scale; it has high-rise apartments sitting on the vast plain, as compared to Canberra's individual homes. And Canberra really contains the capitol, whereas Brazil is still half-governed from Rio. Another measurement might be against conventional cities. It is indubitably pleasant to get away from neon, filth, clangor, power lines, and fried-chicken joints. As a consequence of such considerations, the judgments about Canberra have been various. Historian Keith Hancock found Canberra "a kind of suburban garden parcelled into plots by a network of paths which have no obvious beginning and no visible end." The Duchess of Kent remarked, "It's just a little country town, isn't it? Charming, of course—but just a little country town." Donald Horne perceived much snobbery; there is a "lot of make-believe in Canberra . . . it looks down on the rest of Australia as crude, self-interested, troublesome, ignorant." It has also been called "a city in search of its soul." But Colin MacInnes found it an "authentic federal center with a high concentration of enterprising brains."

CHAPTER 12

Melbourne and Victoria

This will be the place for the future village.
—JOHN BATMAN, UPON CHOOSING
THE SITE FOR MELBOURNE, JUNE 7, 1835

MELBOURNE DIES every night at 11:30—there's not a cat on the streets. The venerable Melbourne Club, with an atmosphere of leather and dark paneling, is the stuffiest institution in Australia, outdoing Adelaide. Financial power, class consciousness, a legacy of Britishness, above all a sense of authentic tradition somehow inconsistent in a city that aspired to be a village only 137 years ago—these are the radiations from Melbourne. "Is Sir Ian in?"; "Dinner tonight at Sir Colin's"; "Sir Roy will see you at ten": knighthood is still in flower here. The town's favorite newspaper columnist, Barry Humphries, writes: "It's the only place on earth where the visitor from abroad can close his eyes and wonder if there really is life before death."

Driving in and out of the city, one sees miles of indifferent architecture; the suburbs are monotonous; the city plan is a dull gridiron determined by the government surveyor who moved in shortly after Batman, a prosperous Tasmanian pastoralist, did. But leafy parks, sweeping freeways, numerous city-enclosed golf courses, and the absence of slums rescue the defects. *One-fourth* of Melbourne proper is parks. The two main streets, Bourke and Collins—not pretentious Parisian boulevards or grand Washingtonian avenues, but simply broad, straight, parallel, mile-long streets—set a tone of settled satisfaction, of complacent bustle, of mercantile potency. This is the hub of the Australian Establishment.

"Sydney is faced to the Pacific coast of America . . . while Melbourne is faced to Europe, our mother and safest friend," observed R. H. Horne, a nineteenth-century writer. The two cities could not be anything but rivals, disputing one another not only in industry, financial power, political leadership, the arts, and population, but also in living styles. Melbourne is mellowly paced, sedate, English or perhaps Bostonian in tone. Sydney, at least by comparison, is cosmopolitan, glittery, New York-like, exciting. In Sydney people take guests to restaurants and in Melbourne they invite them to dine at home. Each city boasts that its way of entertaining is more sophisticated than the other's.

Melbourne nurtured the art of painting in Australia, and most of the luminaries of recent years live there or at least started there, though Sydney, too, has a strong art colony. Good writers seem to prefer Sydney, but Melbourne has the bulk of the book publishers. Sydney has light and water and some charming old crooked streets; Melbourne has theater and a tradition of providing Australia's foremost politicians. The rivalry is intense, but the two cities share wholeheartedly a belief in the pattern of suburban living.

For all its new corporate office towers, Melbourne emanates a quaint English-Australian gentility. The coatroom at the Windsor Hotel is labeled "Cloaks." A showing of a movie is called a "session." The cab drivers are downright deferential, shutting off meters before arrival, rounding out fares in the customer's favor, expecting no tips and visibly grateful when they get an extra five cents. The fare from downtown Melbourne to the new airport at Tullamarine, ten and one-half miles, runs around $3.40.

The new Southern Cross Hotel, with a lobby as big as an airport, has not only a bell captain, U.S.-style, but also a concierge. In hotels, callers tend to come directly to one's room, as in South Africa, rather than arranging lobby meetings. Newsboys are numerous, and papers cost only four cents.

Melbourne, like all Australian cities, has numberless "hotel" pubs, each with brightly striped damp towels laid on the bar to soak up spilled beer and condensation. They serve a brand of beer called Courage. One can see some truly sodden characters in these places, and blowzy women, too. But the trend is away from "hotels." A couple of more modern Melbourne pubs are the Sentimental Bloke, with an acre and a half of carpet, and the bar in the TraveLodge, with seventeen miniskirted waitresses all less than twenty years old. These places play Muzak and cater to women as much as to men.

Dining in Melbourne is a satisfactory experience, by and large—with the accent on the large. Portions are dismayingly big. There are twenty-seven good international restaurants—Ceylon curries, New York cuts, rigatoni, lobster, German dishes, and "natural" oysters served with little dark bread-

and-butter sandwiches—in the center of the city, and many others in the residential areas. Liquor restrictions have come tumbling down in recent years, and most restaurants serve cocktails, wine, and brandy as freely as in Manhattan. If you want to pour yourself a nightcap in your hotel room, any pub will sell you a bottle of good Australian brandy for $3.05.

Shops offer women's coats of suedelike kangaroo skin for around two hundred dollars. In the Army and Navy stores one can still buy digger hats, brim turned up on one side. In St. Kilda, a beachside amusement center reachable on a rickety tram from downtown Melbourne, a long row of delicatessens and shops display marzipans, Black Forest sponge cakes, fruit, and fish; the Melbourne-edited newspapers, in Magyar, Yugoslav, and German, sold in these stores testify to the big colonies of New Australians here. Melbourne abounds in bookshops.

The Melbourne police are said to be the best in Australia; from chief to the lowest cop on the beat they wear made-to-measure uniforms. Yet discipline is somewhat lax in this place where jobs are so plentiful; it is infeasible, for example, to forbid a cop to smoke on duty, and he does. As elsewhere in this country, cops suffer from the Australians' antiauthority complex. John Pringle relates that "a few years ago a New Australian—a young Yugoslav—rescued a Melbourne policeman from the death grip of a certified lunatic while a crowd of Old Australians stood by cheering the lunatic." The police have some problems easily recognizable in the U.S.; on July 4, 1968, two thousand Melbourne University students, protesting the Vietnam war, stoned the American Consulate in Melbourne and broke every single window.

More Melbourne sights and sounds: The label "P" on a car means probationary; a new driver must display it for a year. At the airport (as in Canberra) there are doors labeled "Men," "Women," "Mothers," and "Disabled"—the facility for the latter contains a trapeze with which persons in wheelchairs can maneuver. Most all of them have showers. The presence of the New Australian is much in evidence—driving around, one is suddenly in a community that is all Italian, or all Greek. Collins Street, the Golden Mile, is the downtown finance center, and it smells of crisp banknotes. One buys tickets for Tatersall's Lottery, drawn three times a week, at a big storefront on Flinders Street. On the fringes of the city, the good Colonel Sanders, with his Kentucky Fried Chicken, is present, as everywhere in Australia. The older suburban trains, part of a vast system, might be at home in Birmingham: English-style compartments, doors on each side, green leatherette and worn wood. One also sees, as in Sydney, wrought-iron balconies on many of the older houses; once thought to be Victorian junk, these railings are now prized and preserved as antiques.

A High-Speed History

Destiny seems to have preserved Melbourne from discovery and settlement until the time was ripe; had Captain Cook been able to visit the site of Melbourne and compare it with Sydney, he might well have opted for Melbourne and its rich surrounding land. When Melbourne was belatedly settled, it proved its advantages and grew at high speed from village in 1835 to a powerful city of the world in the 1880's.

Port Phillip Bay, forty miles of almost completely enclosed water on Australia's southeastern bulge, was first entered by the English in 1802. In 1803 Sydney sent out Lieutenant Colonel David Collins with three hundred convicts and a Church of England chaplain, to found a settlement. Collins scarcely bothered to look for a good site, and quickly begged permission to withdraw to Tasmania. Thus Melbourne had a thirty-year respite from occupation and was spared from having many convicts as settlers.* On that questionable basis Collins ultimately earned the honor of having a Melbourne street named for him. Explorers coming overland from Sydney in the 1820's and early 1830's discovered the size and fertility of the Murray River plain, and described grazing land in western Victoria so rich that it was dubbed "Australia Felix."

On the strength of these reports John Batman, the Tasmanian pastoralist, made a deal with the Aborigines at Port Phillip Bay: he acquired 600,000 acres of land in return for a yearly payment of one hundred blankets, fifty knives, fifty tomahawks, fifty pairs of scissors, fifty looking glasses, twenty suits of clothing, and two tons of flour. With Batman came an extraordinary man named John Pasco Fawkner, a convict's son and bookseller in Launceston, Tasmania, who brought fruit trees, seeds, and implements, and soon thereafter opened a hotel that had not a pub but an encyclopedia as its chief attraction. Governor Richard Bourke in Sydney denounced Batman and Fawkner for trespassing on Crown property, but lacked the troops to force them out. And so he capitulated, and named the village they had founded after Lord Melbourne, British Prime Minister of the time. By 1840 the area had eight thousand people and one million sheep, and Charles Joseph La Trobe, appointed by Bourke, governed from a small timber house, still standing in the Domain.

* One convict, by the name of William Buckley, escaped from Collins and stayed at Port Phillip, living among the Aborigines, until the place was finally settled—a feat so unlikely that Australians to this day say that to have a slim chance is "to have Buckley's."

Victoria won separation from New South Wales in 1851, by an act of Parliament, and became a colony with a Legislative Council. Propitiously, gold was found the same year: the colony had offered a reward to anyone who could discover gold, and strikes followed soon after at Ballarat and Bendigo. Melbourne flourished as miners poured in from the world, including American forty-niners who gave the name California Gully to a stream bed near Bendigo. Chinese came too, soon comprising one out of every seven males. American Southerners led parties to lynch the Chinese, and a lot of race prejudice rubbed off onto Australians in the process. Some miners got so rich that before they called for drinks for the crowd at Melbourne pubs they cleared the bar by sweeping off the glasses with their whips, and had it washed down with wine. In 1853 an American entrepreneur sold ice from Boston at fifty cents a pound. Bourke Street, which had had sheep grazing on it in 1845, looked like a London thoroughfare eleven years later. Melbourne passed Sydney in size, growing from 87,345 in 1851 to 540,322 in 1861. At one point there were 187 men for every 100 women in Victoria. So short was labor that La Trobe, by then Governor of the colony, had to groom his own horse.

When the gold diminished, land dealing took over to keep the boom going. A "selection" (homestead) act made millions of acres of good Victorian land available to farmers. However, the graziers already there wanted to keep their vast sheep runs, and did their best to frustrate the intent of the act by creating dummy homesteads and buying up the homesteads of others. Building trades got the eight-hour day in 1856 (in England, the battle to get it continued until after World War I). Melbourne was a world wonder of growth and prosperity. "There is perhaps no town in the world in which the ordinary working man can do better for himself than he can in Melbourne," wrote Anthony Trollope after a visit. Free, compulsory education was begun in 1872. The Melbourne international exhibition in 1880 attracted more than a million visitors, and its awards are still celebrated on the labels of various champagnes and beers. Based on all this optimism, British capital gushed in, feeding a great land-speculation boom. Twelve-story buildings, among the world's tallest, went up; beturreted, movie-set mansions rose along St. Kilda Road.

Then it all went to hell. A widespread strike in 1890, provoked by Melbourne capitalists to break the power of labor, brought months of turmoil and wrecked the unions for years. After that came a drought, then failures by overdrawn businessmen, followed by the collapse of land values, and finally the downfall of overextended banks that had lent money against land. Victoria suffered hysteria, depression, and unemployment. The resulting disillusionment and trauma lasted a generation, and forced Melbourne thereafter to share its financial dominance with Sydney. The comeback, based partly on the great lead-zinc-silver mine at Broken Hill and partly on farming expansion, was slow. Ultimately, a quieter prosperity returned.

Strangely, or perhaps fittingly, the excitement of Melbourne's history died in the 1893 bust. Its twentieth-century story is one of unspectacular growth. A big event seems to have been the Centenary Celebration in 1935, with a London-Melbourne air race (winning time: 70 hours and 54 minutes). In 1942 General Douglas MacArthur, having escaped Corregidor in a torpedo boat and flown to Darwin and Alice Springs, entrained for Melbourne and was met by thousands; on April 18, taking command of the Pacific war, he issued General Order No. 1 from Melbourne. In 1956 Melbourne staged the XVI Olympics with much aplomb in a huge new stadium, now the Cricket Ground. And in 1966 Victoria, dropping her Victorian ways, put an end to the "six o'clock swill," the traditional hour of prodigious beer-drinking between office- and factory-closing time, five-o'clock, and pub-closing time, six. Most pubs now stay open until ten.

*

As he lived, let him die! a base wretch
without feeling:
A bushel of quicklime is all that he's worth!
—VERSE IN THE Bulletin, 1880

Here let us move back a couple of decades in time, and examine a man, more myth than flesh, who to this day affects the Australian consciousness in those places where guilt, rebellion, and pride reside. He is the great Victorian highwayman, the best remembered and most-balladed Australian of them all, Ned Kelly.

Kelly was a bushranger, an outlaw of a kind that flourished in the first half of the nineteenth century, usually escaped convicts who took to the bush and robbed travelers and isolated homesteads. After the gold rush, bushranging became prevalent in the northeastern corner of Victoria. It combined crime with romance, choosing rich English pastoralists for targets. Bushrangers became heroes to the small, mostly Irish selectors (or homesteaders), whose land was being taken away from them, in one way or another, by the richer pastoralists. The police and the government sided with the rich, as they have been known to do before and since in history. Kelly's mother, widow of an Irish dairy farmer, was a selector; so was her father. Ned, born in 1855, began tangling with the pastoralists at fifteen. He "borrowed" a horse, clobbered its protesting owner, and sent the man's wife a package of calf's testicles as a measure of his irrational resentment. By eighteen, Ned had done almost three years in prison for horse-stealing. He became a prospector for a couple of years after that, although cattle tended to disappear from whatever neighborhood he was in, and he was adept at rebranding horses. The police issued a warrant for his arrest, and Ned went into hiding. Meanwhile there was a warrant out for Ned's brother Dan, also a cattle-duffer (Australian for rustler). A drunken constable tried to arrest Dan, failed, and to cover his alcoholic disgrace invented a yarn about being attacked that led to the imprisonment of Ned's mother (who had eleven other children) for three years. This was authentic injustice. Ned conceived a powerful hatred of the police—"a parcel," he wrote, "of big ugly fat-necked wombat headed big bellied magpie legged narrow hipped splay-footed sons of Irish bailiffs or English landlords." Ned and his brother recruited two of Dan's friends, Steve Hart and Joe Byrne, and formed a gang —a gang imbued from the beginning with a Bonnie and Clyde kind of doom.

In October 1878, at Stringybark Creek, Ned and Dan attacked a camp of four policemen sent out to find the Kelly gang, and killed two of them. A third was badly wounded; Ned thought for a long time, then shot him through the heart. "I put his cloak over him and left him as well as I could and were they my own brothers I couldn't have been more sorry for them," Ned later reported. After these killings Victoria panicked. The state Parliament passed a Felons Apprehension Act entitling anyone to kill the members of the Kelly gang on sight. The gang responded, late in 1878, by sticking up a bank in the town of Euroa, eighty miles northeast of Melbourne. Next year they moved across the border of New South Wales and held a whole town at bay for two days before robbing the bank. An anonymous ballad gives the flavor of the event and the times:

They mustered up the servants and locked them in a room,
Saying "Do as we command you, or death will be your doom."
The Chinaman cook "no savvied," his face was full of fear,
But Ned soon made him savvy with a straight left to the ear.

But as the police closed in with ever bigger forces, Ned seemed to know that he was doomed. His resolve to die hard took a weird form. With stolen plow moldboards blacksmithed over a fire in the bush, he and his gang constructed jerry-rigged armor—curved body plates held together with thongs, and for head protection a cylinder with an eye slit. The final shootout came when the gang seized a town called Glenrowan, ruling it from the hotel. Policemen in large numbers laid siege. Ned, with a high sense of tragedy, came out of the hotel in his armor, firing, and was shot in the legs. The cops managed to hit and kill Byrne, then set fire to the hotel, thus burning Dan Kelly and Steve Hart to death.

Sir Redomand Barry, the same judge who had earlier convicted Ned's mother, was assigned to try Ned. "Edward Kelly," he said, "I hereby sentence you to death by hanging. May the Lord have mercy on your soul." Replied Ned stoutly, "Yes, I will meet you there." *Both* men died a fortnight later, the judge naturally and Ned with a rope around his neck. His last words were: "Such is life."

This whole story speaks with a profound eloquence to Australians; Ned Kelly means more to them than Jesse James or Billy the Kid do to Americans. An obvious element in the appeal of the legend is the Robin Hood quality (Kelly would not steal from those who worked hard for little money). It also expressed the resentment of ordinary, hard-working people against a political and social Establishment from which they were excluded. Kelly, as Alan Moorehead notes, made his war on the government, not on individuals.

A disturbing evocation of the legend comes from painter Sidney Nolan, in a series of scenes from Kelly's life. Kelly, though he wore his armor but once in action, is shown only as a symbol, a black rectangle with a slit through which peer, in most of the paintings, a pair of eyes. Through all the paintings looms a feeling of the terror and beauty of the land, and an intimation that Ned Kelly somehow deserved more than a bushel of quicklime.

Megalopolitan Melbourne

In sheer area, Melbourne is one of the biggest cities in the world, measuring 800 square miles in its metropolitan area, as compared to 458 square miles for the American monstrosity, Los Angeles, and 670 square miles for that other Australian overgrowth, Sydney. The population is 2.5 million, half a million short of Sydney and comparable to metropolitan Montreal. Two-thirds of the people of Victoria live in Melbourne. The distance to Sydney is only 440 miles in a straight line, but the distance to Perth is greater than that between London and Moscow. The reasons for its site and growth are twofold: the Port Phillip Bay area is the only place for a port in a thousand miles of coastline, and, lying just south of the Kilmore gap in the Great Dividing Range, it has access to the rich hinterlands of the Murray Valley. As a port, Melbourne has 109 berths and 12 miles of berthage in an area of 20 square miles, all now somewhat handicapped by a newly important limitation. The depth of water over the rock bottom at Port Phillip Bay heads is only 38 feet, not enough for the new ocean leviathans.

*

Visitor: "Does it snow here?"

Cab driver: "Once or twice it has done."

Midsummer (January) temperature *averages* 67.6 degrees Fahrenheit; in winter (July) the average is 48.9 degrees. The sun shines an average of 5.7 hours a day, which is none too much. Melbourne has the makings for smog —factories and cars—and sometimes a great menacing cloud of polluted air hangs over the city, but strong Antarctic winds tend to blow it away. The same winds can also drop the temperature from perhaps 90 degrees in the morning to maybe 55 degrees in the afternoon.

The constructions of man in Melbourne can be both colossal, such as the terra-cotta and gray Cricket Ground capable of seating nearly one percent of the population of Australia,* and flimsy, such as a freeway bridge being built over the Yarra that collapsed late in 1970, killing thirty-five workmen (a post-mortem of the disaster said that the British designers "seemed to have worked largely from intuition"). The Royal Melbourne Hospital, seven hundred beds, is where the first casualties of the Pacific War were brought in the early 1940's. Audiences of as many as seventy thousand hear concerts at the Sidney Myer Music Bowl, an amazing canopy that appears to float above the orchestra. The cavernous new airport at Tullamarine, finished in mid-1970, is Melbourne's way of squeezing out of a humiliating bind; until it opened, Sydney handled big jets on international flights. One more thing must be said about buildings in Melbourne: banks very nearly dominate the scene. The telephone book lists about thirteen hundred banks and branches in the city.

The Royal Botanic Gardens doubtless merit Sir Arthur Conan Doyle's accolade, "the most beautiful place I have ever seen," but one intriguing aspect of them is less horticultural than historical. That is the commemorative trees, ninety-five in all, planted by personages whose names evoke more than a century of time. Among them are Charles La Trobe, Prince Albert, Nellie Melba, Lord Tennyson, Paderewski, Viscount Kitchener, Viscount Jellicoe, the Queen of Tonga, Harold Macmillan, John Diefenbaker, the Duke of Edinburgh, and the King of Thailand. The great asset of the garden —one of three in the world entitled to the adjective "Royal"—is the climate. With no frost, nearly any kind of tree, tropical or temperate, will grow. The

* That is, 120,000; but a new stadium being built is to hold 157,000, surpassing what is presently said to be the world's biggest, Rio de Janeiro's Maracanã.

soil is fertile and the rainfall is a reliable two inches a month the year round. There are five greenhouses ("glass houses" in Australian), where tropical plants are propagated, and exhibited. Three lakes grow water lilies and accommodate water birds, including black swans. It is *de rigueur* in the garden to visit the Separation Tree, an ancient eucalyptus under which the citizenry of Melbourne celebrated their authorization in 1950 to break away from New South Wales.

A comment about suburban sprawl. Obviously, Melbourne has it bad. The typical family here occupies eight times more living space than a London family. Once beyond the fashionable inner suburbs, like Toorak, one sees little but brick and red roof tiles for miles. A man's home is his castle in Australia, and there are hundreds of thousands of castles. Plainly, this is a better way to live than in some city tenement; rose gardens abound in testimony to pride of ownership and contentment. "All a Melburnian wants is a cream-brick triple-front* with a two-tone lawnmower," says one university professor. But no one can drive through, or even fly over, these suburbs —Cheltenham, Moorabbin, Glenhuntly, Alamein, Deepdene, Yarraville, Murrumbeena, and 190 others—without concluding that the place is overextended. It is clear that the old city cannot spread any farther without a new city being founded.

The Benign Hinterlands

The Victorian countryside does not partake of the terrible aridity of the great outback that starts at Victoria's northern and western borders and extends for 1,200 miles north and west. Only a bit smaller than Western Germany, Victoria (87,884 square miles) is Australia's smallest state, apart from the island-state Tasmania. Twenty-five inches of rain (versus the national average of 16½) fall every year on a generally fertile soil. With 3.5 million people, 27 percent of all Australians, Victoria is the most densely settled state. It is also the most industrialized. It produces citrus and other fruit, grain, dairy products, and the country's best wool.

And yet Victoria does summon up the essential down-under, as dozens of painters have proved by their obsession with it. The Murray River, which forms its northern border, is completely controlled by dams, weirs, and locks, so that it is leveled out in steps and navigable by steamers (mainly excursion ships nowadays, but once vital transportation). The river thus provides irrigation, which is the secret of the valley's prosperity. In some places, a pumping system devised in the last century by two brothers from California

* A common style of Melbourne house architecture divides the front into three planes, set back one after another, like stairs tipped over on their side.

reinforces the dams. This water and the natural countryside combine to give the land its productive look. On one hand are vineyards, wheatfields, fat sheep, orange groves, and tan-brick farmhouses with television antennas. On the other hand are plains dotted with melancholy eucalyptuses. This is haunting country.

The natives burst with pride over the Murray Valley. Camping and "caravaning" (touring with a house trailer) are popular here, and the campgrounds offer all amenities. The highways are plentiful and as well paved as, say, West Virginia's. An American tourist experiences the familiar sight of numerous motels. But these places do have some un-American graces. Rooms at the Sanctuary Park Motel in Wodonga are fitted with "breakfast hatches" —small doors through which the management pushes the breakfast that the guests ordered the night before (grilled steak and eggs, thirty cents extra). Little cafés in the area are oddly meticulous about pricing: tomato soup sixteen cents, a single crumpet twenty-three cents, tea thirteen cents, fruit juice seventeen cents.

Victoria's second city, Geelong, is only one-twentieth as big as Melbourne, and being only forty-five miles away will probably join the capital in a big conurbation soon. It is an industrial center (wool and cars), port (wool, wheat, and oil), and home of a splendid boys school, Geelong Grammar. Prince Charles was sent there for a year. Ballarat, third among Victorian cities, establishes once again the point that the bulk of the Australians live in their coastal capitals: it is, with only sixty thousand people, the *second*-biggest inland city in the nation, after Canberra. Ballarat is a gold-rush town that managed to come through the bursting of that bubble without the ugliness attending such towns in the American West, for it has begonia-filled parks, good schools, and a passable art gallery. To the west is basaltic land that grows wheat and Geelong wool, the setting where in the last century farmers and graziers did their elegant best to ape the English landed gentry.

Bendigo, population 45,000, is similar; when the mines—the Golden Square, the Extended Rustlers—shut down, the town turned itself into a place for retired people. It also has an ordnance factory with a big gear-cutting plant. It is ornate, Victorian, beflowered, substantial; its park features a lush fernery and its art gallery a collection of French Impressionists. The director, John Henderson, likes to tell of putting himself out to escort a New Australian around the museum a few years ago, struggling to communicate despite the immigrant's Slavic accent and faulty comprehension. Turned out the fellow was second secretary in the Soviet Embassy in Canberra.

A Melburnian idea of a lark is to go to see the penguins. These flightless birds, a foot high and formally dressed, live on Phillip Island, along the coast, and by day swim out to sea in search of food for their young. Nightly, at a certain moment—Phillip Island natives can predict it with great accuracy—a wave washes up and deposits perhaps ten or fifty or one hundred penguins. They rest a moment, tired from their long swim, and then march up the beach to their burrows. Subsequent waves bring similar groups. Incidentally, the penguins' feathers are glazed so well that the birds land perfectly dry. At the burrows, they disgorge partly disgested fish and plankton into the beaks of their young, who look like balls of fluff. Besides the penguin rookery, Phillip Island also has hundreds of easily visible koalas.

More Victoriana: Healsville, near Melbourne, has a wild-life sanctuary where visitors can walk among emus and kangaroos and see the playful platypus swimming in a glass tank. Gippsland, the eastern end of Victoria, has a Ninety Mile Beach on a spit that encloses charming and little-exploited lakes; the town of Sale, here, supplies the offshore oil drilling platforms in Bass Strait and has grown in population from six to ten thousand, including many Americans. There are fast-growing towns situated on Western Port Bay, an inlet of Bass Strait, which will be able to dock big, new, deep-draft ships, which cannot get to Geelong or Melbourne. Nearby French Island is to be the site of a giant petrochemical complex. By contrast, a town doomed to disappear is Yallourn; it stands ill-situated on the deposit of brown coal (lignite), thirty miles long and five to ten miles wide, which is mined to run generators that supply 70 percent of Melbourne's electricity. Finally, the railroads through all this part of the country run on broad gauge (5 feet 3 inches) except one, the line to Sydney, which is standard gauge (4 feet 8½ inches). Until this standard-gauge track was pushed through in 1962, passengers had to change trains at the border of New South Wales.

An Alluring Gallery of Art

In his office on St. Kilda Road, part of what used to be a mansion and now sprouts drawing boards on every side, Sir Roy Grounds draws the window shade. He does not do so for privacy, or to keep out the sun, but to reveal a paper with a table of figures on it, taped to the back of the shade. "On March 15, 1977, at noon, *noon*," he says, tapping the timetable, "the Melbourne Performing Arts Center will open."

Sir Roy, who is the architect for the Center, predicted in December 1960 that Melbourne's National Art Gallery, also his work, would open on August 20, 1968. It did.

The gallery and the performing-arts halls are really Phase One and Phase Two of the same project, the Victorian Arts Center; architecturally, they will form a harmonious whole. There is about them little of the rash daring of Utzon's sculptural opera house in Sydney, but they do incorporate some strikingly unconventional concepts. The concert halls, to cite an example, will be far underground.

The National Gallery, long since in use, is all blue basalt stone and water. In form it is a parallelepiped, 200 feet wide, 500 feet long, and 52 feet high. A moat surrounds and reflects it, with a simple bridge crossing to the round-arch entrance. One turns to either side to enter the building, for the arch has an inner wall made of a huge hanging sheet of plate glass with water running down the outside to create a waterfall blur. Light for the interior comes from clerestory eaves, rooflights, and three large courts. One court resembles a balconied Elizabethan theater. The center court is a sculpture garden, with works by Rodin and Henry Moore. The third contains fountains that shoot icicle-like jets up at an angle, chords of water that curve into parabolas and break up glittering as they fall. A Great Hall for civic gatherings goes the full height of the building; slender, tapering steel columns hold up a roof of stained glass designed by Leonard French.

The interior is carpeted in gold and fitted with easy chairs of a comfort perhaps never before felt in a museum. Such seduction is strictly intentional. Sir Roy says that the gallery was "not built for esoteric art lovers, but for people who had never been in a gallery." He has in mind the likes of the New Australian laborers who built the museum. "I used to talk to the men on the job, Yugoslavs, Italians, Greeks; they could hardly speak English. I'd say, 'This is being built for you and your wife and kids. I'm trying to get a bloody good job.' "

From St. Kilda Road, on which the gallery fronts, the Performing Arts Center will appear to be a street-level plaza north of the gallery, out of which will rise a 430-foot spire, a sort of cone tapering into a needle. An opera-ballet theater, a playhouse, and an experimental theater will nest under the plaza, to a depth of 115 feet below street level. Construction, which began in 1971, required sinking a sort of cofferdam down to bedrock and then excavating the enclosed mud and gravel to create ten million cubic feet of space for the theaters. This job proved so expensive that Sir Roy was forced to lop one entire concert hall out of the plan. A curious engineering complexity is that in order to keep the structure from floating up through the surrounding mud, it will have to be anchored to the bedrock. The advantages will be acoustical and thermal insulation.

An Animated University

A professor at Australian National University reported a few years ago that of 366 directors and executives of business firms surveyed by him a full 17 percent had attended Melbourne Grammar School. Private schools still count heavily in Victoria; a "Grammar old boy's tie" will take a man a long way. Playing Harvard to this Groton is the University of Melbourne, a public institution like all universities in Australia, but duly venerable, having been set into motion by a twenty-three-year-old chap from Trinity College, Oxford, in 1853. With twenty thousand students on a campus packed with buildings cheek-by-jowl, Melbourne University is badly overcrowded. It is a strong research school. Conversely, a university still growing up is La Trobe, opened in 1967, with one thousand students now and ten thousand anticipated by 1976. The liveliest place, though, is Monash University, founded a decade ago and now enrolling ten thousand students.

The school is named for Sir John Monash, a very admirable Victorian. After taking degrees in arts, law, and engineering at the University of Melbourne, he went into the army and ultimately became commander of the five Australian divisions that fought along the Somme in 1917 and 1918. After the war he took charge of the Victoria State Electricity Commission, at that time opposed by private enterprise as a form of socialism, and opened up the brown coal deposits at Yallourn that now supply Victoria with most of its power.

The university was created from the ground up in three years, 1958–1961. It started out to be a science and technology school, but now has arts, education, economics and politics, medicine and law, as well as science and engineering. Lunch at the Faculty Club—which, in accordance with Australian ideas of democracy, is open to the school's gardeners and janitors as well as its teachers—can be a lively experience. Cocktails and wine are served, hardly the custom at most American universities, and the talk, which is apt to go on until 3:30 in the afternoon, is provocative. The students are lively, too, and they keep stodgy Melbourne in an uproar. One Maundy Thursday they set the city on its ear by staging a mock crucifixion. They have participated in most of the causes favored by radical American students in recent years—sending aid to the Vietcong, for example, marching on Moratorium Day, sleeping-in at the Student Union building in protest to war-industry recruiting on campus, and, last but not least, howling about inadequate space on campus to park their cars.

Some complaints students voiced in a round-table interview were: "The welfare system is no good—they promise free hospitals and then they meet you at the door shaking a can." "The Aborigines in this country live in slavery, working as stockmen two hundred miles from their homes, riding sunup to sundown for bully beef, bread, and tea, and getting paid only once a year." "We are worried because of the trend to the American way of life. There are lots of aspects of America that we don't want transplanted here." Many observers note, however, that in their very complaints Australian students copy Americans.

The dominating building on the campus is the Robert Menzies School of Humanities, nicknamed "The Ming Wing" because some Australians still give Menzies the Scottish pronunciation of "Ming-us." The former Prime Minister's cousin, Sir Douglas Menzies, is chancellor of the university, but the operating president of Monash, as at all Australian universities, is the vice chancellor, J. A. L. Matheson. A civil engineer, he built the school from scratch, but now finds the office burdensome in the same way that American college presidents do. Some of the students are tough Maoists, some are on hard drugs, and Matheson is known to be worried that public reaction to the school's extremists might conceivably force it to close.

Monash students call the University of Melbourne "The Shop." Melbourne students call the University of Monash "The Farm."

A Gallery of Victorians

Victoria's conservative political coloration is felicitously embodied in its Premier, Sir Henry Bolte, a Liberal. He is a solid man with a cannonball head and hands the shape of a spade. Country-born in Victoria, in 1908, he grazes four thousand sheep on an eleven-hundred-acre property, owns and races horses, goes off shooting, and plays golf. It is said that he got into politics because friends were pressing him to enter public life and on the third Scotch he agreed. He has been Premier more than fifteen years. "This is a sovereign state. I am Her Majesty's Premier." He is proud of being the founder of Monash University, but his own formal education ended with graduation from the Church of England Grammar School in Ballarat.

Sir Henry accepts wholeheartedly the principle that foreign investment is vital to Victoria, and encourages it with tax incentives, advice, and assistance. He often goes abroad (seven times to the United States so far) on "Promote Victoria" missions. The results are a spate of new industry, new reservoirs, new dams, new ports, new oil and gas fields offshore in Bass Strait, increased production of electricity. The Premier boasts that Victoria's industries are the country's most modern, so that its wages are higher and savings are far greater per capita. He argues that Melbourne still leads Sydney as a financial power, having the head offices of every bank but one, the head offices of most insurance companies, and the ability to float big stock and bond issues. Bolte is quite aware that Australian premiers have much more power than American governors, and he uses his to the fullest. He must contend for conservative votes with the Country Party and the breakoff Democratic Labor

Party, but managed in the 1969 election to hold his own against an anti-Liberal trend that cost the party votes in every other state. The ministers who assemble around the huge round blackwood cabinet table (14½ feet in diameter, standing on a single steel pedestal) in the Premier's office are all Liberals—no coalition here. Sir Henry, though he swears like a trooper, is as conservative in morals as he is in politics, a powerhouse of Victorian wowserism. "I am as opposed to the legalizing of homosexuality as I am to the introducing of poker [slot] machines," he said in 1970.

*

Gray, lean, swift-talking: such is Sir Ian Potter, who aspired to be a university professor but instead founded one of Melbourne's biggest stock brokerages and now diligently attends to the cultural life of Melbourne and Australia. Australians dote on saving money; Sir Ian says that 28 percent of the national income goes into savings. Everyone has a savings account, but millions of Australians are investors, too, from "penny tremblers"—small speculators—on up. Potter still talks knowledgeably about business; he knows the mining industry well; but his chief interests now are Monash University (he is chairman of the finance committee), the Performing Arts Center (he is a member of the building committee), the Elizabethan Theatre Trust (he is chairman), and Australian opera, ballet, and symphony (he helped send the latter two on recent tours of the U.S.). And, sitting in skyscraper offices carpeted in pepper-and-salt Australian wool, he ponders the nation's problems. How big should Australia be? "When I was young, the parameters suggested ten million. Now I say fifty million. And that's enough. But we cannot bring in more immigrants than a number just about equal to one percent of the population each year, which added to the one and three-quarters percent natural increase will get us to about twenty-five million in the year 2000."

*

A Victorian who holds that pretty much everything is wrong with the picture painted by Bolte is James Ford Cairns, a Labor Member of the federal House of Representatives from the town of Lalor (named for the leader of the rebels at the Eureka Stockade). Cairns holds a Ph.D. in commerce (economic history) from the University of Melbourne, doing a thesis on the welfare state in Australia. He then taught there ten years. He went into politics "to put into practice what I had learned." He early made himself leader of the opposition to the Vietnam war, and later wrote a history of Western intervention in Vietnam since 1847. He proposes "a searching re-examination of our foreign relations, and particularly those with the United States. We must cease to be military camp followers, if we are to have a chance of building a better society in Australia." Cairns is the last remove from a firebrand—he is slow, deliberate, well built, blondish, and youthful, and has fine strong hands. But he talks a toughly critical line. "We have swallowed the myth that this is an egalitarian society, but it isn't. The difference between the wealthiest Australians today and the poorest is greater than it was in the 1930's." On foreign investment: "We are probably paying too much for our development. The country is like a puppy lying on its back, having its tummy tickled."

Cairns occupies a position in Australian politics comparable to that of Eugene McCarthy in American politics, with a similarly small chance of attaining the highest office, though Cairns does not shrink so moodily from power. He has an affinity for youth, and they for him. Cairns perceives the young in Australia as differing more from the Establishment than any recent generation, but in a moral rather than a doctrinaire way. He sympathizes with youth's complaints about the state of education, holding that schools are largely mere purveyors of collections of facts, aimed at ensuring equality but achieving only uniformity. On the subject of race, he says: "We ought to have more colored people," and observes that the "majority of people under thirty-five" oppose white supremacy. Discrimination against Aborigines, he notes, is much stronger in the countryside than in the cities, and is rooted in a white-purity, fear-of-contamination complex. The whites scrub themselves constantly, change their white shirts frequently, and keep Aborigines out of rural hotels and swimming pools because "they're dirty."

*

One Melburnian who proves that a single man can change history is B. A. Santamaria, a dapper, semibald man of sharp intellect, systematized and logical. The son of immigrants from an island near Stromboli, Italy, Santamaria went through law school at the University of Melbourne. In 1942, alarmed at the strength of Communism among labor unions in wartime Australia, he started a clandestine movement, mostly comprised of Roman Catholics, to break Communist power by creating cells to oppose the Communist cells. He succeeded beyond expectation, gathering such a constituency that the Australian Labor Party split and has never since been able to elect a national government. Now the Democratic Labor Party holds the balance of power in many elections, and Santamaria is the eminence behind it.

Though conservative, Santamaria shares Jim Cairns' doubts over the inflow of private capital. He wonders whether foreign investment amounts to "selling out to compensate for our lack of ability to export. We can't live by tapping our bank account forever." On White Australia he says: "We don't want an immigration policy on a racial basis, but we don't want to get into the same situation as Great Britain. We want a unitary national community with a sense of identity." To Santamaria this means that Australia must carefully control the number of incoming Asians, and keep a sharp eye out for their assimilability; Filipinos, he says, are "easy to assimilate, Indians impossible." The Japanese? "People haven't forgotten the war."

On defense, he holds that Australia needs the United States as a friend, but that "there is no such thing as an automatic friend. If you're strong, you have friends; if you're weak, you don't. Client states are treated as client states—which means that they are occasionally flattered, more generally ignored, and not infrequently betrayed." National security is what preoccupies Santamaria most. "Someday the United States will withdraw from this area. China is a problem. The Soviet Union will be a major Indian Ocean power in five years. The Japanese, a major economic power already, will be a major political power. Neutrality is not for us—we can arm, and we should start now. Also, we should have an alliance with Indonesia. Australia can defend itself for less than 7 percent of its Gross National Product—a nation not willing to spend that doesn't deserve to live. But we are," he concludes, "a nation of lotus eaters."

CHAPTER 13

Inside Tasmania

Methinks I see Australian landscapes still,
But softer beauty sits on every hill.
—KIRK HERVEY, DESCRIBING TASMANIA IN 1825

HERE IS A STATE all out of scale, and all out of context, with the rest of Australia. A dab of an island lying 125 miles south of the continent, Tasmania is green, tidy, well watered and well tended, mountainous and sundered by gorges. You can drive from anywhere to anywhere in it, and back, in a day. The sensation, upon flying in from the continent, is like arriving in Costa Rica—all dimensions appear to have shrunk. The railroad seems a toy, with its narrow gauge and 588 miles of track.

The longest east-west distance in Tasmania is 190 miles, and the longest north-south distance is 180 miles; the whole area, including nearby islands within the jurisdiction, measures only 26,215 square miles, about equal to Scotland or West Virginia. This heart-shaped island lies just as far south of the Equator as New York lies north of it. To the west there is nothing but ocean as far as Patagonia.

The people, who number barely 400,000, like to be called Tasmanians rather than Australians, and refer to the rest of Australia as "the mainland." Like Victoria in British Columbia, Tasmania likes to think of itself as "this other England"—a salute, in this case, to its white stone cottages, winding lanes, hawthorn hedgerows, Wordsworthian daffodils, Georgian architecture, and stout British stock. But the British Admiralty Hydrographic Department describes Tasmania as "the most thoroughly mountainous island in the world," so this terrain bears little resemblance to Old England. Equally un-English are the forests of gum trees that cover half the state.

Tasmanians fuss over issues like these: Should the state permit wine bars and night clubs? How much should trucks pay for the use of the roads? Should *Playboy* be banned? (It sometimes is.) There's a slightly archaic air to some of these concerns, and this feeling of being stuck in the past comes on strong at the Legislative Council, one of the more conservative remnants of Australia's colonial period. Its mid-Victorian chambers in Hobart, the capital, are fitted with red-plush chaise longues, a blue arched ceiling, and a full-length portrait of Queen Elizabeth. The quaint qualifications required of voters for elections to this upper house are: minimum age of twenty-five years, ownership (or leasehold) of property, and either membership in a profession or a record of service in the armed forces. Actually, this venerable institution is powerless except to hold up legislation, and its prestige may have been diminished last year when one member was arrested for shoplifting. The authentic lawmaking body is the democratically elected House of Assembly.

This picture of fustiness does not by any means hold true for all of Tasmanian society. Farming methods are modern—apples, for instance, are picked by machine and never touched by a human hand until the buyer takes them from the store in some land across the seas. The motels and hotels are generally more up-to-date than the rest of Australia. Education uses an advanced, think-for-yourself approach in its independent matriculation colleges, where high school graduates study a year before entering universities. But the University of Tasmania, where most of them enter, is, with 2,500 students, too small for the state's needs, although it has a full complement of schools, including law and medicine. It is, one professor explains, halfway between the British and American patterns—not as elitist as in Britain, not as broad as in the United States. All the Australian state universities, incidentally, are in effect campuses of a single national university, since federal support imposes standards, salaries, and uniformity.

Tasmania is the state where the convict heritage looms largest; between 1803 and 1854 it received seventy thousand prisoners, as many as New South Wales, but into a much smaller area. The state's attitude to this background is still typically ambivalent. Most Tasmanians would rather not mention that grandfather or great-grandfather was a convict, even though this is the case with a dozen leading businessmen. Old files of the Hobart *Mercury* are full of perforations where people have managed to remove references to their convict ancestors, and many convict records have disappeared from the state archives.

But, as Tasmanians are ruefully aware, the history of the convicts is of much interest to tourists, and Tasmania wants and gets many tourists, both from the rest of Australia and from overseas. The Tasmanian Museum and Art Gallery in Hobart exhibits cat-o'-nine-tails, gags, handcuffs, balls and chains, yokes, and wardens' cutlasses; visitors are fascinated.

*

The Governor of Tasmania, Sir Edric Bastyan, is one of the three remaining English-born governors of Australian states (the other two are in Victoria and Western Australia). Sir Edric, a military man with a ramrod back, occupies a big Tudor Gothic house with a white stone facing, a ballroom eighty by thirty feet, and elegant gardens in the Hobart Domain—such an imposing edifice that local antiestablishmentarians propose abolishing the governorship and using Government House as Parliament House. The roof of the solarium would have to be fixed first—it leaks.

Apples, Meat, Seaweed, and Crayfish

This fortunate little state has an economy so diversified that it is unlikely ever to suffer a knockdown blow. It is the truck garden of Australia, the orchard of England, and a treasury of minerals, too. Wool, meat, dairy products, fruits and vegetables, mining, metal extraction, and timber products contribute to the economy in roughly equal amounts, and grain and fruit preserving are just behind. This state supplies potatoes for Australia and three-fourths of Australia's overseas exports of apples—big, crisp Tasman Prides,* sent mostly to England. Some single Tasmanian trees produce more than one ton of apples.

Other products of Tasmanian farms are green peas, berries, pears, pigs, fat lambs, poultry, and hops for most of Australia's beer. The state's sheep have historically been Merinos, but in the last ten years a wool grower named Ian Downie, working with the state Department of Agriculture, has developed, from Merinos and Corriedales, a high-quality breed called the Cormo. Its wool, at auction in 1971, brought forty-five cents a pound, seventeen cents more than other wools. A Japanese textile maker bought the whole crop to manufacture it into women's suits. Seaweed is harvested mechanically on the east coast of Tasmania and made into alginate, a thickener for ice cream.

* Another Australian (though not Tasmanian) apple growing popular in the United States is the green-skinned Granny Smith. It gets its name from having been first cultivated by Maria Ann Smith, of Eastwood, New South Wales, in the 1880's.

The sea off Tasmania also produces whopping crayfish, eighteen inches long, with ten legs (but no claws; only fresh-water crayfish have claws). Fishermen catch them in wicker-basket traps; they are frozen and exported to the United States. Tasmanian fishing also includes enormous quantities of scallops, and couta, local name for barracuda. Sport fishermen catch blue-fin tuna weighing up to 250 pounds.

*

Tasmania's declivitous mountains, alpine lakes, high rainfall, and numerous short, rapid rivers give this state no less than half of the water-power potential of Australia. About two dozen power stations utilize this falling water to make 1,240,000 kilowatts of electricity—and make it as cheaply as anywhere in the world. This $370-million system is the "industry behind the industries" of Tasmania. Cheap power has attracted two big electrolytic zinc smelters, a large refinery, which uses alumina sent from Queensland, and a sizable pulp and paper industry.

Tasmania also has western mountain ranges that seem to be mostly minerals. Mount Lyell, developed in 1897–1898, is one of the world's great copper mines. Elsewhere the state produces lead, zinc, silver, gold, nickel, cobalt, and tungsten. Since 1968 it has been exporting iron ore from a remote spot on the Savage River in the northeast corner of the island. In this ingenious operation, the ore, crushed and separated from rock, is mixed with water to form slurry, and pumped for fifty-three miles through a nine-inch pipe to the north coast. There a pelletizing plant removes the water, mixes the ore with additives, forms it into small balls, and bakes them hard. Conveyor belts take the ore out over the open sea and pour it into the holds of ships which are positioned by hawsers secured to the rocky sea bottom. This clever arrangement avoided the cost of building a breakwater and docks, and ships have resisted ninety-mile-an-hour gales without mishap—though they generally put to sea when storms come up.

All this ore goes to Japan, for an ultimate return of $400 million over twenty years. Also going to Japan is the product of another new Tasmanian industry, wood chips. Contracts call for the export of $350 million worth of this raw material for pulp over the next eleven to fifteen years.

The Capital

Every year, the day after Christmas, a score of big sailing yachts tack out of Sydney Harbor and turn south in a 680-mile race to Hobart, where they arrive around New Year's Day. This is a nice symbolic connection between two of the loveliest harbors in the world. Hobart,* with 150,000 people, is a sea-minded city where people in downtown offices can see, just out their windows, the frequent arrivals of merchant ships. The harbor is the estuary of the River Derwent, twelve miles up from Storm Bay. It widens at Hobart enough to accommodate large vessels—the *Queens* were there in their better days. Hobart, founded in 1803, is the second oldest city in Australia, after Sydney. It is a pleasantly provincial place, with sandstone warehouses in the city center dating from the 1830's, and some other good, old, stone buildings—Parliament House, the Theatre Royal, built in 1834 and far more famous for its architecture than for its theater, and an old brewery. A pleasant place in this area is Cat-and-Fiddle Square. So closely are the harbor and the city intermeshed that ships' bows loom over Campbell, Argyle, and Elizabeth streets, and fishing vessels, with nets and green glass buoys on their decks, lend a travelogue look to the place.

Hobart refines zinc, founds steel, prints Chinese silk for export to many parts of the world, makes Cadbury's chocolate. A forthcoming industry, seemingly out of place in this staid town, is a casino. The legal authorization for it was a traumatic procedure, with so many Tasmanians fearing the demoralizing effects of gambling that the conservative upper house blocked the proposition for a while. The House of Assembly bucked the decision to the general public by means of a referendum, which passed. Now the Wrest Point Casino Hotel is going up, at a cost of $10 million, and Hobart hopes to attract hordes of mainlanders to the only casino in Australia. However, another company wants to build a similar, though smaller, hotel-casino in Tasmania's second city, Launceston, which is even nearer to the prospective sinners of Melbourne. This prospect scares many Tasmanians, who just knew that letting gambling in would turn the state into a kind of Nevada.

Forest-clad Mount Wellington provides a stunning backdrop for Hobart. Rising out of the sea for 4,166 feet, this mountain carries snow for several months of the year; a road goes to a lookout on the summit. You can tour Hobart by taxi for eighty cents an hour—geraniums everywhere. Cruise boats go up the Derwent to New Norfolk, an experience featuring such charms as roses, black swans, and picnic hampers. Hobart and the surrounding forested area suffered a terrible conflagration on Ash Wednesday in 1967, when a thousand houses burned down, leaving nothing but a wasteland of chimneys. A good share of the damage, said to reach $500 million, was the result of a dynamite factory's blowing up; the explosion wiped out a cannery, a brewery, and a carbide plant. In the countryside, sheep were incinerated in their paddocks. Now little remains to show that the fire ever took place.

* Named, like Sydney, for the British colonial secretary at the moment of its christening.

Looking Around from Hobart

The orientation of Tasmania from this southern port city goes something like this. To the southwest is the Huon Valley, where most of Tasmania's apples come from; to the west is an area so mountainous and densely vegetated that it is not only unpopulated but virtually unexplored. To the northwest, on the Indian Ocean, is country rich in minerals as well as lovely mountains and national parks. The northern coast of the island, on tumultuous Bass Strait, is a strip of rich flat farmland. Straight north from Hobart is the sheep-raising Midlands valley, leading to Launceston. The northeast is a lightly inhabited corner of the state with good skiing country in the inland mountains; down the east coast are resort towns and snow-colored beaches. The Tasman Peninsula, which was the site of Port Arthur and the prison colony, juts off the southeast coast.

This is mostly clement country, milder even than northern California. The temperature in Hobart averages 61 degrees Fahrenheit in January, and 46 degrees in July. The Midlands, with such English trees as oaks, elms, poplars, and willows, stage a colorful autumn. In high country, such as that of the unroaded Cradle Mountain–Lake St. Clair National Park, a wintry snow scene can look virtually Canadian. The west coast is open to wild west winds and assaulted by heavy rains.

The eucalyptus remains the basic forest tree in this much beforested land, because the conifers that the white man found there when he arrived have all been cut down, and the imported Northern Hemisphere trees are mostly decorative. Conservationists fear that the eucalyptuses are going into pulp and wood chips too rapidly—such a fate does seem ignoble for these three-hundred-foot monarchs. But Tasmania started preserving national parks a long time ago, with the Scenery Preservation Act of 1915. Moreover, much country in the west is unloggable because the terrain, though few mountains are higher than five thousand feet (Mount Ossa, the highest, reaches 5,305 feet), is rent with gorges as deep as three thousand feet. A menace in this mountainous area is a curious phenomenon called the "horizontal." Saplings grow about fifty feet high, blow over, and lie parallel to, but about twenty feet above, the ground. This creates a platform that looks like terra firma, but men walking on it strike weak spots, fall through, land in an eerie vegetable dungeon, and cannot get out.

The animals of Tasmania are few but humorous. The Tasmanian devil is a heavy marsupial, black with white patches and the size of a wolverine, who earned his name by his cry, half-scream and half-snarl. In machine-like jaws, he crunches up everything from carrion to shellfish to straying lambs, feeding a ravenous appetite. He can be tamed if taken young, and makes a contented if ponderous pet. Plenty of these devils remain, protected in national parks. By contrast, the Tasmanian wolf (also called the Tasmanian tiger) is so nearly extinct as to seem mythical. From time to time reports are cabled to the outer world that someone has seen the footprints of a Tasmanian wolf, but no authenticated sighting has taken place in years. And this beast would be easy to recognize: he has tiger-like dark stripes running vertically down his sides and rear haunches; his spikelike tail does not wag or bend; and his jaws will open to a 90-degree angle. He lives (if he lives at all) on small animals caught by chasing them until they falter from exhaustion.

Less of a joke are Tasmanian snakes, all poisonous: the copperhead, the whip, and the tiger. Tasmania has fourteen birds found nowhere else, a mouse-size possum, and a unique marsupial anteater. In high lakes grows a mountain shrimp, straight as a nail, which dates back so far as to make it a living fossil. In the Great Lake, largest of the state's several thousand shallow alpine lakes, trout grow so big that the law requires fishermen to throw back anything shorter than fourteen inches.

The set piece of bucolic beauty in Tasmania is the Derwent Valley, up from Hobart, which raises hops. This crop grows on vines that climb strings to wires strung eighteen feet overhead; to wander among them is to feel like a mouse in a cornfield. The vines are simply pulled down to harvest the hops, which are the fragrant cones that give beer its taste. Hand harvesting used to be the occasion of family excursions to the country for work vacations; now machines do the work. Hops are dried in oast-houses, which stand here and there in the valley. These are brick-and-shingle buildings with steep-sided pyramidal roofs surmounted by chimneys like obelisks.

*

Hobart people disparage Launceston, population 63,000 and 123 miles north, as "Cretinbury-on-Cesspool," but in point of fact it is a more dynamic place than the capital. It has the largest woolen mills in the Southern Hemisphere, and also makes breakfast food, tennis rackets, and boats. It is a city of waterways, up from the coast on the Tamar River. Once big ships could not reach it because of an inconvenient island downriver, but a couple of years ago the Port of Launceston Authority quarried out the center of the island to well below water level, making it like a giant rowboat, then blasted in the sides. Garden Island disappeared, and now ships as big as 55,000 tons can sail up to Launceston.

Near Launceston is Entally, an 1820's mansion now preserved as a national monument. Its builder was Mary Reibey, a girl convicted in England of stealing a ride on a squire's horse, and transported to New South Wales.

On the convict ship she met a young naval lieutenant; they later married, became traders and shipowners, and fetched up with a great Tasmanian estate.

A few other Tasmanian cities stand out for one reason or another. Port Arthur, the old prison colony on Tasman Peninsula sixty-three miles southeast of Hobart, is a monument to misery. Guides take tourists there these days and relate its history with gusto and gory details. Flogging, long terms in solitary on bread (one-half pound in twenty-four hours) and water (one quart), and other degrading punishments were inflicted on this colony's prisoners, mainly repeaters who had committed crimes in Australia after being transported. Nevertheless they put up some lovely buildings with their forced labor. The church, long since roofless but mellowly preserved, was a graceful, light, Gothic building, copied after Glastonbury Abbey, topped with spires at all of its numerous corners. Prisoners were brought to church in blinders that allowed them to see the pulpit but not their neighbors. The old lunatic asylum is now the Port Arthur Town Hall, which leads to endless wry comment. There are ruins of a powder magazine and a hospital, built like the other structures of pink brick and stone. The peninsula is hooked to the main island by Eaglehawk Neck, an isthmus only twenty yards wide. In prison times, hungry dogs were chained on short leashes across this neck, ready to rip the flesh off any escaping convict.

Queenstown, headquarters for the Mount Lyell copper mines, is one of those ecological disasters of the heedless past. You descend on a corkscrew highway through verdant rain forest to a valley where sulphur fumes killed all vegetation until new methods of smelting were introduced in 1922. Sulphur does weird things, brightly staining the rocks in chrome and purple and eating away at tombstones in cemeteries until they look like melted candles. Now patches of green are reappearing around Queenstown, adding new hues to a place often called "hell with the fires out," because it is barren despite one hundred inches of rainfall a year. The economy of the area is picking up—good new roads permit exploitation of minerals once unreachable. Nearby is Zeehan, a lead-zinc-silver mining town which once had ten thousand people, twenty-nine hotels, and a theater where Nellie Melba sang.

A Word on the History

Tasmania was discovered before the mainland of Australia itself. On December 1, 1642, the Dutch captain Abel Tasman put some men ashore at a spot on the east coast not far from what became Port Arthur. They heard voices and saw foot notches cut in a tree with a spacing that suggested a race of giant men, so they scurried back to their ships. In keeping with the strange, unhurried discovery of Australasia, no explorer returned to Van Diemen's Land (which, as we have seen, was the name Tasman gave the place in honor of the Dutch East Indian Governor who sent him) until 1773, when Captain Tobias Furneaux reached Adventure Bay on Bruny Island just south of present-day Hobart. Fifteen years later, Captain Bligh and the *Bounty* put in at Adventure Bay and planted Tasmania's first apple trees. Matthew Flinders, sailing in a small boat with a naval surgeon named George Bass, proved Tasmania to be an island, by going around it, in 1798–1799. In 1803 Lieutenant John Bowen, who was precisely eighteen years old, was sent out from New South Wales to found a colony of convicts. Some pretty rough men, generally the more violent of the convicts, were molded into nation-builders and did a good job. By 1825, when Van Diemen's Land became a colony separate from New South Wales, Hobart was as large as Sydney. Then two circumstances combined to hold Tasmania back. One was the colonization of Victoria, which as we have seen was staged from Tasmania, and caused many people to leave the island. The second was the furious new British determination, at the end of the Napoleonic Wars in 1815, to make Australia take its felons. Tasmania became the "jail of the Empire," and the government in London did not even assume the burden of paying for the jails and wardens and police. One of the worst aspects of the punishment euphemistically known as transportation was the transportation itself. One ship, *George III*, sank in a channel off Tasmania in 1835, and troops shot the prisoners as they tried to jump into the sea. Another, the *Neva*, with 240 women, hit a reef and only twenty-two of the passengers got ashore to start their prison terms. A specialty of Port Arthur was a prison for boys at a locality named, with cold erudition, Point Puer.

Free Tasmanians railed at the "great curse" of transportation, and in 1847 an eloquent preacher and publicist named John West started a movement to end it. By 1853 Britain had agreed. Transportation of convicts ceased, but Port Arthur continued as a prison until abandoned in 1877. On a fluke caused by the slowness and uncertainty of the mails, Tasmania in 1855 became—by a few weeks—the first of the Australian colonies to receive self-government from London. The name Tasmania, assumed at this point to replace Van Diemen's Land, had been in colloquial use since 1823.

*

The Aborigines who occupied Tasmania turned out not to be giants, as Tasman feared, but they were different from the Aborigines on the mainland. They had no dingoes or boomerangs, and their hair was fuzzy rather than silky; possibly they were by origin Melanesians who had sailed to Tasmania from the New Guinea vicinity. The two or three thousand of them were divided into twenty tribes. They wore no clothes, and lived in caves, hollow trees, and tentlike huts. They decorated their bodies with red ocher, scars, and shell necklaces. Their food was shellfish, lily roots, wallabies, fruits, and berries.

From the first, the whites regarded the Aborigines in Tasmania as little better than game to be shot and fed to the dogs. Convicts kidnaped their women. The Aborigines fought back, robbing, burning, and murdering. In 1830 the Governor of the time decided to round them up and isolate them, once and for all. A vivid account of this famous "black line" sweep comes from Charles Darwin, who visited Tasmania six years later and wrote about it in *The Voyage of the Beagle*:

> The whole island was put under martial law, and by proclamation the whole population commanded to assist in one great attempt to secure the entire race. The plan adopted was nearly similar to that of the great hunting-matches in India: a line [of three thousand soldiers and settlers] was formed reaching across the island, with the intention of driving the natives into a *cul-de-sac* on Tasman's peninsula. The attempt failed; the natives, having tied up their dogs, stole during one night through the lines. This is far from surprising, when their practised senses, and usual manner of crawling after wild animals is considered. I have been assured that they can conceal themselves on almost bare ground, in a manner which until witnessed is scarcely credible; their dusky bodies being easily mistaken for the blackened stumps which are scattered all over the country. I was told of a trial between a party of Englishmen and a native, who was to stand in full view on the side of a bare hill; if the Englishmen closed their eyes for less than a minute, he would squat down, and then they were never able to distinguish him from the surrounding stumps. But to return to the hunting-match; the natives understanding this kind of warfare, were terribly alarmed, for they at once perceived the power and numbers of the whites. Shortly afterwards a party of thirteen belonging to two tribes came in; and, conscious of their unprotected condition, delivered themselves up in despair. Subsequently by the intrepid exertions of Mr. Robinson, an active and benevolent man, who fearlessly visited by himself the most hostile of the natives, the whole were induced to act in a similar manner. They were then removed to an island, where food and clothes were provided for them.

Even though, as we have seen earlier, a few lived to return to Tasmania, by 1876 the last of them was dead. They had simply been killed off. All that is left from the genocide of the Tasmanian Aborigines is the habitat group in the Tasmanian Museum and Art Gallery in Hobart.

Back to Tasmania Today

A magnetic figure in Tasmania is the Roman Catholic Archbishop, Guilford Young. He has, in general, stood for the reformist, Vatican II position in Australia. But this complex man lined up with the right-winger B. A. Santamaria in the big Labor Party schism, and in the last year or so he has several times disciplined an angry young priest of his diocese who headed the Tasmanian Vietnam Moratorium Committee.

Archbishop Young comes from Queensland. He got his higher education in Rome during Mussolini's time, and fled Europe for New York just before World War II began. He toured the U.S., and, returning to Australia, was consecrated at thirty-one as the youngest Catholic bishop in the world. He went to Tasmania in 1954, and made a name for himself as a church liberal as well as school-builder. In his white hillside house in Hobart, with a stack of old *Encounters* behind him on a shelf, he made a couple of challenging points. Young, departing from the hopeful and nearly universal position of the politicians, thinks that "Australia is not necessary to the United States. We know we're expendable; the U.S. will become newly isolationist after the Vietnam withdrawal." He also points out that Australia, 27 percent Catholic now, will on projection be one-third Catholic by 1975. Tasmania itself has fewer Catholics proportionately than any other state except South Australia. The Archbishop, admittedly optimistically, holds that "what is happening today is not the death throes of civilization" but rather "the travail of a new age coming to birth." The reason for this hopeful view? "There is a factor X in history, which we may call the mysterious action of God."

*

Tasmanian tidbits: A taxi driver said: "Jews here go to Melbourne for the weekend, the Catholics pray, and the Anglicans stay in bed." Shops open at 9:05 A.M., not 9. Very little marijuana, LSD, or other drugs are used here, one is told. Handsome Georgian architecture prevails among the older buildings because this is one of the older colonies and also because the Victorian style did not reach here until twenty years after it infested England. Tasmania's most famous expatriates are Errol Flynn and Merle Oberon. Not much of the wave of immigration to Australia in recent decades has come to Tasmania; in fact, by a reverse process, Tasmania's young like to leave the place, to go at least as far as Melbourne or Sydney. Only three daily newspapers are published in the whole state.

CHAPTER 14

Adelaide and South Australia

Yes, the Old Bloke makes a good job of them up this way.
—A STOCKMAN COMMENTING ON A SOUTH AUSTRALIAN SUNSET

THE SMELL OF CHANGE, the pervasive sensation of a worn-out Establishment giving way to a new politics—you get that more strongly in South Australia than in any other part of the country. Here, in what has certainly been a mossback milieu, we find a percipient, mettlesome, enterprising, young, and potent new Premier, first fresh figure in Australian politics in a wombat's age. He is Don Dunstan, a Labor politician who came to office in 1970, breaking the solid phalanx of Liberal-Country leadership that then included all the other states and the federal government.* Perhaps he compares with Canada's Pierre Trudeau. Politician enough to dominate the Labor Party machine in his state, he is also an original thinker who draws support from the Adelaide intellectuals. He is married to a lecturer in economics who is part of his brainy circle. Dunstan wears his hair longish, dresses with style, plays Chopin on the piano, and likes to cook. He was born in Fiji, where his South Australian parents were running a business, and was educated in Adelaide's "best" school, St. Peter's, and at the University of Adelaide. Thus he is essentially a scion of the Adelaide oligarchy, which he has now set himself against.

Dunstan owes his election victory to an altruistic gesture by his Liberal-Country predecessor (and current leader of the opposition), Raymond Steele Hall, a man of surprisingly similar views. Hall decided that his party should cease winning elections by virtue of gerrymanders that favored the

* Western Australia went Labor a few weeks later.

countryside electorate, and passed voting reforms that cost him his office. Thus South Australia has two leading politicians expounding radical politics —though Hall's party is divided over him, and about half of it remains attached to conservative views.

Dunstan stands for mild social reform and energetic, state-prodded development. He wants to improve schools and transit, control pollution, and protect consumers. Holding that South Australia's economy is too tightly linked to the automobile and electrical industries, he wants to diversify and export. To these ends he is creating a state development corporation and a merchant bank, pushing the movie industry, and establishing trade centers in four Asian countries. South Australia is only modestly endowed with resources—some iron ore, a south-coast swathe of good farm and vineyard land, plains suitable for wheat or wool (both of which have declining markets). On this resource base, the state historically has done well; Dunstan wants to hold it all together and advance.

The roadblock is the Legislative Council, the upper house of the South Australian Parliament, a body elected under such strict voting qualifications that sixteen of its twenty members belong to the hidebound opposition. Dunstan wants to change this archaic chamber from a "bastion of selfish privilege" to a toothless "house of review," but so far he has failed. He sent up a bill to democratize the manner of election of members of the Legislative Council, but the proposed house of review refused to review itself—and it does have considerable power to delay legislation for years. Dunstan also plans to fight for civil liberties—particularly to curb eavesdropping devices and the general warrant, which permits police to search houses for any purpose or even none. He deplores dossier-keeping and censorship—for example, as we noted earlier, he did not try to block the sale of *Portnoy's Complaint*, the object of much censorial effort elsewhere in the country.

Most of these goals, of course, are radical only in Australian terms, repairs to be made in a society more heavily encrusted with tradition and immobility than its short history would seem to warrant. This is a state that takes immense pride in being the only one with no convict origins. Adelaide boasts that it is more aristocratic and less money-minded than Melbourne. How sweet Adelaide got so staid makes a paradoxically colorful story. Let us quickly run through it.

A Bounder and a Founder

The story starts in London in 1830. The talk of the city, at one point that year, was *Letter from Sydney*, a book by a bounder (also a philosopher) named Edward Gibbon Wakefield, who had just spent three years in Newgate Gaol for abducting an heiress to Gretna Green. His book, which was widely taken to be authentically from Sydney though Wakefield had never been there, dealt with the art of colonization. It detailed errors made earlier in New South Wales, and put forth an idealistic how-to-colonize plan that Wakefield had conceived while doing time in what must have been a rather literary kind of imprisonment. Even as London's theorists, capitalists, and speculators pondered the possibility of using Wakefield's ideas to solve some of England's social problems by sending the hungry and unemployed abroad, news came from Australia that the explorer Charles Sturt had floated down the Murray River to its mouth and found "rich and lovely valleys."

All this had much to do with shaping Adelaide and South Australia as they are today. Economic philosopher Wakefield, the son of a surveyor and land agent, had an Adam Smithian notion that the price of land was the key to successful colonization. If the price was too low, or if the land was free, he thought, penniless laborers would take it and turn themselves into hopeless, struggling peasant farmers. Conversely, if the land was priced high, it would attract purchase by capitalists, who would run it well, and the funds generated from sales could be used to pay the passage of tradesmen and laborers from Britain to Australia. These people could work for the capitalists and eventually save enough to buy land of their own. Wakefield also insisted on migration by people who were respectable, certainly not convicts, and preferably married, to avoid the overly masculine society typified by New South Wales. Soon a group of Londoners excited by Wakefield's ideas formed a South Australian Association to put theory into practice.

The first 546 settlers, mostly English yeoman farmers, went out in 1836. Upon landing they were sufficiently nervous to mistake the raucous laughing of kookaburras for an attack by Aborigines. At length, under a gum tree* at a seaside spot near present-day Adelaide, they proclaimed South Australia a province of the Crown.

If Wakefield seems a bit of an eccentric, he is almost matched by Colonel William Light, the founder of Adelaide. Prophetically, Light (born 1786) was the son of the founder of another city—Penang, the first British settlement in Malaya—his mother being his father's Portuguese-Malay mistress. Light went to sea in the Royal Navy at fourteen, left the service at sixteen, toured France and escaped when the Napoleonic Wars resumed, visited India for a year or so, and in 1808 bought a commission in the British Army. In the Fourth Dragoons he fought in Spain under Wellington for six years, taking part in forty-five actions. Going on half-pay after Napoleon's defeat, he toured Europe sketching. In 1823 he was back in Spain as a lieutenant

* Long since dead, but still preserved by chemicals.

colonel with revolutionary forces fighting the Spanish king, and nearly died of his battle wounds. Next year he met and married Mary Bennet, illegitimate daughter of the Duke of Richmond. Light bought a yacht and they cruised the Mediterranean, ultimately meeting Mohammed Ali, Pasha of Egypt, in Alexandria. This dignitary commissioned Light to create an Egyptian navy. Light left to round up sailors and a ship, and a few years later sailed to Egypt in a new paddle steamer, the *Nile*. While he was in England, Mary, who was prone to wear gold-braided trousers and a white turban with a purple tassel, became involved in a love affair that left her pregnant, and Light chucked her. For a few months Light and a Royal Navy Captain named Joseph Hindmarsh ferried troops from Egypt to Syria. Hindmarsh then returned to England, where the South Australia fever was running high. He got himself appointed Governor of the new colony, and Light was made Surveyor-General.

Fifty years old, and in bad health, Light took command of a small brig and set out for Australia, in mid-1836, assigned to explore fifteen hundred miles of shoreline to find the best location for habitation, plan a city, and then survey 150 square miles of country for settlement. In a mere matter of weeks, he found a lovely city site on a rich plain between the sea and the mountains, laid it out in a design that remains his claim to immortality, and surveyed the main streets. Hindmarsh arrived, only to clash with Light over his choice of site, but Light prevailed. He plunged into the task of making a trigonometric survey of land for settlers, and for a while kept up with sales of plots. Then he was ordered to survey another thousand square miles, and began to fall behind. New settlers could not be put on the land for lack of boundary markers. London complained. Light patiently replied that the head office "reckoned as if this survey should be made in England or Ireland where every facility is given by roads, carriages, provisions, lodgings," whereas he had to transport "tents, provisions, and even water over a country without roads." To Wakefield he wrote: "I am harassed in mind beyond all you can conceive." He resigned, and so did his staff. He was ill and in debt, and to top it off his house burned down, destroying many sketches and his journal of thirty years, not to mention his surveying instruments. He died of tuberculosis in 1839, at the age of fifty-four.

For a few years South Australia suffered headaches that Wakefield never dreamed of. Slow surveys confined new arrivals to Adelaide, where land prices soared to as much as £2,000 an acre. News of such speculative profit boomed South Australia Company shares on the stock market, which used the funds to export more settlers, compounding the problem. Then vigorous and expensive efforts to get land surveyed put the local government so far into debt that the Colonial Office had to bail it out—which was done at the cost of demoting South Australia from a self-reliant province to a Crown Colony. It was thereupon dressed in "Downing Street swaddling clothes," that is, given a Governor, George Grey (whom we shall meet again in a later chapter), and a Legislative Council. Yet by that time 500,000 acres had been surveyed, the 5,000 settlers were moving from city to country, wheat was beginning to grow abundantly, and 200,000 sheep were on the land. Cleverly enough, the colonizers had brought in a group of Lutherans from Brandenburg, who resented the King of Prussia's attempt to unite the Lutheran and Reformed churches. They started South Australia's famed wineries.

Adelaide lies on terrain that slopes from the Mount Lofty Range to the Gulf St. Vincent, a coastal plain 150 miles long and as much as 50 miles wide, all good grain land and accessible to the sea for transport. The colony quickly became the granary of Australia, profiting more than the miners themselves from the Victorian gold rush of the 1850's. Only a decade after settlement, a miller named John Ridley invented a mechanical reaper that came into wide use. A couple of other inventions made it possible to grow grain on land covered with mallee, a scrub eucalyptus. One was the Mullenizer, a great drum that rolled over the scrub to break it down. The other was the stump-jump plow, with springed wrought-iron plowshares that could rise over stumps and roots, and eliminate the need for grubbing them out.

In 1857, a Surveyor-General named George Goyder roughed out a go-no-further line between good grain land, which had at least ten inches of rainfall yearly, and dubious desert. Foolhardy farmers crossed the "Goyder Line" and proved—for a while—that they could raise wheat on eight inches of rain.* But in 1881 nature caught up with this perilous practice, and a drought began that lasted more or less steadily until 1904. Farms were abandoned; the Commercial Bank of South Australia failed. Ultimately science—hybrids, fallowing, and superphosphate fertilizers—restored South Australia's agricultural prosperity.

Goyder's Line marked off the economically significant part of South Australia, but that was only a small fringe of the coast. The unfavored remainder of the colony opened up slowly. Charles Sturt's tortured trek northward in 1844 brought back a report of desiccated salt lakes so frighteningly barren that the colonists were discouraged—luckily, as it turned out—from abandoning wheat raising in the south for dryland sheep raising farther north. About 1860 an intriguing concept led South Australia to offer £2,000 to any explorer who could go all the way from Adelaide to the north coast. The London-Java cable was about to be extended to Australia.

* The average annual rainfall over good U.S. wheat country, specifically North Dakota, is eighteen inches.

The enterprising colonial government proposed to find a suitable north coast terminus and then connect it to Adelaide by almost two thousand miles of overland telegraph. John McDouall Stuart, who had made three expeditions to the north, pushed all the way to the Timor Sea in 1862. "I dipped my feet and washed my face and hands in the sea." On his return trip, privation reduced him to a "perfect skeleton," but he got the prize. The government of South Australia used his explorations to annex the whole Northern Territory in 1863 (not relinquishing it to the federal government until 1911). South Australia also built the telegraph, which linked the major Australian cities to the world, and to instantaneous world news, in 1874.

These explorations finally opened the better parcels of land north of Goyder's Line to sheep raising, inspiring formidable characters like Sidney Kidman, who came to be called the largest landholder in world history. It is said that he could go from Adelaide to Darwin without leaving his own land. He was also, in the eyes of his employees, mean and dishonest. He reputedly fired any man caught lighting his pipe with a match instead of a firebrand, when sitting around an evening campfire, because a man that wasteful must automatically be a shiftless worker.

The Constitution that South Australia got in 1855 was the most radical of all the charters thus far negotiated with the Crown by Australian colonies, reflecting the independence and nonconformism of the free settlers. It specified an elective upper (as well as lower) house, manhood suffrage, and vote by ballot. These wild democratic notions led at first to a measure of chaos: twenty-three governments under eight premiers between 1861 and 1876. But in more recent times, one Premier, Sir Thomas Playford, "the architect of present-day South Australia," managed to rule, on the Liberal–Country League ticket, from 1938 to 1965. At the turn of the century, South Australia voted a thumping five to one in favor of federation, but by the time of the Depression of the 1930's had cause to regret this enthusiasm. The federation had authorized high tariffs that made manufactured goods costly to the farmers; freights to markets were high; so were taxes. South Australia was a "mendicant state." In response to this plight, the federal government started revenue-sharing, and the state has generally prospered ever since then.

Green-Belted Adelaide

Colonel Light wrote, at the end of his life:

> The reasons that led me to fix Adelaide where it is I do not expect to be generally understood or calmly judged of at present. My enemies, however, by disputing their validity in every particular, have done me

> the good service of fixing the whole of the responsibility upon me. . . . I leave it to posterity and not to them, to decide whether I am entitled to praise or blame.

The verdict would seem to be that his was a spectacularly advanced city plan that functioned well for many decades.

Adelaide is named for the consort of King William VI. The Torrens River flows through it, and Port Adelaide is seven miles to the west. Light's central city is a square-mile grid of streets alternately wide and narrow. A big square occupies the center, and four lesser squares (one named for Light) lie near the corners. The inner city is surrounded by a green belt of parklands, which exist to this day. The Torrens runs through the northern green belt, which also contains the Adelaide Oval (for cricket), the Botanic Gardens, the zoo, and the municipal golf links. The major public buildings are all in the center of the city—Parliament House, the public library, the art gallery, the museum, the University of Adelaide, the Royal Adelaide Hospital, and even the railroad station. On higher ground, north of the parklands, is a posh residential area that includes St. Peter's Anglican Cathedral.

Oddly, the problem with Adelaide, which has a population of about 750,000 (depending on where you begin to count), is that it has both too many people and too few. The inner city, way down from its 1915 peak population of 44,000, has too many factories, warehouses, hovels, and even little truck gardens. The City Council is building new blocks of flats and terrace houses to bring back a thousand people a year. On the other hand, the suburbs are overextended, for in Adelaide as elsewhere in Australia almost everyone has his own home, garden, and workshop. As an answer to overcrowding, the South Australian Housing Trust, a state-owned but independent corporation, has constructed the city of Elizabeth, a planned satellite for a planned city, seventeen miles north of Adelaide. Its housing, too, is mostly single homes, forty models rather too cutely varied but so artfully distributed that no street has two houses alike. They are divided into six neighborhoods plus parklands, with many walkways instead of streets, and easy access to shopping and places of work. All electrical cables are underground. The chief employers are a governmental Weapons Research Plant and factories that make cars and sewing machines. Most residents are immigrants, chiefly British.

The traditional adjectives to apply to Adelaide are parochial, decorous, conservative, gracious, provincially aristocratic. The tone was set a century ago by the old pastoralist families; the city has often been compared to a large, prosperous country town; you hear mention of "fifth-generation"

Australians. The police are effective, as befits an orderly town. A couple of years ago one could see astonishing displays of hats on the ladies in the dining room of the now demolished South Australia Hotel: rose petals, pink tulle, white straw with blue ribbons, and turbans, turbans, turbans. The rest of Australia may be on the verge of turning convict descent into a point of pride, but South Australia still boasts loudly that no convicts settled here, and damn few Irish either. The state has an Establishment, and the Establishment's citadel is the green-shuttered, cedar-doored Adelaide Club. Churches are so numerous that Adelaide is sometimes called "The Holy Land." Much architecture, in liver-colored brick or maroon stone, bespeaks a dowdy complacency.

This traditional description is now getting a bit out of date. Industry, technology, and immigration are forming a new, noisy, pleasure-loving Adelaide. The oligarchs are beginning to seem ineffectual . . . so many new people have never heard of them! Managers, experts, technicians are taking over. Long white gloves are going out and barbecue pits are coming in. A symptom of the change is the Adelaide Film Festival, run even-numbered years since 1960—two weeks of new movies, late nights, wine, gaiety, and culture, sponsored by the rapidly evolving Establishment. The city "considers itself a rival to Edinburgh in a furtive sort of way," says Max Harris, the Adelaide poet, critic, and publisher. It is easier to drink, dine, dance, and watch a floor show in Adelaide nowadays than it is in Melbourne.

A typical leader in this new burst of energy is Kym Bonython, best known for his art galleries here and in Sydney. His ancestors, Cornishmen, emigrated in two waves, one to Adelaide and one to found the town of Castine, Maine. Besides running his galleries, Mr. Bonython breeds cattle, operates a speedway, plays drums, serves as a disc jockey in his thirty-third year on a national program, and promotes jazz concerts, once importing Duke Ellington—with some obstructions from White Australia. South Australia's Governor, Sir Mark Oliphant, who was born in Adelaide in 1901, is a scientist, a world-renowned authority on atomic energy. He lives in a cream-stucco, slate-roofed mansion across from Parliament House and the Adelaide Club, and he gets $15,000 a year. A noted Adelaide woman is the Honorable Justice Roma Mitchell of the state Supreme Court, Australia's first woman Queen's Counsel. Another is Mrs. Edna Ayres, the charming and amusing daughter of Sid Kidman. She recalls one of her father's properties being "as big as Holland," 260 miles from one end to the other. A prominent Adelaide author is Geoffrey Dutton, who wrote a book, *Australia and the Monarchy*, which questioned the validity of the royal institution. "We have a revolting attitude of subservience," Dutton says. "We stick to the monarch. We don't want to hurt Mum's feelings." For this sort of thing Dutton was asked to resign from the Adelaide Club.

Sir Thomas Playford, the former Premier, often boasts that South Australia is more industrialized, per capita, than any other state. General Motors–Holden has two plants in Adelaide, and Chrysler Australia Ltd. has another. Other Adelaide industry makes pipes and tubes, chemicals, farm equipment, textiles, salt, plastics, electrical equipment, footwear, clothing, and sheet metal. Adelaide must be a good place to do business. An American named R. Donald Dervin moved to Adelaide from Washington, D.C., in 1961, introduced the soft-bun hamburger into Australia, and by 1968 was selling a million dollars' worth of them every year from fourteen restaurants in Adelaide and Perth.

Adelaidiana: Upon Colonel Light's death the Adelaide Corporation voted an appropriation of twenty dollars a year for raising an annual toast to him, and the Lord Mayor does so on the first day of the annual meeting of the Municipal Council. At the Town Hall Colonel Light is present in a portrait —red coat, gold epaulets, and fawn-colored trousers. Also there, in a glass case, are Queen Adelaide's china and slippers. Sydney oysters are cheaper here than in Sydney, and in the restaurants you can also have yabbies (a small fresh-water crayfish) in vinegar, Canadian fiddleheads, prime Stilton, and papaw-and-passion-fruit sundaes. One thousand Americans live in Adelaide.

On to Nowhere Else

Again, here is an Australian state with a first city and no second city—or third or fourth, at least on the usual scales of population gradation. Next after Adelaide in South Australia is its own satellite, Elizabeth, with 33,000 people, and then steel-making Whyalla, 23,000. But though mostly little more than villages, the remaining towns and the rural population push the state's total close to 1.2 million. They occupy an area half as big as Mexico, yet almost everyone lives in the Britain-size southeastern coastal region, and only five thousand people in the rest of the state. Two long gulfs penetrate the populated area, giving it seaports and a Mediterranean—perhaps more precisely, Greek—character. A large resort island, named Kangaroo for the vast herds early explorers saw, lies at the mouth of Gulf St. Vincent. Place names offer clues to South Australian history and character: Cape Catastrophe, Streaky Bank, Mount Remarkable, Coffin Bay, and, most touchingly, Nowhere Else.

The twelve million acres of productive land in the south are dutifully fruitful, but the north is more interesting. The strike-it-rich towns of Andamooka and Coober Pedy mine opal, that fascinating and supposedly unlucky stone. The largest opal to date was found in November 1969, at Andamooka; it weighed 220 ounces and the Adelaide opal buyer Luka Olah paid $168,000 for it. Japan buys almost all of Australia's opal, to cut and polish the stones and export them to the United States. In a typical deal, a miner might sell some pieces to a dealer for $627, who would resell them to the exporter for $1,200, who would sell them to the Japanese importer for $2,000—when finished and retailed in the U.S., the gems could bring $6,275.

The enormous blue lakes shown on maps of the South Australian outback are, in reality, white salt flats most of the time. Donald Campbell got his racing car up to 403.1 miles per hour on Lake Eyre in 1964. The plains beyond the lakes are mostly barren sand or gibber—clear across Western Australia to the Indian Ocean. This otherwise nearly useless country is therefore ideal for the rocket range that is based at Woomera, 250 miles northwest of Adelaide. This missile-launching site, a well-planned town now twenty-four years old, with water piped from a hundred miles away, has been used lately in the development of the British Black Arrow, a three-stage rocket to put three-hundred-pound scientific satellites into orbits three hundred miles high. Woomera also tracks U.S. space ships—for example, Mariner 9 when it was orbiting Mars. In the northwest corner of the state is another scene of science in the desert, Talgarno, where the Australian-designed pilotless target plane, Jindivik, was tested. Still a third such site is Maralinga, an atomic-testing station in country so flat that the transcontinental express train can be seen approaching for almost an hour. In this vicinity are the Musgrave Ranges, famed for spectacular sunsets. The talk is all about the size of the "properties" (never "ranches"). On one, the distance from gate to house is ten miles.

We cannot leave the South Australian countryside without first having a look at the long thumb of the southeast. Located here is Mount Gambier, which is both a town and an extinct volcano in the craters of which nestle four pretty lakes. One of them, for unknown reasons, turns from blue to gray each March, and back to blue in November. The buildings of the town are made from white coralline limestone quarried nearby; it is so soft that it can be cut with a carpenter's saw. Nearby, on the coast, is Lake Bonney, so polluted by a Kimberly-Clark plant that on any given day one can tell by the color of the water whether the plant is turning out green or yellow toilet paper. Premier Dunstan, who has promised to put through an Environment Act, is particularly concerned about Lake Bonney. But not far away, at Kingston, crayfish are caught by the ton and frozen for export to the U.S.

To the north are vast farms of pine trees, planted since 1886 to provide Australia with softwood. Much farther north is rich country irrigated from the Murray River, as in western Victoria. A diesel-powered paddle steamer, the *Coonawarra*, makes a weekly excursion for 260 miles along the river. Barns in this country are made of stone or brick, testimony to the permanence and stability of the South Australian farmer.

The Wine of the Country

Here we come to wine country—South Australia has two-thirds of the nation's vineyards. And Australia's good wines are among the nation's greatest surprises to the foreigner, a steady joy not yet sufficiently known to the rest of the world. Only a decade or so ago most Australians, fervent partisans of beer, scorned wine as "plonk,"* and drank it mostly as fortified wine intended solely to intoxicate. Now Australians drink light wines as a civilized pleasure, and consume more per capita than any other English-speaking nation, including the United States and England.

Australian wine is never as good as the best French wine, but (which may be more significant) never as bad as the deliberately cheap *vin ordinaire* that so many Frenchmen drink. Vintages are remarkably even; there are few "years" that are strikingly better than other "years." Blending of two wines into one is much commoner here than elsewhere, and generally beneficial. There are delicious dry whites, called Riesling, or sometimes Moselle. The sweeter whites are known as white Burgundy or Chablis—a good white Burgundy is Houghton's. The dryer, more astringent reds go by the name of claret or cabernet; Coonawarra Estate claret is a highly regarded wine of this type. Australia also has rich red Burgundies, much champagne, a tank-fermented sparkling wine called pearl, sherries in five gradations from dry to sweet, and dessert wines—port, muscat, and tokay.

Italians, Greeks, and other immigrants helped spread the recent vogue for drinking wines, but the growers are mostly long-established firms founded by Germans or Englishmen. Fourteen big private companies make the bulk of the wine—Seppelt's, Penfold's, Mildara, Gramp's, and Leo Buring's are names one frequently sees on the bottles. These producers are backed up by six cooperatives and any number of little, one-family wineries. Not much

* Apparently a corruption of *vin blanc*, absorbed into Australian speech in France during World War I.

of their product goes abroad—something like two million gallons a year—but it can be had in all major cities of the world. Seppelt's exports to forty countries.

Half of the fourteen major Australian vineyard districts are in South Australia, the best-known being the Barossa Valley, thirty miles from Adelaide. The road to Barossa runs through squat date palms, silver fields of wild oats on one side and hay on the other, past sheep and cottages with geraniums—all under a high clear sky and against a profile of low gray-green hills. The valley floor is a flat iridescent green, rows and rows of low vines growing in red-brown earth. Gramp's, Penfold's, and Seppelt's all have enormous wineries here.

Broken Hill

South Australia staged the continent's first mining boom, back in 1842, exploiting copper from mines at Kapunda and Burra, not too far from the Barossa Valley. Shares in Burra went from five to two hundred pounds on the London market as the mines paid 200 percent dividends each quarter. Later two mountains of top-quality ore, Iron Knob and Iron Monarch, provided the basis of the blast furnaces, steel plants, and shipyards at Whyalla, heavy-industry center of the state. But the most fabulous mine in this area is, paradoxically, not in South Australia, it is thirty miles over the line in New South Wales, at Broken Hill.

Broken Hill was, and is, so rich that it came to signify the very essence of the idea that a poor man can lean down, pick up a rock, and find himself wildly, gloriously wealthy. All by itself the mine is a substantial chunk of the Australian economy. As late as 1966 Broken Hill produced one-fourth of Australia's metals, and half of its lead, zinc, and silver. Because of its location only two hundred miles from the South Australian coast, Broken Hill has always been economically, if not politically, a part of South Australia.

The country around Broken Hill is a harsh swatch of authentic Australian outback, with nine inches of rainfall a year and seven *feet* of evaporation (that is, in the few ponds, lakes, and reservoirs where that much evaporation is possible). The 150-foot-high hill was named by explorer Charles Sturt, who thought it looked sort of swaybacked. Sheep raisers moved out to that area in the 1850's, and in 1866 James McCulloch, Premier of Victoria, leased (with partners) the sheep station called Mount Gipps, which included the hill in its 900,000 acres and had a homestead only nine miles away. A clue to the context of this time and place is that in Wilcannia, a town not too far from Broken Hill, a favorite pastime in those years was racing camels—

which seems to tell us that the area was settled enough to need recreation, dry enough to require camels, and remote enough to need pack animals.

At that time prospectors, displaced by the end of the Ballarat-Bendigo gold rush in Victoria, were "fossicking" (digging) around the region, attracted by gold-bearing white quartz. But the man most intrigued by the jagged horizon line was Charles Rasp, German by birth and chemist by education, who had mysteriously settled for being a Mount Gipps sheep station boundary rider. An observant man, he saw similarities between Broken Hill and nearby silver mines. In 1883, driving stock to Adelaide, he bought a prospector's handbook, and concluded from it that at Broken Hill he was sitting on a mountain of tin. He and six other men "pegged" (claimed) one eighty-acre and six forty-acre blocks, and chipped in to hire a miner. This fellow, after two years of digging, found not tin but silver. Another discovery of silver on the same property followed soon after. "I believe £30,000 worth of silver was taken out of this spot in a fortnight," Rasp recalled later.

Before that, two luckless members of the syndicate had sold out. Sidney Kidman, the cattleman, with similar lack of faith, unloaded a part of a share of the mine that he had received in return for some steers. Silver turned out to be the least of Broken Hill's assets; it won its fame as the world's greatest lead-zinc-silver mine. Rasp and the remaining partners thereupon founded Broken Hill Proprietary, which grew to be the largest and most ubiquitous corporation in Australia. Broken Hill's population, 30 in 1885, grew to 10,000 in 1889, to 20,000 by the early nineties, and to 30,000 in 1901; it has stayed around that figure ever since.

In 1886 Broken Hill Proprietary brought in William H. Patton, superintendent of the Consolidated Virginia Mine in Virginia City, Nevada. He introduced the Comstock Lode method of mining, shoring up the stopes with imported American timber, which had the saving grace of giving out loud warning creaks before the roof caved in. Thousands of acres of U.S. timber are buried at Broken Hill, but nevertheless "creeps"—caving and earth movement on the surface, caused by the earlier failure to use timber—often wrecked costly mine buildings on top of the lode. The mine paid a million pounds a year in the early 1890's, after the South Australian government built a railroad to get the ore out. Soon Broken Hill's wealth topped that of the entire gold rush of the 1850's. One £200 share grew in six years to a value of £1,250,000.

Then, as the mine deepened, it ran into ores combined with sulphide. The best-known technology for sulphide ore at that time permitted the company to extract only two-thirds of the lead, half the silver, and none of the zinc. Slag heaps of valuable but unextractable metals piled up at the company's smelter in Port Pirie. Finally, in 1912, BHP perfected a bubble-flotation process for crushed ore that got out 97 percent of the lead, 94 percent of the silver, and 92 percent of the zinc. It revolutionized mining both there and elsewhere in the world.

As we noted earlier, Broken Hill Proprietary withdrew many years ago from mining in this area, to concentrate instead on iron, steel, and shipbuilding. The companies now working there are Broken Hill South, North Broken Hill, and Australian Mining and Smelting (controlled by Conzinc Riotinto). These companies mine various parts of the same lode, which is 170 yards wide and 4 miles long. The average grade of ore is lead, 12.3 percent; zinc, 11.7 percent; silver, 4.4 ounces per ton. Exports of lead, zinc, and their concentrates earned $140 million in 1967–1968, and a good share of them went to the U.S. Broken Hill has more minerals in good crystalline form than any other deposit on earth.

These three companies are what remain, after various shakeups, of eleven major companies that once operated in Broken Hill. The early days of their corporate careers were stormy, with strikes and violence in 1892, 1908, 1916, and 1919. A single man could cause a strike; unions were numerous and divided. Then, in 1923, Patrick Eugene O'Neill, driver of a night-cart (toilet) in the mines, conceived the idea of a union of unions, and founded it under the name of the Barrier Industrial Council. Since then, the BIC and the companies, completely ignoring the arbitration process that prevails in the rest of Australia, have set the terms of employment in Broken Hill, and the BIC has gone on to control the town right down to deciding which shopkeepers shall prosper by union blessing and which shall be ruined by boycott. As much as for its wealth, Broken Hill is known for its rigid sociology. For example, every single mine worker is forced to subscribe to the union-owned newspaper, which has the brassy name of *Barrier Daily Truth*, even if this means that three or four copies of the paper get delivered to the same address every morning. The government of the town, in effect, is in the hands of the miners' union, and it shapes every aspect of life. Paddy O'Neill was known for years, until his death, as the uncrowned king of Broken Hill. His chief accomplishment was winning for the union a "lead bonus" (production bonus) that used to run a shilling a week but now comes to $5.50.

English-born Joseph B. Keenan ("Joe is the name, sir") is the current president of the Barrier Industrial Council.

Question: "Is this a company town run by a union?"

Keenan: "Yes, more or less. We're called the Kremlin; it's not true. I'm the boss of the town, yes, but not on Kremlin terms."

Mr. Keenan obligingly gives examples of the strait-jacket conditions of life imposed by the union. No one can get a job in Broken Hill, for example, unless he has lived there for eight consecutive years out of the last ten—this is to "keep wanderers out." Women who marry must resign their jobs in three months. "Too many girls as it is for the work available," says Mr. Keenan. "We don't want married women to take daughter's jobs." There are exceptions—subject to union control. "We allowed in 'foreigners'—Italians, Yugos, Greeks, and Maltese—good citizens, good miners." Prices in shops are controlled by the union's power to declare a store "black" and boycott it. Shops that do not advertise in the *Truth* are likely to be declared black. Union membership is nine thousand—five thousand in the mines, four thousand in aboveground jobs.

The compensation for living with these rules, Mr. Keenan points out, is the "best amenities in the world. We've fought not just for pay and better living conditions, but amenities. Hospitalization, job security, a month's free vacation at the seaside with families, a thirty-five-hour week for miners underground, early retirement with pensions." The companies will lend a miner $8,000 at 2.5 percent interest, for housebuilding. If a man is killed in the mines, no one works the next day. Miners work seven-hour shifts, 8 A.M. to 3 P.M. and 4 P.M. to 11 P.M.; another shift, midnight until 7 A.M., is for maintenance. Boys are usually hired by the mines at seventeen and begin to go underground at eighteen, but only at twenty do they graduate to the status of miners, which is defined as being capable of handling high-explosive gelignite.

The men of Broken Hill appear to enjoy their amenities hugely. They have thirteen clubs, small-town variations in the style of the St. George Leagues Club in Sydney. On a Friday they may gamble a week's wages on the slot machines. For the benefit of the second-shift miners who get off at 11 P.M., some of the pubs* stay open until midnight, which violates the letter of the written law but by analogy obeys the unwritten Australian law that a sailor should be able to get a drink when he leaves his ship. Old people are considerately treated. One street crossing is designated for "AGED PEDESTRIANS."

On Sundays, miners and their families drive down the road to Menindee, a resort town on a series of reservoirs in the Darling River. There, in the midst of the saltbush desert, they swim from beaches, and sail, and fill the air with the din of outboard motors towing water-skiers. Broken Hill's pleasures are hearty ones; miners do not read much, says Allan Coulls, chief of the local library, which circulates only ninety thousand books a year.

* In the early days Broken Hill had ninety-two bars.

Many women find Broken Hill desperately boring; they are forbidden to work, and by a fine old Australian custom, meticulously observed in Broken Hill, their men spend much of their leisure time at clubs and pubs.

*

When Mr. Keenan sits down to "meet the boss," that is, to deal with mine managers, the man he sees most frequently is J. L. Liebelt, who runs the Conzinc Riotinto interests. Mr. Liebelt is president of the Mine Managers Association, which speaks for all the companies in union negotiations. He knows mine labor problems from two angles—his father worked in the mines as a "winding engine driver," that is, windlass operator for a shaft elevator. Keenan and Liebelt do not always succeed in keeping labor peace; miners walked out for six and one-half weeks in 1968. But usually, Mr. Keenan says, "We discuss. One round of discussions lasted eighteen months. Then we in the Council report back to a mass meeting of the membership. Most of the mine managers here know us. Know the town. Have lived here all their lives." Mr. Keenan, who stands every year for election, is a mine timberman who still works underground; besides that, he is a professional musician—trumpet, sax, and clarinet—and president of the musicians' union, too. Much prestige attaches to the presidency of the Barrier Industrial Council—one holder of the job was given the Order of the British Empire.

*

Broken Hill is a town that was wisely laid out, then badly built. Its mining-town psychology gave it an impermanent air. "Anyone could knock up a shanty," recalls Mr. Keenan. Now Sir Maurice Mawby, Chairman of Conzinc Riotinto, has persuaded everyone that Broken Hill's lead, zinc, and silver are good for many decades more, and the town is beautifying itself with gardens, irrigated with water brought by a pipeline from the Darling reservoirs. Houses are still made of "wood and iron," the iron (which is ugly) being galvanized roofing, walls, and fences, but nonetheless many houses are pleasant-looking. They stand on streets metallurgically named Garnet, Chloride, Iodide, Sulfide, Kaolin, Slag, Crystal, Cobalt, and Wolfram.

A hobby of some mine managers is to "go on the land." Mr. Liebelt says, "We buy virgin land, though now it's scarce, borrow from the bank, push the scrub down, put in some sheep, and in fifteen years have a lucrative property. I have twelve thousand sheep." But whereas in the east a grazier can run four or five sheep to an acre, here it takes about twenty acres to a sheep. Properties must cover one or two hundred thousand acres to support six to ten thousand sheep. Driving through the buff-green countryside, one is much afflicted by the dry, red, sandy dust, which penetrates ears, hair, and eyes, and gets positively overwhelming when the wind blows hard; car windows must be kept closed. Broken Hill attempts to defend itself from dust by "protective tree plantations" along its southwest boundaries.

*

A final oddity about South Australia: this state, historically so stuffy and self-righteous, is the only one in the country to experiment with a liberalized abortion law. The law, which permits abortions when two doctors certify that continued pregnancy would gravely injure a woman's physical or mental health, went into force early in 1970. In the first nine months, eight hundred abortions were performed, 38 percent of them on single girls, one of them only thirteen years old. No less than 82 percent of the abortions were justified on psychiatric grounds, which led the Roman Catholic Church to continued attacks on the law for permitting "abortion on demand." The point—once again—is the image of this empress dowager of a state leading the country in experimentation and reform.

CHAPTER 15

El Dorado in Western Australia

Mining attracts the hardier and more self-reliant people.
—SIR MAURICE MAWBY

WHO EVER THOUGHT that anything could be three times the size of Texas? Western Australia is. This prodigious state covers close to one million square miles, and contains almost one-third of the total area of Australia. The state is bigger—to drive this point home—than the entire Mediterranean Sea.

But most of this stupendous terrain is desert, and the population is almost ridiculously small—little over a million people. Imagine what the United States would be like—from the Mississippi to the Atlantic, roughly the equivalent area—if it had only a million people. Distances between communities are vast, and communications, except by air, scant. The dreary endless stretch of road from Perth, the capital, to Port Hedland in the north, is known as the "Madman's Track"—there are only three towns, Geraldton, Carnarvon, and Onslow (population 260), in the whole thousand-mile distance. Until recently no other places existed at all where a motorist could pause for a drink or a meal after 8 P.M., much less a bed. Wayside restaurants and hotels today are mostly run by Greeks, the only people who can stand the loneliness. Similarly, Greeks maintain the isolated railway stations in the Sudanese desert near Khartoum.

Western Australia maintains a Flying Doctor Service, like that at Alice Springs to be described in a subsequent chapter, whereby medical aid is sent by air to isolated communities in the outback, or bush. This organization has its own radio network, which importantly assists communications in other fields. In other realms new concepts and techniques are being constantly advanced. As an example, the Commonwealth government in collaboration with American interests has studied the possible use of nuclear power to blast out a harbor for iron exports in the north.

The Western Australian railways, owned and operated by the government, take a good deal of kidding because their trains are so mortally slow, running to an average speed of thirty-seven miles per hour. One popular ditty, sung by friends to wayfarers as they are about to set out on a journey by train, is "I'll Walk Beside You, Mate." Travel by automobile has been hampered recently by a microorganism with the nice name Desulfovibrio Desulfuricans, which eats into bitumen and destroys road surfacing. One of these bugs is capable of consuming matter equal to its own weight every five seconds. But few roads have pavement, and of the others often the best that can be said is not that they are graded or graveled but merely that they are clearly defined.

Western Australia has one of the historic gold mining centers of the world, Kalgoorlie, 350 miles east of Perth, about which, amazingly enough, Herbert Hoover once wrote a lyrical song. Mr. Hoover came to the goldfields in 1897 when he was a twenty-three-year-old mining engineer, and spent ten years here off and on. The first stanza goes:

Do you ever dream, my sweetheart, of a twilight long ago,
Of a park in old Kalgoorlie where the bougainvillaeas grow,
Where the moon beams on the pathways trace a shimmering brocade
And the overhanging peppers form a lovers' promenade?*

Kalgoorlie is still active today—to understate the case—and every major mining company in the world has an agent or representative on its Golden Mile. Geologists say that it will take at least another hundred years before the wealth of the area has been completely surveyed.

Distances, to repeat, are great in Western Australia. Recently a teenager in a coastal village asked permission from her mother to go to a dance. Permission was refused, because the dance was fifteen hundred miles away. This is lonely and forbidding country, although the local statisticians take comfort in such a detail as that fourteen hundred different varieties of wild flowers are known. In one community, Marble Bar, the heat exceeded 100 degrees Fahrenheit for 160 consecutive days in 1923–1924, a record. Twice in a single week, a couple of years ago, stories appeared in the local press about men missing in the nearby desert. One was a twenty-four-year-old bricklayer, who lived in what is described as "hostile sand country" near

* And so on for eight mellifluous stanzas. Mr. Hoover was supposed to be in love with a local girl.

Derby in the north. "The searchers, including two native trackers, are on horseback, and have taken pack mules with them. It is impossible to travel in this country in a vehicle. There were areas which even a horse could not negotiate." Cases like this give rise to a hearty folklore. Tales are told, as of the Sahara, of intrepid but foolhardly pioneers dying of thirst on the edges of dried-up wells or springs. In spite of its desiccation, this is thought of locally as being "romantic" country.

Western Australia faces the Indian Ocean and the Timor Sea for a fabulous distance—4,350 miles. The state has, more than any other Australian state—although these are also bounded by seas—a true ocean image. The Indian Ocean beckons. Citizens of Perth go to Mauritius or the Seychelles for holidays, broadening their scope, and islanders from the great ocean visit Perth. The United States has several important strategic installations on the Indian Ocean coast, which have particular interest because of the recent upsurge of Soviet naval activity in these waters. Near Exmouth on Northwest Cape is a U.S. Navy VLF (very low frequency) radio station that can communicate with, and guide, submarines under water. From here, in the crunch, would go orders to Polaris subs in the Pacific or Indian oceans to fire their A-3 missiles, each with a range of 2,800 miles. Carnarvon has a tracking station vital to American astronauts; one of its radio towers rises to 1,271 feet, the highest structure in Australia. The bar in the Perth airport is called the Orbit-Inne, because the astronauts passed over it on most of their orbital flights.

Broome, up the coast, an important center for mother-of-pearl fishing before the age of plastics, now concentrates on beef processing. Cattle are driven here on what are called "beef roads." The traveler should never forget that Australia as a whole and Western Australia in particular are still frontiers inhabited by a frontier society.

The Development Factor

Indeed, the principal characteristic of Western Australia today, next to its staggering size and emptiness, is development, which has been prodigious in the last four or five years, particularly in minerals. Scratch any bit of earth in this whole immense region and you have a chance at least to strike unparalleled wealth. Western Australia is a genuine boom area—today's Golconda—and this is what makes it so exciting and vital to its citizens.

This state is outdistancing the rest of the country on any of a dozen indices of growth, among them population, retail sales, personal income, production, savings, and car registrations. Tidal power is being tapped near

Broome and Derby, where what are known as "king" tides have a rise and fall of no less than thirty-nine feet at peak level. On the Ord River, in the tropical north, a $27-million irrigation system makes possible the cultivation of cotton. As far as agriculture is concerned, more than a million acres of land are being reclaimed from the desert every year; the total area of land cleared rose from 22.8 million acres in 1958 to 32.8 million ten years later. Much land hitherto barren has been made fertile by the addition of what are called trace elements (various rare minerals, such as cerium, promethium, terbium, praseodymium, et cetera) to the normal phosphate fertilizer. Wheat production doubled in the five years before 1969. There are more than thirty times as many sheep in the state as there are human beings.

As to minerals, the figures rock the imagination—even the Australian imagination. Mineral production in Western Australia went from $54 million in 1965 to $579 million in 1970. Western Australia has the world's largest known deposits of high-grade iron ore, and substantial quantities of gold, bauxite, salt, nickel, manganese, copper, coal, and tin. The state's first commercial oil field was brought in at Barrow Island, on the north coast, several years ago, with recoverable reserves estimated at 200 million barrels.

One recent discovery in Western Australia is that of rutile, a mineral sand indispensable for the manufacture of titanium, used in nuclear reactors, airplane wings, and jet engines. Another valuable beach sand is ilmenite. Prospectors tread the beaches day by day searching for these and other arcane treasures. The Perth *Independent* has been known to carry sixty solid columns of small-type classified ads with registrations of mining strikes and claims. Everything in the world of minerals is a dizzying adventure.

Iron is king in Western Australia, but the crown prince—and glamor boy—is nickel, needed to harden steel. The mining boom has, naturally enough, induced a great deal of speculation—Australians are great gamblers, anyway—and the state's nickel mines have been the shooting stars of the Stock Exchange. The highest flier in the past few years was Poseidon. The mine was found quite by accident, when a prospecting crew, drilling for water at Windarra in Western Australia, hit nickel ore. The stock, selling at eighty cents, began to quiver and strain upward. Test drilling started, and in due time Poseidon announced that it had proved out several million tons of ore. Crazy to get in on the bonanza, buyers bid the stock up to $57. The price had to fall—instead, it sprinted to $130. Gathering the cheering stockholders together, the management announced that further drilling had confirmed that Poseidon could be a major operation. Early buyers could hardly believe their luck. In two weeks the price hit $200, in eight weeks

$280. The stock came to be known as "the big P." Turbulent scenes took place on the Sydney Stock Exchange. In one melee a broker had an ear torn off. Inevitably, a few professionals got to wondering how a mine consisting of a net of test cores, and absolutely no production, could be worth such staggering amounts. In two weeks the price was back to $212; in another week, $178. A fortnight after that it thudded to $63, and a year later it was down to $37.

Another Western Australian nickel stock with a recent rambunctious history is Tasminex, which rose from $7.20 to $96 a share in a few weeks. Then, its fever gone, it crashed disastrously. "I've had enough!" its owner cried—shortly after its claim was widely photographed as being "a hole worth $180 million." Tasminex has a nickel site about seventy miles from where Poseidon has its base. Still another newly celebrated mine in Western Australia is (as we noted earlier) the one at Kambalda, near Kalgoorlie, owned by Western Mining Corporation Ltd., an omnivorous Goliath. In about 1953 Western Mining decided to expand its operations, which had been based on gold, to base metals. The Kambalda deposits, test-drilled in 1966 after geologists found traces of high-grade nickel sulphide ore in what they call "gossans," or outcroppings, yielded a bonanza. Nickel mining began in August 1967.

That the boom is hugely speculative doesn't seem to cause much concern. Several local authorities are, however, sharply disturbed by the possibly disastrous effects of the mining bonanza on the basic physiognomy of Western Australia. Little thought has been given to the survival of vegetation, birds, and animals. Conservation is neglected in the face of the "insane hurry to get things out of the ground," as one university professor said. So much is being taken out of the ground so fast, that, in the words of another authority, the result could well be the transformation of Western Australia into "a vast disused quarry," before long.

Australians in general are, as we know, markedly materialistic and commerce-minded, but another side to the picture exists as well. Most citizens are possessed of—or by—what can only be called "the Dream," and a perception of this is essential for understanding the country. The "Dream," which cloaks utilitarianism with fantasy, is that of a great fulfilled Australia —on its own, secure, prosperous—with proper attention to human values. The Western Australians in particular want not only to be rich, but to be happy getting rich and happy in their enjoyment of wealth. Moreover, in this concept they consider themselves to be the bellwether for all the rest of the Commonwealth; their strong backs will bring wealth, health, and happiness to all.

Elements in the Background

The first European ever to see Western Australia was Dirk Hartog, a Dutch explorer and merchant, who arrived at Shark Bay in 1616. A subsequent Dutchman gave a swollen little watercourse in the Perth area the name Swan River, because of its black swans; the descendants of these swans are still there. In 1829 a British naval officer, Captain Charles H. Fremantle, landed at the mouth of the Swan and took formal possession of "all that part of New Holland not part of New South Wales." Since New South Wales was already British, the whole continent now became so. At the beginning, Western Australia was known as the Swan River Settlement. Fremantle's name is commemorated by Fremantle, Perth's present lodgment on the sea and the state's most active port.

Clearly the most important event in the history of Western Australia was the discovery of gold (including nuggets weighing 71 pounds and 125 pounds at Coolgardie) and the minerals outburst in 1890–1900. A 350-mile pipeline was built to carry water across the blinding desert from Perth to Kalgoorlie. At one point the population of the goldfields reached 200,000 (versus 21,000 today). The area was known as "the land of sin, sand, sorrow, sickness, sore eyes, and Sir John Forrest" (the unpopular Governor of the time). The most interesting political development in the present century was a strong, defiant move by Western Australia to secede from the rest of the Commonwealth and become an independent political entity. This was caused by resentment at being treated like a "Cinderella" by the other states, but the proposal failed. As of today, Western Australia could not survive without the rest of the Commonwealth in spite of its commanding wealth. One curiosity is that it is the only Australian state without a coat of arms.

Western Australians descend mostly from sound British stock, and, except in the mines, English blood still predominates, along with Scottish, Welsh, and Irish. The number of convicts pitched out into this wilderness was only 9,700 all told.

The Western Australians are extremely sensitive about white supremacy and intend to maintain it at any cost. In the whole of Western Australia there is hardly a single Negro. The local attitude to the Aborigines is clement —provided the Aborigines "keep to their place." In Port Hedland whites can be seen playing pool with Aboriginal boys in the best hotel. Western Australians, asked if amelioration of the white-supremacy concept might come in time, reply defensively. They say invariably that there is no bigotry about the white attitude, no racial hysteria like that in South Africa, and very little personal antagonism to blacks or browns. One remark: "We know that we're part of Southeast Asia, but we prefer to go down the aisle alone." Another: "There's no need for us to create a problem for ourselves. Let well enough alone." Another: "I'm against anything that causes trouble. Why import it?" Still another from a last-ditcher: "I'd rather give up our whole mineral development than give an inch to any black!"

Among white foreign communities the Italians and Greeks are most conspicuous, and a few Turks and Yugoslavs are moving in. Perth has a small Jewish community at Mount Lawley, but it plays little role in civic affairs.

Finally, there should be a word about the Western Australian character and persona. The principal thing to say is that these are typically Australian —only more so. Most men have large aggressive chins, and combine outer toughness with a somewhat tepid interior. Most women are appallingly dressed. Citizens have a considerable regard for tradition, if only because this is one thing they lack. Perhaps most are more progressive in their thinking, less provincial and suburban, than their peers in the east. Many have a deep, sincere humanity, of which they are ashamed. Most are almost embarrassingly gregarious, friendly, and hospitable. This state is, as one newspaper editor put it, "a profoundly English country populated by people remarkably like Americans." But another citizen said, "Don't ever forget—Western Australia is a part of Southeast Asia inhabited by Europeans." It is still frontier country, still shining with the "Dream." People count without ratiocination on a beneficent future in which cultural and even spiritual values will find a proper place.

Then, too, Western Australia goes a bit beyond the rest of the country in its pronunciation of English ("tin sinz" for "ten cents," "to gaow" for "to go," "nawoo" for "no," "males" for "meals," "prem*ice*" for "premise"), and in its use of startling abbreviations in newspaper headlines—"TAS" for "Tasmania" or "PARLT" for "Parliament." One other minor observation: this is certainly not an area where aircraft stewardesses are chosen for looks.

Perth, a Pleasant Small City

This may be the most agreeable of all the Australian state capitals, and it has been called the last "authentic" city in the Commonwealth. Geographically it corresponds to Sydney as San Francisco does to New York. Its population is about 650,000, out of roughly a million for the whole of Western Australia, which indicates why decentralization is a lively issue. For years, poised on the Indian Ocean between sea and desert, Perth was called the most isolated capital in the world, but aviation has made a change—all the major airlines serving Australia stop here on their way to Asia, Europe, and beyond. One remark is that Perth is the farthest capital in the world from Washington, D.C., but that it doesn't have to be—if you could only drive a hole straight through the center of the earth. A common joke characterizing the differences between the Australian state capitals runs like this: What are the first words said to a visitor in each?

Brisbane: " 'Ave a drink, mate!"

Sydney: "What's your bank balance?"

Melbourne: "Where did you go to school?"

Adelaide: "Of what religious persuasion were your parents?"

Perth: " 'Ave a drink, mate!"

The city has eight golf courses, three race tracks, and four legitimate theaters. The audiences do not rise for "God Save the Queen" after performances, as they do elsewhere in Australia. The local university is attractive and soundly run; in seventeen years its faculty has jumped from 15 professors to 58, from 1,500 students to 7,000. Municipal problems are like those almost everywhere else in the world, such as traffic, drunken driving, and a sharply increasing venereal disease rate. This is the sunniest of state capitals, and even in midwinter the temperature seldom goes below 50 degrees; snow is unknown. An evening breeze from the Indian Ocean is called "the Fremantle doctor"; another wind, which yachtsmen hate, is "the southerly buster."

If a person moves out of Perth, people say that he has "gone east," never defining whether the destination is Sydney, Melbourne, or what. The biggest "foreign" colony is the Italian (38,000), followed by Greek (11,000-12,000, once a strong and cohesive group, but split in recent years by the schism in Athens), Dutch (6,000-7,000, split on religious grounds), and Yugoslav (4,000-5,000, split every which way). The city is still overwhelmingly British in tone and context, but American influence is rising. There are 3,900 Americans in Western Australia as a whole. The American consular district centering on Perth is, incidentally, the largest land district in the State Department system. (The one based on Hawaii is bigger, but consists mostly of water.)

Place names within the Perth metropolitan area make a fine hodgepodge from Maida Vale, pure English, to Wanneroo, pure Australian. In the outback are Norseman, Mount Thirsty, The Cups, Overshot, Bungulluping, Mangimup, Cape Naturaliste, Haul-Off Rock, and Double Tank. In fact, Western Australia has many tank towns—double-name places that literally end with "Tank," denoting the most essential feature. Again we see the importance of water or the lack thereof.

Perth has, unexpectably, a hotel, the Parmelia, which is not only the best in Australia but one of the best in the world, fit to rank with the Ritz in Paris, the Gritti Palace in Venice, or even Claridge's in London. The decor—done by a Chicagoan—is striking, the amenities luxurious, and the atmosphere beguiling. Chairs are built for both looks and comfort; carpets are thick, and the hardware dazzling. Brandy snifters are heated, and the bathrooms have bidets.

Ten years ago anybody in Western Australia who drank wine was a sissy, but this is no longer the case. The good restaurants in Perth have copious wine lists nowadays, and the wines are carefully classified, plentiful, and cheap. Rarely does anything cost more than four dollars a bottle. A normal-sized beer costs seventeen cents. Food is inexpensive, too—steaks at the best restaurant in town are $2.25, about half of what they are in Sydney. The pubs are licensed till 10 P.M., and booths are not allowed—this is so that a cop, checking up, can see the whole ensemble at a glance. Even in the best hotels, the floor maids do not wear uniforms but simply ordinary frocks or dresses. Bartenders, as is true everywhere in Australia, are invariably women, and these, too, work in ordinary dress—aprons are unknown. These barmaids are formidable young women, who can get rid of an unruly male customer as smoothly as a bouncer on Third Avenue.

It is difficult to assess social patterns in general. Australians are, in one dimension at least, an extremely formal people, and what is called "society" is rather rigidly put together. Much social life centers on clubs, of which there are multitudes, and white tie is often worn. At even a small affair in a club, the host is likely to make a speech with a microphone. Women, one hears, "are put severely in their place," that is, they work in the kitchen. Nobody has servants. The servant class has utterly disappeared. An odd phenomenon, also to be noted elsewhere in Australia, is that, taking a taxi, the passenger sits with the driver in front; to sit alone in back would be an unthinkable solecism. If a couple takes a taxi, the male passenger may well sit with the driver, while the woman is relegated to the back seat alone.

Games are all-important; Western Australians (like most other Australians) work off their surplus energy in sport, or dissipate it lying prostrate on a beach. One sport little known elsewhere is bushwalking—hiking across the outback. Perth carries a note of blandness, but street scenes can be animated. There are any number of espresso bars, lots selling secondhand automobiles, and shops bursting with radio music. In older days the police used British motorcycles; now, Japanese. Buses have a brace at the rear for holding baby carriages. The newspapers are full of advertisements for "aboveground swimming pools" ("You Can't Beat Our Prices"), and for savings banks which pay 6.5 percent interest per year. But a depositor, to receive this, must give a six-month notice of withdrawal after the first $200.

*

Southeast of Perth, around the jagged elbow of Cape Leeuwin, is the remarkable town of Esperance, near a point appropriately named Cape Arid. Indeed, the hinterland served by Esperance was almost totally useless for cultivation until quite recently, when, as mentioned above, a method was devised for treating the soil with new mineral fertilizers. Here a number of United States citizens—among them Art Linkletter and David Rockefeller—have large properties, called stations. One covers several hundred thousand acres.

A man who has played a critical and creative role in developing Western Australia in the last decade or so is Charles W. M. Court, the Minister for Industrial Development and for the North West until his party fell from power in 1971. Mr. Court is a heavily set six-footer, graying, with a russet complexion and boundless energy. His articulateness is notable. Born in England in 1911, he was brought to Australia by his parents at the age of six weeks. Again we see the rise of the so-called common man—his father was a plumber.

British migrants to Australia were not assisted financially in those days, and the Court family arrived under its own steam. Young Court wanted to be a lawyer, but at that time one had to pay a premium to enter a law firm, so that, he says, he "had to settle for being a chartered accountant." During the war he rose from the ranks to lieutenant colonel, and fought on Bougainville in the Solomons. Entering politics as a Liberal in 1953, he won a blue-ribbon seat at Nedlands, and has held it ever since. He still maintains a partnership in a private accountancy firm, and is an accomplished musician, being an enthusiastic cornet player and member of a local band.

"To get off the sheep's back"—that was his early philosophy. "We're still on it, but we've given the sheep a new back," he adds heartily. His predominant aim for Western Australia is to diversify, encourage industrial development, and, above all, rationalize mineral production. "Activate, activate!" he pleads. "We must come to grips with our great natural resources, harness them to our use!" His approach is vigorously positive. "People said that Perth was the most isolated capital in the world. All that they meant was that it was far away. What we've done is bring it nearer."

Mr. Court claims that Western Australia absorbed private investment capital at the rate of $2 million per week in 1960, $2 million per day in 1970, and can take $1 million *per business hour* in 1980. Total private investment in the state during the 1970's, he contends, may reach $21 billion. "It's magical," he says. "There were three thousand people in the Pilbara area, the size of Britain, in 1959. Now, forty thousand. In 1980, two hundred thousand. We mustn't be frightened of speed. We've never learned to live under prosperity. We're too slow, too easygoing. If something doesn't get in our hair, we'll probably be the richest area on earth in fifteen years. In ten years, we've opened up ten million *arable* acres, not pastoral or grazing land, but farmland. We're putting water in, stock, fences, clearing the virgin bush. And we have found oil—to our horror! It's too much! Found it in the first well we put down. Our program in the next thirty years calls for a most vigorous thrust in metallurgy. Even today, our bauxite goes out as alumina—we're not up to producing actual aluminum as yet. Like South America, we're still largely a raw-material economy. We'll get into aluminum ingots by 1976. Bauxite brings us five dollars a ton, alumina sixty dollars, but aluminum will bring six hundred dollars."

He wrote recently: "Making money is not evil. Tiredness, gutlessness, shortsightedness—these are the cancers."

*

Another remarkable man is Sir Thomas Wardle, Lord Mayor of Perth, known as "Tom the Cheap." Mr. Wardle, who was born in Perth of humble origin, is close to sixty, dark of hair, sharp of face, smallish in stature, sleek-looking, with bright eyes, neat. Mr. Wardle is a merchant—one of the best-known in Australia. Some years ago, while working in a bank, it suddenly occurred to him that the rise of TV would make movie theaters "redundant." Promptly he took a lease on an empty theater, and converted it into a big grocery store. It caught on, largely because the canny Mr. Wardle had another idea—to sell everything at prices 5 percent less than his competitors.

Now he has stores, called "Tom the Cheap," in every Australian state except Queensland, and has become a merchant of almost mythical prowess. In Western Australia, the Wardle stores sell one-third of all groceries sold in the state. "I was very cheeky," he says. "I wouldn't let the banks mortgage me, and I sold for cash." For seven years he couldn't sell cigarettes, because the tobacco companies refused to provide them at a low enough price, but they finally capitulated. In some respects Mr. Wardle's career and methods resemble those of Henry Ford, in whom he has a vivid interest.

Tom the Cheap was elected Mayor in 1967. "I came in as a clean-skin," he says. A clean-skin, in Western Australian slang, is an unbranded calf; in other words, Tom had no commitments to anybody. He was the first mayor in the city's history who had never served previously on the Municipal

Council, and politics as such doesn't interest him at all. "I keep away from politics—I'd never like to be a politician." He belongs to no party, and supports whatever Commonwealth or state government happens to be in power.

His biggest problem is, as he sees it, "to get the best development we can." This is not as easy as might be thought. "Our development came late, so that we can't benefit from experience." Better public transport is an issue; so is more parking space for commuters. The city recently hired a Norwegian expert to work out details of a planned "growth program."

Mounted on one wall of the Mayor's office is a steel case of a four-inch shell fired from the Australian warship *Perth* before it was sunk in the Battle of Sunda Strait in March 1942. The shell case was recovered and presented recently to the city of Perth. What is interesting is that coral still clings to it, and the Mayor, showing it, seems to be indicating that, in Western Australia, a kind of life grows even on dead metal.

*

Langley George Hancock, born in 1909, stout, bespectacled, tough, explosive, ruthless, with cauliflower ears, is probably the richest man in Western Australia and certainly one of the most picturesque. He exemplifies Australian traits which are supposed to be characteristic of the country as a whole, but which are in fact not seen everywhere—drive, durability. His wealth and power derive mostly from mining, and he owns or controls Mount Tom Price, in the Hamersley Range, a fabulously rich iron ore deposit. Other mineral interests include manganese, lead, tin, copper, gold, and asbestos. His agricultural properties are vast as well, including Mulga Downs, a 750,000-acre sheep station in the Fortescue Valley and another—500,000 acres—near Hamersley. Like almost all Western Australians, he is more interested in development than the present accouterments of power.

Lang Hancock, as he is generally known, comes of pioneer stock—of course. His great-great-grandfather, George Hancock, was an early settler north of Perth when this was still part of the Swan River Colony, and his great-grandmother, Emma Withnell, was known as "the first white woman in the north." Her son, Jimmy Withnell, set off the Pilbara gold rush in 1887, when, on the family property, he picked up a stone to throw at a bird and found it to be half-gold. The present Lang Hancock similarly owes part of his fortune to an accident. A vigorous prospector, he flew his own light aircraft everywhere. He was blown off course in bad weather some years ago and was forced to make an emergency landing on what seemed to be a dreary stretch of flat rock. It turned out to be solid iron. Later, as he tells the story, he confesses that he had "a whisper" that iron might be there.

Mr. Hancock is supposed to hold more mineral leases than any man in the world, and, together with a partner, has, as he himself says, "more iron ore than the total resources of the United States and Canada combined." A single company in Japan is his biggest customer. It did not take long to find out from his conversation that he is a fierce, fixed, and tenacious advocate of private enterprise. He resents it extremely that the government takes a large share of mining profits in royalties and taxes, "for doing nothing," and says that "no government man ever found an ounce of anything." Above all he wants to draw foreign money into Western Australian investment and development, and thus personifies the present national mood.

CHAPTER 16

Across the Blazing North

We don't complain of dust unless it clogs the cash registers.
—A BUSINESSMAN IN MOUNT NEWMAN

THE SMALL PLANE dips into the wind, and one sees the desert floor below —ocher, umber, violet, dotted with dimples as well, greenish-yellow small circles, perfectly circular, in perfectly symmetrical procession, like a pattern on a child's dress. Did some sort of vegetation once grow here? Along a cinnamon-colored road, the color of Rome, a bright white car, the only car along unending miles of road, races to meet the plane.

So one arrives at Newman in the Pilbara mining area. Lonely country! The nearest oasis is Weeli Wolli creek, with a few date palms, fifty-three miles away. The nearest community is Nullagine, a shire center seventy miles away, with four or five hundred people, many of them prospectors; here an asbestos mine once stood, now shut down. The car proceeds swiftly from the airstrip to Newman through utter emptiness, the only car on the long straight road. Yet from this car it is possible to telephone New York.

The wheels cast up plumes of maroon dust. The sky seems to be absolutely cloudless; not a stray wisp of cloud, not a shred of white, is visible from one edge of the horizon to the other. The colors of the hills nearby change with the sun—blue in the morning, grayish at noon, green-orange at dusk. A willy-willy, a small twister, or tornado, builds up behind the car. Beside the road lies a bung-arrow, or lizard, two and a half feet long—a baby, says the guide. Growing on the solid, somber hills of iron is a primitive form of vegetation, the spiky spinifex. The car crosses a river, called the Fortescue, but it is invisible—it flows underground. Once a year or so, however, it floods nicely, and the nearby community taps it—the only local source of potable water. "It's O.K. to drink," the people say, "but we have to soften it for laundry."

The rainfall here is ten inches a year in a good year, but some years bring almost nothing. Etiolated white trees, ghost gums, waver fragilely along the roads; fauna in the neighborhood includes wild camels (used for transport on the early stations), bush turkey, and, of course, kangaroos—some ducks, too. Men hunt and shoot. The sights include a shriveled little golf course, and tennis courts where, on account of the ripping heat, play is possible only at night, under lamps. But in winter Newman has a pleasant climate; the temperature can drop to 27 degrees Fahrenheit or thereabouts; taps freeze.

The two dominant mountains are Mount Whaleback (because it is shaped like a whale if you give your imagination a little run) and Mount Newman (3,700 feet), a kind of promontory on the Ophthalmia Range, which got its peculiar name because the man who discovered it, by name Giles, came down with an eye disease called "sandy blight," which nearly blinded him. Whaleback, unnamed ten years ago, is described by the local authorities as the single most valuable real estate property in the world. Its value is said to be $250 million per square mile, and it covers four square miles.

Close to the center of town is a small billboard: "WELCOME TO NEWMAN —FOUNDED 1968." A youthful community indeed! Once this was a cattle station covering a million acres; parts of it still survive nearby. The total population of Newman, this stout little wand in the wilderness, two years after its foundation, is about twelve hundred. The mining company built an airstrip, a railroad, and the town itself, and owns everything in it except the Walkabout Motel—comfortable, sixty-four beds, expensive, always full.

The miners work aboveground (Newman is an open-cut mine) in two ten-hour shifts, six days a week; nonminers in the company's employ work a sixty-hour week as well. At the mine the shifts are 6:30 A.M. to 5 P.M. (half an hour for lunch), and 8 P.M. to 6:30 A.M., and the wage rate varies by the job; the average for sixty hours is $100 to $120 a week. Many men come here for quick money, and like to work overtime; the company has a hard time getting experienced miners or skilled workers. A secretary receives $90 a week here, as against $40 in Perth. A locomotive driver gets $12,000 a year. Workers are strongly unionized, and there are five unions, one tame, four militant.

Housing has—naturally—been a problem. At first prefab houses were brought in from Adelaide, but now houses are built here on the spot. All have steel frames, air-conditioners, electric refrigerators, kitchens, water supply, and sewage disposal. The houses rent for six dollars a month, and furniture is thrown in free. A family moving in needs nothing but blankets, sheets, and crockery. Single men live in two-story dormitories, air-conditioned, and fully furnished; however, they are supposed to wash after their stint in "the hill" in a nearby barracks, not at home. In their dormitories the workers have a mess staffed by a French (no less) firm of "cooking contractors"; full board is fourteen dollars a week. About eleven hundred gallons of beer (sixty-two kegs) are consumed per week—which works out to roughly a gallon per person, not very much.

The Newman community (before the actual town was set up) derives from a long-time Western Australia prospector, A. S. ("Stan") Hilditch, who came out to the region in 1957 searching for manganese. This was forlorn and empty country, still largely unexplored, and he asked some local Aborigines for advice. They pointed to what later became known as Mount Whaleback. They did not know, nor did Mr. Hilditch, that this would be proved to contain 650 million tons of high-grade iron ore. Hilditch came across a kind of ore deposit known as a "banded formation"; he sent it to his partner in Perth to be assayed, and it was found to be hematite with an iron content of 68.8 percent. The highest content ever known is 69.9 percent. Hilditch knew he had a big strike, but at the moment he could do nothing with it, because the Commonwealth government had imposed an embargo on the export of iron ore. This was because the authorities of the time, unaware how much ore the country possessed, thought that Australia should keep a large proportion of its ore reserves at home for purposes of security and defense. When the extent of the iron riches became known, the embargo was lifted, and Hilditch and his partner pegged their claims.

About a decade ago they worked out a royalty agreement with a financial group. They did not get as good terms as Lang Hancock did at Mount Tom Price, but it was enough to enable them to retire nicely. As of today, the company (Mount Newman Mining Company Pty. Ltd.) is owned by the Amax Iron Corporation (United States interests—25 percent), Pilbara Iron Ltd. (a holding company for another Australian mammoth, the Colonial Sugar Refining Company—30 percent), Dampier Mining Company (a holding company for Broken Hill—30 percent), Seltrust Iron Ore Ltd. (a holding company for the Selection Trust, a British amalgam—5 percent), and Mitsui and C. Itoh (a grouping of two Japanese trading companies—10 percent). Selection Trust, to add a complication, owns a portion of Amax, which increases its influence; this is not, however, ostentatiously exerted. A small percentage is held by Australian banks and insurance companies, which marks the first time that institutions in this category have gone into mining ventures.

The Newman mine looks like a hill made of chocolate fudge. It is not, of course, a hole in the ground, but a mountain, rising above the plain. One rides up in a stout vehicle, advancing layer by layer on a series of steep terraces, suffused with dust and perhaps mildly impressed by the fact that, on top at last, one is standing on a couple of hundred million dollars' worth of iron ore. Below are three hundred square miles of terrain solid with mineral leases. Technically the operation of the mine is simple—there's nothing to do except tear the mountain apart and cart pieces of it away; blasts take place continually, and each releases 50,000 to 100,000 tons of hematite. Power shovels seize 15 tons at a bite in their huge jaws. The carting is done by yellow trucks which carry the ore down the terraces; tires on these monsters cost $2,500, and they last about a month. The road is seventy feet wide, but even so accidents occur, if the trucks, fighting the steep grade, slip and turn over, despite their elaborate power brakes. The drivers get $120 a week.

Down the Slope to Hedland

From the chartered airplane flying to Port Hedland, the terrain beneath shows not a sign of life—not a human being, not a road, not a telegraph pole, not a tree. There is perhaps no other flight over territory so limitlessly barren except the one along the coast of Chile—also mining country. A railway does, however, exist, to carry the ore 265 miles from the mines to the port; this was built by a combination of American and Canadian capital, and a subsidiary of American Metal Climax, Inc., New York, holds a 25 percent interest in it.

The Port Hedland airstrip handles a lively traffic. Until a few years ago the planes to Perth or Darwin were too small to carry more than half a dozen passengers, and it could take months to get a reservation out. A welcoming sign says, "PORT HEDLAND—ALTITUDE TWENTY FEET."

A Dutchman named Peter Hedland landed here on a two-ton cutter, the *Mystery*, in 1867, and settlement began in 1893. So Port Hedland is, by the standards of this part of the world, a venerable town, but still raw, rough-edged, vital. The population has grown from three hundred to about three thousand in the past few years. It is usually torrid in the daytime, but a breeze blows at night. The principal problem is, of course, water. Rainfall is about sixteen inches in a normal year; it may not rain for months, then fifteen inches will fall in a single twelve-hour burst, the result of a cyclone in the Indian Ocean passing close to shore. Port Hedland suffers so acutely from lack of water that the townsmen set out tanks to collect dew. Two one-hundredths of an inch of dew comes in a normal night, which people say is a lot. Strips of lawn that have been watered look so unnaturally green that they seem dyed.

Port Hedland is built on a mangrove swamp, and a hook of land stretches into a spit two thousand feet offshore. But to get there, except by boat, calls for an eighteen-mile trip, because of the difficult terrain. Nearby is the Monte Bello Prohibited Area, a group of islands still radioactive as a result of British nuclear tests conducted in the vicinity. There isn't much to see in Port Hedland itself. A good many houses are built on stilts to assist ventilation, because few people can afford air-conditioning; prices are extraordinarily high on goods or services that have to be brought in; a good house costs $50,000 to $60,000. A forlorn small race track stands exposed in the smarting heat, with a dirt track and a Quonset hut for serving drinks; two meetings are held a year, two days each. It seemed quite typical that, even in this metallic Shangri-la, racing should be a formidable preoccupation. Another curiosity is the presence of forty-four-gallon steel drums cut in half; they are used to protect seedling trees. The streets and roads nearby are full of discarded beer cans—people toss the empties out of their cars as they drink and ride. A large shiny white pyramid may attract the attention of visitors—a stockpile of salt mined by a San Francisco company.

There is a well-run motel which does, however, have a defect; page calls are incessant, and can be heard in every room. Nearby is an older, more conventional hotel, which looks like something out of Somerset Maugham: the garden seethes with bougainvillaea, but the kitchen serves bacon-and-egg-burgers and fish and chips. A sign in the bar says, "GENTLEMEN ARE REQUESTED TO WEAR SHOES AND SOCKS IN THE DINING ROOM."

Port Hedland is not in the strict sense a company town; only about 400 people from Newman live here. Mining is, however, its blood. The population was about 1,500 in 1959, about 6,000 in 1969, and estimates call for 30,000 by 1973. Pace, pace! Thirty-four different nationalities are numbered on the labor force—Australians first, then British, then Italians, then Yugoslavs. A few Icelanders, believe it or not, work at Mount Tom Price nearby.

Port Hedland cops are tough. A man picked up for a misdemeanor or minor infraction of the law, not worth bringing to trial or sending to jail, is driven twenty miles out of town on the road to Perth, then pitched out and told to fend for himself. The chances are that he will be picked up by some passing car. If not, he is out of luck, because, in summer, if he cannot hitch a ride and has no water, he could die of thirst or heat exposure.

At Port Hedland's mineral processing installation, enormous yellow machines on railway tracks chew up the ore that descends from Newman into chunks or pellets of manageable size. These fantastic appurtenances are

Japanese in manufacture, and, since Japan is a major market for Hedland ore, it is pleasantly fanciful to think that they are made of what they are working on.

The ore comes in from Newman by train, long solid lines of bucket-shaped cars, 140 cars to a train, eight trains a day. "They will run every two hours when we reach forty-million-tons-a-year production," says a company employee, with Australian confidence. The towering mounds of ore are watered to keep them from blowing away. The plant handling this immense operation is so fully automated that six men can operate the whole thing, but three hundred more are needed for maintenance. One sees such incomprehensible machines as the rotary car dumper, the tertiary crusher control system, the boom station, and the bucket wheel reclaimer. Ore goes out by sea to its markets in Japan, eastern Australia, Europe, et cetera, and is handled by ships which can take loads of up to 72,000 tons. The port is to be enlarged substantially to hold ships with a 100,000-ton capacity, and Hedland will become one of the six or seven ports in the world capable of this. Meanwhile, it is these Port Hedland installations that are largely responsible for the contemporary industrialization of Japan, a fact that augments local Australian pride. Beyond this is the spectacle of Port Hedland itself—such a melange of dreariness, hope, ardor, the Australian striving for identity and fulfillment, the boom-or-bust psychology, and above all the stubborn, indomitable spirit of the pioneer and frontier.

But it's a spartan life for the women in these towns. One hears such remarks as: "If only I could go somewhere where I could wear a hat!"

CHAPTER 17

Darwin and Alice Springs

Minimum Dres (sic) *for Gentlemen in Lounge-Dining Room is Clean Shorts, Long Socks, and Clean Shirt.*

—SIGN IN A DARWIN HOTEL

THE COMMONWEALTH OF AUSTRALIA consists not merely of six states but of a vast region known as the Northern Territory, which has not yet attained statehood because its population is so scant, covers 523,000 square miles, about one-sixth of the total area of Australia, and resembles Western Australia to an extent, but is much less developed. Most of it is emptiness. Sometimes it is called the "Deep" or "Wild" North. There are only a few more than seventy thousand people, including twenty-one thousand Aborigines. It has several cattle stations as big as Connecticut, and American capital controls between 60 and 70 percent of the whole of its pastoral land. Northern Australia belonged originally to New South Wales, but was annexed by South Australia in 1863; in 1911 it was transferred to the jurisdiction of the Commonwealth, where it still is.

The northern headland of the territory, Arnhem Land, has been described as "the most primitive, unexplored, uninhabited country" left in the world. Here thousands of buffaloes still roam near the edges of forlorn seas. Aborigines have carved a special life of their own out of the bitter inland wastes. In spite of its limitless desolation, remoteness, and aridity, Arnhem Land has become a kind of symbol of romance to many Australians who live nearby. Barring the bauxite mine at Gove, the area is not yet ruined by mineral discoveries, cities, or sprouting new settlements. People have the spirit of going out West, as in American frontier days. Even pioneers with prosperous cattle stations in North Australia like to take expeditions into Arnhem

Land—holidays with their families—to see at first hand the spectacle of a region so remote and pure.

Capital of the Northern Territory is Darwin, the principal port of the north, which a local booster pamphlet describes as "the gateway to three million square miles," and "the newest, noisiest [*sic*] city in Australia." In fact, it isn't noisy at all—it is a dead-end city. But, recessed as it is, Darwin somehow manages to be attractive in the way of most Australian frontier towns.

Its isolation is formidable; no other community of consequence exists within hundreds of miles; its sister city, Alice Springs, lies a thousand miles down the "bitumen," or highway. But flight time to Alice on the new jets is only about two hours, and the traveler can get there by road in twenty-six to thirty hours, if lucky; there are rest houses and petrol stations open twenty-four hours a day. The oddly named village, Rum Jungle, lies close by. Actually, Darwin's nearest important neighbor is not on the mainland at all, but is the derelict Portuguese island of Timor four hundred miles offshore to the west, which nobody but an inflamed masochist would ever want to visit twice.

In November, peak of the North Australian summer, the town simmers at an average daytime temperature of 93 degrees, and the water in the hotel's swimming pool goes up to 110 degrees. No one uses the pool, not even children, till dusk, but from then till midnight it is full of handsome young men and women, lolling at their pleasure. The salesgirl in the drugstore, asked when the weather will turn cooler, replies, "About My."

Darwin is built flat; there are only five elevators—lifts—in the whole of the Northern Territory, three here and two in Alice Springs. In the vigorously run hotel, guests inscribe their names in a large ledger, a practice common all over Australia. Air-conditioning is present, but it is somewhat crude and apt to make things too cold—icy. "Darwin rig"—shorts, long socks, shirt—is *de rigueur* for the bar. The dining room has a punkah; its wooden sails give a certain amount of propulsion to the sodden atmosphere. After a day or two the headwaiter will be likely to address you by your first name. Following the almost universal Australian custom, the guest carries his own drinks from bar to table. Partly this is caused by labor shortage. Australians clean their plates meticulously at lunch and dinner; nowhere are such huge meals enjoyed so hugely. Buffalo steaks are a specialty, and milk comes in frozen all the way from Brisbane. Beer is, of course, the universal drink—and how nourishingly good it is! Darwin is, in fact, reported to be the second-biggest beer-consuming city in the world on a per capita basis, after Munich. There are few inhibitions about drinking—or about anything else. A motel bears the nice name "Hot and Cold," and is favored by young lovers. A sign on a filling station on Darwin's main street says, "SWITCH TO CALTEX-ASTRON AND DRINK UP THE SAVINGS." But it is not true, as has been written, that the streets are littered with discarded beer bottles. Darwin is spick-and-span, well kept up, a neat city.

This is the more remarkable because, of course, the prevailing background is so lush and tropical. A marvelously colored red-orange flowering tree, the poinciana, lines some streets, as do clumps of white frangipani, radiant in the sun. At night thunder cracks out of overcast skies like a succession of revolver shots. Darwin has good beaches, but swimming in the sea is impossible for several months each year, when an ugly marine animal that can be dangerous, the sea wasp, hovers in the surf. On the beaches here seashells have been found which geologists estimate to be thirty million years old. Another oddity in a different realm is that many automobiles in Darwin and its vicinity carry a frontal grill known as a bullbar, to fend off kangaroos.

Dingoes, wild dogs, roam the environs of the city, and are pests. They never attack human beings, but they seize upon calves on the outskirts of town if they are *in extremis* from fright or hunger and can find nothing else to feed on.

Darwin, like Newman and Port Hedland, has a great rush of citizens going south at Christmastime; the planes are choked. One somewhat unexpected detail of the city's landscape is that it contains two spectacularly good modern churches, one of them Roman Catholic. Houses are built commonly on stilts, so that there is room to park automobiles underneath. New houses go up all the time, and are expensive—say, $60,000. Once more we see the characteristics of a frontier economy. The local jail is built of galvanized iron; folklore is that the authorities let prisoners out at night to go to the movies, knowing that they are certain to return, if only because there is no place to which they could possibly escape; there's no road except the long track to Alice Springs. Finally among these generalizations one should mention that Darwin shares the country's exuberant mercantilism and will to get ahead in financial terms. This is a city where a man with money can do almost anything.

*

Essentially, Darwin consists of little but a long gently curving main street flanked by residential bungalows. Beyond this it is somewhat difficult to describe what it is like physically, except perhaps to characterize it with the term "provincial" town. Like practically everything else in Australia, Darwin has spread out significantly in recent years, and is growing with the times. Nowadays it measures about fourteen miles from rim to rim, and healthy suburbs stand where there was nothing but bush ten years ago. The population is about 29,000, including half the white population of the whole Northern Territory. The biggest communities are Greek, Italian, and Aboriginal half-breeds, about 3,500 each, followed by Chinese, full Aborigines, Germans, and a handful of Maltese. There are also knots of Filipinos and Malays, who still work—virtual slaves—under an indentured-labor system. The Chinese community dates from the 1850's; the late Mayor, and for many years the grand old man of the town, by name of Harry Chan, was Chinese. The Greeks control something like 80 percent of local business. They dominate the construction industry, avoid politics, trade with avidity, and are exemplary citizens. Darwin's leading citizen and only millionaire is Michael Paspalis, a Greek property owner.

Another distinguished citizen is Tim Bowditch, editor of the local newspapers, the Darwin *News* and the *Northern Territory Times*. He and his managing director, Rod Lever, have provided the community with a high standard of journalism. Mr. Bowditch, a lean, emphatic, and conscientious man, resembles Manchester *Guardian* editors in the old days in England—emancipated, disciplined, fixed in his convictions, unassailably liberal, and a substantial (but modest) power in the community—in fact, its conscience.

Darwin lived on pearling for a long term, but this industry collapsed when plastics replaced natural pearl. Four resources sustain the city now—copper and gold at Tennant Creek, bauxite at Gove Peninsula, manganese and iron at Groote Eylandt, and an important uranium deposit at Batchelor, sixteen miles away. Then, too, Darwin lives on its own commerce as a trading center. Politics need not concern us, but lively complaints are heard that the Commonwealth government holds the territory back by unending bureaucratic needling and too much experimentation. In essence, this community is run by Canberra, and Canberra is far away. The local administrator seemed to be somewhat isolated. His pleasant one-hundred-year-old house (no air-conditioning) was knocked about by Japanese bombardment in World War II, but reconstructed. The Japanese attacked Darwin sixty-four times, but never took it. There has never been a British administrator here—only Australians.

A Glimpse of "The Alice"

We reach now Alice Springs, an attractive small city (population about ten thousand) lying directly athwart the Tropic of Capricorn at two thousand feet of elevation. It has been called the umbilicus of Australia, and it dominates, if anything so small can be said to dominate, the central desert. Approaching Alice Springs the visitor once more becomes acutely conscious of the immense distances of Australia, its unending frugal vistas. In a peculiar way "The Alice," as people in these parts call it, seems to be a land of invention. This city with its banks, bars, gift shops, a comfortable motel, hardly seems real. Yet it has the atmosphere of a flourishing town.

Alice Springs can be extraordinarily hot in the Australian summer. The atmosphere is dry, in sharp contrast to that of Darwin, and the local word is that during Christmas and in the first months of the new year "we usually go over the century mark by three in the afternoon; the hottest period of the day comes after 4:30." Christmas presents and tinsel wreaths seem incongruous when the temperature is 104 degrees.

The Alice Springs area is lonely, rugged country. The city lies not far from what is locally said to be the biggest monolith in the world, known as Ayers Rock, two and a quarter miles long. Physically, the forces of nature operate on a large scale, and a brush fire took place not long ago with a front of four hundred miles. The isolation of the community is, as is natural, marked, and the nearest town of any size is Tennant Creek (population 1,500), 313 miles to the north. Down the southward track are Port Augusta, 800 miles away, and the splendid city of Adelaide, 1,000 miles.

Plentiful legend haunts the story of the railway which connects Adelaide and Alice Springs, through a town named Quorn. This remarkable line was built by a contingent of Afghan camel drivers imported for the occasion, and it is still called "The Ghan" after them. Some descendants of their camels still survive. Passenger trains pass up and down the line twice a week, freight three times. The tracks are not ballasted, and sometimes the berserk weather blows them away. For fourteen days a few years ago Alice Springs was cut off from provisioning—milk, meat, beer—and emergency supplies had to be flown in. The Ghan is the most exuberant of Australian trains. Its bar car carries a grand piano. The maximum speed is thirty-five miles per hour, and one traveler reports that riding through the evening he sensed the "first night out" feeling one gets on transatlantic voyages. A visitor traveling up from Adelaide often brings his automobile with him; this is deposited on an open railway flatcar, and the passenger as a rule prefers to spend most of the time of the journey in his car, not the train itself. Men and women sit out in the open cars and drink beer, tossing the empties along the track.

To repeat—a hot, scored country! Dingoes roam in the derelict highlands near Alice Springs, and dead cattle line the roads. If a calf or steer is trampled to death in an overcrowded truck, its body is simply pitched overboard; if he is merely injured, the beast is shot and pushed to the side of the road. Men get lost, and occasionally die; the average man, if lost in the summer heat, cannot expect to survive more than twelve hours without water. One American prospector died of thirst and exhaustion late in 1969, having lost his way only a small distance from "The Alice." Another, also American, took the wrong turn on his motorbike, and ran out of petrol; he was found two miles from a water bore, still alive after three days, but he died on a rescue plane sent out to fetch him. An Australian schoolteacher crash-landed a glider in the vicinity early in 1970; he survived for several days by drinking his own urine. Another Australian bushwacker died several years ago because his companions did not bother to organize a search—they thought that he had got drunk in the next settlement and decided not to come back.

What makes Alice is, of course, the desert, with purple mountains in the background. The earth is covered with gray green brush and spinifex, small eucalyptuses, ghost gums. The whole area is radiant with the peculiar quality of desert light. Here is the romance of Australia. The city itself—built flat—has a roof line predominantly gray, not red tile as in most Australian towns, because tile is too expensive to bring in. The effect, on a miniature scale, is to remind the visitor of Ibadan, another corrugated-iron city, in Nigeria. Then, too, Alice has, as is always the case in Australia, its suburban aspects; plenty of middle-class ranch houses have sprung up. Alice lies a thousand miles from any ocean, but it has its own river, the Todd. Unluckily, this stream is usually dry, having actually flowed only five times in the last ten years. A handsome war memorial, which commands a height nearby, was built to commemorate a 1963 visit to Alice Springs by Her Majesty Queen Elizabeth II, but the Queen did not have time to have a look at it. The town has an art gallery, a gift shop selling opals, a local specialty, a good-looking modern Lutheran church, a spectacularly modern school, and a swimming pool built to take 290 people a day and used by 540—loaded with chlorine as well as kids. Whites and Aborigines play and pant under trees in starfish clusters. Cops in broad felt hats—in long trousers, not shorts—look like Texas Rangers. A race track is, of course, prominent. The local newspaper, the *Centralian Advocate*, is a curiosity in the world's journalism: it covers the local news thoroughly, but has no wire services—no international or national news whatever.

In general Alice is not particularly tidy—beer bottles and cans dot the streets. The whites say that it is impossible to train the Aborigines to use receptacles. At night, the town gives forth a note of stridency, animation, even wildness—cowboys shout in the streets, children call.

A pleasant restaurant is Luigi's, made out of a refurbished, air-conditioned Quonset hut—chic for this part of the world, and with good wines. In the liquor shops Scotch whisky is sold by the gallon. In the milk bars and pizza stations hot dogs are known as saveloys.

*

The Alice had its birth in the 1870's, when explorers first began to look over the Macdonnell Ranges, where it lies. Its name was once Stuart, and soon after its founding it became a repeater station post in the telegraph line being built north-to-south across central Australia. Sir Charles Todd, the man in charge of building the telegraph, named the town for his wife, Lady Alice. The springs were a persistent water hole in the intermittent local river, which of course is named for Sir Charles. Alice Springs is a headquarters of local government for the Commonwealth, although Darwin is the territorial capital. The local district officials are, as always in Australia, competent and devoted men. Canberra keeps a mildly close eye on affairs, but Alice is too well behaved to bear much watching. As to the economy, Alice lives mostly by being an increasingly popular resort—the weather is marvelous once the crashing inferno of early summer is past.

*

A morning in the law court proved instructive: the magistrate wore no wig (too hot), and during a long session sentenced a variety of Aborigines to minor fines or admonitions for roughhouse or vagabondage during the night—there were no white defendants. Sentences varied from a seven-dollar fine for public drunkenness to four days in jail for disorderly behavior. In general, the Aborigines here seem to be lighter-skinned than in the north, cleaner, more adept. At a nearby settlement, they were being taught the rudiments of sanitation, how to cook on a stove, to clean their teeth, to use a toilet, to bake bread, and to postpone marriage till after the age of fifteen—if possible. Many Aborigines here resent having to learn English. Their chief value to the community is that they are fantastically good trackers out in the bush.

But the most interesting installation in Alice Springs is something else, the post of the Royal Flying Doctor Service. This is a truly seminal organization, whose work has been lately copied in Alaska, Kazakstan, and similar remote, empty places. The purpose is to render medical aid and services to isolated communities or families in the outback. These are given a call number and identical medical kits, packed so that Tube No. 5, let us say, an ointment, is always to be found in the bottom left-hand corner, and No. 6, a vial of penicillin, under the lid on the right. A person afflicted with illness or accident calls in to the Flying Doctor Service at any one of four periods during the day, or may ring a special alarm bell; the service covers 120 communities, 100 cattle stations, 7 settlements, and several missions over an area of 400,000 square miles. The technique is the following. Two doctors are in constant attendance at headquarters, and these, picking up a call, attempt to make a diagnosis and prescribe treatment on the radio. If the matter is serious, one of the covey of doctors on hand may make arrangements to fly out to the patient, and, if necessary, fetch him back to the hospital. An important ancillary function has grown up out of this service, namely, that the Flying Doctors, with their intricate system of radio wavelengths, have become the instrument of almost all radio traffic in the area, not just medical. Last year the Service handled sixty thousand messages.

An important, and secret, American military installation operates at Pine Gap, twelve miles from Alice Springs. This base reportedly is one of two (the other is on Guam) that relay information from satellites keeping watch on the Soviet missile system. Some Australians fear that this base might invite a nuclear attack, in case of war. The two-hundred-man American garrison stays as far out of sight as possible, and never wears uniforms in the town; its members do, however, carry American license plates on their cars, and the local townsmen resent the fact that those bivouacked in neat little bungalows in Alice waste precious water by using it twice a day on their lawns. Australian white supremacists sought recently to make the United States forbid the employment of American Negro troops in these stations, but the effort failed.

You can, if you wish, drive sixty miles in the corrosive heat to a cattle station on the old Hamilton-Downs property. Until lately this covered fourteen hundred square miles, but it has recently been broken up and the operator, Bill Prior, uses only about seven hundred square miles now—enough! The Priors have 4,500 cattle, mostly Shorthorns, which are sold in Adelaide; water comes from ten bores with ten dams, which are dredged-out water holes. They have a cool room, but no refrigeration. Their nearest neighbor lives sixteen miles away, but they can go every so often to Alice—and, as Mrs. Prior puts it in her cheerful voice:

"Alice is noice."

CHAPTER 18

The Splendid Entity of Queensland

I like Brisbane. It has potential, and you can make it be what you want it to be.
—LABOR LEADER JACK EGERTON

ONCE AGAIN—interminable blank distance! This is the second-largest Australian state, covering more than 667,000 square miles or 22.5 percent of the entire continent—intensely variegated, too. Queensland is bigger than the British Isles, France, Belgium, Germany, Italy, and Greece together. Its phenomena range from the great mining complex at Mount Isa, one of the toughest industrial communities anywhere, to the marine marvels of the Great Barrier Reef, which runs for 1,250 miles along the coastline, veritably one of the seven wonders of the world. There are tropical rain forests, dams, peach groves, flat grass tablelands, mountains, scrub, and desert. Several place names give a ring—Cape Upstart, Springsure, Mary Kathleen.

The population is about 1.8 million, and this goes up by 1.8 percent a year, less than the national average. About 88 percent are Australian-born, but this includes a variety of strains—Irish in particular. Queensland is still the "Deep North," and many citizens give a sense of having been burned out by the lazy tropics.

This is the state most richly endowed by nature. Lying across the Tropic of Capricorn, half above and half below, it has the climates to grow sugar, grain, cotton, beef, coffee, peanuts, wool, tobacco, timber, apples, pineapples, macadamia nuts, and dairy products. Its mines spew up copper, coal, lead, zinc, silver, bauxite, mineral sand, gas and oil, manganese, and phosphate. There is adequate room for all this: the state is thirteen hundred miles long, from north to south, and nine hundred miles wide.

Who—or what—runs Queensland? First, the big ranches, some of whose properties are enormous, as big as in New South Wales, covering thousands of square miles in the familiar Australian pattern. Second, such a monolith as the Colonial Sugar Refining Company Ltd., which is the most powerful industrial amalgam in Australia after Broken Hill.

Queensland has a kind of persecution complex. People say, "We don't get a fair shake, we're not appreciated." "We're a branch-office state, a client state." "Yes, we're the coming state, too, but we've been a long time coming." "Blame the drought." "But there's always been a drought."

Puritanism and drinking habits preoccupy the community more acutely than bigger issues. A stipendiary magistrate a while back ordered the destruction of a number of prints by Aubrey Beardsley, and copies of the record *Hair* were seized by the police. The intellectual life of the state is unimpressive. Pubs are not open on Sunday, and motels are not given licenses for Sunday drinking, except in special circumstances. Forty miles out of Brisbane, a tourist can get a drink if he is a bona fide traveler. The temperance lobby is strong. There are three race courses in Brisbane.

Queensland has an extremely strong sense of its own identity and a strong separatist tradition. Yet, paradoxically, Queenslanders are often called the "most Australian" people in the nation—perhaps because they suffer from most typically Australian blights: bush fires, droughts, dust storms, and flies in incredible numbers. Though Queenslanders, like other Australians, are overwhelmingly city-dwellers, the state has a greater psychological attachment to its outback, which brings with it much pride in physical prowess and courage. The state has an unfortunate history of racism that makes it comparable in a way to the American South. The early settlers dealt with the Aborigines more bloodily than anywhere else except Tasmania, and the South Sea Islanders imported to cut sugar cane in the last half of the nineteenth century were treated essentially as slaves. Queensland still has more Aborigines than any other state, about nineteen thousand. When a white man takes up with a black girl, he is said to be "going combo," or "comboing."

At the Top

The Governor of Queensland is a distinguished former judge, Sir Alan Mansfield. He was the Australian representative in the UN War Crimes Commission in London at the end of the war, and the chief Australian prosecutor in the Tokyo War Crimes Trials. He became Chief Justice of the Supreme Court in Queensland in 1956. The story is told of Sir Alan that once after sentencing a man, he kept moving his lips for several minutes.

Explanation: "I knew what he was thinking, and I just kept saying, 'The same to you, the same to you.' " The Governor likes to go fishing, in baggy pants and bare feet.

His appointment to the governorship follows the established patterns of Commonwealth politics—the job is a reward for service, and is given out by a combination of influences in London and Canberra difficult to assess. One thing to note about governors is that they live as a rule in huge enchanting houses, with beautiful lawns and gardens; a really good Government House can be the best hotel in the world. The *de rigueur* first duty for a visitor is to sign the book.

Sir Alan Mansfield, who was born in Indooroopilly, a Brisbane suburb, in 1902, is one of the three native Australian governors in the six states. Three of the governors are still British. This will almost certainly not be true in the future, as most Australians today would prefer to be presided over by a native Australian rather than a Briton.

A Word on Brisbane

Brisbane (pronounced "Brizbun," population about 850,000), gives the impression of being a happily helter-skelter city, full of disputatious citizens. Street scenes are vivid—young women with babies on their backs (no servants, of course), young men swinging in and out of the coffee bars, winding through the crowded streets, fighting a fierce pedestrian traffic, pushing. A big bending slug of a river, with several sigmoid loops, traverses the community. Not far away is Surfers Paradise, a spectacular real estate development along the beach, solid with motels, self-contained flats, rooming houses ad infinitum, and detritus. J. B. Priestley called it a "cardboard Miami." A million and a quarter people spend their vacations here every year. The coastal road is as bad as any average American commercial "strip": gasoline stations, night clubs, signs, and—Australian touch—"choox bars," fried-chicken stands. One advertising spectacular is a giant revolving mug of beer, complete with foam. Surfers Paradise is so totally given over to tourism that it employs pretty meter maids not to ticket overparked cars but rather to insert coins and forfend transgression of the law. Back of this strip, in the mountains, lies genuinely attractive country, Lamington National Park, with waterfalls and Antarctic beeches three thousand years old. From a helicopter over this country, one sees terrain resembling large fungoid-green tennis balls, and sprightly watercraft making wakes like feathers or filets of sole.

Lennon's Hotel in Brisbane is a rewarding place—a landmark of the area for many years. General Douglas MacArthur, on leaving Melbourne, set up his headquarters here, and his name still awakens resounding local reverberations. More G.I.s came to know Australia in this area than any other on the continent, because it was transformed into a huge, outspreading American base. Flying Fortresses operated from a secret airfield on the Atherton Tableland. It was from Lennon's that MacArthur issued his immortal phrase, "I shall return!"

Oddly enough, Brisbane and its hinterland are reminiscent of the Soviet Union in one particular, namely, that the citizens have an abnormal diffidence about culture. They desperately want to be considered "cultured," and the Russian word "*nekulturny*," indicating the pervasive stigma attached to nonculture, would be understood at once. Yet the roots of most citizens are so tenaciously, irreversibly suburban that it is difficult to make the jump. It is not impossible, however—"Up From Suburbia" might be a national motto. Another characteristic is the tendency to stick together. Legislation was proposed a couple of years ago in the local Parliament—but defeated—making it illegal to blackball a candidate for membership in a private club! The concept of mateyness could go no further.

A publisher's salesman says that Brisbane is a hard city for bookselling compared to Sydney or Melbourne, but that it seemed to be opening up a little. Beer is inordinately popular in Brisbane, and if you ask why, beer drinkers will tell you: (1) "It's cheap." (2) "Ever tasted our soft drinks?"

It's strong, too, but served in smaller doses here; the standard is a seven-ounce glass, not eight as in New South Wales. A lad in Lennon's said, "I toike in three quarts after every football game. It's good. It makes you sweat." A nice example of Australian gentility—such a paradoxical country!—is that one fashionable restaurant here gives a man a menu with prices, and his wife one without. The local citizens are good trenchermen, and appetites enormous. Never is a trace of food left on a plate. One curiosity is that *two* potato dishes are ordinarily served with an entree.

For a city of 850,000, Brisbane occupies a vast terrain—more land than all of New York City. The architecture is rather dreary, apart from some filigreed balcony railings and some quaint old buildings on stilts. No well-planned city this—just a grid of improvidently narrow streets. The City Hall, built in 1931, Italian Renaissance style, with a clock tower 320 feet high, contains a big concert hall and a sonorous pipe organ. The suburbs are the predictable row upon row of bungalows, with never a mansion or a shack, but here they are mostly on stilts, with lattice screens to admit the breeze, and corrugated-iron roofs. Palms dot the area. The Observatory is one of the oldest buildings; convicts put it up as a windmill, but it was shortly transformed into a hominy-grinding treadmill, upon which convicts had to labor fourteen hours at a stretch.

It is hot here, in the sense of averaging out high without going above 100 degrees Fahrenheit very often. The business uniform for many men is a white shirt, tie, hat, shorts, and knee socks. You frequently see signs that say starkly, "CASKET." These have nothing to do with the rituals of death; they advertise the state lottery, oddly called the Golden Casket Art Union. This curious appellation comes from the old British-continental practice of raffling off works of art.

The Labor Picture

The first Labor government in the history of Australia was installed here in 1889, which means that Queensland has had this experience for more than eighty years, a record unprecedented for the British Commonwealth or elsewhere. From grandfather to father to son, for nearly three generations, Labor has built itself in. Much of its program has been prudent, self-reliant, and far-seeing. This has never been a reckless party. Communists are rigorously kept out, and every Labor Party member must sign and renew an annual pledge stating that he is not a Communist or Fascist or a member of a Communist or Fascist front party.

Unions are run clean as a scoured pan—no Hoffas here—and exert great power in local politics. Proselytizers, called bush brothers, penetrate the outback to sign up recruits or bring yokels, to be converted to Labor, into the town. It is all quite messianic.

Another obvious and recurrent point to stress is how neatly the Australian tradition of mateship plays into trade unionism, and, from this, Labor politics. The oldest union in Queensland, which became rich early, is the shearers'. Others powerful and prominent are the barmaids, transport, carpenters, even dentists. Nonunion creatures, known as shingle-bums, are peremptorily despised.

Incontestable leader of the labor movement in Queeensland and a powerful figure in his own right is Jack (John Alfred Roy) Egerton, a man with huge hands, a face like a red ox, and an ingratiating appetite for beer. Mr. Egerton was born in 1918 to a farm family in Rockhampton, 640 miles from Brisbane. "I'm a bushie," he says proudly. He has been president of the Queensland Trades and Labor Council since 1957. He came up through the boilermakers, but he is a radio technician by trade. He has attended various labor congresses in Geneva, and likes to play golf and read.

Tommy (Thomas James) Burns, a more pliable man, with an aware, pleased, open face, is Egerton's counterpart. Burns, entirely self-made, was born in 1931, educated at a local grammar school. He got into labor broadcasting, and then became a state organizer for the Australian Labor Party. He derives from a fisherman's family, cut ferns on state farms, grew watermelons, and served in Korea. Articulate, dynamic, this is clearly a man who will go far.

More Men of Brisbane

Premier of Queensland is Johannes Bjelke-Petersen, who is New Zealand born. A successful farmer, an aircraft pilot, a teetotaler, he teaches Sunday school and is an effective, hardheaded businessman. Mr. Bjelke-Petersen has no university degree; as a matter of fact, in the entire Queensland cabinet only two members hold university degrees, the Minister of Justice (who is an M.D.) and the Minister of Labor and Tourism. This government is unique in Australia, a Country-Liberal coalition dominated by the Country Party, which is, of course, Mr. Bjelke-Petersen's party. Generally it is said of Mr. Bjelke-Petersen that he may be the last Premier to represent and express predominantly conservative rural interests.

Vincent Gair, Senator for Queensland since 1965 and Parliamentary leader of the Democratic Labor Party, was born in Rockhampton. He rose to become Australian Labor Party Premier of Queensland in 1952–1957, but he broke with the ALP leadership and has never reacquired control of the state. Senator Gair is a violent anti-Communist and strong Roman Catholic. The Catholic population of Queensland runs to about 25 percent of the whole.

The Deputy Premier, Gordon William Chalk, a vigorous and enlightened personality, was born in 1913 and has been Treasurer of Queensland as well as Deputy Prime Minister since 1965. He rose as Minister of Transport and likes outdoor sports and reading. His nickname is, as it would be, "Chalkie." He has no more than two years of high school, but he is sharp, gregarious, an articulate talker and by all odds the ablest administrator in the state. He wants wider, more fruitful relations with the U.S., and thinks that a predominant British attitude to Australia is that it is still "colonial." He says, "I want good solid-mattress relations with all the world!"

Clem Jones, Lord Mayor of Brisbane, is interesting and extremely able, a man spry and cunning. Born in 1918 at Ipswich and educated in the Brisbane public schools, Mr. Jones is a lively cricketer and a member of the Australian Board of Control for International Cricket. By trade he is a professional surveyor. Urban planning fascinates him, and he has been a member for some years of the Town and Country Planning Association. People say that he is something of a fixer, but he fixes most things well.

Mr. Jones has traveled widely in the United States, and has taught at the University of California at Los Angeles. He is sandy-haired, and smiling—no

Australian nutcracker jaw. Asked how he takes the load off, he replies, "I don't feel that the job is work." Development is his leading problem. An innovator, he has the idea that by doing less one may do more; hence, he has conceived the idea of building new roads to a lesser rather than a higher technical level—so that they will cover a wider network and be useful to more citizens. "Our greatest problem," Mr. Jones concluded, "is lack of sufficient economy to be able to build into it faster than we are."

The Mines of Queensland

Mount Isa Mines has its formidable plant in the western outback of Queensland. The company is owned 53 percent by American Smelting & Refining, and has forty-thousand Australian shareholders who control another 35 percent. Labor relations have been turbulent at Mount Isa, and it is described as the "most unpleasant" community in Australia. All this got started in 1923, when a prospector named John Campbell camped in the dry bed of the Leichhardt River and idly chipped a rock with his hammer. He recognized sulphide of lead, and a "lead rush" began. Ultimately, the treasure of "The Isa" turned out to be copper. The mine has been opened and closed several times as the price of the lead, zinc, silver, and copper that it produced rose or sagged. Ore is smelted here to blister copper, and sent to Townsville, on the coast, for electrolytic refining. Mount Isa's eighteen thousand people live in air-conditioned houses, and drink milk brought a thousand miles in refrigerator trucks.

Mount Morgan is another copper mine that started out to be something else. This hill near Rockhampton was decapitated in the late nineteenth century for its gold, and then turned out to be much richer in copper. After many ups and downs, it still runs, a truly awesome excavation. A sight from airplanes between Mount Isa and the coast is Mary Kathleen, a uranium town built in the mid-1950's just months before uranium mining collapsed all over the world; now Mary Kathleen sits waiting for the price of uranium to rise again.

One characteristic of Queensland mining, it would seem, is that the operators often merely have to take the topsoil off to find the riches. At Weipa, as we have seen, they stripped away a growth of eucalyptus to reveal, red as a flesh wound, an endless deposit of bauxite. In the far west, at Yelvertoft, International Minerals & Chemical Corporation in 1967 similarly found a bed of phosphate fifteen feet thick and fifteen square miles in area, under thirty-five feet of earth. And a hundred miles southwest of Gladstone, at Moura, a dragline with a bucket as big as a barn strips away coal to be sent to Japan.

Queensland, like Victoria, was born by binary fission from New South

Wales. This took place in 1859; Queensland was the last of what are now the six states to become a colony. It was named for Queen Victoria—at that imperious lady's suggestion. Previously the area was known as Moreton Bay, from the name of the original convict settlement, founded in 1824 when New South Wales refused to accept any more of England's criminals. Some of the toughest felons, including men who committed crimes after reaching Australia, were sent to Moreton Bay, but modern Queenslanders are proud to cite descent from these convict-pioneers. Even though New South Wales' Governor Thomas Brisbane (for whom, of course, the capital is named) tried to keep Moreton Bay exclusively a prison colony, free settlers moved in to occupy the most fertile land of Darling Downs. After becoming a colony, Queensland put up in England and Scotland posters reading "WANTED: YOUNG MEN FOR QUEENSLAND," and the population doubled to fifty thousand. Since then Queensland's history has proceeded rather eventlessly, except that in 1915 the state pioneered compulsory voting in Australia, and in 1924 it abolished the upper house of the legislature, making itself the only unicameral state.

Sugar Country

Australia exports more sugar than any nation except Cuba, and almost all of it is grown in Queensland. The cane cutters are all white men, Italians and Maltese for the most part nowadays. This is said to be a unique show of how whites can labor with good health in the tropics. But this has not always been the case. More than a century ago Queensland planters began importing Kanakas (the word means "man" in the Polynesian languages) from the New Hebrides and the Solomon Islands to work the cotton and cane fields. The ship captains that brought the Kanakas were called "blackbirders," and the islanders were worked so hard and paid so little and punished so brutally that ultimately an official inquiry denounced the whole system as tinged with "deceit, cruelty, treachery, deliberate kidnaping, and cold-blooded murder." Under pressure comparable to that of the Abolitionists of the American Civil War, the sugar planters of the north threatened to secede from Queensland, but nevertheless indentured labor was banned in 1904, and the Kanakas mostly sent back. Subsidies, continued to this day, compensated the planters for the extra cost of employing whites. Not that they look white—they are burned to a shade of walnut by the sun and further blackened by soot from the burning of the cane fields, an operation carried out just before the harvest to drive out snakes and clear away brush. Of course, these days machines cut more and more of the cane.

The sugar ports—Bowen, Ayr, Ingham, Cairns, and particularly Townsville, Queensland's second city with 61,000 people, and biggest city in the Australian tropics—preserve a bit of the separatist tradition, disdaining Brisbane. An intriguing place to the north of the sugar ports is Cooktown. An 1873 gold rush to the nearby Palmer River attracted to Cooktown twenty thousand Chinese, who exasperated the whites by sending much gold to China, not to mention the bones of their dead. The Chinese tongs fought with one another, and everybody was set upon by the cannibalistic Myalls, fiercest of the Aborigines. These man-eaters rated the Chinese above the whites because they tasted "less salty and equal to the finest bandicoot." A cyclone flattened Cooktown in 1907, hurting no one because the gold had given out and it was a ghost town. In fact, its destruction did not become known to the world for some time. Now four hundred people live there and hold tight to the real estate on the theory that it will be Queensland's next big tourist town.

The Great Barrier Reef

With an effort, the mind can grasp that this huge reef is no less than 1,250 miles long, and that its area of atolls, keys, and underwater ledges is as vast as the area of Kansas. But it takes far greater effort for the mind to grasp that all this coral was made by tiny polyps, extracting lime from sea water to build the largest structure ever formed by living organisms. How many polyps did the job take? How many years? In the reef shelters live all sorts of amazing, grotesque, and beautiful forms of life, an incomparable phenomenon, beyond anything else on earth.

The reef parallels two-thirds of the Queensland coast—in fact, its seaward side is the official state boundary. In the north it is fairly regular and ten or twelve miles wide, but in the south it breaks into larger banks and platforms, scattered as much as two hundred miles from shore. Most of it is just under water, although low tide exposes some of the crest, and there are, in the reef and the lagoon that it encloses, three thousand islands or islets. The reef is an extraordinary canvas of natural art. The fantasy of the forms, and the colors of the coral (from the air, reddish hues from the algae that encrust it, set off by the ultramarine of the ocean and the turquoise of the lagoons) are extraordinary. For the visitor, the reef itself is quite a sufficient marvel, and he can poke about, at low tide, crunching coral underfoot, with a feeling of endless astonishment at nature's inventiveness.

Yet even more exciting is the underwater life. Coral caves and recesses harbor many hundreds of species of fish and sea animals. Perhaps the oddest is the giant clam, which weighs as much as three hundred pounds, smiles with liverish lips, and acts as host to polyps who mistake him for solid coral. Two kinds of fish kill their enemies by expelling poison through their dorsal spines—the handsome, gaudy lionfish, and the ugly stonefish, which indeed looks like a stone. Another dangerous fish is the Queensland grouper, which can weigh eight hundred pounds and actually stalks divers. Other menaces are the sea wasp, the moray eel, the Portuguese man-of-war, and, of course, the hammerhead shark. There are also repulsively pulpy coral-based creatures: the shell-less snail called nudibranch, and the sea cucumber. Others are as beautiful as their names imply: blue butterfly fish, angelfish, parrot fish, and exotic creatures such as giant turtles and the blood-spotted crab.

The underwater coral is fantastic. It grows in a whole spectrum of colors and infinite shapes—there are staghorn corals, mushroom corals, brain corals, et cetera. Above the water, reef life includes herons, noddy terns, and the unbearable muttonbird, which spends all night engaged in a kind of raucous cooing, if such a thing is possible.

Much alarm prevails in Australia these days over the possibility that the Great Barrier Reef is doomed. Incredibly enough, the reef is under deadly attack, and not by storms or men, but by a starfish. When polyps, which in size are comparable to the eraser on a pencil, extract lime from sea water, they turn it into skeletons which attach to one another to form greater and greater masses. The skeletons are cup-shaped, and the soft, living part of the polyp, attached to the inside of the cup, can emerge far enough to find food. This it does with eight stinger-tentacles that wave plankton into its mouth. Now, for reasons unknown, innumerable starfish of the crown of thorns variety (they actually look more like a small weedy mound) have begun to devour the soft polyps by the billions, sucking them up into the hundreds of little mouths which lie on the underside of the starfish's arms.* Almost two thousand square miles of the reef are said to have already been destroyed.

It was Charles Darwin, incidentally, who first explained how coral reefs are built. The key clue is that the polyp cannot survive much deeper than 180 feet. Therefore the reefs cannot have been built up from a deep ocean floor. Yet some reefs are solid coral for thousands of feet down. Darwin believed, and his theory has been substantiated, that these reefs were started on a rock foundation that lay near the surface of the sea. This foundation then slowly sank down as the busy polyps kept adding coral to the top.

Tourists—more than a quarter of a million a year—get to the reef from four ports along the coast. Many simply swing out in launches for a look or a dive, but more serious visitors tour the reef for days in chartered boats, or

* Parrot fish and angelfish are also coral eaters.

stay at island hotels. Of these islands, Green and Heron are perhaps the best-known since they are both true coral keys. Green Island has a clever sunken observatory, right in the coral, and through portholes visitors can see the whole fishy panorama. Elsewhere, people skin-dive, or swim with goggles, or ride glass-bottom boats. December to April is a bad time to visit, because of cyclones and insects. Ampol Petroleum Company recently created an environmental crisis in Australia by proposing to drill the Great Barrier Reef for oil, but ultimately bowed to public indignation and suspended the plan.

On the Land

Queensland sometimes boasts that it is "the biggest public estate in the world." The point is that, after experiencing many different systems of land tenure from squatting to land-reformist subdivision, the state now leases much of its agricultural area. The typical lease, sized according to use, runs thirty years, after which the government can take it back and cut it up or recombine it.

Some of the land is loamy and fertile. The Darling Downs area supposedly has forty feet of topsoil, and its fields are laid out with the precision of a checkerboard. But most of the terrain is the leathery, limitless outback. Australia exports more beef than any nation except Argentina, and Queensland raises half of Australia's cattle. The favored breed is Brahman crossed with Shorthorns and Herefords. A pitiable resident of the cattle plains is the "brumbie," a once-domesticated horse who has got away and gone wild. Brumbies can outrun any horse with rider, so they cannot be captured, and since they eat more pasturage animal for animal than cattle, they are shot and killed. Kangaroos get the same treatment in Queensland; precisely 6,556,743 of them were "harvested" between 1954 and 1964.

The major pest in sheep-raising areas is the dingo, and he is fended off with a draconian device. Surrounding almost all of the eight-hundred-mile-long tongue of savannah sheep country in south-central Queensland is a wire fence six feet high, with another foot buried underground. This desperation defense cost $2 million when it was built in 1963, and measures 3,500 miles in length. The dingoes get through the dog fence, but in reduced numbers. The real secret of this arid region's success in raising cattle and sheep is the artesian well. Queensland has five thousand "bores" into the Great Artesian Basin that underlies a third of Australia. This water is insufficient in supply and too mineralized to irrigate great areas, but it serves well for watering animals and sustaining humans. Roads in this vast domain are narrow and poorly graded even when paved, and when not paved they are equally unnavigable when dry and dusty or wet and muddy. The Queenslanders' solution is to fly everywhere; they are the most air-minded people in Australia. Sometimes, when big windstorms strike, these air travelers look down on nothing but black dust for hundreds of miles, and the state is virtually blacked out for as much as a day.

Queenslandiana: "Desert" in this state means timbered country—treeless country is called "downs." In the downs, and elsewhere, one can see "magnetic" anthills, dagger-shaped termite houses around seven feet high, with the broad sides invariably running north and south. Actually, it is thought that they are oriented not to the magnetic polarity of the earth but rather to get the morning and afternoon sun. Each hill contains about two million ants. Two botanical wonders are the giant stinging tree, with large, bellicose, velvety leaves, and the ungrateful epiphytic fig, which lodges high in a host tree and then sends down curtains of roots that enclose and strangle it. A zoological wonder is the lungfish, ceradotus, which represents an ancient link in evolution: it has a bladder which it fills with air on the surface of the water, before diving for a swim.

Thursday Island, off the tip of Cape York, is a cosmopolitan dot, inhabited by Europeans, frizzy-haired Torres Strait islanders, Aborigines, Chinese, and Japanese. The main industry is diving as deep as 240 feet for oysters which are destined to be mothers of pearls. Japanese technicians of the Nippo Pearl Company Ltd. implant bits of Mississippi Valley mussel shell, and eventually the oysters produce a cultured pearl. Why is the island called Thursday? The tongue-in-cheek answer is that the strait already had a Tuesday Island and a Wednesday Island, so the next one had to be Thursday. It used to be a fort, with naval guns dominating the strategic strait.

Queensland's little northern towns can be the epitome of gentle tropical life. They look a lot alike, the streets are wide, the air is soft, the houses stilted. In the hotels, one carries one's own luggage and comes to dinner on time or not at all. This can be lotus-eater country; business executives fleeing Sydney's wear-and-tear may settle here and indulge in some such gentle way of living as running a bar. Groups of young hippies live off the dole in beach shacks. Everywhere one sees those trademarks of the tropics: bougainvillaea, poinciana, and frangipani.

Finally, a noble place is Cathedral Cave, in the Carnarvon Ranges National Park, a region of deep gorges and overhanging cliffs. This subterrane measures 270 feet by 70 feet, and is 200 feet high. Of all the caves in Australia that the Aborigines decorated with paintings, this may be the most remarkable in terms of richness and preservation.

*

There is a frontier air about most of the coastal towns outside of Brisbane, but the citizenry bridle if you mention it. A police officer in Townsville reared back at the suggestion and said, "Hardly that—but there's twelve hundred miles of land to the west of us that *is* frontier." Promethean wastes indeed!

CHAPTER 19

New Guinea: Men and Wigs, Women and Pigs

There is a bird-shaped island lying to the north of Australia, with head turned to the west toward the Moluccas, and tail running down to the south-east. This bird-shaped island is Papua and New Guinea, the largest island in the world if you except Australia and Greenland.

—SIR HUBERT MURRAY

NEW GUINEA . . . is that *Australian*? Indeed, the eastern half is, partly an old British colony taken over by Australia, and partly a United Nations Trust Territory administered by Australia. And the western half, once Dutch New Guinea, is now Indonesia's West Irian. New Guinea, hovering north of Australia, is the strand that stopped the Japanese thrust in World War II.

The whole island, 1,200 miles long, measures 312,329 square miles in area; the Australian part alone is as big as California. New Guinea is, amazingly, part of the Himalayan chain of mountains, the place where the eastern end of that great range drowns itself in the Pacific, after having been in and out of the water the length of the Malay Archipelago. Just before the range takes its final plunge, it reaches towering heights; and so in New Guinea, only two degrees south of the Equator, there are peaks rising so far above the snow line (14,600 feet) that they actually have glaciers. The highest mountain, Djaja, in West Irian, reaches up 16,503 feet. Dozens of mountains rise above 10,000 feet, and large areas of productive land lie above 5,000 feet. Vertical country! In some places peaks are rarely seen because of the clouds that constantly surround them; lower down there are rain forests where the precipitation is almost continuous and the moss is two feet thick. Put aside any lingering impression that this island is all fetid tropics: its high, jagged backbone gives it proportionately more mountains than any other island in the world.

But, let it quickly be said, New Guinea has its fetid tropics, too. New Guineans say (though of course it has been said of other places, too) that God created this island on Saturday night, when running out of time He hastily flung down a confusion of marshes, plateaus, volcanoes, and rivers. The southern bulge contains one of the biggest swamps in the world. The Fly River* winds through it for six hundred miles, navigable in a whaleboat, though the straight-line distance thus traversed is only about two hundred miles. A long spur of the drowning Himalayas ends in a curve of islands—New Britain, New Ireland, and Manus. Through some historical foible, Australian New Guinea also includes the biggest and westernmost of the Solomon Islands, Bougainville.

New Guinea trees adapt themselves to their elevation: mangroves and many varieties of palms in the lowland; klinkii pine, laurels, oaks, and beeches on the next level up; myrtles and rhododendrons on the high mountainsides; and grasslands in the alpine areas. Where trees don't grow, the brutal kunai grass takes over, six feet high and sharp enough to cut the skin. It makes good thatch for huts. Much of the animal life resembles the Australian marsupials—tree kangaroos, cassowaries, wallabies, and bandicoots. In the New Guinea mountaintops live at least forty-three distinctive varieties of the bird of paradise. This flamboyant bird is a kind of crow bedecked with crests, breastplates, and plumes of scarlet, moss green, saffron, white, rusty blue, and other colors. Until 1921, when the slaughter was stopped, it was hunted to beautify the hats of European women; villagers still wear bird-of-paradise feathers in various ways. The bird's call is dismayingly raucous. The island also has big crocodiles, innumerable wild pigs, and May flies swarming so densely in the Sepik River that villagers catch and eat them. In surrounding waters are fourteen hundred kinds of fish, good sport and good eating.

*

Soon after you make your acquaintanceship with the Australian part of New Guinea, the 52 percent of the island east of West Irian, individual areas begin to come into focus. The south, up to the highlands, is Papua (pronounced "PAP-oo-a"), an Australian possession, with a population of

* Named not for any insect life there but rather for H.M.S. *Fly*, the little British vessel that first sailed into its mouth.

700,000. The north, including New Britain, Bougainville, and other islands, is the UN Trust Territory, officially known as New Guinea, even though that is also the name of the whole island. The population of this part is 1.8 million. The various subdivisions of both parts are:

1. Port Moresby, the capital, and its environs, on the southern coast of the bird's tail, an area small in size and anthropologically rather uninteresting. Here you find the Motus, whose women tattoo their faces and whose language is one of New Guinea's lingua francas, but the place has little tradition and lore.

2. The land along the Gulf of Papua, west of Port Moresby, and the endless swamps around the Fly River—empty except for some lowland villages and the kind of white man, given half over to adventure and half to drink, that one sees in ports like Daru all over the world.

3. The highlands—a bracing combination of clean air, icy mountaintops, and fine crops.

4. Lae and Madang on the north coast. The former evokes memories of the bitterest battles of World War II, and the richest discoveries of gold in New Guinea; the latter is an area that retains vestiges of the years when the Germans colonized it, plus the influence of missions that have somewhat Westernized the former clansmen.

5. "The Sepik"—that is, the 250-mile stretch of northern swamps and mountains adjacent to West Irian, which has for an axis the muddy, coiling Sepik River, down which float tangled masses of gray-green vegetation. This area is famous for its artifacts, chiefly carvings, and the art bespeaks a violent, magical, superstitious culture.

6. The islands of New Britain and New Ireland, which surpass Port Moresby for progress, prosperity, and economic influence. The Tolai people who live in Rabaul on the Gazelle Peninsula of New Britain are the territory's best educated and most politically potent. Tolai translates to Australians as independent rebel, standing up to the white man. New Ireland, two hundred miles long and an average of seven miles wide, is a strand of surf and coconuts.

7. Bougainville, northernmost of the Solomon Islands, which was arbitrarily placed under Australian control (the other Solomons are a British Protectorate). It has a great, new, wealth-creating copper mine, estimated to be the biggest in the world—and villagers who are fractious.

Uncounted hundreds of small islands, some only dots, surround the bigger land areas. Manus, northern bulwark of the Bismarck Sea, was a major American base in World War II—built up at a cost of $156 million to the point that it sometimes sheltered six hundred ships in its harbor. Then it was abandoned with an unbelievable waste of material and supplies.

The Yam-Eaters

The 2.5 million ulotrichous, or frizzy-haired, people of New Guinea, who combine various proportions of Negroid (or Papuan), Negrito, and Melanesian blood, are descendants of invaders from Asia many thousands of years ago—not much is really known about this. Most of them live in an essentially Stone Age culture, unaffected by white men until as recently as thirty years ago—New Guinea is virtually the last part of the world to be explored. Cannibalism was not unusual until Australian bush patrols combined with Australian law made the practice difficult, and some still persists in the more remote mountains. The bodies were never boiled, in the manner of a Charles Addams cartoon, but rather baked. A trench was dug, and the bottom lined with coals and hot stones, plus a layer of twigs and leaves. The beheaded body was placed on that, covered with more hot stones, and burning coals were raked over the top. The head, however, was boiled, and a deft pull on the neck vertebrae would extract the brain as an appetizer. The meat, as is well known, tastes like pork—hence the phrase "long pig" for a comestible man. Many observers have held that its consumption, apart from appearing natural and enjoyable to the villagers, filled a sharp physiological need. Beatrice Blackwood, an anthropologist who worked in Papua in the 1930's, wrote that "protein shortage is, if not the only, at least a powerful contributary cause of cannibalism." But there was ritual cannibalism, too.

It is probably more significant, however, that the main food of the inhabitants of New Guinea was and is yams. Most people eat ten or twelve pounds of yams—or sweet potatoes, taro, or related starches—every day. It follows that they must be diligent and skillful gardeners, and they are. Men compete in growing big yams, the record being somewhere around twelve feet in length; but these are for ritual, not for food, and women are excluded from the gardens where the necessary magic is practiced to produce a superyam. The very fact of gardening brings with it settlement, which made the people of New Guinea quite different from the nomadic Aboriginal hunters of Australia.

Meat is hard to come by in New Guinea. Villagers sometimes burn patches of kunai grass and then devour the charred trapped corpses of lizards and mice. The big and stupid cassowary is hunted; this bird cannot fly, but it can rip open a man's stomach with one swipe of its large sharp claw. The favored narcotic is the betel nut, fruit of the areca palm. This nut is red inside, green outside, as long as your thumb. It is chewed together with pepper from the betel pepper plant (hence the name), and with lime, which counteracts the laxative effect. Addicts soon get dark red gums and black teeth.

The main point to make about traditional social organization in Papua New Guinea is that it is loose, decentralized, lightly governed, and lacking in hereditary leadership. There are about five hundred clans, roughly based on common ancestry and language, and averaging four thousand members each. There are five hundred linguistically complex languages (seven hundred on the whole island). But thirty-seven of them are spoken by more than ten thousand people each, and since they are somewhat related languages, intercommunication is not completely hopeless. Multilingualism, generally including either of the two main lingua francas, Pidgin and Motu, further eases the problem. Within the clans there are subclans united around their own songs, stories, ceremonies, and family ties. Subclans are further divided into villages and hamlets. Each subclan has a rather impotent chief, and the chiefs jointly form a clan council for such purposes as allocating land. The land is communally owned, but each subclan gets a beneficiary interest in a number of plots, dispersed in little gardens here and there.

The women are "hot of eye and vigorous—they'll tear you apart," according to an Australian journalist. They supposedly know of a plant that is an effective contraceptive. Dress varies widely; women mostly wear kunai-grass skirts, or patches of cloth. Men in many parts of the country feel adequately dressed if they are wearing a *kimbung*, or phallocrypt, that sheathes the penis. Some of these, of gourd or bamboo, are startlingly long —two feet or more. Size is a symbol of status. A common greeting among Chimbu men is to touch one another's genitals—a ritual known to whites as the "Chimbu handshake." Many men have bushy black beards, lending them an uncommonly fierce look.

Warfare once was the way of life among New Guinea clans, the weapons being clubs, spears, arrows, and elaborate shields. Some parts of New Guinea have spooky clan houses full of skulls lined up on shelves to attest to the ferocity of their wars and headhunters. The Australians have mostly stopped the battling by the forthright tactic of moving into an aggressor village and burning down all its houses. The instinct for violence, and the low value placed on life, continue in effect. Writer Jens Bjerre tells of a couple of village men competing to sell potatoes to a white man. One of them casually pulled a club from his belt and with one blow murdered the other—and without a glance at the dead body continued peddling his potatoes. "Killing for them is merely a sport," the white man remarked. "The young men are not really considered worthwhile until they have killed somebody."

Mount Hagen Sing Sing

One of the most bizarre experiences a Westerner can have in the whole South Pacific is to go to a "sing sing" in the New Guinea highlands. Fairly typical was one staged by the Manembi clan, who made it an occasion to give some pigs to the Rogogais. These friendly people, it appeared, had earlier helped the Manembis in a fight, and nothing makes a better gift in this strange high land than pigs—in fact, pigs along with pearl shells are the local currency.

The sing sing began with a signal from a whistle. Forty spear-bearing warriors advanced, dancing with an undulating kneel. Every fourth or fifth man carried a drum, narrow-waisted and black, played by tapping the hide stretched across one end. The warriors' appearance was wondrous and fearsome. From their belts hung, in front, woven reed skirts, and in back fluffy fronds of leaves, known hereabouts as "ass grass." A golden shell was suspended across each man's chest, and above that a chaplet of bars of bark. These bars are marks of wealth, each representing a pig or a pearl shell (*kina*) that the wearer owns. Bodies glistened with tree oil or pig's grease. Under the chin some of the dancers wore green "beards" of a parsley-like foliage, and through the septum of the nose a white bone. Faces were blackened, with white on the nose and outlining the eyes and mouth. Topping it all off were tricorn wigs, typical of these clans, made of black human hair and decorated with a brushlike centerpiece of orange-red and blue feathers from cockatoos, hawks, and birds of paradise. Some of the men carried axes in their belts, and almost all had long spears. The onlooking women, wearing bouffant grass skirts, had painted their faces with red ocher for this ceremony.

Sing sings serve various purposes. Some are simple demonstrations of unity. Some are to reassure people after a death or a tragedy. Sing sings can last a week, stretched out by bursts of suitable oratory. The sing sing is a standard part of the ceremony called *moga,* a pig exchange. Clans trade pigs, incredibly enough, as self-discipline against fighting one another; these beloved animals serve as hostages, and belligerent young clansmen are told, "We can't fight those people—they have our pigs." Pearl shells are traded in the same manner and for the same reason. This complex scheme of debt and credit assures political stability of a sort among the clans. Repayments may go on for thirty years.

Using pigs for currency is rather more difficult than using paper dollars. This four-footed kind of money has to be fed and tended, chores that the highland men assign to their women. A common sight on the roads is a woman walking a pig or two on a leash. Sometimes women suckle pigs. To have fifteen pigs is to be gloriously rich. The *kina* shells are only slightly more convenient as money, since they run to the size of a dinner plate. They come from the coast, and are traded as many as fifteen times before reaching the mountains. Tourists pay ten dollars for *kinas* in shops, but the highlanders buy them with salt and tree oil.

*

Mount Hagen is perhaps the most engaging place in New Guinea, sleepy, faraway, and strange, nestled in a verdant valley. The streets are quick cuts of exotic color. Here we have a topless town—and many of the men are almost naked, too. The population is about four thousand. One-fourth of the people in the town are whites. The market is an energetic scene—fresh vegetables in from the gardens, sugar cane and peanuts, men with grass garlands or circlets of flowers on their heads, betel-nut chewers chomping and spitting, a pig's head on sale for three dollars. A hospitable place to stay is the Hagen Park Motel, and there are several others, all needed to house the tourists who come to the biennial Highland Show, when thousands of villagers get together to sing sing, dance, and play drums.

This town did not exist forty years ago: the very area itself was unknown to white men—completely undiscovered country. Then a pair of gold-prospector brothers, Mick and Danny Leahy, poked their heads over a mountaintop and viewed the wide, grassy Wahgi Valley, containing, to judge from the hamlets and gardens that they saw, a large population. Soon after, they explored the valley by airplane, then walked in and built an airstrip. They never found much gold, but Danny Leahy started a big coffee and tea plantation, took on six or seven wives, fathered twenty children, and lives there to this day. The road from Lae, 350 miles to the east on the coast, was finished only eight years ago, having been built, stretch by stretch, by villagers using only picks, shovels, and bare hands. In 1956 only three buildings in Mount Hagen had iron roofs, the rest all being made of kunai thatch. Only forty-nine whites lived there then. The first shops were opened around 1962. The town's name derives from a nearby 12,392-foot mountain, christened by the Leahy brothers in honor of Count von Hagen, administrator of the German sector of New Guinea in the 1880's. Exploring his domain, Von Hagen once got within forty miles of the mountain. He died in Madang and was buried in a tomb surmounted by a handsome bronze eagle. World War II bombing toppled the eagle, which was subsequently moved to the town that now bears the Count's name.

The Western Highlands District, for which Mount Hagen is the seat of government, covers 9,000 square miles and contains 320,000 people, 5,000 of them white—a fairly dense population. A small area north of the Lagaip River in the northwest is the home of perhaps two thousand people, with whom the government has barely made contact. The Western Highlands voters send nine members to the Parliament in Port Moresby, and rule themselves, in the pattern of the whole country, through nine locally elected government councils. The highlanders tend to vote conservatively; specifically, they do not want independence for Papua New Guinea soon. They fear that the coastal people, with more education, will dominate them. The district's problems, says the district commissioner, Mick Foley, are communications (only eight hundred miles of roads) and education (only one child in five is in a school). The education gap comes sheerly from a shortage of teachers; the people are eager for schooling and happy to provide the buildings by joint effort. Ten religious missions are presently providing the bulk of the schooling—the Seventh-Day Adventists also run a leper colony for 250 patients. Mr. Foley first went to the Western Highlands more than twenty-five years ago, and learned to admire the character of the local population. "They're not as dour or withdrawn as most Melanesian people. One can get contact. We encourage our officers to camp out. These people are more virile than the coastal people." They have no tuberculosis, and little malaria because the valley's elevations—four to nine thousand feet—are above the malaria belt.

*

Tourists are sometimes approached in Mount Hagen by a man wearing the great triangular wig so customary there, and displaying enough wooden sticks dangling from his neck to prove that he is very rich in pigs. What he ardently desires from them is any newspaper they may have. Terrific value for cigarette paper! "A newspaper makes him a millionaire," says Ron Hiatt, a district officer.

The people of this valley eat little else but sweet potatoes, grown, chiefly by the women, in manicured gardens laid out in perfect checkerboards. In the warm valleys, the sweet potato matures in six months, but above nine thousand feet it can take as much as a year. Sweet potatoes sell for two cents a pound. The diet is obviously short on protein, but the highlanders make it up to some degree by occasionally slaughtering a pig, or by buying mackerel for twenty cents a tin. The land is fertile and skillfully handled. After five years of cultivation, it is allowed to lie fallow for five or even ten years, planted with the seeds of the casuarina tree, which returns nitrogen to the soil. When the government buys clan land in order to lease it to whites, it must get approval—a signature or at least an "X"—from every single man in the clan,* for, as we have seen, the land is communally owned. The money is given to agents of the clan, or divided up among members.

When the clans fight, they use bows and arrows, dipping arrowheads (made of human or animal bone) into a dead, rotting pig to provide a slow poison. The disputes are over (1) land, (2) women, and (3) pigs. Since in this valley the clans speak seven different languages, the lingua franca is Pidgin, which the women dislike; they say that it is "heavy on the tongue."

Men and women sleep on the ground, the men in a big central house and the women in nearby huts that also house children and pigs. The hamlets formed by a number of these houses have a central meeting point for pig exchanges, marriages, funerals, and sing sings. Men are entitled to have as many wives as they can buy, the bride price running to maybe eighty dollars,† and each wife tends a garden. In practice, men usually have one wife; women dislike polygamy and use witchcraft against competitive wives. The culture regards women as inferior beings—"a piece of furniture that does housework"; their flesh and blood are thought to be somehow contaminated. On the roads one often sees a man in a wig walking along with an umbrella, his wife following behind without one. Men will not eat with women, though they do accept food from women's hands. The men usually make love to women out of doors. They sing a ritual song, a sort of nasal chant, that serves to announce that they want privacy, and this keeps other people away. At about thirteen boys leave their mothers to live with a teacher or mentor for five years. During this period they are forbidden to touch a woman. This waiting time ends in a coming-of-age ceremony, but boys are not circumcised here as they are in—for example—the Aboriginal society of Australia.

At death bodies are placed in boxes, elevated twelve or fourteen feet, to putrefy, a malodorous process carried out by "morticians" from another clan, who get paid in pigs or shells. After a couple of months the decomposed body is put into a lower box, decorated and painted, and left there until it becomes a skeleton ready for the boneyard.

White men, and their road from the coast that brings up modern civiliza-

* The temptation is to call these groups tribes, but Commissioner Foley says one mustn't. His word is "culture group." The internal political structure is not sufficiently strong or definite to merit the use of "tribe."

† Bride prices have been known to go as high as $5,000. This is, of course, too much for most men, unless they buy on the installment plan. However, the husband gets full use of the wife while making payments.

tion in one-ton trucks, have quite predictably Westernized some of the highlanders. Sweet potato gardens have become plantations of coffee, tea, and pyrethrum, an insecticide derived from the head of a kind of white daisy, which is dried and processed into an oleaginous fluid in a factory near Mount Hagen. The onetime yam-growers simultaneously move from the subsistence to the cash economy, put on Western clothes, and scoot around on Japanese motorcycles (although it is also possible to see perfectly naked men riding motorcycles, carrying bows and arrows). Sorcery is in decline. People who a few years ago did not travel farther than ten miles in a lifetime now go longer distances. Still, the place remains as primitive as the middle of the Congo. Shopping in the stores are girls dressed only in swatches of grass, suspended fore and aft from a belt, as they push their carts around and pick cans from the shelves. Other shoppers are nearly naked men in feather headdresses. On the roads women wear lap laps, unsewn wraps of cloth, and carry one, two, or even three *billims*, which are string-net sacks adequate to hold yams or babies. A common appurtenance is a sort of umbrella or cloak made of pandanus leaves sewed together—good for fending off rain. The people in this area have rather light skins and strong, aquiline noses. Women's cheeks are frequently tattooed.

Coffee is the big cash crop of the highlands, grown by ninety thousand native entrepreneurs in small plots and by about fifty white (mostly Australian) planters on a big scale. But tea is rapidly catching up on coffee here, under the leadership of Ivor Manton, who comes from Melbourne. His tea fields, swamps until he drained them, are so rich that he had to stop using fertilizer—the tea plants grew too fast. "I have 1,350 acres to tea and 650 lads to work it, 90 percent of them bachelors," said Mr. Manton. "We house them, and we have a soccer ground for them, and other recreation grounds, too. We pay the highest tea wages in the world for pluckers, forty-two cents a day, plus food and housing. The day is ten hours." The elevation here is 5,600 feet, which means that the quality of the glistening tea leaves is excellent, for high quality goes with high elevation. Mr. Manton has a large tea-processing plant on the premises, and says that "leaves growing now will be finished tea tomorrow."

The Sepik

From Mount Hagen to Angoram is 115 miles sideways and one mile down: here we come again to sweaty coastal country and the fascinating land of the Sepik River, where the people catch crocodiles with their bare hands. The key words here are sago, artifacts, and beer.

Sago is the staple food, almost pure starch—breakfast, lunch, and dinner for most of the people in this area. To get it, the native men fell any of several suitable varieties of palm tree, strip open the trunk, extract the pith, and pound it to bits. Women knead this stuff with water, which dissolves out the starch. The resulting fluid can be kept wet in sacks, or dried into a flour. It can be served in cakes or as a porridge. One tree may yield four hundred pounds. The river provides plentiful fish to go with the sago, and it all makes for an easy life for anyone who does not mind eating the rough equivalent of white mucilage.

Rice, copra, and coffee are cash crops. The men also get money from itinerant buyers of crocodile skins, which bring forty dollars apiece. Croc hunters find the beast by probing underwater with sticks. They deftly tie the mouth shut with a cord, and bind the lashing tail with another. Another source of cash is artifacts, prized by collectors. This primitive art is chiefly comprised of figures, which can be quite tiny or more than life-size, and masks, which may be carved of wood or woven of fiber, but in either case are decorated with shells, hair, teeth, feathers, and fur. The Sepiks also make stools, shields, headdresses, bark paintings, canoe prows, and, most impressively, great *haus tambarans* (spirit houses) with high carved entrances. Motifs are the crocodile and the hornbill bird, and there are abstract designs as well. The Sepik peoples are endowed with a complex tradition of religion that provides themes for this art, plus much talent for carving and coloring. The carvings generally tell a story of some kind, and often contain sexual symbolism. Though Angoram is certainly an end-of-the-world sort of place, quite a few tourists fly in to buy artifacts, mostly sold at a store run by a local government council; but the bulk of the artifacts are bought by dealers for resale elsewhere.

A great deal of the money thus earned goes for beer. These easygoing people like liquor, and make a potent drink out of coconuts. The European population of Angoram numbers only about thirty, mostly planters. The villagers number between two and three thousand, a floating—literally—population that disappears and reappears in canoes from up and down the wide and muddy Sepik. The old but passable Angoram Hotel, with swishing fans in its four bedrooms, sits on a little hill beside the river, a few minutes' walk from the tiny airfield. Wewak, the big city of the Sepik, is seventy miles away by land, and a road is being built. Presently most people go from Angoram to Wewak by boat fifty miles downstream to the ocean and then west along the coast—a thirty-hour voyage. Pidgin is the universal language here. Parties of bird-watchers come to Angoram from as far away as the United States; one group found ninety-eight varieties in a month.

*

A man put a stone on the ground and shot at it. They all shot at it with arrows and blood came out. It went up into the sky and now it is the moon.

—KUKUKUKU FOLK STORY,
RECORDED BY BEATRICE BLACKWOOD

Twenty minutes from Lae lies the country of the Kukukukus, among whom killing is a fine and satisfying thing, now mostly denied them by the Australians. They have a plant whose branches can be waved before the eyes to make the sight keener before a fight—the same branches, waved over a log, will make it lighter to lift. They know that begonia leaves, heated and rubbed on the skin, relieve pain. They even have a plant to chew before going to sleep, which will eliminate the necessity of urinating in the middle of the night—going outside to do so entails the risk of murder by a watchful enemy. Finally, perhaps most usefully, they know a plant that can be burned to an ash that will substitute for salt, a rare seasoning that they yearn for all their lives.*

The Kukukukus, most dreaded—at least formerly—of all the New Guinea tribes—live in high mountains, and grow their gardens by clearing a bit of the forest. Their best friend, their symbiotic plant, is the bamboo. Cut to include one joint, it makes an excellent cooking pot, the Kukukuku pressure cooker. Mushrooms done this way are said to be equal to the best of French cooking. The bamboo makes both bows and arrows, although the black palm provides a better bow. The bamboo cortex makes a surprisingly sharp knife, formerly used to butcher human corpses. Fashioned into a jew's-harp or an aeolian harp, the bamboo provides music. It also serves as food, torch, container, tongs, and firewood.

The Kukukukus live in scattered hamlets of six houses, typically in family groups of one old couple and a married son per house. The principal house has a conical roof that goes down to within a foot of the ground, a low doorhole for an entrance, and a walled-off circular corridor inside that leads to a door to the main central room. Kukukukus do not call themselves that, preferring to be known as Menyamyas. They number between fifty and one hundred thousand, and occupy a territory bigger than Haiti.

Upon the death of a relative, Kukukukus smear themselves with mud and mourn for four or five days, simultaneously lacerating their skins until blood flows—all in the belief that the dead man's spirit is close at hand scrutinizing

* Another essential of life, Vitamin D, is supplied by the high-altitude sunshine.

the sincerity of the grief. The corpse is then smoked for six or eight weeks, making it a mummy. It is carried to a mountaintop, placed in sitting position on a bench with other recent decedents, all with their heads propped up by arrows so that they can gaze over the valley they knew while alive. Ants and caterpillars eventually reduce the putrefying mummies to skeletons.

That strange, ritualistic musical instrument, the bull-roarer, favored by the Aborigines in Australia, shows up also among the Kukukuku. The *tumbu-lun,* as it is called here, is a flat pipe tied with a bark string to a stick. Swung in a circle over the head, it makes an awesome drone. This serves to keep evil spirits away from the initiation ceremonies of boys into manhood—if a woman hears it, the spirit of the *tumbu-lun* makes away with her.

Sweet potatoes, grown in a laborious digging-stick cultivation that consumes the bulk of the day's hours for the bulk of the Kukukukus, are sufficient for most of their meals. The yearning for protein, though, leads them to hunt small wallabies, anteaters, birds, and even snakes. They have traps that cause a log to fall on the animal victims. Fish are stunned and caught by throwing pounded derris root (basic ingredient of rotenone) into a pool.

The Kukukukus make a cloth of bark, as elsewhere through the South Pacific, but do not decorate their clothes or their habitations very much. They make effective stone adzes and clubs, with heads in a lethal starfish shape. If they were ever to run out of meat, they could, it would seem, find a fat anthropologist behind any tree in the vicinity; New Guinea has proved to be a fruitful place to go for material for a Ph.D. dissertation.

The Cargo Cults

New Guinea seen through Western eyes is an amazing place, but the Western world seen through New Guinean eyes is nothing less than supernatural. The outer world is the source of the wondrous materials and products—food, weapons, cars, textiles, and baubles in infinite variety—that pour from the holds of ships and planes, described by the white men as "cargo." To the villagers, the origins of these highly desirable marvels are utterly mysterious—a ship appears on the horizon, an airplane materializes from heaven. Soon envy creeps in—the Europeans possess the secret for obtaining cargo, it is said, and won't tell the New Guineans. Sorcerers arise who claim that if they are duly worshiped and rewarded they can practice the magic that will produce the cargo. From this ridiculous premise, accepted blindly by villagers again and again in New Guinea's history, comes that weird phenomenon, the "cargo cult."

The oddest of these cargo cult explosions is the one that took place in

1964 on the island of New Hanover—a place particularly susceptible to this sort of hoax because it had been so impressed, as well it might, by the stupendous amounts of cargo brought to the region by the Americans during World War II. New Hanover, like the rest of New Guinea, was about to elect its first representatives to the territorial Parliament; simultaneously, as it happened, a United States Geodetic Survey team was in the area making maps. Some whimsical American suggested to the New Hanoverians that they should vote for the President of the United States, Lyndon Johnson—certainly he could deliver the cargo! The idea caught fire instantly. New Hanoverians admonished the electoral officers that regardless of who was on the ballot they would vote only for Lyndon Johnson. Simultaneously, as an alternative, they took up collections of money to *buy* President Johnson outright. One night the navigation lights of a French airplane appeared in the sky, and hysteria prevailed on the island. Johnson was arriving, and bringing the cargo! When the plane flew on without landing, the furious cultists charged that Australia had stolen it. In Washington, President Johnson, himself preparing for an election, heard of this tribute to his leadership from an Australian diplomat, and remarked that he was too busy to go to New Hanover, but would gladly send Barry Goldwater.

The Johnson cargo cult, it is pleasant to report, had a happy upshot. A Roman Catholic missionary, the Rev. Bernard Miller of Toledo, Ohio, persuaded the cultists that the cargo they really needed was not material goods but American know-how. On the organizational framework of the cult, its members then founded a United Farmers Association. Under its auspices, they have planted 100,000 coconut trees, started a sawmill, and provided themselves with a bulldozer to build roads and a motor vessel to transport their produce.

Usually, however, when a cargo cult leader gets a sufficient grip on a village's credibility, the people stop gardening and other productive work—why slave over a yam when bounteous food will arrive any minute? In one case cultists built a large garage to house the automobiles due in the cargo destined for them. In another they built a mock airport, complete with control tower. Australian district officers keep a sharp ear out for rumors of cargo cults, and attempt to head them off. They fear that cargo cults are dangerous because they represent envy, hopelessness, and frustration. Another dark aspect is that cultists often adopt a warped form of Christianity; one told his followers that Christ was a Papuan, and that the Europeans had suppressed this information by tearing out the first page of the Bible. The government has many times taken local leaders to Australia to show them how the contents of cargoes, manufactured goods, are unmysteriously turned out by human hands in factories and then loaded on ships to be taken to New Guinea. But most of the cultists remain convinced that cargo has a supernatural provenance.

*

One inscrutable cult in New Guinea goes by the unlikely name of the Hahalis Welfare Society. Its field of operations is the small island of Buka, just across a narrow passage from the northern tip of Bougainville. The founder of "The Welfare," as it is commonly called, is a burly, handsome man named John Teosin, now thirty-three, the product of a good education by American Roman Catholic priests in Buka, and later in government schools in Rabaul. This training won him a position of leadership in Hahalis, a village twenty-three miles up the Buka coast from the straits, when he was only sixteen. The Welfare's first goal was to force the government to build a road to the straits over which to truck out the village's main product, copra. Teosin achieved this goal, by a perfectly flabbergasting method.

Hahalis, it seems, had a sex problem: the old men, by reason of seniority, got all the young girls, and the young men had to wait. Hahalis also had a motivation problem—no one could see any really good reason to work. Teosin's solution, in 1961, was to start what soon became famous throughout New Guinea as the Hahalis Baby Garden. The town built a two-story house big enough to contain two hundred tiny cubicles, and stocked it with a corresponding number of toothsome young local girls, aged twelve and up. In return for productive work for the Welfare, young men were authorized to disport themselves among these lovelies, and the more of them they made pregnant, the better. The children became the property of the Welfare. White blood was prized—half-breed children were "easy to educate," said Teosin—and quite a few white men helped to fertilize the Baby Garden.

The Welfare quickly became such a dominant institution that Teosin decided his people could dispense with the official local government, which seemed chiefly interested in collecting taxes. Hahalis men clashed bloodily with government patrol officers. Teosin was jailed for a while. But the Australian Administrator in Port Moresby perceived that "European civilization and the government" had been deficient in developing Hahalis, and proceeded to build the road that Hahalis wanted. Soon the Welfare's copra trucks were churning down to market. The Baby Garden was reorganized, and opened with an exhibition of sex acts for the benefit of invited guests, the members of the local government council. In fact, Teosin has several times used sex orgies performed in public (or the threat of doing so) to bludgeon the government. But he himself, married in a Catholic mission church years ago, stays strictly away from the Baby Garden.

Such is politics in Buka.

Some Towns and Cities

PORT MORESBY was chosen for the capital of combined Papua New Guinea after the war because it was the city least flattened. Even so, Port Moresby has been mostly rebuilt since then, and it has some attractive modern architecture and decent hotels. There are about 41,000 people in all. The look of the place is agreeable for the tropics. There are hills; eucalyptuses dot the landscape; the waters of the fine harbor are predictably turquoise. The temperature is bearable, never over 97.3 degrees Fahrenheit, and the rainfall is moderate (and varied: between twenty-three and seventy-two inches a year). The New Guineans in Port Moresby now wear mostly Western clothes, but one can still see pretty laughing girls in raffia skirts with flowers in their hair—a contrast to the drained-out, thin-blooded white women. Pidgin is the language heard on every hand. There is no television here or anywhere else in New Guinea.

There is still a Papuan village on stilts over the water at Hanuabada, the main settlement in the area before the whites arrived. A lot of the houses are made of an ugly material that the Australians call fibro—fibrous asbestos cement.

The Sogeri Rubber Plantation lies twenty-eight miles from Port Moresby and eighteen hundred feet up in the hills. Lisle Johnston, the manager, says that he employs 250 local men as tappers, paying up to twelve dollars a month plus housing, blankets, matches and tobacco, and family keep. On up the road are even bigger plantations.

*

RABAUL, meaning "place of mangroves," main city of New Britain, has been the setting for tremendous violence, both natural and man-made. The harbor is a caldera, the product of some thunderous prehistoric explosion of a volcano, later breached by the sea. Subsequent eruptions threw up three of the volcanoes (now dead) that adjoin the harbor, called North Daughter, the Mother, and South Daughter (the Father stands fifty miles down the island). Newer volcanoes still threaten Rabaul. One of them, Vulcan, was born during three days of smoke, explosions, steam, and ash-falls in May 1937, as the population watched in terror. The most recent blow, however, was not an eruption but a Force 8.4 earthquake in July 1971. Tidal waves in the area swept half a mile inland, and the Rabaul waterfront was badly knocked about.

Rabaul's fine harbor outweighs its volcanic perils; but—just in case—vulcanologists are posted on the mountainsides to listen for any rumble and shout "Get out!" if necessary. Half of New Guinea's three thousand "*kong kongs*," Chinese descendants of laborers and house servants brought by the Germans, live in Rabaul. Rabaul exports sweet-scented copra and cocoa, much of it raised by the energetic Tolais, for whom this is the big city, though the population is only 10,500. During World War II, the Japanese swiftly captured Rabaul and converted it into a fortress so strong that the Americans and Australians never even tried to retake it, but instead waited until the surrender in Tokyo. The bombproof bunker of the Japanese naval commander still stands in the center of Rabaul, now deserted after having served briefly as a movie theater. Japanese-built defense tunnels lie under the whole town, and at nearby Kokopo are the seaside caverns that the Japanese excavated as ports for their supply barges.

*

You reach WEWAK on a plane with white stewardesses serving black passengers. Visible from above are many circular pools, bomb craters blasted out during the war. The town has lovely safe beaches, on a long spit of sand, and an ocean boulevard washed by a fresh breeze. Wewak lies behind what the local people call a "rain shadow"—that is, mountains on the windward side catch most of the rainfall—so Wewak is not as wet as nearby areas. One street has an odd-sounding name: Kenny V. C. Avenue; it celebrates a private named Kenny who got the Victoria Cross for his gallant capture of a Japanese gun position here.* Wewak has: (1) the most expensive motel in New Guinea, at nineteen dollars a day; and (2) Leo Arkfeld, the Roman Catholic Bishop, who flies his own plane all over the Sepik to attend to his flock.

*

LAE took advantage of being bombed to bits to relocate, moving from the coastal flats to a bench above the Huon Gulf. Though the city is new, big trees close over above the streets, and parks and gardens dot the city.

* The Japanese returned here (and elsewhere in New Guinea) after the war to open the mass graves of their thousands of war dead, cremate the bones, and take the ashes back home.

The market sells such temptations as smoked flying fox. On the beach, nearly covered by sand, is the hulk of a Japanese battleship. A number of Americans live here, and the town is booming with various light industries. Lae also reaches out to the gold-rush country of the 1920's, around Bulolo, and to the land of the once-dreaded Kukukukus.

A Short and Simple History

Moresby and Murray, General MacArthur, General Adachi, and Margaret Mead—these are some of the names that attach themselves, in the Westerner's mind, to New Guinea. The Spice Islands, just west, attracted Portuguese colonizers in the early 1500's, and a governor of the Moluccas was the first to sight the New Guinea mainland. After inspecting the residents he named the island Papua, from a Malay word meaning "frizzy-headed." A Spanish explorer, coming along later, descried a coastal resemblance to African Guinea, and gave the island the name that stuck. Three centuries of eventless history then drifted over New Guinea until the Dutch, branching out from Indonesia, took the western half of the island, establishing the bisecting border at 141 degrees east longitude, which remains the boundary to this day. About that time, British Naval Lieutenant Charles Yule landed from the schooner *Bramble* a bit up the coast from present-day Port Moresby to claim the eastern end of the island for Great Britain. An air of improvisation attached to this adventure; nobody remembered to bring a Union Jack, so Yule drew one with a pencil and paper, and nailed it to a handy tree. The tars on the beach sent up three cheers, but pianissimo, "lest too much noise should attract the natives." Unluckily, the sharp-eared natives were attracted anyway. Yule prudently tried to leave the beach, but his boat overturned in the surf. A cutter was sent to the rescue. It, too, broached, leaving fifteen unarmed Englishmen on the shore to be captured. And captured they were—until the *Bramble* managed to get boats through the surf to save them. Yule courageously waited until all his men were off the beach. Then—the natives having conveniently stripped him of his clothes—he dived into the waves and swam to his ship. He blandly named the beach Cape Possession. But so slow was the pace of exploration that it was not until 1873 that Captain John Moresby found the fine port that is presently the capital of New Guinea, and named it in honor of his father.

The next colonizer was Queensland, then a British colony and now, of course, an Australian state. The imperious Queensland Premier of the time, Sir Thomas McIlwraith, was worried by German agitation for the annexation of eastern New Guinea. He cabled London, urging England to grab New Guinea; failing to get action, he sent an agent to Port Moresby to do so. Gladstone, Prime Minister in England, scowled at the colony's attempt to colonize. Queensland was not "fit to rule," he said. The rebuff shocked all Australia. In 1886, under further pressure from the Australian colonies, Britain seized Papua while allowing the Germans to take the rest of eastern New Guinea.

Britain ran the possession listlessly, but it established the principle that the villagers' life and right to their land should be left intact. Missionaries brought their dubious boons, suffering great perils in the process; two of them were spectacularly slaughtered and consumed. When Australia confederated in 1901, Britain gladly handed the place over to the new nation. Under an intelligent and energetic administrator, Sir Hubert Murray, New Guinea was left more or less as it was. This policy is the root of present-day accusations that Australia did not get started soon enough in educating Papuans for life in world society now. But Murray was conforming to the demands of Australian unions that black labor must not be developed and brought into White Australia. On balance the welfare of the Papuans seems to have been foremost in his mind; later, retired, he fought Canberra's attempt to make Papua an "asset" to Australia, and opposed a whipping-of-natives measure proposed in Parliament. While Administrator, he set up the system of Australian *kiaps* (Pidgin for district officers), who explored the territory, cut down cannibalism and tribal warfare, and kept the missionaries from overly disrupting village customs.

A month after World War I began, German New Guinea slipped easily into Australian hands: a few troops clashed with a volunteer militia of German planters on New Britain, and overcame them at a cost of six dead—first of the sixty thousand Australians killed in that war. At Versailles, Australia's Prime Minister Hughes demanded and got a League of Nations mandate to the former German colony. Australia took it over to "promote to the utmost the material and moral well-being" of its people, but promptly announced that the territory would have to be self-supporting, and to ship all its products through Sydney. Australians took on the former German plantations and ran them with indentured laborers, "recruited" from their homes and paid threepence a day, and susceptible, in the absence of their wives, to what was shudderingly known as "sexual depravity." The only event of note in the next two decades was the discovery of gold in the mountains up from Lae; Guinea Airlines was founded to fly cargo in and out, including entire gold dredges, part by part, and was the biggest-volume cargo airline in the world up to that time.

World War II

For millions of Americans, the first day they ever thought about New Guinea was January 21, 1942. That day the Japanese bombed two towns on the island; in March they made their first landings; and soon the war communiqués made household words of such remote places as Rabaul, Lae, Wewak, Port Moresby, Buna, Kokopa, the Owen Stanley Range, and Bougainville. In May, having taken Rabaul, the Japanese assembled a fleet to sail around the eastern end of New Guinea and seize Port Moresby. As it steamed into the Coral Sea, the assault force met a big American fleet, centered around two aircraft carriers. The opposing ships in that battle did not come within sight, but their planes fought savagely. The Japanese turned back—first augury of their eventual doom.

The Japanese decided to take by land what they could not take by sea. Over a six-thousand-foot pass in the Owen Stanley Range, north of Port Moresby, they poured troops far outnumbering the defending Australians, who fell back almost to Moresby. But the Japanese had outrun their supplies, and the tide of battle turned. Papuan villagers, the Fuzzie-Wuzzie Angels, rather reluctantly carried supplies in and wounded soldiers out.* That saved Moresby for good, but the Japanese still held Rabaul with ninety thousand men, and had fifty airfields in the New Guinea jungle. They stabbed back, attempting a convoy from Rabaul to Lae that was wiped out by three days of attacks by American and Australian planes in the Bismarck Sea. Left isolated in the mountains back of Lae, the Japanese held out savagely for two years, until the middle of 1944. Meanwhile, the Americans built up their stupendous base on Manus, the island where anthropologist Margaret Mead lived while she wrote *Growing Up in New Guinea*, and, after the war, *New Lives for Old*. One million Americans were funneled through this base.

General MacArthur deemed the enemy sufficiently under control so that he could transfer his headquarters from Brisbane to Hollandia, the capital of Dutch New Guinea, on the north coast just west of the border. Soon he was landing on Leyte, in the Philippines, and the New Guinea campaign was essentially over. The Japanese at Rabaul were simply bypassed, and remained until after the war was over. Elsewhere—on Bougainville, on the parts of New Britain outside of Rabaul, and at Wewak on the north coast of New Guinea—Australia's General Thomas Blamey fought on against the

* The first published novel by a Papuan, *The Crocodile*, by Vincent Eri, is the story of one such carrier.

105,000 Japanese troops there. In the end, the Japanese General, Hatazo Adachi, came out of the bush so weak that he had to be carried, and handed over his sword to an Australian colonel. Fifteen thousand Australian troops were killed or wounded in New Guinea, and fifteen thousand New Guineans were killed—plus one hundred thousand pigs.

After the war, the League of Nations Mandate was reconstituted as a United Nations Trust Agreement, and in 1949 the Australian Parliament passed the Papua–New Guinea Act, which thereby became the territory's Constitution. It joined the northern and southern halves of eastern New Guinea into a single administrative unit, which now has a common Parliament, Supreme Court, and civil service. The UN scrutinizes Australia's performance in the trust territory by means of a visiting mission every three years, and prods the colony toward self-government. How this works, in terms of developing education, the economy, and the political system, is the subject of the next chapter.

CHAPTER 20

Niugini: The Future Nation

Hark and behold our stone age is swaying and groaning,
Right beneath your mighty step of pain,
Haltingly and stubbornly resisting and frowning,
But forever and ever in vain.

—A. P. ALLAN NATACHEE, MAKEO POET

WE HAVE NOW GRASPED that the eastern half of New Guinea is Australian; we must proceed to grasp that it will not be Australian much longer. The territory is slated for independence some time in the next decade.

The idea raises many questions. An island-nation may make some sense; one sliced down the middle by a boundary that came from the whim of some forgotten Dutchman is certainly less logical. It is equally unnatural to reach east and include a couple of islands from the Solomons. And what is enclosed in these artificial political-historical borders has no particular coherence—future fragmentation seems quite possible. Furthermore, independence may well sacrifice the law and order that the Australians imposed, which might seem a fusty argument, except that this law and order replaced cannibalism, tribal warfare for the fun of it, and casual murder. The slender new nation will also expose itself to the possibility of a cold world's raising duties against its products; it will be vulnerable to losing its markets just when it should be opening up bigger ones; and Australia will be under less obligation to subsidize it, as she has been doing at a recent rate of $100 million a year.

In reflection of these considerations, powerful forces oppose independence. Almost all of the conservative highland villagers are against it. The white Australian plantation owners also object. And one can correctly surmise that the managers of the huge Conzinc Riotinto copper mine in Bougainville would rather stay under Australian law.

Nevertheless, Papua New Guinea is inevitably going to be a nation of its own, perhaps as early as 1976, for the forces in favor of independence are much stronger than those against. The Australian government has long since committed itself to the goal of New Guinean nationhood. The United Nations presses continuously for it. The strong nationalism of most of the educated natives of the territory works for independence. The consequence of all these pressures is a slow boil of passions and politics. Let us examine the panorama in more detail.

*

Australia's problem of letting go in New Guinea is ticklish now because the government made no preparation for education and self-government during all the long decades before the end of World War II. It was almost as though Australia deliberately steered itself to its present embarrassing position of possessing the last important colony in the world*—a colony bigger in size and population than many full-fledged members of the United Nations. In the process, Australia managed to fetch up with the last significant territory administered under the UN Trusteeship Council.†

Until the early 1960's, government in Australian New Guinea lay in the hands of an all-powerful Administrator appointed by the Department of External Territories in Canberra. He ruled through district officers backed up by patrol officers, in turn backed up by village authorities called *luluais* and *tultuls*. A more or less fictitious Legislative Council, composed mostly of prominent white businessmen and missionaries, lent advice. Local government councils—black men in white shirts sitting submissively around a table—assisted the district authorities. The Minister for External Territories in Canberra kept tight control of the whole show. Then came a memorable visit, in 1962, of a United Nations Mission to New Guinea, headed by Sir Hugh Foot (now Lord Caradon), last of the great British colonial governors (Jamaica, Nigeria, Cyprus). The mission censured Australia for dragging its

* If one accepts the fiction that Angola and Mozambique are provinces, not colonies, of Portugal.

† Which since the war has successfully terminated the mandates in Togoland, Cameroons, Somaliland, Tanganyika, Western Samoa, and Ruanda-Urundi; the only remaining trust territory besides New Guinea is the group of Pacific islands administered by the United States.

feet in developing New Guinea,* and demanded: (1) creation of a house of representatives with one hundred members elected by universal adult suffrage; (2) education through university level of one hundred Papuans and New Guineans to be administrators for the territory; and (3) a survey of the country's economic possibilities by the World Bank.

Thus prodded, the government proceeded, with vim and great goodwill, to get an assembly elected. Patrol officers took on the prodigious task of enrolling every last discoverable tribesman. In some cases, as one might expect, the tribesmen thought that the registration was for the purpose of singling out people to be taxed or murdered, but the more general reaction was wild, uncomprehending fervor. Explaining democracy, voting, and the principle of representation was almost comically problematic, but the patrols did their best, eloquently displaying maps of the capital and pictures of the House of Assembly.

The campaigning was vigorous and inventive. In a hinterlands New Britain constituency, a candidate named Lima Larebo promised, should he be elected, to recruit the doctors of Rabaul to go to the countryside and give the villagers injections that would turn their skins white. Some white candidates took new names with more appeal to the local voters; Peter Murray became Pitamari, and John Pasquarelli became Master February. One candidate campaigned by holding up an egg and assuring voters that it contained the embryo of an American soldier—upon winning, he would hatch the egg and the Americans would take over, which was, it is inspiring to note, thought to be a good thing. Another candidate cited just one impressive qualification: he had, in his lifetime, killed nine men. This New Guinea—what a culture clash!

Patrol officers took ballot boxes to every village. Enthusiasm reigned. Some voters walked for days to cast a ballot. One man who was wanted for murder could not resist showing up to vote, and was duly arrested. The process took a month, early in 1964, and when it was over Papua New Guinea had a new House of Assembly of sixty-four (not one hundred) members, ten of them appointed by the government rather than elected. The Rt. Hon. William Philip, Viscount De L'Isle, V.C., P.C., G.C.M.G., G.C.V.O., K.St.J., and Governor-General of Australia at the time, came to open the new Parliament. For a second general election in 1968, the size of the House was raised to ninety-four, still including ten appointive members.

This House of Assembly was, and remains, a rather toothless body, gain-

* Of course, the mission had to confine itself to the trust territory, and could scarcely set foot in Papua, but the logic of its criticism and proposals obviously applied to Papua, too.

ing only a little every year in the powers allowed to it by the Australian raj. But the system of which it is a part is the framework for the advance of the territory toward self-government and independence, and the territory's leaders work mostly within it. Let us meet a few of them.

The Not-Very-Angry Mr. Guise

Described as "widely hated among the Europeans" and "one of the angriest Papuans," John Guise is a docile, charming man of fifty-seven who scared the planter class a few years back by raising the idea of nationhood, but turned out to be a force for the most moderate kind of change. Guise, one of whose grandfathers was English, was born in a village near Milne Bay (on the eastern tip of New Guinea), and schooled by an Anglican mission. At twenty-six he was "top boy" at one of the stores of the Burns Philp Mercantile company, which dominates New Guinea. During the war he was drafted for road building, which led him to join the police as a sergeant and go on to become, in 1955, a village-affairs expert for the Department of District Administration. In 1960, when the Australian government decided to let six elected Papuan and New Guinean members into the old Legislative Council, Guise won the Eastern Papua seat. By then he had been, as a visiting policeman, to Brisbane, Sydney, and London (for the coronation of Queen Elizabeth); now he went to Kenya at Jomo Kenyatta's invitation, to Pago Pago for a conference of Pacific islanders, to New York as a UN adviser, to London again for an Anglican General Synod. In the Legislative Council he preached a program of reform—more education, help for village farmers, more authority for the local government councils, equal pay for equal work, the employment of native magistrates, antidiscrimination laws. Modest enough—but it upset the mossbacks. He won election to the House of Assembly when it was formed, and at once became leader of the elected members. He pushed the case for Papuan–New Guinean unity, proposing the name "Niugini," which looks like another way of spelling New Guinea, but is really a felicitous combination of words from local languages that jointly mean "stand of coconuts."

Certain members of the House of Assembly are now ministerial members in charge of, for instance, public health, stock and fisheries, trade and industry. But Guise never took a ministerial post: instead, he was elected the first island-born Speaker of the House. Just before taking office, he announced that for the ceremony he would shun a Western jacket in favor of a white bark tapa cloth over his shoulders. The switch infuriated highland members of the House, because tapa cloth is a coastal mode—so Guise sent someone out for bird-of-paradise feathers, much worn in the highlands, and pinned them to the costume. Adding a *kina* shell on a necklace, a black cape, and a long white Westminster wig, he unified Papua, New Guinea, and old England with this one grand symbolic gesture. As his wife, who wears the blue face tattoos of the Motu people, looked on, Guise took office asking God's guidance for them both—"simple village people," in his words. In 1971, the Papua New Guinea government made its first international contact on its own. Guise and a group of members of the House visited Djakarta, pointedly disdaining to check in at Canberra first. Guise never went past the fourth grade, but he now holds an honorary Doctor of Laws degree from the University of Papua and New Guinea.

*

Guise floated up and out of Parliamentary politics when he became Speaker, but while he was still a partisan his heart was with the only party that has so far managed to hang together in the territory, the Pangu (an acronym of Papua and New Guinea) Pati (Pidgin for party). This group joins public servants, students, teachers, intellectuals, and radicals, plus more grass roots than any other aggregation, and criticizes the government. With only ten seats out of ninety-four, its main function, however unintentional, is to provide most of the other elected members with something to oppose. Pangu's opponents, highlanders, planters, and uncommitted members of the House, banded together after the 1968 election as "The Independent Group," and in 1970 formed a party called Compass. The party's main purpose is to stall independence as long as possible.

Chairman of this conservative group is Oala Oala-Rarua, one of the few tall, heavily built men of Papua, where people tend to be short and wiry. He is the son and grandson of pastors for the London Missionary Society. Some of his nine brothers (he also has two sisters) have become pastors, too. Mr. Oala-Rarua taught for a while, managed to study and travel in the United States and Europe, and got into politics as a founder of the Pangu Pati before the 1968 election. Soon "there were disagreements in the party. I resigned. Some say I was expelled." His qualifications—among other things, he speaks English much better than most Australians—quickly levitated him into the post of assistant ministerial member for the Treasury. "I had more experience. I was a teacher by profession."

As Oala-Rarua sees it, Papua New Guinea feels "no fierce, urgent desire to toss Australia into the sea." The reasons for this are that: (1) apathy, abetted by lack of education, is the prevalent mood; (2) Australia provides vital funds for the territory; and (3) Australia provides a good administration with no serious exploitation. What does Australia get in return for the funds it spends here? Goodwill, a market, and raw materials, says Oala-Rarua. "There is no nationalism as such, as in Africa. There is no Communism either; there have been attempts, we've kicked them out of the trade unions, but there is no organized party." As for independence: "We look forward to it, though it is not a general feeling. Quite a lot of people are against it, especially in the highlands. They fear being taken over by the city people; they feel they are protected by the Australian government; they fear all good jobs would go to the coastal people, who have contact with the outside world. And the majority of the planters want the Australians to stay."

In sum, Oala-Rarua holds that the territory is getting ahead at an acceptable speed. "My children certainly have more opportunity than I had. They learn English from the word go" (although "only about a quarter of the children in the country at large even get into primary school"). He thinks that "the Administrator is right when he says we already have a large measure of self-government."

*

A couple of impassioned young men of Rabaul are John Kaputin, twenty-nine, the territory's most rousing orator, and Oscar Tammur, also twenty-nine, leaders of the Mataungan* Association, which is a sort of political party that wants to rule by setting up a district government of its own, bypassing the official one. The issue is land. The Gazelle Peninsula, site of Rabaul, has the best volcanic land in New Guinea, much of it held by Australian planters as an inheritance from the freehold system that prevailed under the German administration. Kaputin calls the planters "white pigs who have grown fat on my country." Responding slowly to the land hunger of the exploding Tolai population, the government in mid-1970 planned to resettle some of the Tolais on 302 plots carved from vacant plantations held by the administration. Without waiting, Mataungan squatters dashed in and seized the land. Blaming the land shortage on the lack of action by the Gazelle Peninsula Local Government Council, which has some white members, Mataungans by the thousands refused to pay taxes, putting the money into escrow pending Council reforms.

Prosecuting the tax-evaders, the government fined Tammur thirty dollars for refusing to pay sixteen dollars in taxes, and jailed him when he refused

* Meaning "Be alert."

to pay the fine. Tammur, a bearded teacher and copra grower who speaks fluent English, Pidgin, Toli and Mandik, is a Pangu Pati Member of the House of Assembly, but that did not save him from jail. He is a fiery backer of independence now. Kaputin, talking with John Gorton when the former Prime Minister visited New Guinea in 1970, told him that Mataunganism is "nationalism in the raw state."

*

Other redoubtable leaders dot the New Guinea scene. Albert Maori Kiki, secretary of the Pangu Pati, says right out loud: "We have hatred for the white man in our hearts." Michael Somare, a teacher, journalist, and Parliamentary leader of the Pangu Pati, is another angry young man. One fabulous early member of the House of Assembly is a Scotsman named Ian Farley Graham Downs. He went to New Guinea as a district commissioner in the Eastern Highlands, but resigned in 1956 to become a coffee planter. In the House he spoke up vigorously for highlands interests. He campaigned by papering his district with handbills in Pidgin that read:

YUPELA HARIM. VOT LONG
ELEKSION. DOWNS NAMBA WAN

When the returns came in, Downs was indeed No. 1. A less forceful member was Handabe Tiabe, elected by the Huri people of Tari in the Southern Highlands. He spoke only Huri, and sat through four years of sessions, which were mostly in Pidgin, bewildered but smiling broadly.

*

The man who occupies the position of the world's last high-level colonial governor—here tactfully called Administrator—is Leslie W. Johnson, a veteran Australian civil servant. The House of Assembly, he says, has the power to "pass laws about anything except a few reserved subjects like defense and external affairs, but the laws are subject to veto by the Administrator and the Governor-General of Australia." In practice, Mr. Johnson points out, the veto has been used only twice in six years. In one case, the House passed a law transferring control of the public (civil) service from the Australian Ministry for External Territories to itself—plainly a patronage grab. Another, says Mr. Johnson, was a "technical matter of mining legislation." There is a touch of play-acting in such maneuvers. The House of Assembly's ministerial members "meet in a cabinet called the administrative executive council, which formally advises the Administrator," but they are "not yet fully responsible for government action."

Mr. Johnson, a sensitive and professional high-level civil servant, is articulate and aware of the territory's touchiest problems. Land tenure—as we have seen in the case of the Mataungan rebels in New Britain—is one of them. "We operate on the system that land belongs to the natives, and that's it," he says. All the land is owned by somebody other than the government, usually communally, and if the government wants this land, it has to buy it with the consent of all the co-holders. The natives cannot sell the land to individuals or corporations, but only to the government, which can then lease it.

For the more than $100 million a year spent in New Guinea, what does Australia get in return? Mr. Johnson replies: "Most Australians would say, 'Nothing.' The white man's burden. But Australia gets defense—not such a valid point since World War II—and a stable neighbor, and a sense of humanitarian service. And of course we are under pressure from Australian companies that have property here."

The Administrator plays down the differences between Papua and the New Guinea Trust Territory. "Legally, Papua is an Australian colony, and New Guinea is a trust territory of the United Nations administered by Australia. But in human terms, they are administered as one—my writ carries equally. They have one Parliament and one public service. They have a single educational system and a single budget. There is no problem of apportionment of funds because funds are apportioned on a basis of need."

*

Dr. John T. Gunther will probably be known, when New Guinea becomes independent, as the father of the nation. The New Guinean and Papuan leaders that he has helped to form—Guise is typical—are to be found all over the territory, and they are fantastically loyal to him. Born in northern New South Wales, Gunther went to medical school at Sydney University and planned a career in industrial medicine, but the war took him to New Guinea, where he served in the Royal Australian Air Force. Entering government service, he became Director of Public Health in the territory, then rose to be Deputy Administrator. But he never moved up to Administrator because of the political string-pulling that goes on in Canberra. This may have been all to the good, for Dr. Gunther got the fulfilling task of founding the University of Papua and New Guinea, and serving as its first vice chancellor (which in Australian terms is head man). One recent New Year's Eve he said, "I haven't seen a winter in fifteen years." Such are the diligence and creative energy of this man.

Sitting on one of the orange seats in the university auditorium, a room of rough stone walls and a ceiling in the shape of a pyramidal tent, Dr. Gunther talked for a while about his school. The university started its first classes in makeshift rooms in 1966, began construction of its airy, modern buildings in 1967, and occupied them in 1969. The staff includes twelve professors and ninety other teachers and functionaries. The enrollment in 1970 was 780, two-thirds black and one-third white; Dr. Gunther hopes for an eventual ratio of eight blacks to one white. Entry requires four years of high school *plus* one year of prematriculation study—and still 38 percent of those who enter drop out. All the blacks are on scholarships: $200 a year for tuition, $160 for board and room, $100 for pocket money. The territory has five institutions of "tertiary" education—a technology school in Lae, an administrative college, an agricultural college, a medical and dental college, and a teachers college—but only the university grants degrees. The university library had forty thousand books on shelves, forty thousand not yet catalogued, and a set of copies of busts from the British Museum—Benin bronzes and Greek-Roman classics.

Dr. Gunther is, naturally, a mine of New Guinean lore. "There is not much left of the territory that white men have not walked over, but near Angoram recently a professor from here met people who had never seen a white man. Light skin is not generally the result of intermarriage with whites; the people around Port Moresby are, it is true, often lighter in skin color and straight-haired, but that is apparently because Malay traders came here long ago and influenced the heritage. We avoid the use of the word 'native,' except as an adjective, and 'indigene.'* They call themselves black, though they range in actual color from puce to Bougainville ebony. A bit of headhunting still goes on in the remoter areas—also eating Grandma because you love her. There used to be a brain disease, *kuru*, that mystified the doctors in New Guinea for a long time. It was finally traced to cannibalism. The cannibal himself would die—not right away but two or three years later."

* This is certainly a vexed question in New Guinea. Sir Hugh Foot's United Nations Mission decreed that the use of the word "native . . . must be eliminated." Government publications scrupulously avoid it, and writers often try to sidestep the word by saying "local people," "villagers," and the like. Other new books take the view that "native" means what the dictionary says it means, and use it throughout. In ordinary speech, whites use "native" functionally and naturally, and the Tolais of the Gazelle Peninsula call someone from another part of New Guinea a "foreign native." "Indigene" is, of course, an absurd pedantic euphemism.

*

Early in 1971, the Minister for External Territories, Charles E. Barnes, said that Australia would accept without reservation any date for self-government that the Papua New Guinea House of Assembly might choose. On the face of it, a rosy picture indeed—here is a colonial power cheerfully bending every effort to let go gracefully. But in Canberra one quickly learns that letting go involves excruciating problems, all related to the timetable. Australia seems to have a choice of cutting New Guinea adrift either much too soon or much too late, with no sensible compromise between these extremes.

The separation will come too soon if:

• The central government is not sufficiently strong and respected to restrain secessions and divisions.

• Education is not well enough advanced to supply replacements for the seven thousand Australians who hold most of the top jobs in the public service.

• Foreign investment ($50 million a year) declines sharply out of lack of confidence.

• The House of Assembly cannot develop more seriousness and responsibility. (One of Speaker John Guise's priorities is to hold down drinking on the job by members of the House of Assembly.)

• The highlanders, half of the population, continue to oppose independence.

But separation will come too late if:

• Nationalism grows to the point of impatient and possibly bloody rebellion.

• Dissension among the parts of the territory grows to the point of messy disunity at the moment of independence.

• Delay costs Australia credibility with the United Nations and the world, and makes it look like a nation hanging onto a colonial empire.

The trick, says one official in Canberra, is to "get out with cheers as our flag goes down and theirs goes up." Some trick; the dangers of both too soon and too late are quite real. Some of the black New Guineans are talking tough; Leo Hannet, a Bougainville poet and playwright, says, "The day of the *kiap* is over. As for the planters, they will have to go. But we must be fair. We must give them back their beads and axes." Education is still deplorably deficient; 72 percent of the people ten years old or more are illiterate; only about 220,000 children go to primary schools, and only

1,600 graduate every year from high school. The government still relies on mission schools for the bulk of primary education.

The sharpest dangers of all, no doubt, involve disunity and threats of secession. When a new United Nations Mission visited the territory in 1971, several hundred angry tribesmen at Wapenamanda in the highlands nearly broke up a meeting as they shouted down suggestions of self-government—they even opposed flying the United Nations flag next to the Australian. This sort of thing gives the Papuans of coastal New Guinea a feeling that numerically strong but backward neighbors are retarding their nationhood, and the attitude of the Mataungans on New Britain is that they'll go it alone into independence, rather than wait for the mossback highlanders. Many people in Bougainville also yearn to secede; one leader openly asked the 1971 UN Mission what the UN would do about it if Bougainville pulled out. The mission chairman said that he "hoped the situation would not arise."

Former Prime Minister John Gorton, on his 1970 tour of the territory, had to argue constantly that secession would damage the seceders. "The other thing which has been spoken of is self-government now, self-government for New Britain. . . . Would it not be well for each man to sit down in his own home and think what he really wants and what advantages he can get from being a part of the territory?" Part of the thinking in Bougainville is that the single biggest industry of the territory, the $350-million Conzinc Riotinto of Australia copper mine, is located there, and by secession the island can keep the resulting prosperity to itself. Gorton countered this concept by stressing the possibility that Papua is on the brink of a big oil find, as a consequence of some discoveries in the gulf, and will have some prosperity of its own to share before long.

How to let go of New Guinea has increasingly become a political issue in Australia. The leader of the Labor Party, Gough Whitlam, made a flamboyant tour of the territory early in 1970, and won the applause of the people of Papua and New Britain by proposing a firm timetable: self-government in 1972, independence in 1976 (both territorial election years). Ten thousand cheering people mobbed Whitlam in Rabaul. It was this successful maneuver that forced Gorton to visit New Guinea six months later, but as he prepared to go, planters rushed to Canberra to plead with him not to set any dates for independence. So he confined himself to assurances that it would come eventually but positively. "I do not speak of self-government in 1972 or in any calendar that you may mention," he said, and "anyone who seeks to say so . . . is dangerously simplifying the problem." Gorton won his share of applause in the conservative highlands.

The machinery that Australia uses to guide Papua New Guinea to independence is the Westminster Statute, employed by Britain in the decolonialization of nations all over the world—Nigeria, Trinidad-Tobago, India, even Australia itself in the last century. An appointive Legislative Council is created, later liberalized with elected members, then supplemented or replaced by a more representative House, which in turn is liberalized by increasing its size and the proportion of elected members, and by giving it more and more power. Where the territory stands now is this: The House of Assembly, the intended seat of power, has ninety-four members. Ten are appointed by Canberra; all of these are "European" (that is, white Australian) officers of the administration, who are supposed to give the house stability and know-how. Sixty-nine are from "open" electorates of the voting public at large—sixty-one of them happen to be Papuans or New Guineans, and eight Europeans. The remaining fifteen are from "special" electorates, meaning that they must be educated persons. Four of these are Papuans or New Guineans, and eleven Europeans.

Administrator Johnson says that this House of Assembly is "more than halfway to self-government." To be precise, the House and specifically its ministerial members have taken power (subject to veto) in the areas of primary and secondary (but not tertiary) education, public health, posts and telegraphs, territory revenue, coastal shipping, prisons, registration and use of land, town planning, and some other lesser functions. Canberra reserves final authority for the judiciary, the enforcement of law and order, internal security, higher education, external affairs, and external and large-scale development projects in agriculture, transport, and forestry that are financed by Australian funds.

Quirky factors in this political entity, half-colony and half-nation, are citizenship and customs. Residents of the trust territory are Australian Protected Persons, while residents of the old colony of Papua are Australian citizens. Yet not even the Papuans are allowed to move to Australia; this is one more application of the supposedly nonexistent White Australia policy. Papua New Guinea is also cut off from Australia by tariffs, though mostly low and preferential ones, similar to those conceded to Canada.

How much does race matter in the territory? Socially, the bars are dropping. Discrimination prevailed at pools, theaters, hospitals, and clubs until the mid-1960's, but a Discriminatory Practices Ordinance now works against this sort of thing. The biggest step, perhaps, was the 1963 abolition, under United Nations pressure, of laws that forbade blacks to drink and censored movies that might purvey uppity ideas. Opening the pubs to everyone forced the more prejudiced planters and businessmen to form private clubs, but in general race relations in the territory are easy and relaxed. Still, it is the kind of place where you are likely to hear a white planter say, "Some of my best mates are coons."

One grinding irritant remains. A decade ago, the administration began to employ Papuans and New Guineans in the public service, hitherto a preserve of Australians. At first the pay for the blacks was the same as for the whites. But as more and more blacks were hired, the administration perceived that it was: (1) building up a high salary bill for the future independent country; (2) creating a class of people who in local terms were supersalaried; and (3) pressuring such commercial companies as Burns Philp, W. R. Carpenter Ltd., and Steamships Trading Company by vastly exceeding their low pay scales. Accordingly, the government in 1964 cut the pay of the black public servants (who now number thirteen thousand) by 60 percent, while leaving the pay of the white Australians (who now number seven thousand) just what it was. This could be rationalized: the Australians had needed skills, and would quit rather than take a cut. But the widespread effect was unequal pay for equal work. Papuan and New Guinean members of the House of Assembly howled, and it fell to the unhappy Australian officials holding the appointive seats—at that time including both Dr. Gunther and Mr. Johnson—to defend the measure. Administrator Johnson now says, "It is still a sore point, and will get more so."

The practical facts of land tenure also rub the wrong way. Put in terms of bland official totals, 96 percent of the territory is "native or ownerless," while the administration owns 1,300 square miles and leases 5,000, and only 850 square miles is given over to "expatriate freehold," meaning white planters. Put another way, however, it turns out that only half of the land under commercial agriculture is cultivated by Papuans and New Guineans. Similarly, although blacks got the majority of individual loans made in 1969 by the New Guinea Development Bank, the white planters got more than half of the $5.5 million lent that year.

None of these issues is fully ablaze. But their presence helps explain the posters one sees on the bulletin boards of the University of New South Wales in Sydney: "NIUGINI LIBERATION NEEDS YOU! For the autonomous development of New Guinea. Redistribution of land. Economic, social, and political freedom." Radical students scent that New Guinea can be a cause.

*

We have seen that education in Papua New Guinea is barely stumbling along now, that schools were left entirely to missionaries until after World War II, and that there was not a single New Guinean university graduate until lately. In the face of this bad record, Australia, on urging by the

World Bank, made a tough and controversial decision in 1964—namely, that education would still take a back seat (with a goal of universal but low-level literacy), and that the stress would be put on economic development to enable the new nation to stand on its own feet. The money would go to roads, ports, communications, airports, incentives to industry, training in trades and agriculture.

All this is now getting enormous results, the Department of External Territories in Canberra contends. The idea is to raise agricultural exports, by means of two successive five-year plans ending in 1973, to about $90 million a year. The basic product is the traditional coconut, made into copra by splitting the husks and sun-drying the meat until it can be extracted and further dried in a furnace fueled by the husks. Copra provides coconut oil for food, soap, and cosmetics. Other crops are cocoa, rubber, oil palm, and—as we saw earlier—most notably, tea. Coffee is a big item; New Guinea supplies all of Australia. But increased planting is discourged because the market is saturated.

The dense forests of the island supply fine woods for plywood, and seventy sawmills are now in operation. Beef cattle thrive in the highlands. Tapioca has been brought in from Africa; here it is called manihot. A large proportion of the world's pyrethrum comes from around Mount Hagen. Gold mining produces a dribble of money, but the Bougainville copper is the real gold of the territory; copper exports alone are approaching the value of all agricultural exports put together.

The economic development plan pushes tree planting of all kinds, and encourages villagers to increase their share of commercial agriculture, even though by 1973 their share of copra exports, for example, will be only $9 million as compared to the white planters' $14 million. In general, most of the profit from the new (and old) enterprises in New Guinea goes to Australian and foreign businessmen, not to New Guineans.

There are social consequences which go along with this. Once people living in a subsistence community come into contact with a cash community, they are committed to change. The native culture gets shoved overboard in the process. Garden plots have to be consolidated willy-nilly. A system of family land inheritance replaces that of clan ownership. With money coming in, the New Guinean will want a permanent, European-style house, rather than a shack made of *pit pit* (sugar-cane fiber). The cash-cropper may buy a motorbike or a car. In short, life will change from the agricultural to the industrial, and the villagers will say good-bye to the yam and the sing sing. The government will benefit as well; it cannot tax a man in the subsistence economy, but it can certainly nail a cash-cropper.

Five Open Questions About New Guinea

- How much will it cost Australia after independence?
- Will it end up as a military dictatorship?
- Any chance of a Biafra here?
- Will an independent New Guinea form an alliance with West Irian and Indonesia?
- How far can a nation go on coconuts?

Four Curious Tidbits About New Guinea

The *Papua-New Guinea Post-Courier*, published in Port Moresby, is printed in both English and Pidgin.

The shillings and pence that used to circulate in New Guinea were often pierced so that they could be strung on a necklace for easy access and safekeeping.

The U.S.-based Summer Institute of Linguistics is translating the Bible into all available Papuan and New Guinean tongues—which involves first converting the nonliterate languages into written forms. American students work at this task in pairs in remote villages, and the result counts as a Ph.D. thesis.

When a village disobeyed its leader's orders, the government provided him with a tape recorder. He then taped the same orders and played the tape at full blast throughout the village. The stratagem produced instant obedience.

*

When Papua and New Guinea join as an independent country, the name will probably be Niugini, as proposed long since by John Guise.* The House of Assembly has formally adopted a committee report supporting the name, as well as a flag of red and black, bearing a white Southern Cross and a bird of paradise. The House also adopted (over administration objections) a committee recommendation favoring a new site for the nation's future capital—a place called Arona near Kainantu, in the Eastern Highlands. Thus, amid fears and doubts, New Guinea proceeds to acquire the accouterments of national life. And the most distinctive part of the national equipment,

* A popularity poll a while back plumped for Pagini as the new name. It won out narrowly over Paradesia.

if adopted as predicted, will be the choice of Pidgin as Niugini's official tongue.

Is this surprising? Most Americans and Englishmen seem to think that Pidgin is a sort of baby talk for traders dealing with primitive South Sea Islanders—the word itself apparently derives from "business." But in fact, particularly in New Guinea, Pidgin has long since attained a subtle and adequate Melanesian-style grammar and a sufficient vocabulary. There is even a move afoot to rename the language "Neo-Melanesian." Pidgin is the lingua franca of the territory—your hotel is likely to provide a "Do Not Disturb" sign that reads, "*Yu No Ken Kirapim Man I Slip*"—"You Cannot Interrupt the Man [in this room], Who Is Sleeping." More importantly, Pidgin is one of the three official languages permitted in the House of Assembly, the others being English and Motu.* One radio channel in Port Moresby broadcasts in nothing but Pidgin, and the New Testament has been published in this language.

To the English-speaker, Pidgin is tantalizing—enough of the words are close enough to English to provide a drift of the sense. Your ear has to make the connection between, for instance, "*guvman*" and "government," "*bagerap*" and "bugger up," or "*samting*" and "something." Learning a basic vocabulary of connectives is useful. "*Bilong*" ("belong"), also spelled "*bolong*," "*bilog*," "*long*," and "*blong*," may be Pidgin's commonest word, denoting the whole area of possession or attachment. Thus, "*meri bilong enaderfelo man*" is "another man's wife"—"*meri*" ("Mary") being the generic word for women. "*Felo*" ("fellow"), also spelled "*pela*," is perhaps the next commonest word, and it means not only "a man" but, more broadly, "piece" or "thing" or "kind." "*Gutpela kaikai*" might be translated "good kind of food." Plurals are often made by duplication: "*ol dei ol dei*" *is* "every day."

Here are the Ten Commandments in Pidgin, as published by the Alexishafen Catholic Mission in 1937:

1. *Mi Master, God bilong yu, yu no ken mekim masalai end ol tambaran.*
2. *Yu no ken kolim nating nem bilong God.*
3. *Yu mast santuim sande.*
4. *Yu mast mekin gud long papamama bilong yu.*
5. *Yu no ken kilim man.*
6. *Yu no ken brukim fashin bilong marit.*
7. *Yu no ken stilim samting.*

* The Motus, the main tribal group around Port Moresby, provide another territorial lingua franca much used by police, and known as Police Motu. In Motu, "Do Not Disturb" is "*Mahuta Basio Nadikaia.*"

8. *Yu no ken lai.*
9. *Yu no ken duim meri bilong enaderfelo man.*
10. *Yu no ken laik stilim samting.*

Some odd Pidgin words (and perhaps apocryphal, because whites cannot resist inventing additions to this colorful language) are these: "*pickaninny namba wan bilong queen*": Prince Charles; "*grass bilong hed*": hair; "*mix-masta bilong Jesus Christ*": helicopter; "*die bokus*": coffin; "*bokus bilong teeth yu hitim teeth bokus i cry*": piano.

The Other End of the Island

Just to frame the picture of Papua New Guinea a little more precisely, let us briefly examine the neighbor to the west. The Indonesian half of the New Guinea island is that country's seventeenth province, and its capital is Djajapura, née Hollandia and known for a time in the early 1960's as Sukarnapura. West Irian has between 750,000 and 1,250,000 people—nobody knows for sure. Perhaps 320,000 of them live in the highlands.

The Dutch got a tenuous claim to western New Guinea in 1714, when a contemporary sultan threw it in as part of a deal. Its jungles and declivities did not compare in wealth with Java and Sumatra, and Holland scarcely gave the place a thought. As late as 1938 there were only four hundred Dutchmen in all of Dutch New Guinea. The colony served chiefly as a prison camp for insurgent Indonesians—about fifteen thousand between 1927 and 1962. Many of them were friends of Sukarno, whom the Japanese put into power by sponsoring the Republic of Indonesia in 1945. After the war, the Netherlands tried to get the old Dutch East Indies back, but both the United States and Australia supported Sukarno, and the Dutch were left with the scraps—that is, New Guinea. Belatedly, they tried to make something of the place (as Australia was beginning to do next door), half in the hope that Sukarno would fall and the Netherlands could reclaim the Indies. A governor moved into the handsome house that General MacArthur had built for himself in Hollandia while commanding the Pacific campaign. Thirteen thousand Europeans came in to develop the colony, and for a while the Dutch spent around $25 million a year in development. To keep the Indonesians from getting their hands on New Guinea, the Dutch rather haplessly tried this and that: an exchange of technicians and students with Australia that might beef up the case for joining the two halves of the island; a New Guinea Council, elected by 100,000 tribesmen, that might lead to home rule; a promise of eventual independence. But the

Dutchmen's hearts weren't in it; Sukarno seemed to know that, and stepped up pressure to redeem what the Indonesians called West Irian.* There was some military skirmishing—Indonesian paratroopers against twelve thousand Dutch troops. By 1962 self-government in Dutch New Guinea had got to the point that seven political parties were contending at elections, and not by any means did everyone in the Dutch colony wish it to be turned into an Indonesian colony. But the American diplomat Ellsworth Bunker, serving as a United Nations mediator, studied the conflict and decreed the transfer. Australia approved, feeling that Sukarno was eventually going to have West Irian and consent would avoid bad blood. Planters in the Australian half of New Guinea howled that the move brought "Communism to the borders of Australia." By way of compromise, Bunker gave Indonesia only "administrative control" pending a plebiscite to see how the West Irians liked it. This "act of free choice" was held in 1969, and the Indonesians rounded up a number of tribal chiefs who duly voted that being an Indonesian province suited them just fine.

The impression West Irian has given in the last decade is that of a country on the skids. Bribery and corruption—a UN report even called it "plunder"—prevailed. Power plants, transport, machinery of all kinds broke down. Schools declined until in one case a single teacher had a class of 280 pupils. Food ran short. Quite a few West Irians fled across the unpatrolled border to Australian territory, where each city now has a small colony of West Irians. Some of them, to the concern of Australian authorities, were anti-Indonesian rebels belonging to the Operasi Papua Merdeka—the Free Papua Movement, Papua in this sense meaning the whole island of New Guinea. In the western district of Manokwari, twelve thousand tribesmen rose in arms, and the Indonesian Army took a couple of years to put them down. Particularly before Sukarno was toppled, Australia was sufficiently worried over its new neighbor to spend $60 million building up the territory's military defenses, including a $9-million barracks at Lae for the Pacific Islands Regiment of Papuans and New Guineans (with mostly Australian officers). Shots flew across the border now and then. Education in West Irian is said to be going tolerably well now, partly as a consequence of an effort to teach all children the Indonesian language. A university, called Tjenderawasih, meaning "bird of paradise," was founded in Hollandia-Sukarnapura-Djajapura even before eastern New Guinea founded its university. But Tjenderawasih developed poorly, and has been attended mostly by civil servants.

* Irian signifies "hot climate." In prefixing it with West, Sukarno implied that the Australian part was really East Irian, and that he might like to grab that, too.

*

> *The greatest need of New Guinea is time: time to teach the young, time to stabilize the legend, time for the young to grow old, time to cement the scattered fabric of its evolutionary thoughts, time for planning and reflection, time to build an ideal and a constitution, and to eliminate the tenacious restraints of the darkness from which it is emerging.*
>
> —OLAF RUHEN, IN Mountains in the Clouds

But there is no time. The machinery of the modern world cannot be stopped. Australia and the United Nations have decreed that Niugini will be the 128th nation on earth. Anticolonial Asians and Africans in the UN, often much to the irritation of some Australians, hammer at Australia to speed the process. The Soviet delegate to the General Assembly once asked sarcastically whether Australia intended "to develop the [Stone Age] natives to, say, the Bronze Age with the same slowness as humanity generally has progressed." As a matter of fact, former Prime Minister Robert Menzies said a decade ago, when the independence boom began, that "if in doubt you go sooner, not later" toward independence.

One interesting possible relationship, Australian statehood, went by the board in the process of settling for independence. The arguments for statehood, a concept pleasing to the white planters on the island, were that Australia needed New Guinea for defense, that independence was going to end in failure, and that in this manner Australia could once and for all wipe away the tarnish of the White Australia policy. In the end, it was the race problem that Australia could not swallow. More than two million blacks would suddenly become one-sixth of the population, with the right to elect Senators and Representatives to the federal Parliament, and with freedom to go to the continent in search of jobs and better lives. So Australia never got a seventh state. Another possibility that caught fire for a while in the late 1950's was union with Dutch New Guinea, but Indonesia, already planning to take that colony, frowned, and Australia did not press the point.

So independence it is—the exact shape unforeseeable. Strategically, the new country will lie safe between stout Australia on the south and the Territory of the Pacific Islands,* an American trust, on the north. A possibility of external conflict lies along that unnatural western border, the

* The Marianas (including Guam), the Carolines (including Yap, Ulithi, and Truk), and the Marshalls (including Eniwetok and Kwajalein).

141st meridian, particularly because New Guinea is likely to advance at a pace that will set up an enviable contrast with West Irian. Internally, "Niugini" may quite conceivably split into "coconut republics," perhaps with the islands of New Britain, New Ireland, Manus, and Bougainville seceding from Papua New Guinea. This could be bloody, but the present leaders seem aware of the danger. "We do not wish to see in our country the things that have happened in Africa," says John Guise. A happier prospect is that we shall see, in writer Grenfell Price's nice phrase, "how quickly head-hunters could become vote-hunters, cannibals conservatives, and sorcerers statesmen." Australia, which separated itself from England without rancor and with no zeal for breaking every last tie, might be just the country to provide a similarly agreeable experience for "Niugini." Certainly some interrelationship, perhaps slightly comparable to that of the United States and Puerto Rico, will prevail for a while. Australia will provide "foreign aid," and, by supporting the Pacific Islands Regiment, internal security. But the day will come when Australia will have to cross its fingers and launch the new nation.

CHAPTER 21

New Zealand: High Alps and Walking Birds

. . . this small country at the bottom of the world . . .
—SIR KEITH HOLYOAKE

THE CONVENTIONAL first stop for the visitor to New Zealand is the biggest city, Auckland, or perhaps the capital, Wellington, or even Christchurch, the main city of the South Island. But if you want the most startling experience that the country affords, go as quickly as possible to the Hermitage, halfway down the length of the South Island. From the delicious warmth of this gracious, government-run hotel you step out into the crisp, cold air and hear . . . the thunder of avalanches! The bottom of the world takes on a strange excitement; here we reach a land—remote, oceanic, tidily homogeneous in culture—that ranges from high-alpine to subtropical.

The Hermitage, whose bar turns out a particularly potent gimlet,* is a long, low building of stone and dark wood, with 140 rooms. Hotels run by private enterprise in many countries might take lessons from the Hermitage's scrupulous instinct for hospitality and efficient management. Its main asset, though, is its stunning view of Mount Cook, black-flanked, double-peaked, upper slopes piebald with snow. At 12,349 feet, this mountain is New Zealand's highest, but it is only one of 223 peaks on the South Island that reach 7,500 feet, part of an icy spine that makes itself a presence everywhere on the five-hundred-mile-long island.

There are South Islanders who have never seen snow close up, but have

* As made there, two-thirds vodka, one-third maraschino liqueur, a dash of grenadine, juice of half a lemon and half an orange—shake, add a cherry.

known it all their lives as the frosting on the range. So dominant are the mountains that in places a man can stand on a summit and see the whole girth of the island, Tasman Sea to the west and Pacific Ocean to the east. Mount Cook itself, though beautiful at sunset when the side light pinks the snow, is a mean mountain to climb. High gales scour it down to glassy ice, and climbers must employ full alpine paraphernalia—crampons, ropes, guides. Three-day blizzards and omnipresent avalanches are perils; fifty-three people have been killed so far on Mount Cook's slopes. Sir Edmund Hillary practiced on Mount Cook before he conquered Everest.

The flight in to the Hermitage aboard Mount Cook Airlines ("Fly the world's most scenic airlines," says the sign at Christchurch airport) takes you over two lakes, one of glacial water, a deep slate color, and one of rain water, a pale lucent green-blue. From the hotel, buses climb a terrifying road so placed on the razorback that it falls off steeply on *both* sides. The destination is an unearthly height where nothing grows, and rock and snow make a black-and-white landscape of chilling beauty. There are also ski planes that depart from the Hermitage, circle stupendous peaks, and then land high, high up on one of the slopes, where one steps out onto the slow flux of Ball Glacier or Tasman Glacier. Some daring sportsmen use the flight as a lift so that they can ski for *fifteen* miles back to the Hermitage. Mount Cook is called Aorangi, "cloud-piercer," by the Maoris. All this is part of 173,000-acre Mount Cook National Park, which is one of ten in New Zealand that together occupy no less than one-thirteenth of the country's land area. Skiing, from July to September, is popular on dozens of exciting snowfields the length of the Southern Alps, as this range is called.

The South Island recreates not only Switzerland but also Norway. Deep, long fiords notch the entire southwestern coast, protected from man's commercial greed by being enclosed in the three million acres of Fiordland National Park. The most spectacular of these is Milford Sound, with sheer cliffs, brilliant sky and sea, and a rain forest below (which gets two hundred inches of rain a year). A dramatic tunnel through the mountains brings the highway to the head of this channel, where Sutherland Falls drop 1,904 feet. Higher up and farther inland, the pattern of narrow water is repeated in many finger lakes, with patches of dark green forest around them.

Another mountain range in the south of the South Island is fittingly named the Remarkables, and at its feet is Queenstown, one of the island's summer resorts. From the airplane, a rough-and-ready DC-3 with the luggage stowed in the back of the cabin, the immobile sheep standing on the edge of the airstrip seem like stone markers. Queenstown stands on Lake Wakatipu, which has waters of a paralyzing coldness that seems to deter no one from water-skiing and swimming in the summer. An inexplicable and ominous characteristic of this lake is that it rises and falls two or three inches every fifteen minutes. A substantial village of stone buildings and churches, Queenstown had ten thousand people during gold-rush days a century ago; now it has sixteen hundred year-round residents and twenty thousand summer residents.

On the road north, bracken on the hills looks from a distance like fungus or moss. Dogs herd sheep, letting them disperse and then driving them together with such skill that the pattern of movement seems like a ballet. The valley floor is multicolored green; circles of glassy rock shine in the sun. On the highway, cars tow house caravans and sometimes boats as well.

Arrowtown, the next settlement north, a semi-ghost town, has a museum that was a bank in the region's gold-rush days. Gold worth £86 million sterling went through this building, some of it mined by seven hundred Chinese who had deserted ships to join the rush. An old sign flaunted by the bank says, in Chinese, "We sell Hong Kong currency. We buy gold dust. We give money on deposit. And give good interest." More than forty thousand tourists go to Arrowtown every year, and a good many, armed with picks and pans, still find a bit of gold in the river.

*

New Zealand is an end-of-the-earth sort of place, a pair of islands and associated islets lifted to their present heights, after an adventuresome geological career, as recently as five million years ago. With Patagonia and southern Chile, it is the southernmost land area in the world, quite appropriately the base for the U.S. Navy's explorations of Antarctica, whose shores lie fifteen hundred miles to the south. Here is authentic isolation. A wry, symbolic signpost on the northernmost cape of New Zealand reads like this: "Bluff [southernmost tip of New Zealand] 745 miles, Equator 2,065 miles, Sydney 1,065 miles, Suva 1,030 miles, Panama 6,579 miles." New Zealanders say that London is halfway between New Zealand and New Zealand—in other words it is about twelve thousand miles away no matter whether you go northeast or northwest. The logistics are such that New Zealand is detached even from Australia: the natural sea route from New Zealand to England is through Panama whereas the natural sea route from Australia to England is through Suez.

New Zealand's land area is 103,736 square miles: it compares in size with Italy. Of the two main islands, the South Island is the bigger by about fourteen thousand square miles. But whereas the South Island is roughly a long rectangle, the North Island is looped and pronged with bays and peninsulas. The combined lengths of the two islands are about a thousand miles, and the shoreline, indentations and all, measures just short of ten thousand miles. The dividing water is Cook Strait—once again a name drawn from the stalwart British captain who first closely explored these waters. It is narrow, less than twenty miles, yet with tumultuous seas. In an amiable way, North and South Islanders perpetually dispute the merits of their respective terrains. Statistically, North Island has the lead. Auckland lies in the north of that island, and Wellington, the capital, is on the southern tip of it. The North Island has more than two-thirds of New Zealand's population, which is pushing three million. It also has more than half of the nation's sixty million sheep. Incidentally, domestic animals, including cattle, outnumber human beings in New Zealand by twenty-five to one, a ratio probably not exceeded by any other country in the world.

The country as a whole bears some resemblance to an archipelago and includes a number of smaller islands. Stewart Island, a spot you could drive around in an afternoon if there were a road, lies just south of South Island, and the Chatham Islands, considerably smaller, lie 530 miles to the east. Some uninhabited islets with nice names—Three Kings, Snares, Bounty, Antipodes (which is straight through the center of the earth from London), and others—poke up through the ocean offshore to north and south. As overseas territories, New Zealand possesses the Tokelau Islands and Niue Island, dots in the Polynesian South Pacific about two thousand miles to the northeast, near Samoa. New Zealand also administers a 60-degree wedge of Antarctica, Ross Dependency, which contains the U.S. bases of McMurdo and Little America. The Cook Islands, a group of fifteen pin-points between Samoa and Tahiti, used to be New Zealand territory, but are now self-governing, with much tutelage and protection from the mother country. Rarotonga, one of the southern tier of pretty, elevated, fertile islands of the Cooks, is the torrid capital. The northern tier consists of coral atolls. All are vulnerable to fierce hurricanes, and a New Zealand government ship *Moana Roa* visits them regularly.

*

New Zealand gives the impression of having been put together from lava, pumice, graywacke (a local gray sandstone), and rich alluvium, vegetated with grass, evergreens, and ferns. Punctuating this landscape are the white sheep, which seem like maggots when you look down from an airplane. Man's constructions are of wood, by and large; the frame house of the American West was brought to New Zealand by gold-rushers from California a century back, although here it was generally roofed with corrugated iron. Lumber, in villas, bungalows, and country houses, still predominates heavily over masonry. The geology, too, shares Californian characteristics. New Zealand, like that state, is on the "mobile belt" around the Pacific, where the earth's crust buckles and breaks. Something like four hundred earthquakes shake the nation every year, about a hundred of them noticeable without instruments. A quake at Napier in 1931 killed 255 people.

To the Maoris, the Polynesians who won christening rights to New Zealand as its first discoverers, the islands looked variously long, bright, and cloudlike. They named it Aotearoa, a musical word meaning "land of the long white cloud."* The loose Polynesian language permits of other translations, however, and (according to *A Dictionary of Maori Place Names*) Aotearoa could also mean "continuously clear light," "land of abiding day," or "long white world."

The more prosaic appellation "New Zealand" is the contrivance of the Dutch East Indies governors who dispatched Abel Tasman in 1642 on the voyage that took him to the shores of Tasmania and New Zealand. His name choice for the latter was Staten Landt, but his superiors preferred Nieuw Zeeland, after a province in Holland. The melodious Maori language, which is somewhat overloaded with vowels for the newcomer to pronounce without some practice (viz., Pukengerengere, Ngawhakapakoko, Tauherenikau), provides the bulk of New Zealand place names, but British nostalgia for heros (Nelson, Wellington), and old-country cities (Hastings, Plymouth) provides hundreds of others. Assorted capes have graphic names: Cape Foulwind, Cape Turnagain, Cape Runaway, Cape Kidnappers.

*

The South Island, as we have seen, drops precipitously into the Tasman Sea on a rainy, windy, sparsely inhabited West Coast. The chief phenomenon here is Franz Josef Glacier, which glides down to only nine hundred feet above sea level, well into the relatively warm rain forest, before melting. The flatter east coast provides grass for 25 million sheep and good soil for grain. The island's charming cities are there, too.

The North Island is all juts and spits and gulfs and bays. A protuberance

* Unkind Australians, who are prone to consider New Zealand a bit dull, say that the word means "long white shroud."

reaches north like a strand of taffy pulled away from the bulk of the island; no spot on the length of this peninsula is more than twenty miles from the sea. At the point where it joins the rest of the North Island, harbors carved in from east and west narrow the isthmus to only three-fourths of a mile, and this nexus is the sensible and scenic setting for Auckland, New Zealand's biggest city and main port. All is fairly flat here and for a hundred miles to the south of Auckland—then the country rises to volcanically active elevations of between three and nine thousand feet, and they dominate the rest of the island.

This country is prone to convulse, rumble, boil, hiss, gurgle, seethe, tremble, and blow up. Lake Taupo, the result of an explosion a few thousand years ago, is the world's largest volcanic lake, and a warm one, too, with a hundred beaches. Pumice from that explosion still covers much of the ground. Something harrowing is always happening in these parts. A Maori village was completely buried in 1886. In 1953 Mount Ruapehu cracked to release its crater lake, which foamed down to carry away a railroad bridge just as a train approached; 151 people were killed. In May 1971 the same mountain erupted for eight days. The city of Rotorua, on whose golf course steam vents are the hazards, is the tourist center for this volcanic region. At the nearby Whakarewarewa Thermal Reserve, geysers spout up fifty to a hundred feet, and mud boils in whirling, greasy patterns. The Maoris cook food by lowering it into boiling pools of water. Houses pipe in steam for doing the laundry, and the same steam, which as George Bernard Shaw said "smells like Hades"—he might have said rotten eggs—pours forth from a thousand spout holes. A sign on the road, where steam drifts across, says, "VISIBILITY HAZARD." A quarter of a million people visit Rotorua every year, one-third of them from abroad.

Six miles from Lake Taupo, at Wairakei, which has a splendid government hotel similar to the one at Mount Cook, all this superheated natural energy is put to practical use. In this long, twisting valley at the bottom of a trough of pines, hundreds of wells—four, six, and eight inches in diameter, and 570 to 4,000 feet deep—penetrate the earth to bring up live steam under high pressure (225 pounds per square inch) that operates turbines to drive thirteen generators. Much water comes up with the steam, and it is cleverly removed by shooting the mixture through a circular loop, wherein centrifugal force separates the two components. No engineers are visible at this inferno, but white plumes of steam rise everywhere from stubby chimneys. Concrete silencers hold down the roar.

One of the wells, the Rogue Bore, is an out-of-control hellhole. Begun as a nine-inch bore in 1960, it struck steam of such force that the engineers had to try to stopper it. They poured in grout (cement and gravel), but pressure built up so high that the well blew out thousands of tons of grout and the rig besides. Vibration and hissing steam reamed out the bore to a bigger diameter; the engineers tried to kill it by pumping in cold water, and dropping in concrete blocks. Nothing worked; the constant trembling of the earth and the explosive steam and mud made the sides keep falling in and enlarged the hole until it was two hundred feet across. Every few minutes mud shoots into the air to geyser heights. Now it would cost $250,000 to kill the Rogue—and ruin a gripping tourist attraction: this roaring, sizzling, twenty-four-hour-a-day baby earthquake.

The whole belt of volcanic convulsion runs, 20 miles wide, for about 150 miles. White and pinkish sinter—silicon and calcium from evaporated geyser water—frosts the rocks in waterfall-like terraces. Tikitere, of which Shaw said, "I would willingly have paid ten pounds not to see it," is a weird and vaporous badland that matches the translation of its Maori name, "hell's gate."

The Plants

The flora and fauna of New Zealand, like those of Australia, are the freakish products of a long, separate evolution. Here plants and animals are of yet another displaced and antediluvian type, and for the same reason—separation from the "World Continent." There is a theory that seventy million years ago Australia and New Zealand were linked through a long-sunken land mass in the Tasman Sea, which lies between them. This hypothetical continent (which, in turn, may have been linked with Asia) is called Tasmantis. Certainly New Zealand has been isolated since then. Although seeds can cross oceans, and ferns, a plant of great antiquity, grow widely throughout the world, New Zealand has ferns of varieties found nowhere else. In short, the vast majority of New Zealand's plant species are endemic to the country. There are, to be sure, tantalizing contradictions. The lancewood, a tree of supposedly New Zealand–Australian origin, is found in South America, and many fuchsias found in New Zealand are also found in America. But the eucalyptuses and acacias that are dominant among Australian trees are mysteriously missing, except where introduced by man.

The New Zealand trademark is the giant ponga (pronounced "punga") fern. In this country, as nowhere else, ferns grow as trees, reaching sixty feet. The ponga's fronds are, says the poet A. R. D. Fairburn:

> *. . . shaped and curved*
> *like the scroll of a fiddle: fit instrument*
> *to play archaic tunes . . .*

The soil of New Zealand is ideal for forests, and probably half of it was forested before man arrived to burn and cut it; even now, about a quarter of the country is still wooded. The native trees, running in size between ponderosa pine and California redwoods, make imposing, cathedral-like forests. The kauri, which can be sliced in planks as wide as seven feet, is an evergreen softwood that grows straight and even for sixty feet before it branches. Except for some protected stands, this North Island tree has been nearly wiped out by fire and logging. Several still exist with girths of up to forty-seven feet and ages up to twelve hundred years. Other lofty evergreens, still growing strongly in the mountains, are the podocarps, softwoods of various species—rimu, miro, matai. The tree of the higher altitudes, especially on South Island, is the southern beech, a New Zealand native hardwood that sheds a bountiful pollen.

An exotic aspect of New Zealand forestry is the cultivation of plantations of trees literally called exotics, because they came from abroad. Chief among these is the radiata pine, brought from California about fifty years ago; others are the ponderosa pine, the Corsican pine, the lodgepole pine, and the Douglas fir. During the Depression, these trees were planted at a furious rate, using men who would otherwise have been unemployed. In New Zealand soil, and with New Zealand rainfall, these foreign trees grow twice as fast as they did where they came from. Well tended by the New Zealand Forest Service, radiata pine reach 125 feet in height and 38 inches in diameter at only forty years of age. Native forest still outranks man-made forest by ten to one in area, but the exotics, growing so fast, account for more than half of lumber production. New Zealand has the largest man-made forest in the world.

One oddity in New Zealand is the cabbage tree, a slender, spike-leaved plant whose shoots can be cooked and eaten—they taste like leeks. Not much else of New Zealand's specialized plant life is interesting and edible except the Chinese gooseberry, or kiwi fruit.* This plum-sized morsel, which is exported to the U.S. among other destinations, has a skin that in appearance is like the nut of a coconut. Peeled off, it reveals a soft, sea-green core that can be eaten, black seeds and all, without alarm. It tastes like a pear, but tarter.

The Animals

Three points about New Zealand fauna:

There are *no snakes.*

Only one mammal existed in the islands before man arrived, and that

* Properly *Actinidia chinensis,* a native of the Yangtze Valley.

was an insignificant bat. New Zealand's isolation started before the age of mammals, or even marsupials, began.

The dominant form of native animal is the flightless bird, in amazing variety.

*

Most notable of these birds is the brown, hen-size kiwi, the country's national bird, found only in New Zealand. It is so characteristic that New Zealanders call *themselves* Kiwis. Hairy-feathered, whisker-faced, stumpy-winged, this bird clumps on solid-boned legs through the forest in the dead of night—most human Kiwis have never seen the bird except in the Auckland Zoo. The kiwi smells out grubs and worms with nostrils on the very tip of its six-inch beak, and the kiwi hen lays five-inch eggs that weigh one pound, a fourth as much as she does. Kiwis are now very rare.

A bird of the same order, Apteryges, but built more like an ostrich, was the moa, now extinct. Some of these were veritable giants, twelve feet tall, with legs like a grand piano's. Darwin, who visited New Zealand aboard the *Beagle* in 1835, concluded that moas evolved only in the absence of predatory mammals—and it was precisely a predatory mammal, the early Polynesian settler, who finally wiped them out by killing them for food.

New Zealand has, or has had, flightless or nearly flightless geese, ducks, eagles, parrots, parakeets, and rails. One of the parrots is the kakapo which hitches its way through branches with its beak and talons, and having gained sufficient height glides to another tree.

The New Zealand kea, though, is a bird of different inclinations. Nesting high in the Southern Alps, this unflappable parrot, brightly feathered, swoops down on sick sheep and rips away live flesh. To humans, the kea is friendly and insatiably curious, but a pest. It steals TV antennas, windshield wipers, shoes, and pens, and it enjoys letting the air out of tires.

A reptile of distinction is the tuatara, a lizard that died out elsewhere 135 million years ago, but survives here as a living fossil. Its body temperature averages 52 degrees Fahrenheit, and it can go an hour without taking a breath. The tuatara has no ear opening and no penis, but in partial compensation it has a light-sensitive area on the top of its head that functions as a sort of a third eye. Another oddity is the toheroa, a dubiously edible shellfish that buries itself in the sand of the North Island's Ninety Mile Beach. The public is allowed to dig toheroas, by hand only, during a two-week season in August or September, "the months of the broken fingernails." The limit is ten per person—all this to prevent the toahera from becoming extinct. Still another oddity is the weta, a cricket with a fourteen-inch legspread.

*

This flora and fauna formed the fragile prehistoric ecology that man proceeded recklessly to upset. Forest fires, used by Polynesian moa-hunters to scare the birds into spearing range, and used by English settlers to clear land for farms, denuded half the timbered area. As for the imported fauna, "the history of animal introductions is strewn with tragic mistakes, one leading on to the other," says the *New Zealand Official Yearbook*. Rabbits, six of which can eat as much as a sheep, turned out to be capable of reducing vast areas of grassland to desert. Stoats, ferrets, and weasels, brought in to kill rabbits, decimated kiwis and other native animals instead. American elk,* Australian opossums, goats, pigs, rats, mice, and even sparrows similarly thrived and unbalanced the ecology. The red deer's voracious browsing made it such a pest that the government fights it strenuously with air-dropped poisoned carrots, and with helicopter gunships manned by trained hunters known as "meat hawks." As for rabbits, the goal is extermination, by similar methods, at an annual cost of four cents per acre of the country. Several importations, however, were harmless or beneficial. The thar (pronounced "tar," and also spelled "tahr"), a Himalayan mountain sheep, and the European chamois are good game animals in the high country. And the sheep and the cow, though erosion-makers, are the uncomplaining providers of most of New Zealand's prosperity. But the authorities remain deeply worried. What might happen if the carpenter ant reached New Zealand? Or foot-and-mouth disease? Or—shades of Eden—the snake?

*

> *I believe we were all glad to leave New Zealand. It is not a pleasant place.*
>
> —CHARLES DARWIN

For once the great naturalist was quite wrong; he appears to have been rather upset by watching two Maoris rub noses. The New Zealand climate is temperate and oceanic; the occasional hot winds from Australia or cold

* Sent by Teddy Roosevelt as a decorative animal for the southern fiordlands.

blasts from Antarctica lose their zip before arriving. The prevailing westerlies, the winds that made these latitudes known to sailing ship skippers as the Roaring Forties, give both islands breezy coasts. Gusts of sixty miles an hour or more hit Wellington an average of thirty days every year. The same winds bring heavy rainfall—more than one hundred inches a year—to the entire West Coast. Elsewhere, annual rainfall measures between twenty and sixty inches, plenty for all kinds of farming. The temperature runs around 61 degrees in January, and 43 in July. Obviously the top of Mount Cook gets very cold, and in general the cities are colder than Australian cities during their winter. The climate gets cooler as one goes south which means an occasional light frost in Auckland and Wellington, and as many as thirty-six hard frosts a year in Christchurch and Dunedin, on the South Island.

Tale of Four Cities

"Dunedin and Christchurch live on last year's income. Wellington lives on this year's income. Auckland lives on next year's income." So goes a New Zealand saying about the four main cities. Another comparison: Dunedin was founded by Presbyterians, Christchurch by Anglicans, Wellington by merchants, Auckland by pirates.

*

DUNEDIN, which is the ancient name for Edinburgh, has a statue of Robert Burns in the center of its octagonal main square, and the people go ice curling in the winter (on high mountain lakes)—none of which necessarily makes it a wee bit o' auld Scotland. The town was founded in 1848, at the end of a narrow gulf on the southeast coast, by a nephew of the poet Burns, together with three hundred settlers belonging to the Free Kirk of Scotland, a schismatic group of Presbyterians. They had adopted the colonizing principles of Edward Gibbon Wakefield, the Newgate Gaol philosopher who provided the inspiration for the colonization of South Australia. That is, Dunedin and the surrounding province of Otago were to reproduce the social pattern of English country life, with squires, doctors, lawyers, pastors, artisans, and peasants, and this social order was to be preserved by making the price of land prohibitively high, preventing democratic ownership. Moreover, the land was to be farmed, not turned into sheep runs. Some fleeting thought was even given to the banishment of Scotch whisky, but cooler heads prevailed. Although only twelve years later some of the stuffier

Scotsmen were so comfortably settled that they were calling themselves the "Old Identity" of Dunedin, the plan was doomed. The land cried out to be grazed, not cultivated; worse yet, gold rushes throughout the 1860's attracted a lot of rough Irishmen to Otago, which in turn brought roads, banks, dancehalls, commerce, gambling, industry, prosperity, and democracy. The Old Identity, as historian Keith Sinclair put it, became the New Iniquity.

Still, when Dunedin was only twenty-one years old and had only thirteen thousand residents, the good Scots duly founded New Zealand's first institution of higher learning, the University of Otago. When the gold rush ended, sheep raising was so firmly established that Dunedin could carry on as a commercial center, with woolen mills and mutton exported via the country's first refrigerator ship, which was named *Dunedin*. Up went stone and brick buildings. St. Paul's Anglican Cathedral came to rival the Presbyterian First Church in size. Nowadays, democratic suburbs, with bankers and laborers cheek-by-jowl, cover all the surrounding hills, and the population is 110,000. Yet Dunedin is something of a backwater, living in the shadow of the old Victorian buildings that its earlier prosperity built.

*

CHRISTCHURCH, two hundred miles up the East Coast from Dunedin, is a place that grows flowers until the mind boggles. The main civic organization is Christchurch Beautifying Association (Inc.), and woe to the burgher who does not surround his house with roses, azaleas, chrysanthemums, daffodils, snapdragons, and flowering trees. Factories, too, must landscape the premises with flaming gardens or suffer contumely. The idea is to make Christchurch as much as possible like the country from which it originated; as a local poet once put it, " 'Tis England where an English spirit dwells." The result is an extremely prepossessing city, particularly where the river Avon* flows through an immaculate park. A local joke is that this small stream is the source of the Pacific Ocean.

Newspaper headlines call this city "CHCH" for short; American Navy sailors, who have for years used Christchurch's Harewood Airport as a jumping-off place for Operation Deep Freeze in Antarctica, call it "Chi-chi." This is a city of imitation-English schoolboys in boaters and starched collars, of eleven hundred factories, and of a tradition-encrusted (already!) university, Canterbury, that has outgrown its Gothic buildings in the nar-

* Named for the Avon in northern Scotland, not the Avon of Stratford, England.

row central streets and is moving to a spacious modern campus out of town. The Christchurch *Press* is 110 years old, a record few U.S. newspapers can match.

Christchurch and the attendant Canterbury province, which dominates the South Island and runs as far west as Mount Cook, is another brainchild of the inveterate colony-founder Wakefield. Morality and practicality were intertwined in his plan to acquire land cheaply (for blankets and beads from the few resident Maoris) and sell it dear, making a profit that would build schools and cathedrals, import more God-fearing citizens, and in general avoid the lawless and unstructured society that Wakefield perceived to be growing in Australia. His collaborator in this case was the Archbishop of Canterbury, serving as president of the Canterbury Association of Settlers, which had been formed by John Robert Godley, a young graduate of Christ Church College, Oxford. One-fourth of the first fifteen hundred settlers were men of sufficient wealth to pay three pounds sterling an acre for land. The first 773, who called themselves "Canterbury Pilgrims," arrived in 1850 aboard the *Charlotte Jane*, the *Randolph*, the *Cressy*, and the *Sir George Seymour*. To this day these vessels are reverently capitalized in Christchurch newspapers as "The First Four Ships."

Dame Ngaio Marsh, now seventy-two, the mystery-story writer who created detective Roderick Alleyn, is Christchurch's most world-famous resident. She does not know precisely what her parents had in mind when after the given name "Edith" they added the middle name "Ngaio," a Maori word for "clever," or "light on the water," or "little bug." Christchurch lives from its manufacturing and industry, plus the commercial benefits of Canterbury sheep raising and export via Lyttelton,* the city's harbor, reached by rail and road tunnels under an inconvenient hill. The population is 260,000, making this New Zealand's second-biggest city, but it is still a low, ground-hugging place. Forty miles of good beaches lie to the north.

*

WELLINGTON, as the capital, draws civil servants and bankers and politicians from all over New Zealand, but the atmosphere is not so much that of a capital as of a city in its own right. There are touches of San Francisco and Rio here. Obsession with government is not all-pervasive, as it is in Washington.

* Captain R. F. Scott's base for his expedition to the South Pole in 1912, which ended in his death on the return leg.

This city is built along the shores of a splendid, round bay, six miles across, with a narrow entrance to Cook Strait on the south. Most of Wellington sits on the narrow western foreshore, or on adjacent fill land reclaimed from the sea, or on the slopes of the steep enclosing hills. Houses hang on cliffs. Transport is managed by frighteningly vertical streets, thigh-strengthening paths, flights of steps, and a cable car that goes through a tunnel. Only two routes lead out of town, which prevents Wellingtonians from having weekend houses to the extent that New Zealanders do elsewhere. Geography thus forces a sense of unity and coherence on Wellington, making it a city of some urbanity, intellect, and culture. Partly in consequence of the diplomatic community, one hears foreign languages in the coffeehouses. The national ballet, opera, and orchestra perform here frequently. Alexander Turnbull Library, the nation's best, is at hand. For these inducements, many people accept life in high-rent inner-city apartments, rather than the suburban houses universally preferred elsewhere.

Here again, and even more emphatically, we encounter Edward Gibbon Wakefield. Wellington was another of his projects,* and to this one he came personally and stayed; his grave is in the Bolton Street Cemetery. The colonizers cast about for industries (whaling, for example) to develop the place in the Wakefieldian mold, but in the end settled for luring the national capital away from Auckland in 1865, on grounds of centrality, and with help from the South Island cities. That brought banks, insurance companies, shipping. Wellington became the city that agitated hardest for national self-government, and the capital where the world's first welfare state was drafted. Now all political power centers here.

Squeezed by its site, blustery Wellington has spilled over into a bedroom suburb called Hutt Valley, around the bay, and between them these cities hold 310,000 people. There are more people in Upper and Lower Hutt than in Wellington proper. It adds up to a metropolis by New Zealand standards, but pretty small as world cities go. The harbor was early dubbed Port Nicholson, soon shortened to Port Nick. The Maoris pronounced it "Poneke," and named a tribe the Ngati-Poneke. Nowadays Wellington comes just after Auckland in the number of city-dwelling Maoris. This is a city of fresh air and salt spray. Houses creak a lot, from earthquakes and powerful gales. If anything stands in this town, it's because it cannot be blown down or shaken down. Ropes are strung across midtown intersections to steady people in the wind, as on a ship. But new techniques in earthquake-proof construction are letting the city start to build up instead of out.

A popular confection in Wellington is an ice cream called hokey—vanilla

* Which in this case had the support of the Duke of Wellington.

with bits of honeycomb. Crime is low—only one murder last year. There is little chance of a criminal getting away, because it is hard to get out of the country. The novelist Katherine Mansfield (1888–1923) spent girlhood summers at Day's Bay, on Port Nick's eastern shore. The ferry *Maui* sails daily from Wellington for Christchurch, arriving ten hours later. The basic architecture consists of charming, rather simple wooden houses. Parliament is a curious, Greek-colonnaded building; never finished, it flies on one wing, with a central entrance far off-center. The other wing will never be built; on its site the government is constructing an amazing steel-and-concrete building in the shape of an inverted bucket, to provide Parliament with the space that it needs. A sight that delights visitors and embarrasses Wellingtonians is the government office building, said to be the world's largest wooden structure; the local opinion is that it should be proper masonry. Also of wood, and exceedingly graceful, is St. Paul's Cathedral Church. Wellington is busy building high-rises and highways, including a six-mile downtown expressway that costs $8,830,000 a mile. Seven hundred and seventy-five more acres have been "won," as the New Zealand expression has it, from Port Nicholson by filling it with rock.

The Mayor of Wellington, Sir Francis Kitts, is in his fifth term of three years each. His hobby is visiting other Wellingtons. "There are forty-three Wellingtons in the world, and I have visited fifteen. This is the biggest. Wellington, India, has about fifty-four thousand people. There are thirteen Wellingtons in the United States, and I have visited five. Wellington, Kansas, is the largest. Whenever I feel depressed, I read a clipping about myself from a paper in Wellington, Ohio." Sir Francis has won all the recent elections by huge majorities. The Mayor is a colorful orator and a powerhouse of a politician.

*

In AUCKLAND, a pretty girl rides by on a motorbike, singing into the wind, as if to express her delight at living in this metropolis, which with 615,000 people is by far New Zealand's biggest city. Auckland is a city neither English nor Scottish in tone; it is a rambling, vigorous, sophisticated, open city of many influences. Among these are the urban Maoris, who number about sixty thousand, and, together with forty thousand other South Sea islanders, make Auckland the biggest Polynesian city in the world. Instead of some tiresome British hero, a towering Maori warrior, club in hand, is depicted in a bronze statue on Queen Street. Often, you see a Polynesian man wearing a *lava lava*, wraparound skirt, in downtown Auckland. The exhibition of Maori artifacts in the War Memorial Museum is interesting and incomparable—it includes a full-size carved Maori meeting house.

In Cornwall Park graze sheep and cows, surrounded by the city. Telephone dials are numbered backward; the "9" is where the "1" usually is. In the South Pacific Hotel, a comfortable place that provides each room with a small refrigerator containing bottles of milk, the bellboys are stout girls, and if the guest tries to lift a bag, a girl seizes it, saying, "But I'm *paid* to do this." The valet wears golf socks and shorts, and the bar, as everywhere in New Zealand, serves the smallest whiskey since prewar Vienna, five-eighths of an ounce.

Auckland's situation is lovely enough to be compared with those of Sydney and Rio and Naples. In form it is essentially an isthmus, connecting the bulk of the North Island to the long northern peninsula. This gives Auckland a double harbor, one on the Tasman Sea, used for light-draft traffic chiefly to Australia, and the other on the Pacific Ocean, used for ships to Asia, the United States, and England, via the Panama Canal. All this is complicated by bays, necks, basins, capes, and indentations impossible to describe. Suffice it to say that one geographical juncture requires a bridge, so that this city, like Sydney or San Francisco, has a soaring span to adorn the natural setting. Though built not long ago, in 1959, its four lanes quickly proved too few for the traffic—Aucklanders said the city was "too big for its bridges." A Japanese firm, employing principles used in tanker construction, added ingenious roadways to the bridge which doubled its capacity. Aucklanders call them "the Nippon clip-on."

Waitemata Harbor, the Pacific port, and outlying Hauraki Gulf are the scene of big thousand-yacht regattas. In the gulf is Rangitoto Island, a volcano extinct only eight hundred years. The island symbolizes Auckland, and gives rise to a Wellingtonian slur that Aucklanders are, owing to their excessive bustle and enterprise, "Rangitoto Yanks." Privacy-loving residents of Waiheke Island, beyond Rangitoto, commute to work in Auckland by hydrofoil. Some of the harbor islands still license prospectors to search for gold. Fee: twenty-five cents. Beaches abound in such numbers that they are rarely crowded, even on the warmest days of the October-April season. The Tasman coast, to the west, provides immense rollers for surfing.

Low volcanic cones, not necessarily dead, rise here and there in the city proper, and they are often used as parks. Most of them are curiously terraced, the work of Maoris who lived on them, and used them as fortresses, two centuries ago. Auckland housing is doggedly surburban: wooden bungalows set on quarter-acre plots—or, latterly, fifth-acre plots. A house on a promontory, such as the side of a volcano, has great status. There are splendid villas in the high, chic parts of town. Central heating is not needed—electric radiators, run on cheap current, will do for cool spells. The quarter-acre obsession has forced Auckland into an awesome spread; it measures about twenty by thirty miles. A beflowered showplace is Ellerslie race track.

Many downtown streets are narrow, because an early governor had done some time in Egypt and concluded that narrow streets would reduce the glare and heat of the sun. On Queen Street, one might surmise that the main business of the city was department stores—or, if not that, bookshops. The sidewalks have a civilized innovation, a center line to divide pedestrian traffic. You must remember to keep to the left, like the street traffic. An ambiguous street sign says, "NO STANDING AT ALL TIMES." Once each cycle, traffic lights stop vehicles in all directions, and pedestrians, upon the sound of a buzzer, can cross the intersection diagonally if they wish.

What keeps Auckland going? Meat freezing, wool storage, and the docks that load these commodities are the main traditional industries. Near the city is a steel works and a rolling mill. Other plants manufacture fertilizer, used in enormous quantities in New Zealand. In essence, the sheep keeps Auckland going.

CHAPTER 22

New Zealand: Pakeha and Maori

I went to New Zealand, but it was closed.
—BBC JOURNALIST CLEMENT FREUD

THE STATE-RUN LOTTERY in New Zealand decided a few years ago to try a special inducement, a drawing with a grand prize of $120,000. To the puzzlement of the lottery's organizer, the tickets sold rather slowly. At length he found out why: the average New Zealander couldn't conceive of having or spending a sum as large as $120,000.

This is a nation of low-burning ambition, wholesome lives, limited intellectuality, dogged egalitarianism. New Zealand is not much given to hero worship. "Never mind" is the national motto, afternoon tea is the national ceremony, a jolly weekend is the national goal. "All of our problems can be painted in water colors, compared to the stronger colors of other countries," says W. A. Pyatt, the Anglican bishop of Christchurch. An Australian editor says that his idea of a fitting punishment for a foul felon is to "sentence him to New Zealand without option of a fine!" In 1970 the arrivals of "immigrants intending permanent residence" were outnumbered, 26,825 to 29,822, by "New Zealand residents departing permanently."

But nothing could be more erroneous than to picture this as a nation of mediocrity. Its accomplishments are many. It has built a conservative, working welfare state on an agricultural economy—specifically on the Romney sheep. It has won the world's highest standard of living after the United States and Canada. It has a stable, if static, society. And it joins Pakeha (white*) and Maori (Polynesian brown) in a degree of harmony that all other biracial nations can envy.

* The word comes from the Maori language, and also means "goblin" or "spook."

*

Few exercises are more hazardous than singling out "national characteristics," but we must make a try. Certainly the New Zealander is a person who counts on the government to make his life secure. He stresses society and cooperation over individualism and competition. New Zealanders form themselves into committees as easily and automatically as a platoon falling into step. Government is a tool to solve social problems—but if this is socialism, it is an undoctrinal, un-Marxist kind. Capitalism prevails in much of the economy, but it is said to be an ever "nicer" form of capitalism. The result is a minutely worked-out welfare state, which we shall observe in detail presently.

With this stress on a cooperative society goes a fierce egalitarianism. Social classes are visible, but not on the multilayered British model. Some pastoralists in Canterbury attempt to set themselves off as a rural aristocracy; prominent men take pride in being knighted by the Queen. But the only suggestion of an Establishment is a fitful collusion of the Federated Farmers, the conservative National Party, and the Returned Services Association, a war veterans group. Official links between church and state, vital for a classic Establishment, are missing. "Old boys" from the private schools do not club together to dominate one field or another. Birth is not sufficient to establish status. Servants are virtually unknown. Neighborhoods mix artisans, laborers, businessmen, and professionals. A man calls his boss by his first name. "We are an egalitarian society, though very conservative," explains Bishop Pyatt. "We all know each other so well." Democracy is carried to the ultimate: almost anyone with a smidgen of a reason can get in to see the Prime Minister personally, and he can see the other ministers even more readily. Egalitarianism also discourages what New Zealanders call "ritual tipping"—they tip only when they receive some special, or especially good, service. Student representation in the administration of a university, an idea newly arrived in the U.S., is old practice in New Zealand, and a partial explanation for the infrequency of student protests and riots.

Living as they do a jillion miles from anywhere, New Zealanders are inevitably somewhat insular. A newspaperman in Wellington explains that "we haven't got a continent—we live in an ocean." The outside world has historically consisted of England—just England; New Zealand was the "most loyal" dominion, tranquil, prim, a "corner of an English vicarage." Sometimes the Britishness of New Zealand astounds even Britons—although, as in Australia, New Zealand has its quota of young rebels who will not rise when "God Save the Queen" is played in the theaters. One solid reason for insularity is the difficulty of travel. To conserve foreign exchange, the government limits the expenditures of vacation travelers abroad to $600 a month, up to a maximum of $1,800. In any case, New Zealanders, operating in a low-price economy, find travel excruciatingly expensive, except to Australia, and of course airline distances are great. Overseas newspapers take six weeks to reach New Zealand by ship mail; local newspapers do not take much interest in international news.

A corollary of insularity is what Colin MacInnes calls New Zealand's "non-love" affair with Australia, the nearest civilization. One member of the New Zealand Parliament explains the relationship this way: "New Zealand feels, first, envious; second, somewhat frightened—they're slicker than we are, and they'll do us in—and, third, somewhat inferior. Sydney is to us what New York is to the Canadian. We think of it as another kind of universe where one has a sense of living dangerously—murder, auto accidents." It is this ambivalent feeling which possibly lures some New Zealanders to Australia, perhaps to live in Sydney's King's Cross section. But New Zealanders hold their own with Australians in sports, satisfying their need to be "one up on the Aussies." The New Zealand–Australia relationship is not like that of Canada and the U.S. Both down-under countries produce meat and wool, so that they compete with one another for markets, and Australia does not dominate the New Zealand economy as the U.S. does Canada's.

New Zealanders simply will not tolerate high-density housing; every man has his quarter-acre. They're a house-proud people, the furnishings chosen with care and taste. And although the average person lives modestly, his house and well-treated garden can be charming. The sputter of the lawnmower is the standard New Zealand noise. Going with house and garden is a car—one out of three persons owns one. Fifty thousand automobiles are assembled every year in no less than eighteen plants; but prices are so high that many people have to drive vintage cars. There are even some 1924 Maxwells around, and owners tend to keep the car that they buy for ten, twenty, or even thirty years. A related obsession is the beach or mountain weekend house, called a "bach" (pronounced "batch"). This is all part of the outdoor life that New Zealanders are mad about—although one environmentalist, writing in the *Official Yearbook*, damns the "pathetic weekend escape to the countryside, which chokes the roads and spreads a rash of substandard huts and garbage around every beauty spot."

Finally, there seems to be a troubled side to the New Zealand character. A humorless prudishness frequently prevails. When a traveling art exhibit brought Marcel Duchamps' sculptures, *Fountain*, made of a urinal, and *Please Touch*, a foam-rubber breast, to Christchurch, Councillor P. J. Skellerup kept them from public view, saying, "I don't mind a bit of good, clean fun in the art world, but you have to draw the line somewhere." Movies are censored, though not harshly; *Ulysses* was shown on the suggestive condition that the two sexes must view it separately. The public serving of liquor has suffered all the tiresome restrictions of Australia and more; "licensed" means that an establishment may serve wine only, and even "fully licensed" restaurants, though they may serve hard liquor, have to insist that the customer order a full meal before they will bring a cocktail. The abortion laws are strict, and so rigorously enforced that girls go to Australia to get abortions. Prisons are harsh, with occasional riots and singularly tough solitary punishment for the "intractables."

The reality of New Zealand contrasts with its Victorian assumptions. Gambling is endemic: $210 million a year goes into race-track betting and lotteries. Drunkenness is a problem referred to five times in the *Official Yearbook*. Among beer drinkers, New Zealand stands fifth in the world, at 194 pints per head per year (and the beer drinkers bellow, "That's not good enough! We must drink our way to first!"). The little town of Westport once had eighty-two pubs in a single mile. One in eight children is born out of wedlock, and in many more cases the bride is pregnant on her wedding day.

One-third of all New Zealanders require sleeping pills, and the total bill for tranquilizers and mood pills runs to ten dollars per person per year. The former Governor-General, Sir Arthur Porritt, who is also an eminent surgeon, finds the amount of pill-popping "horrible." Psychologists speculate that New Zealanders are neurotic for lack of incentive in the welfare state. The suicide rate, however, is not high: 8.8 per hundred thousand of population, as compared to 10.9 in the U.S. and England, 19.6 in Sweden, and 29.3 in Hungary. Some adjustments are being made to reduce the hypocrisy of blue laws whose intent is wildly contradicted by practice. Bars may now stay open until 10 P.M., eliminating the vomitous "six o'clock swill" that used to take place daily in New Zealand (as in Australia) when bars closed at that hour. And (as in Australia) a government-approved Totalisator Agency Board runs off-track betting in place of the former illegal bookies.

Zubin Mehta, the conductor, found much to deplore on a visit to New Zealand, which in his view is "living in the England of the last century. If you want to go out on Sunday, forget it! The food is awful. Lamb is a delicious meat if cooked well, but the New Zealanders ruin it. In New Zealand, you have to go out of town to find Indians. They and the Maoris all live in suburban slums. I took the Israel Philharmonic on tour there. We had to fill out forms that were insulting. There was a place marked 'Race?' The orchestra has a lot of Polish-Jewish violinists—the best violinists come from Poland. They filled in the question about race with 'Human.' "

And yet, to keep perspective, these shortcomings are essentially the normal contradictions of any country. On balance New Zealand is benevolent, responsible, one of the least corrupt nations of the world—modest, too. New Zealanders are proud of their moral position, and feel that their influence on foreign affairs is larger than their size because of it.

The Historical Background

New Zealand's prehistory is a maddening mixture of firm facts, probabilities, and contradictory mysteries. A probability is that the Polynesians were originally Asian Caucasoid, modified by Mongoloid and Negroid blood as they moved eastward through Indonesia and Melanesia to the Pacific islands of Hawaii, Tahiti, and Easter Island. Certain it is that they became good canoemen, capable of sailing at least a few hundred miles, well out of sight of land, in canoes that could carry 250 people. Certain it is, too, that their canoes began to take them to New Zealand more than a thousand years ago. But there is much mystery as to whether, on those voyages, they were lost, or deliberately seeking new lands to colonize (which might explain their bringing women), or perhaps even consciously sailing to islands already discovered and reported upon by an earlier traveler.

It is established, from carbon dating, that Polynesians lived in various places along the New Zealand coast by A.D. 1000. But the Maoris (rhymes with "dowries") have a tantalizing legend that their ancestors arrived in a number of big outrigger canoes about twenty-four generations ago, a date calculated to be 1350. It is known that there were two Polynesian civilizations in prehistoric New Zealand, one a Stone Age culture based on hunting the moa, and the other the more advanced stage of civilization that the first Europeans found here. The temptation is to equate the first scattered arrivals with the moa hunters, and the big canoes with higher Maori culture, but new scholarship casts doubt on it, chiefly questioning the concept of a specific fleet of canoes in 1350. The thought now is that the landings were occasional but continuous, and that the moa-hunter culture evolved into the Maori culture.

The pre-Pakeha civilization of the Maoris, a handsome people of light brown skin, was the highest in Polynesia. They were an agricultural people, artistic, religious, and warlike. For adzes and clubs, they crossed the Southern

Alps to the West Coast for a kind of translucent jade known in New Zealand as greenstone. They built, on numerous hilltops, a kind of conical fortress called a *pa*. They found flax growing in New Zealand, and learned to make it into baskets and clothing. For meeting houses and the prows of canoes, they practiced wood carving that ranks high in primitive art.

Day-to-day life revolved around the cultivation of the sweet potato, the taro root, and the yam. For other food they ate fern roots, birds, fish, and one another. The Maoris were notorious cannibals, keeping people in pens to fatten them up, and eating all shipwrecked sailors. Tribal organization was based on the family, then the subtribe, with a common ancestor, and finally the tribe, with a set of distant common ancestors who, according to legend, would have all arrived in the same canoe. The canoes, incidentally, all have names, and to this day it is common for a Maori to speak of descent from the Tainui canoe, or the Te Arawa canoe, or the Tokomaru canoe. The characteristics of the religion were, first, many gods but no supreme god, and secondly, a powerful sense of *tapu* (the origin of the English word "taboo"), which served to enforce customs and the law.

Above all, the Maoris loved warfare. Charles Darwin reports, in *The Voyage of the Beagle*, the case of a missionary who after much argument had nearly persuaded a certain Maori chief not to go to war with a nearby tribe. Then the chief discovered that his barrel of gunpowder was going bad, and would be worthless if not used at once. He immediately declared war. It is a likely speculation that English intervention, far from leading the Maoris to extermination, was what saved them from exterminating one another.

*

A great exterminator in the first half of the nineteenth century, when the white colonization took place, was Te Rauparaha, chief of a tribe seated in an area fifty miles south of Auckland. In 1818 he led his tribe south on a bloody trail of conquest, and established them on Kapiti Island, in the Tasman Sea near Wellington. There Te Rauparaha traded with American and English whaling ships for muskets, the weapon that was turning Maori battles from club fights into highly lethal warfare. Having terrorized the tribes of the North Island, Te Rauparaha sailed off, in his canoes with fearsome carved figureheads, to dominate the South Island, too. The battles ended with feasting on the bodies of the vanquished. In 1829, when South Islanders at Akaroa killed one of his best lieutenants, Te Rauparaha chartered a British sailing vessel called the *Elizabeth*, and with his warriors sailed for Akaroa. There the local chief was lured aboard by the ship's captain, who promised to sell him guns for gunpowder. Te Rauparaha seized the chief and sent his men to sack the town and capture its leaderless tribesmen. They were stuffed into the *Elizabeth*'s hold and taken to Kapiti on a bloody voyage during which many of them were tortured and killed.

The scandal of this exploit and pressure from Christian missionaries forced the reluctant British government to take action. In 1840 the Treaty of Waitangi was signed formalizing British rule. Te Rauparaha was one of the chiefs who signed it. The chiefs apparently thought that they were getting the protection of the distant British Queen in return for allowing the Crown to buy Maori land if the tribes wished to sell. The chiefs had held a two-day debate and were not entirely naïve—word had reached them of the British extermination of the Aborigines in Tasmania; but in the end they decided there was no turning back the clock—the British were there. Within three years Te Rauparaha began to have regrets, as he watched the white colonizers grab land under their interpretation of the treaty. He became so defiant that Governor George Grey arrested him and imprisoned him aboard naval ships for eighteen months. Then Grey released him, provided him with the uniform of a British naval officer and an American Army sword and scabbard, and returned him to his tribe. It is to be feared, judging from a drawing, that Te Rauparaha looked a bit ridiculous, with his epaulets, his hawk-nosed wizened face, painted in whorls, and his rakish naval cap. He died, at seventy-nine, a year later.

We have already met Governor Grey, briefly, as the redoubtable official who forced the colonists of Adelaide from the huddled protection of the town to the productive rigors of farming the land. That episode over, in 1845 Grey was assigned to shape up New Zealand in similar style.

Grey, born in 1812, son of a lieutenant colonel in the 30th Foot, was a Governor who governed. From Sandhurst he had gone into exploring in Western Australia, where the Aborigines speared him in the hip. He ruled New Zealand despotically but efficiently from 1845 to 1853, buying Maori land for the Crown cheaply and selling it dear to the settlers, but nevertheless winning Maori admiration by building hospitals and schools and by taking such an intellectual interest in them that even today the best collection and translation of Maori proverbs is one of his published works. He virtually stopped intertribal warfare, and turned many Maoris to the commercial cultivation of potatoes and wheat for export to Australia. In 1852 he suddenly promulgated a New Zealand Constitution more democratic than those of the Australian colonies, giving the country self-government only a dozen years after the British takeover at the Treaty of Waitangi. Then Grey charged energetically off to South Africa to be Governor of Cape Town (where he thwarted a formidable Kaffir rebellion), returning to New Zealand in 1861 when London (with Grey concurring) deemed him vital to win the Maori Wars.

The Maori tribes, astonished at how fast their land was going into the hands of the whites (by pressured purchases and all manner of legal trumpery), had in 1858 ominously joined together in their first nation, and elected a king. This potentate reigned from the area south of Auckland that is known to this day as the King Country. The place where the Maoris most ferociously resisted the land buyers and surveyors, however, was the area called Taranaki, south of the King Country. There in 1860 the Maoris burned the British settlers' farmhouses. The war had started. Three thousand Imperial troops and colonial militiamen responded by devastating a Maori village. A Maori war party from the King Country joined the Taranaki fighting; the white forces attacked Maori *pas*; there were a couple of pitched battles; but neither side won and an armed truce began.

Grey, taking charge of the war, tried threats and conciliation, building a menacing military road from Auckland to King Country, and at the same time ruling for the return of some Maori land. The Maoris, uncertain of his intentions, attacked again in Taranaki in 1863, and soon suffered a sharp counterattack. Grey decided to press from the north. The British General, Duncan Alexander Cameron, moved into King Country aboard small gunboats on the Waikato River. He attacked a *pa*, turning his howitzers and Enfield rifles against the Maoris' flintlocks, sporting rifles, and spears. The Maoris held out three days, until they were down to firing wooden bullets, and then charged out. One hundred and fifty of them were killed, but at least as many more escaped.

This equivocal victory for the Pakehas should have ended the war, except for an outlandish conseqence of the earlier Christianization of the Maoris. In 1862 a certain Maori Christian claimed that the Angel Gabriel had appeared before him in a vision leading him to found a religion that was both Christian and Maori. It combined belief in a hierarchy of angels with cannibalism, and worship of the Trinity with an incantation—*hau hau*—that would render the members of the sect invulnerable to British bullets. At their services, the *hau hau* people danced around a sort of Maypole surmounted by an Englishman's severed head. An Anglican missionary who attempted to stop this heresy was killed and his blood drunk in his own church; they even ate the missionary's eyes.

Bitterness increased when the New Zealand Parliament, in 1863, authorized confiscation of Maori land, thus loosing on the scene speculators who had a vested interest in taking over as much Maori territory as possible. The war bumbled on, but was virtually over. The British troops, who admired Maori courage and chivalry, disliked fighting for the settlers' land hunger, and, except for a regiment, were withdrawn by 1866. Thousands of Maoris still held out in the King Country, excluding settlers and booze, but on such amiable terms that they continued to grow wheat and trade it for European goods. By 1868 Grey, anxious to end the conflict, had indulged in such excesses of zeal (he himself leading an attack on a *hau hau* village) that the Colonial Office dismissed him from the governorship.

The Maori Wars were over by 1872, the epic story of New Zealand, a bit remindful of the American Indian Wars. The result was that the settlers got the bulk of the land of New Zealand, and they proceeded to put it to production of wool, while waiting with a certain hypocritical sympathy for the Maoris to die out. About two thousand Maoris had been killed, and about one thousand Englishmen. The Maoris called it "the white man's anger" and "the fire in the fern."

After the wars, George Grey spent a dozen or so years in London, a doughty advocate of imperialism, and then retired to the island of Kawau, off Auckland. In 1876, the central government abolished the provincial governments (Otago, Canterbury, Taranaki were examples of these) that Grey had written into his Constitution of 1852, and he came storming out to run for Parliament. By the next year this lonely, forceful, eloquent figure was again leading New Zealand, as Prime Minister. His program was radical for the time: manhood suffrage, universal education, triennial election of Parliament, legal recognition for trade unions, compulsory government purchase of large estates, a tax on land, and popular election of the Governor (then as now a Crown appointment). He achieved some of these reforms, and all but the last were later passed. He also founded the reformist Liberal Party, later to be a main shaper of the country. But land profiteers managed to bring him down from the prime ministry. He served, respected but inconspicuous, as a plain M.P. until 1894, and died in London in 1898.

*

We now begin to scent the origins of the New Zealand welfare state, as a shrewd, gargantuan, genuinely reformist politician named Richard John Seddon comes into view. The politics of New Zealand before and after the Maori Wars were the politics of land tenure. As might be expected, the land had fallen into too few hands; access to land was the name of the problem.

Seddon, a Lancashireman, went out to Australia to work in the Melbourne railway shops, and caught gold fever when the great Bendigo gold rush began. This in turn led him to gold mining on New Zealand's West Coast, and thence to election as the area's Member of Parliament in 1879. He became one of George Grey's Liberals, and in 1892, after consulting with that old man, he accepted the prime ministership. He and his cabinet were strongly influenced by the ideas of John Stuart Mill, Henry George, and Edward Bellamy, ideas also current in Australia at the time.

The Liberals' first answers to the country's inequities were graduated taxes on income and unimproved land, accompanied by the removal of property taxes on everything but land. Then, instead of selling Crown land, the government began to lease it, on the theory that freehold led to speculation and high prices that froze out small farmers. For small farmers, the Liberals passed cheap-loan acts that freed them from having to pay interest, which ran up to 15 percent. For labor, the government devised an Industrial Conciliation and Arbitration Act that put disputes with management into a court and removed the need for strikes; not a single one occurred from 1894 to 1906. The conditions of labor were reformed right down to guaranteeing that shopgirls could have chairs to sit in.

A Legislative Council, the upper house, typically opposed the reforms, but during the 1890's it was reduced to impotence by assorted maneuvers, leading finally to its abolition in 1950; New Zealand now has one of the world's few unicameral legislatures. Seddon established penny postage, and—rather reluctantly—made New Zealand the first country in the world to give women the vote.* In a ninety-hour session of Parliament in 1898, Seddon put over governmental old-age pensions, long before the U.S. Social Security Act of 1935. And all the while he skillfully fought off New Zealand's bluenoses, who pressed for prohibition on the drinking of alcohol. Seddon died in 1906.

All this reform met with singular success. Foreigners came to New Zealand and admired it, and the fame of its prosperity and high standard of living spread round the world. To be sure, two economic factors, quite unrelated to the country's political organization, were in the background. One was the breeding of the New Zealand Corriedale sheep, a cross of the Merino and the Lincoln, and a prolific producer of both wool and mutton (though now largely supplanted by the Romney). The other was refrigeration, at the packing plants and on ships, that opened sales of New Zealand lamb, mutton, beef, and butter to the British market. One more point about this period: it turned New Zealand from a colony into a nation. In the 1890's New Zealand shared political characteristics with New South Wales, Queensland, and Victoria, and even considered federating with Australia; by 1907 it was clearly on its own as a British Dominion.

* Two lesser jurisdictions already had woman suffrage: Pitcairn Island and Wyoming.

*

The turn-of-the-century euphoria ended just before World War I with the Liberals breaking away to right and to left. The right prevailed from the war until the Depression, a period of eroding prosperity that left the standard of living about where it had been in the 1880's. By 1935 New Zealand was ready for the left-wing alternative, the Labor Party that had been growing steadily for two decades.

No single figure—no Roosevelt—stands out in the turbulent epoch of reform that followed, although Walter Nash proved brilliant as Minister of Finance, and then first New Zealand Minister to Washington, and Peter Fraser turned out to be a politically skillful wartime (1940–1949) Premier. The measures that restored prosperity (along with the rising price of wool and mutton, and later the effects of the war) were nonrevolutionary, Keynesian repairs to the system. The Reserve Bank was nationalized and given the power to lend to the government. Farmers got subsidies, and the state took over the marketing of their produce. Union membership was made compulsory. A Social Security Act, with improved old-age pensions, family allowances, sickness and unemployment benefits, and so on, was passed. The Department of Health started a medical services system. And some beginnings were made toward economic diversification.

New Zealand's experience in World War II was a strangely sour one. With utter loyalty to Britain, she sent her 2nd Division, under General Bernard Freyberg, to Egypt, and it fought with bravery and skill in Greece, Crete, North Africa, and Italy. Tempted to bring the troops back to the Pacific after Japan attacked Pearl Harbor, New Zealand nevertheless stayed in Europe, defending Britain, while the U.S. was in the South Pacific defending New Zealand—and while New Zealand was single-mindedly growing food to feed Britain. In 1943 the frustrating feeling developed that the 2nd Division had been too long in Europe, but that it was too late for it to join the Pacific fighting. The soldiers were then brought home on long furloughs, during which they developed resentments against the large number of men busy growing and shipping foodstuffs, whom they considered shirkers. Many troops refused to go back to the distant European theater, and in the end New Zealand was left without a role there or a voice in the Pacific.

After the war, in 1947, Parliament ratified the Statute of Westminster, passed in 1931 by the British Parliament to grant complete autonomy to members of the British Commonwealth. New Zealand has simply never been in a hurry to cut itself off from England, though accused of "prolonged adolescence" and addiction to "maternalism." It accepted English governors long after Canada, Australia, and South Africa insisted that their governors be from their own countries. Not until 1968 did the National Party remove the Union Jack from the platform at party gatherings.

The Welfare State

The standard old-age pension paid in New Zealand (mostly without a means test, such as Australia requires) is $715 a year—a figure that raises a lot of questions. Is this piddling pension the measure of the New Zealand welfare state's prosperity?

The answer is that the pension is only the beginning of the benefits. To begin with, a married couple would get almost double $715. A dependent child would add about $500. A cheap, government-subsidized mortgage, probably paid off earlier, would guarantee home ownership for most New Zealanders, and property taxes are likely to be only $50 to $100 a year. For those without houses, apartments rent for as little as $40 a month. The main scourge of old age, medical bills, is removed by free hospitalization and state-guaranteed doctors' fees. A pensioner, or any other New Zealander for that matter, can get the services of a general practitioner for $1.50. "The fear of illness has been removed," says Dr. Wilton Henley, a surgeon at Auckland General Hospital. If the pensioner has sufficient savings or small investments or part-time work to push his income to $2,000 a year, he will have an income equal to that of a worker in a dairy processing plant—enough to live on in New Zealand. The aged and infirm get other benefits. If incapacitated, they are cared for in hospitals, not nursing homes, until death if necessary. If they can stay at home, Meals on Wheels brings food. "The care of old people is fantastic in New Zealand," says Sir Arthur Porritt.

Yet the cushioning of old age is only the beginning of the boons provided to New Zealanders by their government. The family benefit program gives mothers $1.50 a week for each child, and allows for borrowing against child benefits in order to finance a house on a low-interest government loan. Veterans (depending partly on whether or not they were wounded) get car loans, clothing allowances, incapacity allowances, and free passes, first-class, on the New Zealand Railways. A gallantry award brings in $1 a week, and the Victoria Cross $200 a year. Farmers get loans, cheap fertilizer and pesticides, transport subsidies, and dispensation from the standard 2 percent payroll tax. Other boons of the welfare state are profit-sharing, university educations at trifling cost, government-ordered wage boosts to keep pace with inflation, a commitment to total employment that works in practice,* subsidized life insurance, and numerous government jobs (one-fifth of all workers

* In 1969 only 2,082 persons collected unemployment benefits.

are in the civil service). But it is not quite a cradle-to-grave system: there is no funeral allowance.

The money cost of this comes from taxes, and the rates are steep. Typical income taxes for a family with two children run from $484 on a total income of $3,500, to $4,171 for a single person with a total income of $10,500. The top bracket (50 percent) on taxable income for a single person is reached at only $12,000, as compared to $22,000 in the United States. To most people, however, these tax rates are no particular hardship; only one million people pay any taxes at all, and they rarely get into the upper brackets because wages and salaries are low. The basic wage of a lathe operator, for instance, is $2,500, while even the Prime Minister gets only $17,000. The class called "Monied Farmers" clears $6,000 to $12,000 a year. Per capita income is $1,440, which is the seventh highest in the world. Low income, in turn, is no particular hardship because prices average out so low. The stiff $370 for a black-and-white television set is balanced out by a loaf of bread at 16 cents, lamb at 32 cents a pound, butter at 30 cents, sugar at 9 cents, and a pint of milk at 4 cents. No wonder New Zealanders eat an incredible amount of food per person per day, 3,358 calories, the highest in the world, including 242 pounds of meat per person every year.

Such is the balance in material things. On the philosophical scales, the welfare state wins stout support from the majority. The people come first in this country, they say; the economy is subordinate to their welfare. They feel that they have an unquestionable right to be well off, to have not only full employment but *more* jobs than jobholders. All of New Zealand was profoundly shocked in the bad year of 1968, when unemployment reached seven-tenths of one percent. The welfare state has eliminated slums, unnecessary disease, sweatshop labor, monopoly, and poverty. The country has shown itself to be admirably ready to experiment, using the government as a utility. Yet the government has not become an ogre; electorates are small, single votes still count, and Members of Parliament are accessible to individual voters. The idea of human dignity as a right—of decent employment and adequate health care—pervades the philosophy. Is this regimentation? "No," says a rich industrialist, "we are more individualistic than any other dominion." Sir Arthur Porritt concurs: "At first initiative was stifled, but now the individualism of the more enterprising people is as strong here as in countries without the welfare state." The new Prime Minister, John Marshall, argues that the government's objective is merely "to remove the insecurity caused by ill health, old age, and unemployment. When you take care of a man's medical care and unemployment, the risk of his losing his money and falling on his face is less acute. A man can look at life here without fear. So a man can dare to have more initiative, be more experimental." Sir Keith Holyoake,

Marshall's predecessor, says: "When I was a young man in Parliament, I, a conservative, of a conservative family, was worried by the possibility that social welfare would stifle initiative. But I have come to the conclusion that it has not damaged private initiative in New Zealand."

However, one minister, Duncan MacIntyre of Lands, Maori Affairs, and various other portfolios, holds that high income taxes are a definite curb on incentive. "The concept of social security was originally to 'build a floor,' so nobody would be destitute. Now, to finance the floor, we have to put on a ceiling, that is, heavy taxation. So there is no incentive to work." Doctors, who often feel themselves the victims of a welfare state, have generally fought against this welfare state, too, but New Zealand medicine has nevertheless managed to gain pre-eminence in heart surgery and neurosurgery, and the country pioneered in intrauterine transfusions of fetuses for Rh incompatibility or anemia. Doctors come from abroad to learn certain operations in these fields.

The argument against this utopia contends that only luck, specifically the idiosyncratic English hunger for lamb and butter that has prevailed until now, holds it together. Tough times would reveal its weaknesses. And, this argument continues, the cushioned life takes a toll in lack of individual incentive. With everyone, but most prominently labor and farmers, appealing to the government for support and protection, some other force—namely, the market—ultimately has to be allowed to make the economic decisions. There is supposed to be a demoralizing me-firstism about people coddled by a welfare state; if a person dies on Friday night, it is said, his body will be left until Monday, when the workers' weekend is over.

"I don't think socialism holds us back, but we don't display much zest," Bishop Pyatt admits. "As for social security, we are not the world's leader. We were when it began, but other people have overreached us. We have been a success because we're small, and because the bureaucrats are not dead-handed."

One criticism is directed at the indignity of the compulsory nature of health care, which seems to assume that the average New Zealander will shoot his wages on the race track and leave his sick children untended. Compulsory unionism is another target, for it is said to concentrate power in the hands of union officials who would be more responsible to their members if they had to struggle to enlist them and keep the union going.

The Maoris Today

The Maoris, as we have seen, were supposed to die out after the wars of the 1860's, and the population duly sank as a result of European tuberculosis, measles, and typhoid, until it hit bottom at 42,000 in 1896. Then, perhaps owing to heightened immunity to disease, Maori numbers began to rise until now there are 220,000* of them—more, probably, than in the palmiest times of prehistory. They form 8 percent of all New Zealanders, and with a birth rate of forty-four per thousand they are increasing twice as fast as the Pakehas.

Once again, the central question here is the preservation of the culture and identity of the original occupants of a country against the seductions of white technology and urbanism. The Maori has a preservable culture, for it is based on agriculture. The Maori defends his heritage with spirit, born perhaps of the honorable fight he put up in the Maori Wars. Thus, though the word "Maori" means merely "ordinary," the Maoris are in fact an extraordinary people, respected for their courtesy, virility, assertiveness, grace, wit, dignity, and athletic prowess. Many New Zealanders claim more Maori blood than they really have in order to be identified as Maoris instead of as whites.

Maoris feel strong kinship obligations—every Maori is "cousin" to another. They value the spirit of *aroha* (affection or love or pity for others), and they are proud of their mellifluous language, though most also speak English, the language used in schools. The King Country survives, a paper kingdom within the nation; currently reigning is Queen Te Ata, wife of a prosperous Maori dairy farmer. With it goes a powerful church, Ratana, Christian-Maori plus faith-healing.† But Maori nationalism is negligible. Tribalism has declined to the point that many enthusiastic Maoris do not know their own tribal descents, but tribal customs are strong enough that even radical young Maoris treat their elders with much gentleness and respect. Hospital patients' beds are always thronged with visitors, but there are few Maoris in geriatric hospitals; the dying aged go back to their villages for loving attention.

On the other hand, the Europeanization of the Maori has gone so far that all of them—in strong contrast to the Aborigines of Australia, or the New Guineans—are in the money economy. Most work at unskilled and menial jobs, but there are also many big and small farmers, schoolteachers, mechanics, sheep shearers (the finest), nurses, and heavy-machinery operators, and quite a few doctors, lawyers, accountants, and dentists. Long since, certain Maoris have risen to the top of New Zealand society. Sir Peter Buck (whose Maori name was Te Rangi Hiroa) was a medical doctor and politican who turned to Polynesian anthropology and became, before his death in 1951, a professor at Yale and head of the Bishop Museum in Honolulu.

* Defined as persons with one-half or more Maori blood. The total rises to 350,000 when persons with less than one-half Maori blood are included.

† Mormons are also winning many Maori converts.

He is only one of several Maoris knighted for distinguished professional careers.

Of Maori houses, 73.8 percent have washing machines, 80 percent have refrigerators, 78.5 percent have flush toilets, and 61.2 percent have TV sets. The proportion of Maoris who live in cities has risen from 10 percent in 1936 to more than 50 percent, the biggest concentration being in Auckland, which on projection will be 29 percent Polynesian by 1990. Even the common Maori diseases nowadays seem European: gout, obesity, hypertension, and diabetes.

Putting Pakeha and Maori together, one gets a very peculiar national combination: one the reserved, British-descended white, concerned with butter, skiing, pensions, and gardening; the other the warm, unbuttoned, brown Polynesian, concerned with sex, song, relatives, and the land that he lost. Yet the harmony of this relationship, though overadvertised, is indisputable. Pakeha and Maori mingle physically, mentally, and culturally. They josh and argue in the pubs. The Maori collection in Auckland's War Memorial Museum, with its huge canoe, carved storehouses, greenstone adzes, and fishnets a mile long, is a monument of Pakeha pride in Maori culture, and no one likes to visit it more than the citified Maoris. New Zealand is unquestionably the beneficiary of two great traditions. Intermarriage is commonplace, Maori men to Pakeha girls as well as the other way around. In the Wellington area, more than half of Maori marriages are to Europeans. The percentage of persons with Maori blood is rising steadily.

Blatant racial prejudice is definitely bad form throughout the country. "Only a few far-out individuals practice discrimination here," says Matt Te Hau, Maori lecturer at the University of Auckland. Yet there can be no doubting who is up and who is down in New Zealand. A gentle condescension, or at least a naïve sentimentality, prevails among the whites. A visitor may hear a Pakeha lady gush, "Have you seen our Maoris?" Pakehas tell one another stories of Maori ignorance such as that Maori mothers hold their children's noses between their knees to sharpen them, and that they bury bloody rags because fire is for cooking and it's bad to use sacred fire to destroy filthy objects.

Prominent doctor: "Our Maoris are wonderful with their hands, proud of being Maoris, delightful people."

"Do you ever invite any of them to dinner?"

"Actually, very few of them are culturally adequate."

One serious judgment is that most of the credit for harmonious relations belongs to the Maoris, for being willing to put up with these attitudes. But let it be quickly added that most white New Zealanders know more about, and care more about, Maori culture than Americans do about Indian culture.

They have respected Maori virtues and power for more than a century and are proud of their relations with the Maoris. The essential tolerance springs from New Zealand's classlessness and basic decency. Many Pakeha high school students, for example, take the time to learn at least a smattering of the Maori language, and to appreciate its poetry.

*

Maoris get their say in Parliament through four members elected by more-than-half-blood Maoris. To assure this quota, the country is divided into four special Maori electoral districts which have no relation to the Pakeha districts. In addition, Maoris can, and do, stand for and win seats from Pakeha districts, though paradoxically they cannot vote for themselves in these cases. Currently seven or eight part-Maoris hold Pakeha seats. The Maori Sir James Carroll ran for office at various times on both rolls and once served as Acting Prime Minister, and pipe-smoking Sir Peter Buck rose to be Minister of Health. Presently, a Maori woman, Mrs. Tirikatene-Sullivan, daughter of an illustrious (and knighted) M.P., is the member for the Southern Maori District. She is a strikingly handsome woman, with shoulder-length black hair and beautiful hands. Zealous and articulate, she got into politics as her father's secretary, and won by 81 percent of the vote. Maori M.P.s have always been members of the Labor Party, and Maoris in general vote 70 percent pro-Labor. This segregated system of special Maori electorates, in use since 1867, is under constant attack. Critics say it is racist and tokenist, and makes Maoris second-class citizens. The most pragmatic proposal for improvement is to increase the number of Maori districts, because the Maori population has grown so swiftly since the 1867 apportionment. Dr. I. H. Kawharu, a social anthropologist at the University of Auckland and a Maori, says: "It never occurs to a Maori to be anything but a Maori. If he can't make a contribution as a Maori, he wants to know what's wrong with the system that does this to Maoris. So he wants more Maoris in Parliament, not more whites *talking* for Maoris. He doesn't want to lose consciousness of his identity."

Sometimes the Maori M.P.s are dismissed as the "little brown mandate," and the laws passed by Parliament for the benefit of Maoris have an air of being gifts. The Maori Social and Economic Advancement Act of 1945 financed Maori development in farming, put Maoris fully into the Social Security System, and wiped out legislation discriminating against Maoris. The word "native" was abolished from official lingo in 1947. Yet the Department of Maori and Island Affairs cannot seem to avoid a paternal "us and them" tone in official statements. It employs 782 wardens to curb "excessive drinking" among the Maoris. Various relationships are proposed for the indigenous people and their Western successors: integration, symbiosis, assimilation, coexistence. The Maoris seem to want to be both in and out of the white culture, symbolically integrating the washing machine with the *marae*, the still-prevalent traditional place for meetings and oratory. Sentimental Pakehas purport to value the Maori culture, but the official policy of integration is, at bottom, that Maoris should be like whites. The stress is on apprenticeship for trades, and the beneficial effects of YWCAs, and the like.

As a consequence, articulate Maoris seem more than a little irritated over their role in New Zealand, while admitting that basically they are treated better than any other minority in the world. They complain of everything from "alienation in their own land" to occasional discrimination in barbershops and movies to "mutilation of Maori place names" by announcers on the radio. Mrs. Tirikatene-Sullivan cites the case of a Maori girl who tried to register at ten hotels and was refused by three of them. But Mrs. Tirikatene-Sullivan also boasts that "we are the world's most successful plural society, or multiracial society, except possibly Hawaii." A great periodic outcry arises over how to overcome South African racial prejudice when New Zealand's Rugby team, with many Maori teammates, goes to Cape Town to play. Recently South Africa agreed to classify the Maoris as "honorary whites" for visa purposes, which made the Maoris more furious than outright exclusion would have. Racism, perhaps, is increasing a bit as Maoris change from distant farmers to city-dwellers, often in ghettos. One-third of all persons in prison are Maoris, which would seem to be an indication of educational shortcomings and a lack of good job opportunities.

The Pakeha land grabs of the past century still rankle. Of New Zealand's sixty-six million acres, Maoris now own only four million, less than they should even in proportion to numbers. A land tenure map of the North Island shows scrappy patches of Maori land indicated in yellow amidst a sea of Pakeha freehold land in green. A new land act, passed in 1967, makes it easier for Maoris to sell to Pakehas, and Maori radicals darkly interpret this as another land grab, this time, they say, on behalf of American companies that want it for oil and other minerals.

Maoris also suffer deficient education, partly because they tend to leave school at fifteen, the end of the compulsory period, and partly because 27 percent of them attend special, segregated Maori schools that are inferior to the state schools (the Maori schools are now being rapidly integrated into the state system). Out of ten thousand students at the University of Auckland, only one hundred are Maoris, one-eighth of what the ratio should be.

Note on the Maori Language

Here is a language ingratiating to the ear, confusingly homonymic, rich in syllables, a source of place names. You hear it frequently on the streets of Auckland. It is uniform throughout New Zealand, and all Maoris speak it. A surprising aspect of Maori, which like Hawaiian is a dialect of Polynesian, is that it gets along quite well without any of the sounds indicated by *b, d, j, l, q, s, v, x,* and *z*. Owing to the scholarly efforts of the missionaries, Maori can be—and is—written and printed. Strangely, the sound that the missionaries denoted as "*wh*" is more or less like "*f*." The name of the aforementioned Dr. Kawharu is pronounced "KAFaroo." Maori is by no means Pidgin, but it has adopted and transliterated innumerable English words. "Tin" is "*tini*," "pork" is "*poaka*," "broom" is "*puruma*," "Christmas" is "*Kirihimete*." "*Wiwi*" comes from French, but it means "Frenchman," not "yes-yes." Thousands of Maori words are homonyms. "*Te-Hokioi*," for example, called "the most mysterious word in the Maori language," means "symbol of love," "symbol of guidance," "symbol of war," and "I shall return." "*Rangi*" means "arrange in rows," "heaven," "period of time," "sky," "tune," and "weather."

CHAPTER 23

New Zealand: Politics, Grass, and Potters

They grizzle and groan, but they've got nothing to grizzle and groan about.

—AN AUCKLAND TAXI DRIVER

SIR KEITH HOLYOAKE, Prime Minister from 1960 until early 1972, ran New Zealand longer than any other leader except the reformer Seddon. He made this record partly because he possesses two characteristics that New Zealanders greatly admire* in a politician: broad, strong shoulders, and an education achieved on his own, without benefit of college. The first proves that he has "used the shears"—that he knows how to raise sheep; the second, that he is not too "airy-fairy" to understand the needs of the ordinary people.

These barefoot-boy traits, of course, quite misrepresent Sir Keith's character taken as a whole. In office, he proved able, powerful, sound and markedly adept at steering away from mistakes. His ancestry goes back to a headmaster at Rugby in 1687, but a more pertinent forebear may have been an English great-granduncle who was a Chartist, an Owenite, and a Secularist—a mid-Victorian Socialist. Some of this spirit of social revolt crossed the ocean with almost every New Zealand settler.

Because his father was ill, Keith Jacka Holyoake, third of seven children, had to leave school and go to work on the North Island family farm at the age of twelve, taking full adult responsibilitiy for running the place. Self-reliance and faith in free enterprise were bred into him by this experience. For further education, he got tutoring from his mother, who had been a

* In addition to a first name that his countrymen seem to prefer above all others to give their male children.

teacher, and took correspondence courses. He became, and remains, an important farmer (dairy products and tobacco). Farmer-organization politics led him into national politics, and election to Parliament in 1932 as its youngest member. In 1936 he and other politicians hooked together the National Party from the remnants of the right wing of the old Liberal Party, and in 1949 they beat Labor and came to power. Mr. Holyoake served until 1957 as Minister of Agriculture—a long run in what is regarded as a deathtrap post—and then took over as party leader. The Labor Party regained power from 1957 until 1960, with Walter Nash as Prime Minister. Then the National Party, under Keith Holyoake, won the government again.

At one point Sir Keith studied elocution, discarding a New Zealand accent in the process, and his oratory is so persuasive that on one occasion a Speaker of the House was stirred to drop his decorum and cry, "Hear, hear!" Holyoake also has a talent for mimicry. In public he is courtly, even pompous, and well groomed; he has a fine, haughty mouth. In private he is warm, hearty, and self-deprecatory all at once. Queen Elizabeth knighted him in June 1970, the first New Zealand Prime Minister to be so honored. His wife, a former girl athlete, shares his political zest. They have five children. He is a man with few other interests than politics, but after he underwent a prostate operation in 1970 it was generally assumed that he would step down to let a younger man lead the National Party in the November 1972 elections. And he did, resigning a few days before his sixty-eighth birthday, February 11, 1972. His successor, inevitably, was Deputy Prime Minister John Marshall, fifty-nine, a man of the same political cut, with a record of twenty-five years in Parliament, nineteen of them in the cabinet.

In office, Sir Keith operated with beguiling informality. He used to walk to work without a bodyguard, and often stopped at the Chinese greengrocer's on the way home. In his childhood, to avoid confusion with a cousin of the same name, he took the nickname "Kiwi," and still has it. Because he is over sixty-five, he collects a social security pension like anyone else. His home phone number, 44-797, is listed in the Wellington book, and anyone who dials it can speak directly to him. "I hope I'm not disturbing you," said a caller during Holyoake's last year in office. "Not at all," he replied. "Just working away at some cabinet papers." To some American visitors in his office, through the windows of which one could see seagulls sitting on a flagpole, he said, "Thank you for coming to such a teeny-weeny country."

*

New Zealand accepts the British Queen as her own, and the Queen exerts her largely fictitious powers through a Governor-General. For practical purposes, all sovereignty rests with the New Zealand Parliament, which can make laws that bind itself with constitutional force, and then quite blandly amend them. At bottom, government in New Zealand rests simply on a great public consensus, rather than a coherent written constitution.

As we have seen, the upper house was quietly buried in 1950, the provinces, equivalent of states, having been abolished long before. The country is simply too small to need much subdivision. Jurisdiction drops directly from the federal level to the counties, of which there are 106, abetted by boroughs for urban areas and town districts like townships. A borough with twenty thousand or more inhabitants becomes a city. Backing this up is a labyrinthian system of no less than 657 local authorities—pest destruction boards, underground water authorities, electricity and gas boards—many of which require elected officials and entail endless elections. Voting is not compulsory (though registration is), but in important national elections turnouts often reach 80 or 90 percent.

Bureaucracy is rampant and paper work endless. "It takes three times as long to get anything done by a government office here as it does in the States," says an American resident of Wellington. The outstanding exception is the Inland Revenue Department, which provides simple tax forms, help and cooperation in filling them out, and fast tax refunds.

The Governor-General until lately has been Sir Arthur Espie Porritt, appointed in 1967 as the first native-born New Zealander to hold that job. He was born in 1900, educated in medicine at the University of Otago in Dunedin and at Oxford. He captained the New Zealand Olympic team in 1924 in Paris, where he won a bronze medal, and in 1928 in Amsterdam. As a surgeon he rose to president of the British Medical Association and of the Royal College of Surgeons. He served as surgeon to King George VI from 1946 to 1952, and as Sergeant-Surgeon to the Queen since then. In office, he toured New Zealand from the Tokelau and Cook Islands to the South Pole. Sir Arthur was succeeded at the beginning of 1972 by Sir Denis Blundell, also a New Zealander, who had been serving as his country's High Commissioner in London.

The Leader of the Opposition

Norman Kirk weighs twenty stone, 280 pounds, quite enough to displace John Marshall, and that is what he aspires to do as leader of the Labor Party. As far as shunning the more uppity kinds of education, the best he can boast is that he left school at fourteen. While pursuing further knowledge by reading seven books a week, he earned his living operating a factory engine. He got into politics as Mayor of Kaiapoi, near Christchurch, which gave him a shot at running for Parliament from Lyttelton, Christchurch's port, in 1957. He won the seat, and by 1965 was Labor Party president and Leader of the Opposition—a fast rise, due in part to his eloquence as a television speaker. He is forty-eight years old, married, and has five children.

Labor has been in power only three years in the past twenty-two, but it remains strong because it devised the brilliant reforms of the late 1930's and because most workers belong to it. A three-seat switch in the 1969 election would have given the government to Labor. In a general sort of way, Labor is supposed to speak for the "socialist alternative," but in practice it fully accepts the free-enterprise component of the New Zealand mixed-economy system. It has specifically dropped nationalization of industry as a goal. The National Party, in theory, is a rightist supporter of private initiative over government regulation, but it in turn accepts state operation of part of the economy. Pragmatically, this means it has the support of most farmers—in fact, one-half of the Nationalist Members of Parliament are farmers.

Given this consensus on over-all goals, elections have to be fought over the question of how to achieve the goals. Kirk attacks the National Party administration for running the country by rigid "cabinet rule." The ministers, meeting privately, set policy and make decisions, without consulting the backbenchers, who are then marshaled into line to vote for what the cabinet wants, in short and uninformative sessions of Parliament. The cost, he says, is low prestige for Parliament—which to an outsider, listening to New Zealanders "grizzle and groan," in the Auckland taxi driver's phrase, seems to be the case. Kirk's remedy is longer sessions and freer debate. As to the economy, Kirk holds that reliance on the traditional customer, Britain, to buy wool and food is too risky; New Zealand "must rethink her policy in the light of her position in the Southwest Pacific and of changing patterns of trade inside the Commonwealth." Kirk contends that the country "should be exporting carpets, textiles, and garments instead of raw wool, prepacked processed foods instead of carcass meat, leather goods instead of hide and skins." Yet he puts reforms in the welfare and educational systems ahead of immediate economic development. "We are more nationalistic than the National Party," says Mr. Kirk. "We put more emphasis on the redistribution of wealth. The responsibility of government is to create equality of opportunity, regardless of wealth." The Labor Party's problem, he says, is that it historically stood for the right of the blacksmith's son to become an architect, but after he did so, no incentive was provided by Labor for the architect to stay in the party. "We've had to rebuild the party."

No doctrinaire is Mr. Kirk, nor was Sir Keith Holyoake either. Astute and dominant, through cabinet rule, Holyoake balanced pressures successfully for a decade—pressures that come, for example, from the Federated Farmers, the Federation of Labor, the Manufacturers Federation, the Association of Chambers of Commerce, and the Public Service Association. For a time Holyoake had a Minister of Labor so seductive that he almost stole the unions out from under the Labor Party. The Nationalists' close call in the 1969 election, though, seems to indicate that something is amiss. The farmers are worried, naturally enough, by the prospective loss of British markets, and sometimes feel that their party is not doing enough for them; the Taranaki branch of the Federated Farmers even called upon Holyoake to dissolve his government. One notable National Party man, incidentally, is Sir Leslie Munro, former President of the United Nations General Assembly, now serving as a humble backbencher. Another is Robert Muldoon, the Finance Minister, a forceful character who aspires ultimately to be Prime Minister, but had to settle for election as deputy party leader in the early 1972 caucus that chose Marshall for the top job.

The universal criticism of the New Zealand political system is that it puts a premium on excessive caution. A perennial example is the question of prohibition. The politicians considered this to be such a hot potato that they tossed it to the public in the form of a referendum held every three years, in which the voters get to choose among the outright banishment of booze, the present style of licensed pubs, or complete government control. (Usually about 30 percent of the voters choose prohibition, but this proportion is falling slowly.) Individual members of Parliament cannot try bold initiatives, but must loyally vote with their parties. The passion for ordinary men, rather than experts, in politics provides just that—homespun types who take care of their constituents' requests and attempt no leadership. Submission to pressure groups is commonplace. One issue that did stir emotions was Vietnam. Sir Keith sent New Zealand troops there. Labor soon began to demand that they be withdrawn, and in August 1971 Sir Keith agreed to get them out by the end of the year.

The Ombudsman

Like the four countries of Scandinavia, New Zealand has an ombudsman, a watchdog to make sure that private citizens get treated fairly in their relationships with their government. By the nature of their jobs, a certain percentage of bureaucrats anywhere in the world turn into petty tyrants—dictatorial welfare workers, red-tape artists, discourteous postal employees, overzealous tax collectors. New Zealand, using a system that basically originated in Sweden one hundred years ago, gives the man with a grievance a chance to get justice without hiring a lawyer and making a costly court case out of it. He can go to the office of Sir Guy Powles, the Ombudsman, whose jurisdiction covers not only the various branches of the state bureaucracy but also the utilities run by the government, such as the railways, the telephones, and the electric power supply.

The system works like this: A complainant must set down his gripe in writing, and accompany it with a two-dollar fee. The Ombudsman is entitled to reject any complaint he considers to be unwarranted. On complaints that he accepts, the Ombudsman runs an investigation that is kept private and deliberately informal, although he can summon and examine persons on oath, and has access to government premises and records. He must inform a government department that he is investigating it, and give it a chance to defend itself. He has guaranteed access to cabinet ministers, and the right to go to the Prime Minister if his recommendation is not acted upon. "We've never quite got to the crunch as yet," says Sir Guy, the pressures of public opinion being sufficient always to get a remedy at a lower level. Most department heads say, "Goodness, did we do that?" and make amends.

The Ombudsman can rule against any illegal act by a civil servant, and, beyond that, against any decision that appears to him to be unreasonable, unjust, or oppressive. If such a decision is made in conformity with a law, the Ombudsman can deem the law improper. Finally, and even more broadly, he can simply pronounce a decision to be wrong, an "elevated use of a plain old English word," as Sir Guy puts it.

Sir Guy, a tanned, sophisticated man with white-gray eyebrows and hazel eyes, operates with delightful simplicity, employing a staff of six that costs only $28,000 a year, and writing his reports with much candid use of the first person singular. Most of the investigation, he finds, can be done by mail. In a typical year, 1969, he received 620 complaints, many from Maoris, and investigated 285 of them. He found 66 to be justified, obtained satisfaction for the complainant in 56 of these by the mere act of investigating, made recommendations in the cases of 6 others, and dropped 4. The biggest number of justified complaints was against the Social Security Department, with the Post Office next, and the State Services Commission (industrial accidents) third; only one was against the police.

The complaints are over the sort of thing that makes people furious with bureaucracy everywhere. Two businessmen exploded when asked to answer the question "Race?" on a form as they departed from a New Zealand airport. Sir Guy agreed (on the basis of his own travels) that the question was not asked by other countries, and that it could be offensive, but accepted the government's argument that the answer was needed for statistical reasons. A woman sought to bring to New Zealand her mother, an Anglo-Burmese who also had children living in England. New Zealand immigration policy requires that in such cases all of the children have to be living in New Zealand before the parent can be let in. Sir Guy persuaded the authorities to make an exception.

The White New Zealand Policy

To go from Australia to New Zealand is to go from the cosmopolitan to the provincial, and the reason quickly dawns on the traveler: Australia is a rich melting pot of European cultures, and New Zealand, barring the graceful Maoris, is almost wall-to-wall British—not a bad stock, of course, but in this case frightfully homogeneous. During the two decades when Australia was absorbing its polyglot New Australians and their pizzas and paellas and potato pancakes, New Zealand was assisting a few thousand Britons a year to join the earlier immigrants from the same place. The only cautious exception was the Dutch, 26,000 in all, plus pockets of Austrians, Americans, Hungarians, Germans, as well as ten thousand Chinese who immigrated in considerable numbers in the last century, a sizable colony of Indians, and a number of Yugoslavs who make wine. There are conspicuously few Greeks and Italians. The Dutch, by the way, run many restaurants, markedly improving New Zealand's choice of foods. In the last years of the 1960's, as we have seen, the country suffered a net outflow of population of up to six thousand a year (mostly to Australia). It must be added at once, however, that with a high local birth rate New Zealand managed not only to keep up with Australia in population growth rate, but even a little ahead, from 1951 to 1966. This is a fast-growing country!

Now New Zealand has decided to bring people in rapidly, but with much more racial trepidation than Australia. Manufacturers are crying for workers, and an easier labor market would slow inflation. Americans seem to be particularly desirable, provided they are not black, or Hawaiians of dark skin. With a giddy feeling of experimentation, New Zealand is also subsidizing the fares of workers from France, Belgium, Italy, West Germany, and Switzerland, as well as Holland. Sir Keith Holyoake says that they will "add a new dimension of strength and vitality to New Zealand."

Decisions as to who may immigrate are made, one by one, on the administrative level, by issuing entry permits. Formerly persons of "British birth" were not required to have permits, British birth being defined as descent from native-born (not naturalized) British subjects, and any British subject who was "an Aboriginal native or the descendant of an Aboriginal native" was specifically excluded. This was a little too blatant; anyway, the permit system is sufficiently broad and arbitrary. Anyone denied a permit can appeal to the Minister of Immigration, who is not required to explain his decisions. In general, though, the decisions are based on "assimilability"—and New Zealanders are notorious for their ability to distinguish people who are "not like us." Prime Minister Marshall, a soft-spoken, sun-bronzed man who put in many years in the touchy job of Immigration Minister (and was simultaneously Minister of Labor, Minister of Overseas Trade, and Attorney General), says: "We seek to maintain a homogeneous society."

The color bar has one gaping breach. Cook Islanders, whose Polynesian homelands constitute a "self-governing territory in free association with New Zealand," are admitted as New Zealand citizens, and islanders from Western Samoa, a former New Zealand trust territory and a nation on its own since 1962, are admitted at the rate of fifteen hundred a year by a special arrangement. These islanders form a colony of nearly forty thousand, mostly in the older section of Auckland, where they crowd densely into housing vacated by Maoris moving to better areas. Freshly arrived islanders have a reputation for drinking, violence, and trouble with the police, but their children are said to settle in well. A problem of this migration is that it tends to drain the islands of their richest and most talented people, who prefer Auckland's bright lights to small-island boredom. New Zealand requires that Samoan girls, before immigrating, must prove by a medical test that they are not pregnant. The girls object to this as "social stigmatization," which indeed it would seem to be, since scores of Australian girls go untested to New Zealand every year to have illegitimate babies inconspicuously in the free government hospitals.

One final note on this complex race and migration problem, where some people are decidedly more equal than others. Australia admits Maoris freely, but demands a visa for Cook Islanders, who are equally New Zealand citizens. New Zealand, conversely, raises no barriers against black Papuans, who are Australian citizens, but these same Papuans are not allowed into Australia, despite their citizenship, without a permit.

The Economy

Grass! English grass, growing in ten thousand meadows. Or natural tussock, covering the hillsides. To this country, grass, turned into wool, lamb, and mutton by that four-footed factory, the sheep, or into milk, butter, cheese, and powdered milk by that equally industrious animal, the cow, is like oil to Kuwait. Beautifully, simply, and endlessly, the soil has poured out the wealth that let New Zealand live its easy, cushioned life. Every New Zealander—man, woman, child, Pakeha, Maori—is backed up by two dozen tireless animals busily getting fat or producing milk or extruding a valuable fiber. The land is, to be sure, extraordinarily well tended. Cobalt and superphosphates are added in the tiny proportions that energize the soil like the discharge of an electric eel. The country leads the world in the use of airplane-dropped top dressing on pasture land. Planes operating off of *eight thousand* airstrips drop fertilizer on five million acres of land every year. The soil, in fact, has been completely rebuilt from the condition in which the first English settlers found it. Considering that the two islands are both mountainous, the New Zealanders have managed to use an amazingly high proportion of it: two-thirds.

The most typical case of a product raised to the English taste is the fat lamb ("fat" because they look blocky, not because the meat is fatty). Americans will accept meat from a lamb that weighs as much as forty-five pounds, dressed, but the English pay enough more per pound for baby lambs, only three months old, that New Zealand aims to ship lamb carcasses at just thirty-two pounds. At Invercargill, which with fifty thousand people is the most southerly city in the world,* five *million* fat lambs are slaughtered every season, between early September and the middle of May. The men in the meat works are a doughty crew, slitting the throats of the lambs and hanging them on moving chains. These independent men will quit in a flash if they don't like the "tucker" (food) in the "tucker box," the slaughterhouse lunchroom.

Farmers breed sheep by putting a ram in a paddock with the ewes for almost six weeks, which is certain to include two menstrual cycles for each ewe. The gestation period is 148 days, give or take a few; thus a sheep raiser may breed the ewes in April so that they will drop their lambs in August and reach the slaughtering age of three months by November to hit the English market for Christmas. A lamb is a lamb until it is eight months old; then it becomes a hogget, and at sixteen months a mature sheep. Good sheep land in New Zealand supports ten sheep to an acre, poor land one sheep to ten acres. A farmer needs at least two thousand sheep to make a profit, and a big farm may have eight thousand. The huge sheep stations of the past, broken up, as we have seen, in the 1890's, occupied as much as fifty thousand acres. Now stations average two or three thousand acres.

About half of the country's forty-four million acres of farmland is leased

* Provided that Chile's more southerly Punta Arenas is defined as a town, not a city.

from the Crown, and about half owned outright. The price of good sheep land is $150 an acre, and of poorer land $60 or $70 an acre. In general, the South Island raises sheep and grain; the North Island breeds sheep more intensively, and yet specializes in dairying. By law milk processing companies are cooperatives. At Te Rapa, south of Auckland, one of the fifty plants of the New Zealand Cooperative Dairy Company uses 400,000 gallons of milk a day, an amount so big, the manager says, that "we mine our own coal, we need so much for the steam processing." Eight hundred farmers supply the raw milk, getting thirty-two cents a pound for the butterfat content, and the product, powdered milk, is sent to Southeast Asia—some also to, of all places, Denmark. The workers wear white caps, white overalls, and white boots; they get $36 for a forty-hour week, and the factory manager makes $5,000 a year. The machinery, fully automated, came from West Germany.

*

Lying ahead for this economy of wool and meat and cheese is something that could be akin to disaster, and its initials are EEC. After Britain joins the European Economic Community, a wall of tariffs will eventually rise to shut out New Zealand's products. The thought causes anguish. One New Zealand politician, visiting London early in 1970, called the EEC a "gigantic swindle of the British public." He passionately asked, "What has happened to our ancient dignity and pride of race? Our Queen and all she stands for as a focal point of Commonwealth loyalty are being sacrificed for a few pieces of silver. Will her robes be divided among the directors of the great international moneymakers of Wall and Threadneedle streets? The cause of the British housewife and the New Zealand producer are the same cause. We must unite and march together so that we can continue as brothers to toast as our sovereign lady, the Queen. God bless her."

Farm products form nearly 90 percent of New Zealand's exports; it is the world's largest exporter of butter, and for many years the largest exporter of meat. All told, farm exports bring in $1 billion a year. Twenty percent of the Gross National Product is exported, as compared to 4 percent in the U.S. Almost half of these exports go to Britain, including four-fifths of the butter,* cheese, and lamb. The loss of these markets would be a dreadful blow. During negotiations in mid-1971, the continental members

* The British are mad about butter. They eat almost 20 pounds per capita per year, along with almost 12 pounds of margarine. Americans eat almost 11 pounds of margarine, but only 5½ pounds of butter.

of the European Economic Community agreed to let Britain continue buying these New Zealand products during a five-year phaseout after Britain's entrance into the EEC. Finding new markets for butter, cheese, and lamb may prove difficult. To most of the world, particularly New Zealand's Asian neighbors, these are luxury foods, to be consumed only in small quantities. In other markets, where she could compete powerfully, there are import restrictions. New Zealand farmers could put a pound of butter on U.S. tables for 40 percent less than domestic prices. New Zealand's other agricultural exports, happily, are in less peril. Three-fourths of its beef goes to the United States and Canada, at high prices. Mutton goes to Japan for sausages. Big buyers of wool are Britain and other European countries, the United States, and Japan, but of course wool suffers ever-growing competition from synthetics.

Luckily, ten years of De Gaulle excluding Britain from the European Economic Community gave New Zealand a breathing spell in which to plot new incomes. The Comalco aluminum smelter at Bluff is, in effect, an exporter of electricity from the numerous hydro plants in the Southern Alps. Here electric power, added to alumina (from Australia), makes aluminum, to be sent to Australia, Japan, and elsewhere. Radiata pine is exported as lumber and pulp. Iron sands, found along hundreds of miles of the New Zealand coastline, have succumbed to a technology that permits smelting it into iron for the local steel industry, and for export to Japan. Sand also yields titanium and ilmenite. Oil and gas have been found off the coast of Taranaki, on the North Island, in big enough quantities to give New Zealand hope for self-sufficiency. Presently New Zealand imports oil worth $100 million a year from the Middle East and Indonesia; now, with these discoveries by British Petroleum, Shell, and Todd Consortium (a company backed by one of the few millionaires in New Zealand), it may be able to start a petrochemical industry. A similar economy might come from a proposed shipping line; until now all the country's export shipment has been left to the British. Tourism, too, is a developing possibility; Americans departing from the West Coast can get Hawaii, Samoa, Fiji, Tahiti, Australia, *and* New Zealand all on the same airline ticket—taking the Tahiti leg aboard Air New Zealand.

New Zealand might also become a workshop country, along the lines of Sweden; already it manufactures goods of a variety all out of proportion to its small population. Wire, nylon cloth, bathtubs, hydraulic trench diggers, acrylic paint, TV tubes, gin, thermostats, bicycles, road rollers, ships, adhesives—these are some of the products of New Zealand factories. Exports of manufactured goods (newsprint, farm machinery, woodworking equipment) reached $100 million in 1969—not bad. Most of it went to Australia, which has a limited free-trade agreement with New Zealand. But Europeans now buy New Zealand lawn mowers, and Singapore buys New Zealand carpets.

The spread of socialism in New Zealand is perhaps best measured by how much business the government runs, and it runs a lot; telephones, radio and TV, mines, railways, natural-gas distribution, hotels, domestic and international airlines, insurance, electricity. The power goes from the cheap hydroelectric sources in the South Island to the big consumers on the North Island through a unique, 500,000-volt submarine cable, twenty-five miles long, under Cook Strait. The Bank of New Zealand, the country's biggest, which competes directly against commercial banks, is government-owned. "I hold all the shares," says Minister of Finance Robert Muldoon. Sometimes, though, the state pioneers in some industry, and then turns it over to private enterprise. The government discovered how to make steel by pelletizing the iron sands of the West Coast of the North Island, and set up a private company to carry on from there.

On the other hand, the government stays completely out of farming. The whole dairy industry, for example, is based on one-man farms, working through cooperative marketing organizations. Two minor industries of note are brewing (the DB Export beer is strong and hearty) and wine making (the whites are superb, and the New Zealanders are slowly being weaned away from their dreadful fortified reds).

Pottery, Painting, and the Enzedbeecee

> *We are a young nation with enough leisure, education and material security to start looking for a culture of our own, and we want more human values than usually found in suburbia.*
>
> —HELEN MASON

New Zealand frets a good deal over its cultural development, lamenting, for example, that such a writer as Katherine Mansfield and such a painter as Frances Hodgkins felt, in the early part of this century, that they must work out their careers in London and Paris. Ernest Rutherford, later Lord Rutherford, Nobel prizewinner and first man to split the atom, was another New Zealander who had to go abroad, to Cambridge, before he could do the work that won him fame. Perhaps the same might be said of Sir Edmund Hillary, but of course he had to go to where the highest mountain is before he could climb it.

But of late the country seems to be a quite adequate home for artists, poets, dancers, writers, and musicians. Strangely, though, the pre-eminent art is pottery. In fifteen years, New Zealand has come to the fore as the workshop of dozens of highly talented potters turning out jugs and bowls and jars in huge variety and quantity.

Kilns and studios abound. Great events shake the pottery world from time to time, such as the arrival of expert Japanese potters to teach and demonstrate. In turn the local potters go abroad, most frequently to Japan but also to England, the United States, and Mexico. Their work shows Japanese and Maori influences.

The Professional Potters Association has about a hundred members, a leading light being Helen Mason, who also edited the *New Zealand Potter* for many years. Mrs. Mason went to Fiji a few years ago and lived in a village there for a month, working with Fijian potters. In her house-studio in the bush fifteen miles west of Auckland, she still uses techniques and motifs that she learned in Fiji. She can produce $350 worth of pottery from one firing of her kiln, even though she consciously holds prices low because "we want people to use our things every day. If they break a dish, they come back and buy another." She also teaches the potting craft: "A youngster will arrive on my doorstep and stay on for a year to work with me."

Painting in New Zealand inspires much lyricism about the quality of the light. The poet A. R. D. Fairburn calls it a "hard, clear light" that "reveals the bones, the sheer form, of hills, trees, stones and scrub. We must draw rather than paint, even if we are using a brush, or we shall not be perfectly truthful." Landscape, rather than the figure, has been the customary theme of the New Zealand painter, from Charles Heaphy, official artist and draftsman of the New Zealand Company in 1840, to Colin McCahon, a present-day South Islander. Painting has a respectable history in New Zealand. In the Auckland City Gallery, the National Art Gallery in Wellington, and the Hocken Library in Dunedin, many of the paintings are unusual, specifically because they are not derivative. Distance kept artists from firsthand knowledge of French painting. The Auckland gallery has a large collection of European Old Masters. Peter Bromhead, the bearded, long-haired curator, says that his eighteenth- and nineteenth-century Italian collection is "better and larger" than Melbourne's. This gallery also has sculpture by Rodin, Maillol, Epstein, Henry Moore, and others.

A lively private gallery in Auckland is the Mill, a century-old building that once housed a flour mill. While a folk singer performs, the people of Auckland buy art and craftwork. One Auckland gallery owner, Barry Lett, contracted with twelve leading artists to do prints, which he sells in forty-dollar sets (one from each artist) to "get away from the idea that art is for people with money." Paintings here are much cheaper than in Australia.

*

The press in New Zealand (about twenty daily newspapers) must by law be New Zealand owned—no Lord Thomsons or Rupert Murdocks allowed here. The result is a constricted ownership that, among other defects, leaves the Labor Party without daily-newspaper support. A narrow and conservative press. NZBC (pronounced "enzedbeecee"), the government-subsidized New Zealand Broadcasting Corporation, is scarcely more venturesome. The rows that it gets into are usually over what it refuses to air, rather than what it does air on its four TV and forty-four radio stations. New Zealand viewers, who have had television only since 1960, now get: one channel only, no color, a surfeit of American programs, and the obligation of paying a license fee of thirteen dollars a year. They even have to put up with commercials, but only on Tuesday, Wednesday, Thursday, and Saturday. Broadcasting hours are 2 P.M. to 11 P.M.—midnight Fridays and Saturdays.

Enzedbeecee has a much-admired ninety-piece symphony orchestra, which broadcasts and also plays in concert halls all over the country. The New Zealand Ballet Company and the New Zealand Opera Company, both government subsidized, also play to the whole country and pull enthusiastic full houses. The theater is mainly amateur, but well attended.

New Zealand has had any number of competent male writers, but the internationally notable aspect of the country's literature is its domination by women. Katherine Mansfield was a master of the short story; Ngaio Marsh is a ranking writer of detective stories; Janet Frame plants broad themes of tragedy in a New Zealand setting; and Sylvia Ashton-Warner has won over the world with her poetic, moving, and touchingly funny novels, such as *Spinster*.

New Zealanders take their sports obsessively, and with approximately equal dedication to watching and participating. Rugby football is virtually the private property of New Zealanders, whose revered All Blacks won fifteen straight annual "Tests" with the few other nations that play this occult game (Australia, France, South Africa, and Britain). The other big spectator draw is horse racing, not only galloping but also trotting and pacing. This little country has five thousand brood mares, producing stock so good that one horse was recently sold to some Americans for a reported one million dollars. But when New Zealanders aren't watching, they're doing. What they do best is fish for trout, which are plenteous; climb mountains, which are also plenteous; and sail in the beautiful bays. They also have a special thing about camping.

*

There is abroad in the world today, particularly in the United States, a dark frustration, a feeling that the quality of life is deteriorating and progress is illusory. In most U.S. cities, safety, civility, standards of all kinds, decline in spite of the speeches and promises of the politicians. The citizenry despairs, frustrated by the vast immobility of an overgrown system. Perhaps a summary judgment of New Zealand is that it is happily free of this curse. Probably because of its smallness, government does respond to the people's needs. The individual is protected. People are not afraid. Land tenure is well handled. Taxes are high, but used in ways that are visibly beneficial, or at least not destructive.

New Zealand: you would not think you'd want to live there, down at the bottom of the world, twenty tiresome hours by jet from Kennedy Airport. But if you did live there, you might enjoy it hugely.

CHAPTER 24

How Australasia Fits with Asia

Australia is anchored off Asia and cannot be towed away, no matter how awkward its Asian neighbors may become.
—PROFESSOR J. D. B. MILLER

WITHIN RECENT MEMORY, Australia and New Zealand were essentially detached parts of Europe, filially linked to England by blood and loyalty and the teak-decked vessels of the P. & O. Line and the New Zealand Shipping Company. Asia might be physically on the doorstep, but in the Australasian public consciousness it was as remote as Venus. Then Japan, hungry for resources and markets, decided in 1941 to incorporate Australasia by war into the Greater East Asia Co-Prosperity Sphere (as Japan euphemistically called its plan of conquest). The might of England, based in Singapore, crumbled in a few moments. The might of the United States, assembled with panicky speed in the Coral Sea, rescued Australia and New Zealand from certain invasion. After the war India, Pakistan, and Burma opted to become republics. China, for decades dismissed as a famine surrounded by Western exploiters, emerged as a heavy, hostile, Communist power, with atomic bombs and a population on the order of fifty times that of Australasia—all not much farther away than the distance between Sydney and Perth. Dienbienphu fell. Then the revived Japanese economy proceeded to buy Australasian produce in gulps so voracious that Australians nowadays ruefully refer to their country as "the Japanese quarry." Nice irony here—the defeated Japanese gained after defeat a good deal of what they set out to achieve by war. Finally, the United States failed to win the war in Indochina, raising Australasian fears that American power in 1971 was no more reliable than English power in 1941. Is an attack on Australasia still equivalent, in the U.S. view, to an attack on Ohio, as Walter Lippmann once put it?

So now Australia and New Zealand look to England from a position less daughterly than cousinly, and to the United States with gratitude for past favors tainted by doubts about whether the United States can be, or even wants to be, a stout ally. And they view Asia, large and close and omnipresent, with fascination, apprehension, and a good deal of incomprehension. These two countries share geography with Asia and history with Europe, and they sense an urgent problem of deciding how the twain shall be made to meet.

*

Australia's navy still sails "Her Majesty's Australian Ships," and New Zealand has a "Royal New Zealand Air Force," but the process of separation from Britain—begun with federation in 1901 for Australia, and with Dominion status for New Zealand in 1907—is now virtually complete. Way back in 1919, Australian Prime Minister William M. Hughes asserted his country's independence from Britain, demanding, "What is there that we cannot do?"; the same year New Zealand independently signed the Charter of the League of Nations.

The hard ties that remain are in trade and investment. The United Kingdom buys $400 million worth of Australian wool, meat, grain, fruit, sugar, and ores per year, and sells Australia $700 million-plus worth of machinery, electrical equipment, vehicles, and chemicals. These figures amount to about one-seventh of Australia's exports and one-fifth of its imports—which is, of course, a steep decline from decades past when the U.K. was Australia's major supplier and customer. From New Zealand the U.K. buys $380 million worth of lambs, wool, and butter, and to New Zealand it sells $208 million worth of cars and assorted manufactures, thus holding its traditional position as most important trader both ways. As we have seen, Britain, upon entering the European Common Market, will eventually cut its purchases of New Zealand lamb and dairy products. Yet the British still control almost half of overseas investment in Australia, and a great deal in New Zealand.

The relationship between Australia–New Zealand and the United States has always been a pretty easy one. World War II, drawing hundreds of thousands of American G.I.s to Australian staging bases, produced a generation of Americans half in love with Australia. American history and geography are well known in both countries. The Brisbane *Courier Mail* runs a quote from Jefferson on its masthead; ordinary Australians and New Zealanders speak of U.S. states and cities as familiarly as they do of their own. There is a closeness based on the three countries' similarities as former British colonies built largely by people of British stock.

When Australia and New Zealand initiated and signed the 1951 ANZUS (Australia–New Zealand–United States) treaty for mutual defense in the Pacific, they pointedly shunned British participation. It was, in fact, the first pact ever negotiated between members of the British Commonwealth and a foreign power. Americans may not think about ANZUS very often, but it has been a sort of religion down-under. "ANZUS is critically important to us because it contains a formal recognition by the U.S. that an armed attack upon Australia or its territories or its defense forces would be dangerous to the United States' own peace and safety," says Australia's former Foreign Affairs Minister Leslie Bury. A concept often evoked in these two nations is that the U.S. is a "Pacific country," as, of course, they themselves are. New Zealanders are quite capable of quipping that their country is "the fifty-first state," while realistically recognizing that New Zealand is not indispensable to the U.S. An Australian official says, "There is very little feeling that the U.S. is Big Brother, breathing down our necks."

Trade with the United States is a strong link, too. U.S. purchases from Australia, chiefly beef, run to more than $500 million a year, and its exports to Australia (transport equipment, machinery, chemicals) are more than $1 billion. Trading with New Zealand, the U.S. imports wool, meat, and other products worth something under $200 million, and exports airplanes, tobacco, chemicals, computers, and so on, worth about $75 million. American investment there is relatively low.

The Vietnam war, by the time it wound down, had become a severe irritant in relations between the U.S. and Australia and New Zealand. The troops they had sent to fight there represented, in bald terms, an IOU cashed by Washington for past and future protection—or, as one radio commentator put it, the two countries "sacrificed twenty-year-olds as an insurance premium to the American alliance." The Prime Ministers of Australia and New Zealand, paying the premium, had to follow the U.S. lead at every twist and turn of the war, while, for domestic consumption, they tried to make it appear that the initiatives were theirs, or at least that they were amply "consulted" by Washington. When the U.S. escalated, so did they. Former Prime Minister Harold Holt allied himself strongly with President Johnson, and when Johnson renounced his job (and, implicitly, his faith in his policy), the Australian government was left with egg on its face. President Nixon's decision to begin pulling U.S. troops out of Indochina forced Australian and New Zealand leaders to mumble that they just happened to be planning to do the same thing.

Beyond that, the two governments try to weigh the extent to which the U.S. pullout leaves them vulnerable to Communist China—or even, should history repeat itself, to Japan. In January 1970, Vice President Spiro Agnew went to Australia and New Zealand, and tried to reassure both countries that "the United States will keep its treaty commitments. Our policy is neither one of gradual withdrawal from Asia nor of unwarranted intervention in Asian affairs."

Relations with Washington are the No. 1 concern of the foreign affairs departments of both countries. And both have been run for many years by parties that represent rightist, pro-American positions. They suffer assorted slings and arrows. Senator Fulbright says: "Both Australia and New Zealand have been rewarded with lavish praise and gratitude from the U.S. Gratitude for what? For making a tiny contribution to what they themselves consider their own defense."

The Brown-Skinned Neighbors

For a bunch of Anglo-Saxons like the Australians and New Zealanders, though, diplomacy with Britain and the United States is easy compared to relating to the neighbors. The near neighbors are friendly. Australia (fearing to do otherwise, lest it create a next-door enemy) helped Sukarno grab West Irian in 1962, and felt its judgment justified when the agreeable government of General Suharto replaced Sukarno. The Australians managed to remain quite unperturbed over the fact that Sukarno's ouster required the massacre of 300,000 Indonesian Communists and sympathizers.

The future nation of Niugini will doubtless be an Australian client state, and the new countries of the near South Pacific are amicable. Melanesian Fiji (population: 519,000—many of them, to be sure, Chinese and Indians) gets along passably well with partly Polynesian New Zealand, 1,149 miles away. So does Western Samoa. The stout little South Pacific nation of Nauru (area: 8 square miles; population: 6,500) seems favorably disposed to its large southern neighbors, at least until its mines of phosphate, exported to New Zealand for an average income of $6,000 per capita per annum, run out in 1990.

Malaysia and Singapore, sister members of the dissolving Commonwealth, are power bases land-linked to tumultuous Indochina. Britain, confessing its helplessness to sustain Singapore, virtually withdrew in 1971, and the United States, singed in Vietnam, would like to settle for monetary support only—namely, commitments to repair naval vessels in the Singapore dry-docks. It seems to be up to Australia and New Zealand to establish a credible medium-power presence there, both in a military way and as a Eurasian force for collaboration and sanity.

Then there is Japan, once mortal enemy, now foremost customer, third-largest industrial power of the world, harborer of vaulting ambitions, land of inscrutable yellow men who may want to emigrate to White Australia but on the other hand may be perfectly content to use it as a quarry. Just as enigmatic is the People's Republic of China, which may aspire to occupy Australia's empty spaces, or, conversely, may be a lucrative market for Australian goods. Many Australians visit China as tourists, and Australian ships call at Chinese ports. India, Pakistan, and Ceylon relate to Australia and New Zealand as fellow members of the Commonwealth, but they are more strongly inclined toward neutralism and have less critical attitudes toward Communism. There is envy, too, based on the unignorable fact that the Australians have been able to make so much out of their barren continent. As Australians helped India with the Pakistani refugee problem in mid-1971, one Indian official turned to an Australian aid administrator in Calcutta and blazed: "You bloody big white Australian. You bloody bastard. Get out of here. Damn your bloody big rich country for its great help." This was an irrational explosion, but it demonstrates one Indian attitude toward Australia.

Thus, since World War II, Australia has been drawn into Asia, partly by the opportunity to secure a measure of dominance, partly to be a helpful neighbor, partly as a half-thought-out "forward defense" strategy. The Far East, as Australians illogically refer to it, has become what it really is, the Near North. The Australian population build-up is a conscious response to the dangers of being an empty continent in crowded Asia. Government leaders and journalists increasingly visit Asian countries. The weekly *Bulletin* scrupulously covers Southeast Asia, Fiji, and the Philippines, in a department called "The Neighborhood," and prints a column called "This Week in Japan." The Australian diplomatic service is said to be doing a highly skilled job of reporting and representation in its Asian embassies, particularly Tokyo. The Sydney and Melbourne symphonies play in Asian capitals, and the seven short-wave stations of Radio Australia broadcast in Japanese, Malay, Mandarin, Thai, Indonesian, and Vietnamese.

Australia and New Zealand make such contributions as geodetic surveys for the Philippines, water systems for Vietnam, military training for Asian officers. Both also founded and take part in the Colombo Plan for economic aid: Australia spent $160 million up to June 1968, chiefly in Indonesia and

Pakistan, but also in such remote spots as Brunei, Nepal, and Bhutan. In fact, according to Prime Minister McMahon, Australia's foreign aid is proportionately higher than the United States'—.56 percent of the GNP as compared to .38 percent for the U.S. New Zealand, typically, ran dairy projects in Bombay and Dhulia in India. Both countries provide higher education for Asians; more than twelve thousand Asian students are regularly enrolled in Australian universities, and up to mid-1969 New Zealand had brought in 2,662 Asians for college educations under the Colombo Plan.* A criticism of this effort is that the Asians are often pushed into courses that are underenrolled rather than courses they want, and go home to unemployment because they are miseducated.

*

> *We Australians have been for long an unbearable collection of Pommies, but may now become a rather likable collection of second-rate Japanese.*
>
> —PROFESSOR GEOFFREY SAWER

Japan is a word that has popped up again and again in this book on Australia and New Zealand, chiefly as the engine of the Australian boom. Japan buys over one-fourth of what Australia exports, taking wool, iron ore, nickel, copper, bauxite, coal, grain, and meat. Australia, therefore, is greatly dependent on Japan—a thought that causes much wry comment. "It was bad enough being run by the Brits and the Americans," says an Australian journalist, "but at least we could talk to our bosses in English." Australia still has a higher standard of living than Japan, but the Japanese have better technology, and are thus in the position of being able to decide, for example, whether they will continue to import and then smelt Australian

* The regional organizations in this part of the world are confusing and overlapping. The Colombo Plan (so called because it was set up at a meeting in Colombo, the capital of Ceylon, in 1950) tries to do for non-Communist Asia roughly what the Alliance for Progress tries to do for Latin America. Members, besides eighteen Asian nations, are Australia, New Zealand, Canada, the United Kingdom, and the U.S. The South East Asian Treaty Organization (SEATO), which includes the United States, is the primary defense mechanism. The United Nations Economic Commission for Asia and the Far East (ECAFE), backed by the Asian Development Bank, undertakes such projects as the utilization of the waters of the Indus and Mekong rivers. The Asian and Pacific Council (ASPAC) promotes solidarity among Korea, Japan, Taiwan, the Philippines, Malaysia, Thailand, Australia and New Zealand. The Association of South East Asian Nations (ASEAN) is a consultative group which includes Thailand, Indonesia, Malaysia, Singapore, and the Philippines.

iron ore, or whether they will let the Australians handle part of this profitable business of making their own ore into steel.

Australian euphoria at every new billion-dollar contract with Japan is not quite enough to make the Australians *accept* the Japanese. The Australian National University in Canberra teaches the Japanese language, and so do some high schools, but only about eight hundred Australians are learning the language, nothing like as many as commerce demands. Back of all this is that old White Australia policy. High-ranking Japanese businessmen have to go through an elaborate procedure to get a visa to visit Australia, and as a rule those who settle there for business reasons are allowed to stay only three years. The bars are high enough so that at any given time only about seventeen hundred Japanese have residence permits. As of early 1971, only 717 Japanese had acquired Australian citizenship; by and large the Japanese may not emigrate to either Australia or New Zealand. These are powerful and poisonous ironies in what has been called "the first European country to be largely dependent on an Asian nation." The Japanese Ambassador in Canberra, Shizuo Saito, in a book published in Tokyo in mid-1971, criticized Australian immigration policy, and charged that the Australians are unwilling to have warm and friendly relations with the Japanese.

The volume of Japanese imports from Australia is huge and growing—from $470 million in 1966 to $1.1 billion in 1970. What Japan sells to Australia—cars, cameras, electronic goods, textiles, and machinery—amounts to only half of this sum, but the imbalance does not bother Japan. It has a big (if growingly reluctant) customer, the U.S., which buys more from Japan than it sells to Japan. To complete this triangular relationship, U.S. sales to Australia are double U.S. purchases from Australia. In short, the Americans give dollars to Japan for Toyotas and Sonys; then the Japanese give the dollars to Australia for wool and iron ore; then the Australians give the dollars back to the Americans for airplanes and computers—it works something like that. Japan is also important to New Zealand, as its third-biggest customer.

Besides buying Australian raw materials, the Japanese are increasingly investing in Australian ranching, mining, and manufacturing—zippers, TV sets, microwave equipment, ball bearings. They plan to push their investment stake from $120 million to $420 million, much of it in fifty-fifty deals with Australian companies—an arrangement more amenable to Australians than the branch-office operations that the English and Americans prefer. Partnership might ultimately reach diplomatic levels. With complementary economies, Australia and Japan have common interests in keeping Japanese exports high, and preserving favorable markets—which may indicate a need for a formal alliance.

Australasia in the South Pacific

Some characteristics of the smaller islands of Melanesia and Polynesia are these: their economies are mostly feeble; they are a drain on the treasuries of their parent nations, chiefly Britain, the U.S., New Zealand, and France; and from these indifferent parents they can all get (or have already got) autonomy (except for France's jealously held possessions). A widely accepted hypothesis is that Australia and New Zealand should take responsibility for the social and economic advancement of all these islands, except France's. As a matter of fact, the two countries already exercise an important stewardship. The currency of Nauru, for example, is Australian, and Australia controls 70 percent of the foreign investment in Fiji. New Zealand takes charge of the defense and international relations of the Cook Islands, and New Zealanders still staff many government departments there. New Zealand sends Niueans and Tokelau Islanders to medical, dental, nursing, and agriculture schools of the University of the South Pacific in Fiji. Various free-trade pacts are in force. Both Australia and New Zealand resist the immigration of islanders, for essentially racist reasons, but this at least spares the islands from being stripped of their most talented and ambitious people. The machinery for organizing the islands is the South Pacific Commission, created in 1947 by Australia, New Zealand, Britain, France, and the United States.

The Trans-Tasman Relationship

For more than a century, Australia and New Zealand had an amazing diplomatic relationship with one another: they talked only through their representatives in London. Not until mid-war, in 1943, did they exchange high commissioners. Now, according to former Prime Minister Holyoake, they are probably more intimately related than any two other governments in the world.

The two nations cannot trade in great volume, because many of their products—wool, meat, butter—are the same. Still, Australia manages to sell New Zealand around $160 million worth of cars, steel, medicine, gasoline, and chemicals every year, and New Zealand sells Australia around $75 million worth of newsprint, lumber, fish, and peas—all under a free-trade agreement. New Zealand was originally administered from the colony of New South Wales, and was once considered to be a possible member of the Australian federation—it even took a tentative part in talks that led to federation. As late as 1969 a cabinet minister in New Zealand had to rebut proponents of union with Australia. To people in other parts of the world (many of whom are so uninformed as to think that Australia and New Zealand *are* politically united), the advantages of union in facing the world might seem imperative. But most New Zealanders take tremendous pride in their country's independence, and simply won't hear of union. Besides, they think it would upset their delicately balanced system of subsidies and welfare. Australians don't seem to give the idea much thought at all. When Sir Keith Holyoake visited Canberra in 1970, he was rather conspicuously ignored by the Australian press and public.

Still, New Zealand often takes Australia's lead, and the two countries have been united since 1944 by the Anzac Agreement.* This rather vaguely pledges each to keep in close touch with the other, through a secretariat, on matters of regional interest.

Militarily Speaking

Anzac military policy is to assert the two countries' determination to defend themselves while realizing that the U.S. must provide the bulk of their protection. They know that they do not have the population to fend off a big attack, and hope that the U.S. will forever regard Australasia as a vital bastion of mutual defense.

The main strategic issue is "forward defense" versus "armed neutrality." "Forward" means Singapore and Malaysia. Anzac forces have been there ever since the British war against Communist guerrillas in Malaya in the 1950's, and for a long time they took the comfortable role of backing up Britain. In other words, forward defense *depended* on Britain—on British command. Then, in 1967 and 1968, Britain, overstrained, announced that it would pull out. Australia and New Zealand boldly declared that they would take over the military responsibility in that area, and they did. The boldness began to fade in 1969 when President Nixon proclaimed in his Guam Doctrine that the United States would try to coexist with Asian Communists after the Vietnam war ended. This seemed to leave the Anzacs alone in Singapore-Malaysia, not so much as a considered decision, but to plug the hole the British left. To put a good face on the matter, Australia, Britain, Malaysia, New Zealand, and Singapore invented yet another acronym, ANZUK, signifying a joint military force in Singapore-Malaysia that includes a submarine on rotation from Britain's Royal Navy.

* An extension of the earlier collaboration in the Australia–New Zealand Army Corps in World War I.

"Armed neutrality" amounts to withdrawal from forward bases in favor of a flexible, mobile force based, probably, in northern Australia. The Labor Party favors this approach. The essence of this strategy is that the home force could stop any small conventional attack; therefore an aggressor would have to attack in such force as to constitute a sizable war, and the U.S. would have no choice but to come to Australasia's aid. This is a posture of weakness, which probably cannot be helped given the two countries' small populations; it creates a sense of insecurity. Nowadays the alarming possibility is that in some major dispute Australia and New Zealand could become principals, instead of loyal little allies in Great Power conflicts. A variation of armed neutrality is the proposal for an Israeli-like semimilitary society, in which every citizen is a soldier; such a nation, though small in population, can be fearfully dangerous to attack. The difficulty with this approach is that it sacrifices the delights of the consumer society, and requires persuading people that they are living in a fool's paradise. Prime Minister Gorton toyed with this idea for a year, but dropped it in favor of "forward defense."

Toward these somewhat ambivalent defense goals, Australia, at least, has made a persistent effort in the 1960's to strengthen itself. The size of the services grew from 112,000 men to 133,000. The defense budget doubled in five years to $1.2 billion, 4.3 percent of the GNP. The first peacetime draft, for two-year terms of service, was begun in 1966. Russian interest in the Indian Ocean, evidenced by fleet maneuvers there, brought a strong Australian response. The navy spent $40 million for berths for submarines (it has three, with six on order) and escort vessels at Cockburn Sound, near the Northwest Cape. Here there is also an air force base, as well as the U.S. Navy communications station mentioned earlier.

The Australian Navy's largest vessel is the carrier *Melbourne*,* equipped with Skyhawks; there are also three guided-missile destroyers and a couple of dozen smaller ships. The Australian Air Force has Canberra bombers, 110 Mirage fighters, and numerous transports and trainers. In 1963 the air force ordered twenty-four American F-111s, but then backed away after eighteen such planes crashed in the U.S. Only late in 1971 did the government finally decide to accept the planes, and in the meantime the cost had risen from $229 million to $344 million. New Zealand's armed forces have four frigates, a squadron of Canberras, and a total of 13,000 men; $85

* This is the ship that sliced through an American destroyer, the *Frank Evans*, during night maneuvers in the South China Sea in June 1969, killing seventy-four American sailors. Two officers from the *Evans* were later court-martialed and convicted for negligence.

million a year, or 2 percent of the GNP (versus 2.3 in 1960), goes into defense. Men are subject to conscription, but draftees need serve only fourteen weeks.

Australia provides the real teeth for ANZUK: forty-two Mirages at Butterworth Air Force Base in Malaysia—nearly half of the troops in the command; New Zealand has some transport planes and a battalion there; and between them the two countries keep one naval ship in or around Singapore. When Australia committed troops to Vietnam, New Zealand felt obliged to commit a token force of 500, later raised to 750. Australia had three battalions of men in Vietnam. Both countries have now withdrawn all of their combat troops; Australian losses in the war were 487 dead and 3,000 wounded. By fighting in Vietnam, incidentally, both countries were involved for the first time in a war not entered on Britain's behalf.

*

To pull the threads together, Australia and New Zealand seem to be increasingly responsible in an area of decreasing danger. The struggle in South Vietnam taught the U.S. the perils of getting mired in distant guerrilla wars, and neither Australia nor New Zealand, as American allies, would repeat the experience. But the domino theory of Communist encroachment on Australasia has been somewhat discredited, and the danger from China, which worried Australasians for so long, now seems more clearly to be a factor of the Russia–China–United States equation. The United States pullback will leave Australasia more exposed but freer to aid and protect Southeast Asia. Yet the United States will keep its base in Guam and its attachments to Korea, Japan, the Pacific Islands Terrritory, and Australia and New Zealand themselves—in short, it will not disappear from Asia. Japan may develop a foreign policy aimed at Asian stability, and Australia and New Zealand will benefit both from the lead that Japan may give and from the possibility of allying themselves in some way to it. Two factors will give Australia and New Zealand new responsibilities and opportunities in the Pacific area: the end of their adolescent dependence on Britain and the United States, and the inevitable termination of colonial relationships throughout the Pacific islands. The two nations will remain relatively helpless, simply from lack of population, but they should be able to work more effectively in their Asian environment, and worry less about the possible perils it contains.

CHAPTER 25

Some Thoughts in Conclusion

If you are looking for the Utopia of the 20th Century, it is there Down Under.

—ASIA MAGAZINE

AUSTRALIANS are knockers and scoffers, and when the poet Robert Heanley speaks of them as a people who will prove to be "a living bridge between east and west," by and large they find such talk a pretty piece of nonsensical idealism. Yet—to repeat and emphasize a point touched upon often in this book—the major fact of present-day Australasian life is that two historically British nations have been forced by geography to become political and sociological parts of the vast and varied Asian and Pacific region. This represents not only a belated abandonment of pro-British snobbery, and an equally belated recognition of the possibilities that the neighborhood affords Australia and New Zealand; it is also an acknowledgment of the brute fact that Europe, specifically the European Economic Community, is casting Australasia out of its trade arrangements. Australasia is being both pushed and pulled into Asia. The consequences will transform both countries.

1. Economically, the link to Japan can only grow closer. What is not clearly realized in much of the world is that Australian prosperity is now a component part of Japanese prosperity; the two nations have common interests—such as opposing U.S. barriers to the importation of Japanese goods—that could lead to a formal alliance. As a consequence of this tight link Japan would react to Australia in three ways: by selling Australia more goods, such as the heavy machinery that now comes from England, by investing more in Australia, and by sharing its great technological resources with Australia. This sharing would mean more intensive processing of Aus-

tralia's raw materials before they are shipped to Japan. If the European Economic Community takes away from Australasia its English market for butter and meat, the certain result will be termination of the trade preference that both nations have always extended to Great Britain.

2. Politically, closer ties to Asian neighbors should have the effect of making Australasia less defensive—literally. The emphasis in foreign policy will shift from the military to trade and aid. If China becomes more of a market, it should be less of a threat. Perhaps in collaboration with Japan, Australia and New Zealand will feel obliged to reduce the stunning contrast between their wealth and the poverty of Indonesia and some of the Pacific islands. The three nations have the means and technology to help in development and education on a scale much bigger than at present. Indonesia and Australia, in particular, have an existing friendship not necessarily to be expected from nations of their sharply contrasting cultures.

3. Sociologically, the White Australia policy must eventually go by the boards. Beyond a doubt the Japanese will politely but insistently press for treatment equal to that accorded to Englishmen. Japan's pollution alone may drive the Japanese to emigrate, and it is also quite possible that Australia may find itself pleading for skilled Japanese immigrants. Australia, if not New Zealand, may also become desirous of its share of the stream of skilled and educated Filipinos who presently emigrate in droves to the United States and Canada. What should become clear to Australians is that the greatly increased immigration of Japanese, Hong Kong Chinese, Filipinos, Indians, Pakistanis, American Negroes, and so on will not trouble, but rather enrich, a nation where currently only one person in one hundred is not white. Closer relations to the various kinds of Asians will also require changes in Australasian education, specifically much more teaching of Japanese and other languages.

*

Are these prospective developments a little too visionary? Is Australia (plus, in a lesser role, New Zealand) ready to be a catalyst as well as a junior partner to Japan and a senior partner to her poverty-ridden neighbors?

To judge from their politicians, the answer is "not yet." Australia's cautious Prime Minister McMahon seems to want to steer clear of possibly dangerous adventures. The opposition Labor Party, partly inspired by the Ping-Pong initiative of the Chinese in April 1971, but also reflecting a traditional Labor position, proposed that Australia recognize Peking and help it get a seat in the United Nations. Mr. McMahon replied that Australia's "major objective" was to keep Taiwan in the United Nations, and that recognition of China was not a paramount concern. McMahon thus shared with Nixon the rebuff delivered by most of the world's nations when they cast Taiwan out of the United Nations as part of the process of admitting the People's Republic. He was still holding basically to something resembling the old domino theory, contending that China's ideology is the promotion of people's revolutions, and that if relations with China became relaxed or friendly, Australia might ultimately be left surrounded by Communist nations.

The bulk of Australians would seem to be with the Prime Minister, fearful of China and Communism generally. Here, however, we get back to the Australian character, and particularly to a strange aspect of it. One civil servant who has profoundly studied his fellow citizens feels that Australians have a deep-seated fear that the European occupation of Australia will be only momentary, that tomorrow they could be pushed into the sea, that their domain cannot be expected to last, that they are essentially alien to this continent—it was never in the cards for them to stay. This philosophy, if indeed widespread, might make Australia an easy conquest. On the other hand, instead of reinforcing the White Australia policy, it might encourage Australians to collaborate with their neighbors. They would be good at it if they really tried because white Australians relate easily, even enthusiastically, to dark-skinned immigrants on a one-to-one basis. The trouble has not been racial, but the fear of being engulfed.

Joining Asia will have to involve, most importantly, recognition of the People's Republic of China. The grounds for fearing China are certainly not unreasonable. But the reality of the Chinese threat has to be weighed off against the benefits of getting along better. It is also to be argued that even if Communist China is the most apparent threat, there is little point in relatively weak nations like Australia and New Zealand making a show of belligerence at a moment when Britain has withdrawn protection and the United States is lowering its level of commitment in Asia. Over and over in Australia one hears the questions, "How far would the U.S. go to protect us? Would it get into a major war for us?" Many Australians think not.

Moreover, neutralist and nonaligned nations in Southeast Asia might concede Australia and New Zealand a little more scope for leadership if the two took a less suspicious stance. Australia has been criticized by a newspaper in Thailand for creating "the impression that the basis of Australia's relations with the Asian region is apprehension and unease"; critics of present policy argue that this should not be the case. Some Australasians find it difficult to square the tough anti-Communist pacts, ANZUS and SEATO, with the Australian–New Zealand need to be a closer neighbor to Asia.

In New Zealand, criticism of the big-power alliance policy takes another twist. This most remote nation, it is argued, should assume that it is of very little interest to possible aggressors, and adopt a Swiss-style policy of nonalignment. This would mean weaker ties to Australia and recognition of China, and might clear the way to sales of meat, butter, and wool to the Communist nations of Eastern Europe, and to Russia, when England stops buying these commodities.

Despite political caution and the ordinary man's reluctance, the overriding fact is that the forces of economics in Japan and Europe have pushed Australia and New Zealand into an unpredictable multiple marriage with the countries on and near the Asian continent. They are, by virtue of possessing economies several times stronger than those of their near neighbors put together, the natural fount of leadership in this sea of brown and yellow faces.

*

Australians and New Zealanders, we are repeatedly told, do not hold their own cultures in high regard; things are done better "overseas," they say, and what is well done at home was really not worth doing in the first place. Many Australians believe, with the English writer James Morris, that their country's origins are unsavory, its history disagreeable, its suburbs hideous, its politics crooked, its buildings plain, its people's voices rasping, and its art movement spurious. The world originates, and Australia and New Zealand follow. As a general observation, they do lag behind the United States in attitudes and concerns by somewhere between two and twelve years; an American senses something of the Eisenhower era in present-day Australia. This lag implies a nation not in a rage, not frustrated, not angry (at least yet), a nation that still sets a slower pace and avoids widespread dissension, a nation that can still afford complacency and reserves ample time for play—to this extent the lag is a blessing; may the future never arrive!

But in point of fact, Australians and New Zealanders should be happy for reasons better than merely not being in the plight of the U.S. The more positive reasons for national satisfaction are the genuine accomplishments of both countries. What an achievement, for example, the full-employment economy is. This is a system that values what human beings do, and assures them of a chance to do it. So much needs to be done that labor must be imported, and the newly arrived labor creates needs for still more to be done. Obviously, these economies, particularly New Zealand's, may stumble, but they will always be better for being guided by the national determination that a man or a woman can train for a job and then *get* a job. Moreover, the availability of work is probably related to the low rate of crime. Fewer homicides are committed in all of Australia in a typical year (the rate runs around two hundred or less) than in Atlanta alone, or Baltimore, or Dallas—and much fewer than New York City, which has nearly two thousand.

Another achievement (and how the social critics of Australia and New Zealand will dispute this one!) is suburbia. Granted that the suburbs of Melbourne and Sydney are too extensive and monotonous, granted that new cities should be created before allowing these monsters to get bigger, granted that the "mod-cons" (modern-construction houses) are banal, granted that suburban life may be bound by television, gossip, and high-interest mortgages—it is nevertheless a respectable accomplishment to have two nations housed this well. Not much can be said against a garden unless it becomes a total obsession. A house is, by and large, likely to be a better place to live in than an apartment. And unlike the United States, Australia and New Zealand do not have painful contrasts between suburbs for the rich and center-city slums for the poor. The two countries have few rich, few poor, and few slums. In the 1960's, when Australia attempted to imitate the United States in a war on poverty, only 8 percent of the population met standards of poorness that applied to 20 percent of the people of the United States.

More broadly, the world must respect Australia, and perhaps New Zealand even more so, as places where one of humanity's most ancient ideals, democracy, manages to function better than in most of the rest of the globe. The leaders do not get assassinated; the streets are not full of tumult. Small population, no doubt, has a lot to do with this; a man can reach the politician who represents him. The average Australian or New Zealander does not delude himself that he can affect the course of the world, and the world may eventually snuff out his dreams. But in the operation of his own country, he still feels that he has at least a slender grip on the handle of his own fate.

Acknowledgments and Bibliography

If John Gunther had settled down to write these acknowledgments, he would, I do not doubt, have thumbed through the record he kept of persons interviewed, and after that he would have run an eye along his shelves of books about Australia and New Zealand. Then he would have been forced to conclude that this book is in debt to more people than it is possible to list. For example, the number of persons he talked with, each of whom contributed a greater or lesser part of the book, is five hundred and five. This does not include hundreds of other informed people whom he met briefly on social occasions or in the course of travel. The books and booklets that Gunther and I collected add up to almost two hundred. So I will start this, as Gunther might have, with gratitude to the contributors of the facts and insights of which the book is made—and despair over how to do justice to them all.

Sir Patrick Shaw, who headed the Australian delegation at the United Nations when the Gunthers started their trip, and John V. Scott, the New Zealand Ambassador to the United Nations, sent them off with full and lucid briefings, introductions to figures high in government, and excellent advice about other people whom they might consult. Thanks must be extended to the members of the government in both Australia and New Zealand who gave interviews to the Gunthers, the Governors of the states of Australia, the United States Ambassadors to both countries, and the various United States Consuls who were hospitable and informative. Without the invaluable help of all these people this book would never have been written.

To greet the Gunthers on arrival was Anthony Paul, then editor-in-chief in Australia for the *Reader's Digest*, a magazine with which Gunther had enjoyed a close association for many years and which published an article by him about Australia. Mr. Paul put the resources of the *Digest* in Sydney at their disposal, introduced them to his colleagues all over Australia, and gave them welcome hospitality. Mrs. Bryce Fraser, a member of Mr. Paul's staff in Sydney, was exceedingly helpful, and Alex Freeleagus in Brisbane, John Bulbeck in Western Australia, John Bennetts in Canberra, Lindsay Ellis in Darwin and Alice Springs, and Peter Cole-Adams in Melbourne were of invaluable assistance.

Sir Colin Syme, chairman of the board of Broken Hill Proprietary, opened doors for the Gunthers in Melbourne and in the whole mining world. John Dorrance, then second secretary of the American Embassy in Canberra, shared the insights he had gained from his experience and study of New Guinea. In New Zealand, Paul Tipping of the Department of External Affairs accompanied the Gunthers on all their travels, smoothing the way and providing information in the process. In New Guinea, the man who helped Gunther most was his namesake (but no relation), John Gunther, Vice Chancellor of the University of Papua and New Guinea (a "most glorious human being," in Jane Gunther's words), who briefed them, arranged interviews, laid out an itinerary, and provided many contacts there and in Australia. A chance meeting at an airport put the Gunthers in touch with Captain Percival Trezise, a pilot and, more relevantly to the author's purpose, a man interested in and knowledgeable about the Aborigines.

A few others must be singled out: some because their discourse with Gunther (or with me) ranged helpfully beyond the set scope of an interview; others because they provided the kind of hospitality that allows the outsider to see a little distance inside the society he is studying; still others because they supplied information for substantial parts of this book. These benefactors include Donald Horne, John Pringle, Geoffrey Dutton, Lady Lloyd-Jones, Mrs. Edna Ayres, Miss Sheila Scotter, Mrs. Ronald Stewart, Sir Keith Park, Sir James Plimpsoll, W. C. Wentworth, Thomas Larkin, George T. Walker, Luke Hazlett, Sir Frank and Lady Packer, and Clem Jones.

Quite a few of those mentioned in the preceding paragraphs, having been interviewed by Gunther, were kind enough to see me too when, later, my wife and I toured Australia, and I talked to at least another fifty people. I want to express a special indebtedness to my wife Deborah for sensitive reporting and observation while we were in Australia and New Zealand, for criticism of the manuscript that forfended some egregious errors, and for creating an atmosphere propitious for writing. Another Forbis, a distant cousin unknown to me until I met him in Auckland, also helped. He turned out to be a professional journalist, and much of the material in the chapters on New Zealand is the result of a happy collaboration with John Forbis, who supplied many of the facts and verified others. In Australia, assistance of this kind was ably given by Geraldine Kirshenbaum, a skilled researcher formerly with *Time* magazine. Margaret Butterfield, a Harper editor, helped tighten and shape the book, and the meticulous eye of Richard Passmore, another Harper editor, caught many redundancies, contradictions, solecisms, and other mistakes.

For certain verses used in this book, printed with permission of the copyright owners, I would like to thank: (1) Angus and Robertson Pty. Ltd. and author A. B. Paterson for lines from "Waltzing Matilda" (on page 6), taken from *The Collected Verse of A. B. Paterson.* (2) Ure Smith Pty. Ltd. and Ronald M. Berndt, Professor of Anthropology at the University of Western Australia, for his translation of the verse beginning "Up and up soars the Evening Star" (on page 77), taken from *The World of the First Australians,* by Professor Berndt and Catherine H. Berndt. (3) Hill of Content Publishing Co. for a couple of lines from "Jim Jones" (on page 18) and a verse of "Herbert Hoover's Love Song" (on page 204), taken from *Great Australian Folk Songs,* collected by John Lahey. (4) The Viking Press for two lines from "The Arctic Ox (or Goat)" (on page 119), from *O to Be a Dragon,* by Marianne Moore. Copyright © 1958 by Marianne Moore. First appeared in *The New Yorker,* 1958. (5) The Department of External Territories for the lines beginning "Hark and behold" by A. P. Allan Natachee (on page 264). (6) The Estate of A. R. D. Fairburn for a quotation from "Conversation in the Bush" (on page 290), published by Penguin Books.

By way of bibliography, a number of books were significantly helpful in providing background knowledge about physical characteristics, history, politics, sociology, and culture. The principal over-all reference works used were the *Australian Encyclopaedia* (ten volumes, Angus and Robertson, Sydney, and Michigan State University Press, Lansing, 1958), Osmar White's *Guide to Australia* (Heinemann, Melbourne, 1968), *Yearbook Australia 1969* (Commonwealth Bureau of Census and Statistics, Canberra), *New Zealand Official Yearbook 1970* (Department of Statistics, Wellington), *Australian Handbook 1971* and *Australian Facts and Figures* (Australian News and Information Bureau, Canberra), the *Encyclopaedia Britannica*, and the *World Almanac 1971* (Newspaper Enterprise Association, New York).

A number of periodicals and newspapers were essential sources of information. Among them the *Bulletin* and the *Sunday Australian*, as well as Robert Trumbull's dispatches in the *New York Times*, provided up-to-date news, as did the *Australian Weekly News*, published in San Francisco. Equally indispensable were the many articles and news stories which had appeared in recent years in literally dozens of newspapers and periodicals, both English and American. Much useful information was also obtained from pamphlets, guidebooks, speeches, and brochures.

Listed below are most of the books which John Gunther and I enjoyed and found useful:

AUSTRALIA

Abbie, A. A. *The Original Australians*. Reed, Sydney, 1970.

Australian Economy, The. The Treasury, Canberra, 1970.

Baker, Sidney J. *The Australian Language*. Sun Books, Melbourne, 1970.

Bergamini, David. *The Land and Wildlife of Australia*. Life Nature Library, New York, 1964.

Berndt, Ronald M. and Catherine H. *The World of the First Australians*. Ure Smith, Sydney, 1968.

Blainey, Geoffrey. *The Rise of Broken Hill*. Macmillan of Australia, South Melbourne, 1968.

———. *The Tyranny of Distance*. Sun Books, Melbourne, 1966.

Boyd, Robin. *The New Architecture*. Longmans, Croyden, Victoria, 1963.

Brash, Donald T. *American Investment in Australian Industry*. Australian National University Press, Canberra.

Clemens, Samuel Langhorne. *Following the Equator*. Harper & Bros., 1899.

Clifford, Beverley, and Barbara Richards. *More Than a Harbor*. Murray, Sydney and Melbourne, 1969.

Cobley, John. *The Crimes of the First Fleet Convicts*. Australian National University Press, Canberra, 1970.

Commonwealth Electoral Law. Chief Electoral Office, Canberra, 1966.

Commonwealth Scientific and Industrial Research Organization, *Annual Report*, 1968–69.

Coulls, A. "Charles Rasp, Founder of Broken Hill." Unpublished paper, 1952.

Covell, Roger. *Australia's Music*. Sun Books, Melbourne, 1967.

Crawford, R. M. *Australia*. Hutchinson University Library, London, 1952.

Darwin, Charles. *The Voyage of the Beagle*. P. F. Collier & Son, New York, 1909.

Davies, A. F., and S. Encel (eds.). *Australian Society: A Sociological Introduction*. Atherton Press, New York, 1964.

Durrell, Gerald. *Two in the Bush*. Collins, London, 1966.

Elkin, A. P. *The Australian Aborigines*. Anchor Books, Garden City, New York, 1964.

Establishing a Business in Australia. Bank of New South Wales, Sydney, 1968.

Farwell, George. *Around Australia on Highway One*. Nelson, Melbourne and Sydney, 1966.

Finemore, Brian. *Painting*. Longmans, Croyden, Victoria, 1961.

Gordon, Richard (ed.). *The Australian New Left*. Heinemann, Melbourne, 1970.

Gritscher, Helmut, and Craig McGregor. *To Sydney with Love*. Nelson, Melbourne, 1968.

Hallows, John. *The Dreamtime Society*. Collins, Sydney, 1970.

Hancock, Sir W. Keith. *Australia*. Tri-Ocean, 2nd ed., 1930.

Harvey, Frank R. *Theatre*. Longmans, Croyden, Victoria, 1965.

Herman, Morton. *Early Colonial Architecture*. Longmans, Croyden, Victoria, 1963.

Hood, Kenneth. *Pottery*. Longmans, Croyden, Victoria, 1961.

Hope, A. D. *Selected Poems*. Angus and Robertson, Sydney, 1963.

Horne, Donald. *The Lucky Country*. Penguin, 2nd rev. ed., Ringwood, Victoria, 1968.

———. *The Next Australia*. Angus and Robertson, Sydney, 1970.

Howitt, Alfred William. *The Native Tribes of Southeast Australia*. Macmillan, London, 1904.

Hughes, Robert. *The Art of Australia*. Penguin, Harmondsworth, England, 1970.

Huxley, Elspeth. *Their Shining Eldorado*. William Morrow, New York, 1967.

Idriess, Ion L. *The Cattle King*. Angus and Robertson, Pacific Books, Sydney, reprinted 1967.

Kaberry, Phyllis. *Aboriginal Women Sacred and Profane*. Blakiston, Philadelphia, 1939.

Keesing, Nancy (ed.). *Transition*. Angus and Robertson, Sydney, 1970.

King, Philip Parker. *Survey of Australia 1818–1822*. Reproduced by the Libraries Board of South Australia, Murray, London, 1969.

Knorr, Hilde and Hans. *Religious Art in Australia*. Longmans, Croyden, Victoria, 1967.

Lauder, Afferbeck. *Let Stalk Strine*. Ure Smith, Sydney.

———. *Nose Tone Unturned*. Ure Smith, Sydney, 1966.

Lawrence, D. H. *Kangaroo*. Penguin ed., Harmondsworth, England, 1968.

William Light. Libraries Board of South Australia, 1966.

Luck, R. K. *Modern Australian Painting*. Sun Books, Melbourne, 1969.

McGregor, Craig. *Profile of Australia*. Henry Regnery, Chicago, 1967.

Melville, Robert. *The Legend of Ned Kelly*, with paintings by Sidney Nolan. Viking Press, New York, 1964.

Miller, J. D. B. *Australian Government and Politics*. Duckworth, London, 1959.

Moorehead, Alan. *Cooper's Creek*. Harper & Row, New York, 1963.

———. *The Fatal Impact*. Harper & Row, New York, 1966.

Mountford, Charles P. *Aboriginal Art*. Longmans, Croyden, Victoria, 1961.

Mulvaney, Derek John. *The Prehistory of Australia*. Praeger, New York, 1969.

Murphy, D. F. *The Australian Wine Guide*. Sun Books, Melbourne, 1966.

O'Grady, John. *Aussie English*. Ure Smith, Sydney, 1969.

Parr, Lenton. *Sculpture*. Longmans, Croyden, Victoria, 1961.

Pearl, Cyril. *Beer, Glorious Beer!* Nelson, Melbourne and Sydney, 1969.
———. *So, You Want to Be an Australian.* Ure Smith, London, 1968.
Perkins, Kevin. *Menzies, Last of the Queen's Men.* Rigby Limited, Adelaide, 1968.
Pike, Douglas, *Australia: The Quiet Continent.* Cambridge University Press, Cambridge, 1970.
Preston, Richard (ed.). *Contemporary Australia: Studies in History, Politics and Economics.* Duke University Press, Durham, 1969.
Pringle, John Douglas. *Australian Accent.* Chatto & Windus, London, 1965.
Reed, John. *Australian Landscape Painting.* Longmans, Croyden, Victoria, 1965.
Rivett, Rohan. *Australia.* Oxford University Press, Melbourne, 1968.
Scott, Ernest. *Australian Discovery by Sea.* Vol. I, J. M. Dent & Sons, London, 1929.
———. *Australian Discovery by Land.* Vol. II, J. M. Dent & Sons, London, 1929.
Seidel, Brian. *Printmaking.* Longmans, Croyden, Victoria, 1965.
Shaw, A. G. L. *The Story of Australia.* Faber & Faber, London, 1966.
Snowy Mountains of Australia, The. Nucolorvue Productions, Mentone, Victoria, nd.
Splatt, W. J. *Architecture.* Longmans, Croyden, Victoria, 1962.
Trollope, Anthony. *Australia.* Republished by the University of Queensland Press, Brisbane, 1965.
Turner, Ian. *The Australian Dream.* Sun Books, Melbourne, 1968.
Van Sommers, Tess, and Unk White. *Sydney Sketchbook.* Rigby Limited, Adelaide, 1965.
Ward, Russell. *The Australian Legend.* Oxford University Press, Melbourne, 1966.
———. *Australia.* Walkabout Pocketbooks, London, 1969.
White, Patrick. *The Vivisector.* Jonathan Cape, London, 1970.
———. *Voss.* Longmans, London, 1965.
Whittington, Don, and Bob Chalmer. *Inside Canberra.* Rigby Limited, Kent Town, S.A., 1971.
Wright, Judith. *Selected Poems.* Angus and Robertson, Sydney, 1963.
Younger, R. M. *Australia and the Australians.* Rigby Limited, Adelaide, 1970.

NEW GUINEA

Bjerre, Jens. *The Last Cannibals.* Michael Joseph, London, 1956.
Blackwood, Beatrice. *The Technology of Modern Stone Age People in New Guinea.* Oxford University Press, Oxford, 1950.
Champion, Ivan F. *Across New Guinea from the Fly to the Sepik.* Landsoune, Melbourne, revised 1966.
Clune, Frank. *Prowling Through Papua.* Angus and Robertson, Sydney, 1948.
Davies, Donald M. *Journey into the Stone Age.* Robert Hale, London, 1969.
Durack, Elizabeth. *Face Value.* Ure Smith, Sydney, 1970.
Essai, Brian. *Papua and New Guinea: A Contemporary Survey.* Oxford University Press, Melbourne, 1961.
Fiske, E. K. (ed.). *New Guinea on the Threshold.* Australian National University Press, Canberra, 1966.
Handbook of Papua and New Guinea. Jacaranda Press, Brisbane, 1969.
Hastings, Peter. *New Guinea, Problems and Prospects.* Cheshire, Melbourne, 1969.
Lea, D. A. M., and P. G. Irwin. *New Guinea: The Territory and Its People,* Oxford University Press, Melbourne, 1967.

Mallord, Ann. *A Traveller's Guide to Papua New Guinea.* Jacaranda Press, Milton, Queensland, 1969.
Murray, Sir Hubert. *Papua of Today.* P. S. King & Son, Westminster, 1925.
Price, Sir A. Grenfell. *The Challenge of New Guinea.* Angus and Robertson, London, 1965.
Ruhen, Olaf. *Mountains in the Clouds.* Rigby Limited, Adelaide, 1963.
Ryan, John. *The Hot Land.* Macmillan of Australia, South Melbourne, 1969.
Salisbury, R. F. *From Stone to Steel.* Cambridge University Press, Cambridge, 1962.
Simpson, Colin. *Adam with Arrows.* Praeger, New York, 1968.
Souter, Gavin. *New Guinea, the Last Unknown.* Angus and Robertson, London, 1964.
White, Osmar. *Parliament of a Thousand Tribes.* Heinemann, London, 1965.
Williams, Maslyn. *In One Lifetime.* Cheshire, Melbourne, 1970.

NEW ZEALAND

Armstrong, Ala. *Say It in Maori.* Seven Seas, Wellington, 1968.
Ashton-Warner, Sylvia. *Bell Call.* Simon and Schuster, New York, 1964.
———. *Spinster.* Simon and Schuster, New York, 1959.
Bigwood, Kenneth and Jean. *New Zealand in Color,* Vols. I and II. A. H. and A. W. Reed, Wellington, 1961 and 1962.
Brewer, Ian H. *Te Rauparaha.* R. E. Owen, Government Printer, Wellington, 1966.
Brown, Gordon, and Hamish Keith. *New Zealand Painting: An Introduction.* Collins, London and Auckland, 1969.
Buck, Sir Peter Henry. *Vikings of the Pacific.* University of Chicago Press, Chicago, 1959.
Cape, Peter. *Artists and Craftsmen in New Zealand.* Collins, Auckland and London, 1969.
Condliffe, J. B., and W. T. G. Airey. *A Short History of New Zealand.* Whitcomb and Tombs Limited, Christchurch, reprinted 1968.
Duff, Roger (ed.). *No Sort of Iron.* Art Galleries and Museums Association of New Zealand, Christchurch, 1968.
Grey, George. *Ko nga Whakapepeha me nga Whakaahuareka a nga Tupuna.*
Growth and Development of Social Security in New Zealand, The. Social Security Department, Wellington, 1950.
Jackson, Keith, and John Harré. *New Zealand.* Thames and Hudson, London, 1969.
Keam, R. F. *Volcanic Wonderland.* A. H. and A. W. Reed, Wellington, 1965.
Maori Place Names. A. H. and A. W. Reed, Wellington, 1962.
Maori Proverbs. A. H. and A. W. Reed, Wellington, 1963.
Mason, Helen. *10 Years of Pottery in New Zealand.* The New Zealand Potter, Wellington, 1968.
National Parks of New Zealand. R. E. Owen, Government Printer, Wellington, 1965.
Oliver, W. H. *The Story of New Zealand.* Faber & Faber, London, 1968.
Poole, A. L. *Forestry in New Zealand.* Hodder and Stoughton, Auckland, 1969.
———. *New Zealand Forestry.* R. E. Owen, Government Printer, Wellington, 1964.
Powles, Sir Guy. "The W. Clifford Clark Memorial Lectures." Reprinted in *Canadian Public Administration,* June, 1966.
———. *Report of the Ombudsman.* Government Printer, Wellington, 1969.

Royal Commission of Inquiry. *Background Paper*. Social Security Department, Wellington, 1969.

Shadbolt, Maurice. *The Shell Guide to New Zealand*. Whitcomb and Tombs Limited, Christchurch, reprinted 1969.

Sinclair, Keith. *A History of New Zealand*. Penguin, Harmondsworth, England, rev. ed., 1969.

Index

Abbie, Andrew, 72, 73, 74*n*
Aborigines, 3–4, 14, 17, 44, 66–89, 104, 107, 173, 183–84, 208, 222, 225, 228, 231, 238, 241, 246, 307, 315; and alcohol, 72, 80, 81–82, 83–84; art, 75–77, 88, 241; education, 75, 79–80, 84, 86, 87; health, 74, 86; Institute for Aboriginal Studies, 85, 98–99; land, 84, 87, 88; languages, 17, 69, 71, 79, 81, 85, 86; National Tribal Council, 87; origin, theories of, 73–74; racism, 74–75, 80, 83–85, 184, 327; religion, Christian missions, 66, 74, 85; religious beliefs and magic, 67–69, 75, 76, 77, 78, 82, 89; sexual customs, 67, 68–69, 78, 84; song and dance, 77–78, 82
Adachi, Hatazo, 260, 263
Adelaide (Aus.), 31, 63, 187–94 *passim*
African immigrants, 44
Agnew, Spiro, 154*n*, 338
agriculture: Australia, 14, 30, 95, 121, 124, 176, 177, 190, 206, 230; New Guinea, 246, 250, 252, 253, 277; New Zealand, 307, 310, 311, 312, 314, 315, 328; *see also* cattle raising; dairy industry; sheep raising; individual commodities
alcohol: Aborigines, 72, 80, 81–82, 83–84; Australia, 142, 231; New Guinea, 253, 273; New Zealand, 304, 317–18; *see also* beer; wine
Alice Springs (Aus.), 203, 223, 225–29
Allen, Jan, 45
Altman, Dennis, 34
alumina (aluminum oxide), 112, 114–15, 213, 330
Anderson, Judith, 58
animals: Aborigines and totemic relationship, 67, 68, 69, 78; Australia, 1, 4, 8–10, 12, 124, 180–81, 207; New Zealand, 4, 290, 291–92, 293; *see also* individual animals
Antarctica, 7, 286, 287
anteaters, 10, 181, 255
Anthony, Douglas, 101
Antill, John, 59
Anzac Day, 35, 93
Anzacs *see* military forces and defense (Aus. and N. Z.)
Arab immigrants, 48, 49
Arnhem Land, 222–23; Aborigines, 66, 76, 77, 84, 222
art: Aborigines, 75–77, 88, 241; Australia, 53–59; Maori, 306; New Guinea, 245, 253; New Zealand, 4, 331–32
Ashton–Warner, Sylvia, 333
Asian and Pacific Council (ASPAC), 340*n*
Aspden, David, 57
Auckland (N.Z.), 284, 287, 289, 294, 297, 298–300
Australia, name given to, 23
Australia Day, 22, 35
The Australian, 41, 64–65, 123

Australian Alps, 13–14, 143, 150
Australian Capital Territory, 7, 148, 154–55; *see also* Canberra
Australian National University, 153–54
Austrian immigrants, 326
automobile industry, 95, 98, 122, 125, 126, 303, 342
aviation (Aus.), 123–24, 241; Air Force, 344; Royal Flying Doctor Service, 203–04, 228–29
aviation (New Guinea), 261
aviation (N.Z.), 328, 330, 331; Air Force, 336, 344
Ayers Rock (Aus.), 76, 226
Ayres, Mrs. Edna, 193

Baker, Sidney, 39, 48*n*
Ballarat (Aus.), 27, 28, 161, 167, 198
banking and insurance (Aus.), 93, 94, 95, 123, 172, 218
Banks, Joseph, 20
Banning, Walter, 152
Barnes, Charles E., 273
Barry, Sir Redomand, 164
Bass, George, 183
Bathurst (Aus.), 81
Batman, John, 157, 160
Bastyan, Sir Edric, 177
bauxite, 2, 16, 84, 112–17 *passim*, 206, 213, 222, 225, 230, 236, 340
beer, 40–42, 162, 177, 181, 196, 223, 233, 304, 331
Belgian immigrants, 326
Bellamy, Edward, 31, 310
Bendigo (Aus.), 27, 28, 161, 167, 198, 309
betel nuts, 246–47
Bhutan, 340
birds: Aborigines and totemic relationship, 69; Australia, 4, 11–12, 16, 181, 207, 239; New Guinea, 244, 253; New Zealand, 4, 292, 293; *see also* individual birds
Bjelke-Petersen, Johannes, 235
Bjerre, Jens, 247
Black, Niel, 74
Blackwood, Beatrice, 246, 254
Blainey, Geoffrey, 4
Blair, Harold, 88
Blamey, Thomas, 262–63
Blaxland, Gregory, 23
Bligh, William, 25–26, 183
Bluff (N.Z.), 115, 116, 330
Blundell, Sir Denis, 322
Boer War, 35
Bolte, Sir Henry, 171–72
Bonner, Neville, 88–89
Bonython, Kym, 193
boomerangs, 70, 71
Botany Bay (Aus.), 20, 21, 132, 139
Bougainville, 244, 245, 262, 283; mineral resources, 115, 116, 245, 265, 274
Bourke, Richard, 160
Bowditch, Tim, 225
Bowen, John, 183
bowerbirds, 11
Brasília (Brazil), 156
Brisbane, Thomas, 237
Brisbane (Aus.), 63, 231, 232–34, 238
Brisbane *Courier-Mail*, 63, 65, 336–37
Broken Hill (Aus.) and Broken Hill Proprietary Ltd.: mining, 95, 113, 116–17, 143, 162, 197–202, 218, 231
Bromhead, Peter, 332
Browne, Coral, 58
Brunei, 340
Buck, Sir Peter, 315–16, 317
Buckley, William, 160*n*
buffaloes, 16, 222
Bulletin, 45, 63, 65, 83, 104, 162, 339
bull-roarers, 77, 78, 255
Bunker, Ellsworth, 281
Burdick, Eugene, 68, 70, 71, 79
Burke, John O'Hara, 24, 74
Burma, 94, 335
Burns, Thomas James, 234–35
Bury, Leslie, 337
business and industry: Australia, 95, 109, 122–24, 194, 212, 219; Australia, foreign investment in, 1, 2, 98, 104, 107, 113, 114, 116, 117, 122, 123, 125–26, 215, 218, 219, 236, 241, 337, 341, 346; Canadian investment in, 219; German investment in, 122; Great Britain, investment, 2, 116, 123, 125, 126, 218, 336, 341; Japanese investment in, 2, 114, 122, 125, 126, 218, 241, 341, 346; New Zealand, 323, 330–31; New Zealand, foreign investment in, 273, 336, 337; U.S. investment in, 2, 113, 114, 117, 122, 125, 126, 218, 219, 236, 337, 341; *see also* economy; labor; trade
Butler, Constance Lee, 32

Byers, Bernard, 46
Byrne, Joe, 163, 164

Cairns, James Ford, 99, 172–73, 174
Caldwell, Zoë, 58
Calwell, Arthur, 47
camels, 24, 197–98, 217, 226
Cameron, Duncan Alexander, 308
Campbell, Donald, 195
Campbell, John, 236
Canada, 340*n*, 347; business and trade, 219, 275, 330
Canberra (Aus.), 7, 36, 63, 98, 146–56; Academy of Science, 152; Australian National Gallery, 155; Australian National University, 153–54; National Library of Australia, 152, 154; Parliament House, 149, 152
Canberra *Times*, 63, 64, 147
cannibalism: Aborigines, 238; Maori, 306, 308; New Guinea, 246, 261, 264, 272
Carroll, Sir James, 317
Casey, Sir Richard Gardiner, 110
cassowaries, 11, 244, 246
cattle raising: Australia, 83, 121, 177, 205, 222, 230, 240, 336, 337, 340, 342; New Zealand, 293, 303, 310, 329, 330, 337, 342, 349; *see also* dairy industry
censorship, 60, 61–62, 100, 187, 304
ceramics (N.Z.), 332
Ceylon, 339
Chalk, Gordon William, 235
Chan, Harry, 225
characteristics, personal: Australia, 33–39, 132, 207, 209, 211, 233, 234; Maori, 315; New Zealand, 301, 302–05
Charles, Prince, 38, 167, 280
Chifley, Joseph Benedict, 95
China (mainland), 335, 345, 348; and Australia, 2, 106, 108, 121, 174, 339, 347, 348; and New Zealand, 2, 348, 349
China (Taiwan), 340*n*, 348; and Australia, 106, 108, 348
Chinese immigrants, 28, 29, 161, 225, 238, 241, 259, 286, 326, 347
Chipps, Don, 62
Christchurch (N.Z.), 284, 294, 295–96
Christmas Island, 7
Churchill, Winston, 93, 94, 95, 98, 99, 110
Church of England, 66, 294, 296
Cilento, Diane, 58
climate: Australia, 4, 16; New Zealand, 4, 293–94
coal, 112, 113, 115, 117, 143, 206, 230, 236, 340
Cobley, John, 21
Cocos Islands, 7
coffee, 252, 253, 277
Collins, David, 160
Colombo Plan, 339–40
Colonial Sugar Refining Company Ltd., 218, 231
Comalco Ltd., 114, 116, 330
Commonwealth Scientific and Industrial Research Organization (CSIRO), 124–25
Communism (and Communist Party), 339, 345, 348; Australia, 92, 95–99 *passim*, 173, 234; Indonesia, 281, 338; New Zealand, 269; *see also* China (mainland)
convicts, 4, 20–23, 26, 29, 30, 182, 183, 208, 233, 237; heritage, 31–32, 35–36, 176–77, 193
Conzinc Riotinto of Australia Ltd., 114, 116, 199, 201, 265, 274
Cook, James, 19–20, 36, 57, 61, 130, 287
Cook Islands, 287, 327, 342
Coolgardie (Aus.), 30, 208
Combs, H. C., 86–87
copper, 112, 113, 115, 116, 178, 182, 197, 206, 214, 225, 230, 236, 245, 265, 274, 277, 340
copra, 252, 257, 259, 277
cotton, 121, 206, 230, 237
Coulls, Allan, 200
Country Party (Aus.), 92, 94, 95, 97, 100–01, 235
Court, Charles W. M., 212–13
Court, Margaret, 88
cricket, 53
crime rate (Aus.), 350
crocodiles, 10, 16, 252, 253
Cudlipp, Hugh, 64
Curtin, John, 94, 95
Cutler, Sir Arthur Roden, 50, 139–40
Czech immigrants, 48

dairy industry (N.Z.), 310, 314, 327, 329, 330, 331, 336, 342, 349
Dampier, William, 19, 67

dance: Aborigines, 77, 78, 82; Australia, 58–59; New Guinea, 248, 249; New Zealand, 333
Darling River (Aus.), 14, 23
Darwin, Charles, 127, 184, 239, 292, 293, 306
Darwin (Aus.), 36, 223–25, 226, 228
Davis, Jack, 88
Deakin, Alfred, 45
defense *see* military forces and defense
Defoe, Daniel, 31
De L'Isle, William Philip, Viscount, 266
Democratic Labor Party (Aus.), 92, 97, 108, 173
Dervin, R. Donald, 194
desert (Aus.), 3–4, 12, 13, 15, 16, 227
dingoes, 9, 16, 72, 224, 240
Dobell, Sir William, 53, 55–56, 136
Donnellan, Frank, 71
Downie, Ian, 171
Downs, Ian Farley Graham, 270
dress: Australia, 34–35, 134, 209, 223, 234; Maori, 298; New Guinea, 247, 248, 249, 250, 252, 255, 258
drinking *see* alcohol
Drysdale, Russell, 56, 57
dugongs, 10, 72
Dunedin (N.Z.), 294, 295
Dunstan, Don, 62, 186, 187, 195
Dutch East Indies, 19, 182, 288; *see also* Dutch New Guinea; Indonesia; Timor; West Irian
Dutch New Guinea, 260, 262, 280–81, 282; *see also* West Irian
Dutton, Geoffrey, 193–94

eating and food habits: Aborigines, 70–71, 72; Australia, 48–49, 140–41, 158, 167, 192, 223; Maori, 306, 309; New Guinea, 246, 250, 253, 255; New Zealand, 313
economy: Australia, 2, 31, 43–44, 49, 94, 95, 98, 104, 123, 125, 126, 349; Colombo Plan for economic aid, 339–40; New Zealand, 327–31, 349; *see also* business and industry; trade
education: Aborigines, 75, 79–80, 84, 86, 87; Australia, 95, 98, 104, 107, 169–70, 173, 176, 340, 347; Maori, 318; New Guinea, 250, 265, 266, 268, 269, 271–72, 273–74, 276–77; New Zealand, 295, 312, 340, 347
Egerton, John Alfred Roy, 230, 234
Egypt, 121
Elizabeth II, Queen, 37–38, 100, 227, 321
Elkin, A. P., 67
eucalyptus, 4, 10, 12, 121, 143, 180
Eri, Vincent, 262*n*
Eureka (Aus.), 28, 29
European Economic Community (and trade), 329–30, 336, 346, 347
Evatt, Herbert Vere, 96–97, 110
exploration, early, 18–20, 23–24, 182–83, 260
Eyre, Edward John, 24

Fadden, Arthur, 100
Fairburn, A. R. D., 290, 332
Fairfax, John, 62, 63
Fairfax, Sir Vincent, 62, 63
Fairfax, Sir Warwick, 62, 63
Fawkner, John Pasco, 160
Fiji, 42–43, 338, 342
Finch, Peter, 58
fish and seafood: Australia, 141, 178, 181, 238–39; New Guinea, 244, 255; New Zealand, 292–93, 333, 342
Fisher, Andrew, 93
Fitzgerald, T. M., 107
Flinders, Matthew, 23, 183
Flynn, Errol, 185
Foley, Mick, 250, 251*n*
Foot, Sir Hugh (Lord Caradon), 265, 272*n*
football, 51–52; *see also* rugby
forestry and related industries: Australia, 4, 13, 121, 151, 177, 178, 180, 196, 230, 241, 277; New Guinea, 244, 253, 254; New Zealand, 290–91, 330, 342
Forrest, Sir John, 208
Frame, Janet, 333
France, 21*n*, 326, 342
Fraser, Malcolm, 105
Fraser, Peter, 311
Frazer, Sir James, 67
Fremantle, Charles H., 208
French, Leonard, 57, 152, 169
Freud, Clement, 301
Freyberg, Bernard, 311
Fulbright, J. William, 338
Furneaux, Tobias, 183

Gair, Vincent, 235
George, Henry, 31, 310

geography: Australia, 6–7, 13–16; New Guinea, 243–44; New Zealand, 284–90 *passim; see also* desert; mountains; outback; volcanoes and earthquakes
Germany: German immigrants, 28, 47, 225, 326; investment in business and industry, 122; New Guinea, colonization, 245, 259, 260–61
Gladstone, Herbert John, 261
Gladstone (Aus.): mining, 114, 115, 116, 236
Godley, John Robert, 296
gold: Australia, 23, 24, 25, 27–28, 30, 113, 115, 116, 161, 178, 190, 206, 208 214, 225, 236, 238; New Guinea, 245, 260, 261, 277; New Zealand, 286, 309
Goolagong, Evonne, 88
Gorton, John Grey, 65, 102–05, 106, 122, 270, 274, 344
Gorton, Mrs. John Grey, 103
Gove (Aus.): mining, 80, 115, 222, 225
government: Australia, 5, 29–30, 31, 90–111; New Guinea, 265, 266–67, 268, 270–71, 273, 275, 276, 278; New Zealand, 5, 297, 302, 307–14 *passim*, 317, 321–25 *passim*, 331; *see also* individual political parties
Goyder, George, 190
grain, 121, 167, 177, 187, 190, 206, 230, 307, 309, 329, 336, 340
Grainger, Percy, 59
Great Australian Bight, 15
Great Barrier Reef, 230, 238–40
Great Britain, 340*n*, 348; ANZUK, 343; Boer War, 35; and New Guinea, 260–61; and Malaya (Malaysia), 343; newspapers, 62, 64; and Singapore, 94, 335, 338, 343, 345; South Pacific Commission, 342
Great Britain and Australia, 29, 35, 36, 37–38, 336, 345; British influence, 37, 38, 40, 60, 91; discovery and colonization, 4, 19–23, 25–26, 27, 29–30, 182, 183, 208, 233, 237; immigration, 22–23, 27, 28, 30, 47, 48, 50, 96, 188, 189, 193, 208, 220, 294–95, 337; investment in business and industry, 2, 116, 123, 125, 126, 218, 336, 341; land, ownership of, 88, 161; trade, 1, 27, 121, 177, 336, 346, 347; *see also* convicts
Great Britain and New Zealand, 294, 295, 302, 307–09, 336, 345; immigration, 326, 337; investment in business and industry, 336; land, ownership of, 328–29; trade, 2, 310, 311, 314, 323, 329–30, 336, 347, 349
Great Dividing Range, 13, 143
Greek immigrants, 48, 200, 203, 209, 210, 225, 326
Greenway, Francis, 26, 130
Greenway, John, 70, 71, 83*n*
Greer, Germaine, 42
Grey, George, 190, 307–08, 309
Griffin, Walter Burley, 148–52 *passim*, 155
Guam, 282, 345
Guise, John, 267–68, 271, 273, 278, 283
Gumpilil, David, 58
Gunther, John T., 271–72, 276

Hagen, Count von, 249
Hall, Peter, 137
Hall, Raymond Steele, 186–87
Hamersley Range (Aus.), 15; mining, 113, 114, 116, 214, 218, 220
Hamilton, Jim, 79
Hancock, George, 214
Hancock, Sir Keith, 92, 156
Hancock, Langley George, 214–15, 218
Hannet, Leo, 273
Hargraves, Edward, 28
Harris, Max, 193
Hart, Steve, 163, 164
Hartog, Dirk, 208
Hasluck, Sir Paul M. C., 75, 102, 103, 108, 110–11
Hawke, Robert James Lee, 109
health: Aborigines, 74, 86; Royal Flying Doctor Service, 203–04, 228–29; Maori, 314–15, 316; *see also* social welfare
Heanley, Robert, 346
Heaphy, Charles, 332
Hedland, Peter, 219
Helpmann, Sir Robert, 58–59
Henderson, John, 167
Henley, Wilton, 312
Hervey, Kirk, 175
Hesling, Bernard, 48
Hiatt, Ron, 250
Higgins, Henry Bourne, 93
Hilditch, A. S., 218
Hillary, Sir Edmund, 285, 331
Hindmarsh, Joseph, 189

Hobart (Aus.), 176, 177, 178–80, 184
Hobart *Mercury*, 63, 176
Hodgkins, Frances, 331
Holt, Harold E., 33, 99–100, 101–02, 104, 337
Holyoake, Sir Keith, 284, 313–14, 320–24 *passim*, 326, 342, 343
Hoover, Herbert, 204
Hope, A. D., 61
Horne, Donald, 34, 51, 65, 146, 156
Horne, R. H., 157–58
horse racing, 52–53, 220, 304, 333
Howitt, A. W., 69
Howson, Peter, 85*n*
Hudson, Sir William, 144
Hughes, William Morris, 93–94, 261, 336
Humphries, Barry, 157
Hungarian immigrants, 48, 326
Hutchinson, Max, 57
Huxley, Elspeth, 11, 78, 153
hydroelectric power (Aus.), 13, 95, 143–45, 178

Icelandic immigrants, 48, 220
immigration: Australia, 12, 20–21, 22–23, 27, 28, 29, 30, 44–50, 52, 94, 95, 96, 98, 101, 102, 107, 123, 125, 140, 142, 161, 172, 173, 174, 188, 189, 193, 200, 203, 208, 209, 210, 220, 225, 237, 238, 241, 326, 337, 339, 341, 342, 347; New Zealand, 288, 294–95, 301, 326–27, 337, 341, 342; *see also* racism
India, 335, 339, 340; Indian immigrants, 174, 326, 347; trade, 121
Indochina, 335, 337–38; *see also* Vietnam war
Indonesia, 8, 174, 280–81, 282, 338, 339, 340*n*, 347; Communism, 281, 338; trade, 121, 330; *see also* Dutch East Indies; Dutch New Guinea; West Irian
Iran, 121
Iraq, 121
Irish immigrants, 28, 96, 193, 208, 295
iron and steel, 2, 112, 113–14, 116–17, 122, 178, 197, 199, 206, 214–19 *passim*, 220–21, 225, 330, 331, 240–41, 342
Italy, 114; Italian immigrants, 1, 47, 48, 52, 200, 209, 210, 220, 225, 237, 326

Japan, 340*n*; Japanese immigrants, 49, 174, 241, 339, 341, 347; and U.S., 113, 341, 345, 346; *see also* World War II
Japan and Australia: 174, 339, 345, 347; investment in business and industry, 2, 114, 122, 125, 126, 218, 241, 341, 346; trade, 1, 2, 39, 113, 114, 115, 121, 177, 178, 195, 221, 236, 335, 340–41, 346–47
Japan and New Zealand, 345, 347; trade, 2, 330, 340, 341
Jeanne Marie, Sister, 88
Jensen, Harry F., 136
Johnson, Leslie W., 270–71, 275, 276
Johnson, Lyndon B., 101, 102, 151*n*, 256, 337
Johnson, Roger, 155
Jones, Clem, 235–36

Kaberry, Phyllis M., 68
Kalgoorlie (Aus.): mining, 30, 113, 115, 117, 204, 208
Kambalda (Aus.): mining, 113, 115, 207
Kanakas, 231, 237
kangaroos, 1, 4, 9–10, 16, 69–70, 224, 240
Kaputin, John, 269
Kawharu, I. H., 317, 319
Keeling Islands, 7
Keenan, Joseph B., 199–200, 201
Kelly, Dan, 163, 164
Kelly, Ned, 58, 162–64
Keneally, Thomas, 61
Kidman, Sidney, 191, 193, 198
Kiki, Albert Maori, 270
Kimberley Mountains (Aus.), 15
King, Philip Parker, 71
Kirk, Norman, 322–23
Kitts, Sir Francis, 298
Kiwis, 4, 292, 293
koalas, 9, 10, 168
Koman, Rudy, 57
Korea, 345
Korean War, 89
Kukukukus, 254–55, 260

labor (Aus.), 43, 50, 94, 122–23, 125, 349; Aborigines, 79, 80, 83; Arbitration Commission, 104, 108, 109, 122; convicts, 22, 23, 233; indentured labor, 225, 231, 237; strikes, 31, 95, 161, 199; unemployment, 94, 98, 123;

labor (*cont'd*)
wages, 50, 93, 122, 123; *see also* immigration
labor (New Guinea), 261, 276
labor (N.Z.), 310, 313, 314, 315, 326
Labor Party: Australia, 43, 80, 91, 92–97, 98, 100, 102, 106, 107–09, 111, 173, 234, 344, 347; New Zealand, 311, 317, 321, 323, 333
labor unions: Australia, 30–31, 93, 95, 96, 109, 122, 161, 173, 199–200, 217, 234, 261; New Zealand, 269, 314
Lachlan River (Aus.), 26, 143
Lae (New Guinea), 245, 259–60, 261, 262, 281
Lake Eyre (Aus.), 14, 195
land: Aborigines, 84, 87, 88; Australia, 27, 29, 30, 84, 87, 88, 121, 125, 161, 212, 213, 240; Great Britain, ownership, 88, 161, 328–29; New Guinea, 247, 250–51, 269, 271, 276; New Zealand, 294–95, 307, 308, 309, 310, 318, 328–29, 334; U.S., ownership, 88, 125, 212; *see also* agriculture
Lane, William, 31
Lang, John Thomas, 94, 131
languages, 36, 39–40; Aborigines, 17, 69, 71, 79, 81, 85, 86; Maori, 288, 315, 319; New Guinea, 245, 247, 251, 253, 278–80
La Pérouse, Count Jean-François de, 21*n*
La Trobe, Charles Joseph, 160, 161, 165
Lauder, Afferbeck (Alistair Morrison), 40
Launceston (Aus.), 179, 181
Lawler, Ray, 58
Lawson, Henry, 90
lead, 112, 113, 116, 117, 178, 197, 198, 199, 214, 230, 236
League of Nations, 261, 263, 336
Leahy, Danny, 249
Leahy, Mick, 249
leisure and recreation, 33–34, 37, 192; *see also* sports
Lett, Barry, 332
Lever, Rod, 225
Lewis, Essington, 95, 116
Liberal Party: Australia, 43, 92, 94, 95, 97–107, 109, 235; New Zealand, 309, 310, 311, 321
Liebelt, J. L., 201–02
Light, William, 188–89, 191–92, 194
Lippmann, Walter, 336
literature, 60–61, 333; *see also* censorship
Lutherans, 74, 190
lyrebirds, 11

MacArthur, Douglas, 94–95, 162, 232–33, 260, 280
Macarthur, John, 25, 26
McCahon, Colin, 332
McCarthy, Frederick D., 85
McCulloch, James, 197
Macdonnell Ranges (Aus.), 15, 228
McEwen, John, 101, 102–03
McGregor, Craig, 132, 145
McGuinness, Bruce, 87
McIlwraith, Sir Thomas, 260–61
MacInnes, Colin, 152, 156, 303
MacIntyre, Duncan, 314
McKern, Leo, 58
McMahon, William, 85*n*, 102–03, 105–07, 108, 147, 151, 340, 347–48
Macquarie, Lachlan, 22–23, 26
Malaysia, 225, 338, 340*n*, 343, 345
Maltese immigrants, 200, 225, 237
manganese, 116, 206, 214, 225, 230
Mannix, Archbishop Daniel, 94
Mansfield, Sir Alan, 231–32
Mansfield, Katherine, 298, 331, 333
Manton, Ivor, 252
Manus, 244, 245, 262, 283
Maoris, 4, 288, 289, 293, 296, 297, 298–99, 301, 305–09, 314–19, 325, 327; appearance and dress, 298; art, 306; cannibalism, 306, 308; education, 318; health, 314–15, 316; languages, 288, 315, 319; religious beliefs, 306, 308, 315, 319
Marsh, Ngaio, 296, 333
Marshall, John, 313, 314, 321, 322, 327
Mason, Helen, 331, 332
Matheson, J. A. L., 171
Maurice, R. T., 13
Mawby, Sir Maurice, 116, 201, 202, 203
Maza, Bob, 87
Mead, Margaret, 260, 262
Meadmore, Clement, 57
Meale, Richard, 59
Mehta, Zubin, 304–05
Melanesia, 342
Melba, Nellie, 59, 137, 149, 165
Melbourne (Aus.), 3, 8, 28, 31, 52, 140, 157–66, 187, 350; Monash University, 170, 171; National Art Gallery, 54,

57, 77, 168; Newspapers, 54, 63, 64; Performing Arts Center, 168–69; Royal Botanic Gardens, 165–66; University of Melbourne, 170–71
Melville Island, 79, 81–82
Menzies, Sir Douglas, 171
Menzies, Sir Robert Gordon, 35*n*, 95–101 *passim*, 103–04, 107, 110, 150, 171, 282
Methodists, 66
military forces and defense (Australia), 152, 344; Aborigines in, 89; Air Force, 344; Anzac Agreement, 343; ANZUK, 343, 345; ANZUS treaty, 337, 348; Korean War, 89; Navy, 336, 344; SEATO, 340*n*, 348; U.S., agreements and forces, 205, 229, 337, 340*n*, 343, 344, 345, 348; Vietnam war, 100, 101, 107, 108, 152, 337, 345; World War I, 35, 93–94, 261; World War II, 35, 89, 94, 95, 174, 243, 259, 262–63, 335
military forces and defense (N.Z.), 312, 336, 344–45; Anzac Agreement, 343; ANZUK, 343, 345; ANZUS treaty, 337, 348; SEATO, 340*n*, 348; U.S., agreements and forces, 337, 340*n*, 343, 345, 348; Vietnam war, 324, 337, 345; World War I, 35, 93; World War II, 311, 335
Miller, Rev. Bernard, 256
Miller, J. D. B., 335
mineral resources and mining: Australia, 1, 2, 3, 30, 95, 96, 104, 112–18, 125–26, 178, 197–202, 204–08 *passim*, 213–21 *passim*, 225, 230, 236, 336, 340–41; New Guinea, 115, 116, 245, 260, 261, 265, 274, 277; New Zealand, 115, 286, 309, 330, 331; *see also* individual minerals
Mitchell, Rona, 193
moas, 292, 293, 305
Mollison, James, 55, 56, 155
monarchy, attitude toward, 37–38, 100, 193–94
Monash, Sir John, 170
Monash University, 170, 171
Moorehead, Alan, 11, 51, 61, 164
Moran, Francis Patrick Cardinal, 96
Moresby, John, 260
Mormons, 315*n*
Morris, James, 349
Morrison, Alistair, 40
mountains: Australia, 13–14, 15, 143, 150; New Guinea, 243; New Zealand, 284, 285
Mount Cook (N.Z.), 284, 285
Mount Gambier (Aus.), 195
Mount Hagen (New Guinea), 248–52
Mount Isa (Aus.): mining, 113, 230, 236
Mount Kosciusko (Aus.), 13, 24, 145
Mount Lyell (Aus.): mining, 178, 182
Mount Morgan (Aus.): mining, 113, 236
Mount Newman (Aus.): mining, 113, 114, 117, 217–21 *passim*
Mount Tom Price (Aus.): mining, 113, 114, 214, 218, 220
Mount Whaleback (Aus.), 217, 218
movies, 58
Muldoon, Robert, 331
Mulvaney, D. J., 74
Murdock, Sir Keith, 62, 63, 64
Murdock, Rupert, 63–64
Murray, Sir Hubert, 260, 261
Murray River and Valley (Aus.), 4, 14, 23, 24, 143, 144, 160, 166–67, 188, 196
Murrumbidgee River (Aus.), 14, 23, 143
Musgrave Ranges (Aus.), 15
music: Aborigines, 77–78, 82; Australia, 59–60; New Guinea, 248, 249, 251, 255; New Zealand, 333

Namatjira, Albert, 88
Nash, Walter, 311, 321
Natachee, A. P. Allan, 264
Nationalist Party (Aus.), 94
National Party (N.Z.), 302, 312, 321, 323, 324
Nauru, 338, 342
Nepal, 340
Netherlands: Dutch immigration, 210, 326; *see also* Dutch East Indies; Dutch New Guinea; Indonesia
New Britain, 94, 244, 245, 258–59, 261, 266, 269–70, 274, 283
New Guinea, 7, 243–83; alcohol, 253, 273; appearance and dress, 247, 248, 249, 250, 252, 255, 258; art, 245, 253; birds, 244, 253; cannibalism, 246, 261, 264, 272; cults, 255–58; education, 250, 265, 266, 268, 269, 271–72, 273–74, 276–77; emigration restrictions and racism, 46, 261, 275–76, 282, 327; government, 265, 266–67, 268, 270–

New Guinea (*cont'd*)
71, 273, 275, 276, 278; and independence (Niugini), 263–79, 282–83, 338; land, 247, 250–51, 269, 271, 276; languages, 245, 247, 251, 253, 278–80; mineral resources and mining, 115, 116, 245, 260, 261, 265, 274, 277; people, 245, 246–49, 272*n*; religion, Christian missions, 250, 256, 257, 259, 261, 267, 268, 276, 279; religious beliefs and magic, 245, 246, 251–57 *passim*; sexual customs, 247, 251, 253, 257; song and dance, 248, 249, 251, 255; World War I, 261; World War II, 94, 95, 243, 245, 256, 259, 260; *see also* West Irian
New Hanover, 256
New Hebrides, 237
New Holland, 19, 23, 208
New Ireland, 244, 245, 282
New South Wales (Aus.), 7, 9, 20, 28, 29, 44, 116, 127, 133, 140, 143–45, 148, 183, 208, 222, 236–37, 342; Aborigines, 66, 83; convicts, 22, 23, 25, 26, 237; *see also* Sydney
newspapers: Australia, 37, 48, 62–65; New Zealand, 303, 333
New Zealand, 1–5, 284–334, 335–50 *passim*
New Zealand and Australia, 303, 342–43, 349; military forces and agreements, 35, 93, 337, 338–39, 340*n*, 343, 345, 348; trade, 330, 331, 342
nickel, 2, 112, 115, 117, 178, 206, 207, 340
Niue Island, 287, 342
Niugini, 267, 338; *see also* New Guinea, and independence
Nixon, Richard M., 337–38, 343, 348
Noble, Rev. Ames, 88
Nolan, Sidney, 53, 54–55
Norfolk Island, 7
Northern Territory (Aus.), 7, 30, 66, 115, 191, 222–29; Aborigines, 86, 222, 225, 228
Norton, John, 38*n*
Nullarbor Plain (Aus.), 15

Oala-Rarua, Oala, 268–69
Oberon, Merle, 185
oil *see* petroleum
Olah, Luka, 195
Oliphant, Sir Mark, 193
Olsen, John, 57
O'Malley, King, 58, 146, 148
O'Neill, Patrick Eugene, 199
opals, 116, 195
outback (Aus.), 15, 36, 38, 166, 195, 210, 231

Packer, Sir Frank, 62, 63
painting: Aborigines, 75, 76–77, 88, 241; Australia, 53–57; New Guinea, 253; New Zealand, 4, 332
Pakistan, 335, 339, 340; Pakistani immigration, 347
Papua, 244–45, 260, 261, 266*n*, 271, 274, 275, 276, 281; *see also* New Guinea
Paspalis, Michael, 225
Patton, William H., 198
Paul VI, Pope, 35, 57
Pearl, Cyril, 41, 49*n*, 62
pearls and mother of pearl, 205, 225, 241; shells as curency, 248, 249, 251
penguins, 167–68
Perth (Aus.), 4, 15, 17, 209–11; newspapers, 63, 206
Peters, Lance, 58
petroleum, 117–18, 125–26, 168, 206, 230, 240, 274, 330, 342
Petrov, Vladimir, 96
Philippines, 339, 340*n*; Filipino immigrants, 174, 225, 347; trade, 121
Phillip, Arthur, 21–22, 74
Phillip Island, 167–68
phosphate, 116, 230, 236, 328, 338
pigs, 248–49, 250, 251, 263
Pilbara (Aus.): mining, 113, 114, 117, 214, 216–19
plants: Australia, 4, 8, 12–13, 204, 207, 241; New Guinea, 254; New Zealand, 4, 290–91
platypuses, 1, 10, 72
Playford, Sir Thomas, 191, 194
police, 28, 36, 159
Polish immigrants, 1, 48
Polynesia, 305, 342
population: Australia, 8, 28, 36; New Zealand, 2, 287, 315, 326
Porrit, Sir Arthur Espie, 304, 312, 313, 322
Port Arthur (Aus.), 180, 182, 183
Porter, Hal, 61
Port Hedlund (Aus.), 219–21

Port Moresby (New Guinea), 245, 250, 258, 260, 262
Portugal, 260
potatoes, 177, 246, 250, 255, 306, 309
Potter, Sir Ian, 172
Powles, Sir Guy, 325–26
press *see* newspapers
Price, Grenfell, 283
Pringle, John, 145, 159
Prior, Bill, 229
Pugh, Clifton, 57
Pyatt, Bishop W. A., 301, 302, 314

Queensland (Aus.), 7, 29, 230–42, 260–61; Aborigines, 66, 79–80, 231, 238, 241; convicts, 23, 25, 233, 237; mineral resources and mining, 113, 115, 116, 117, 230, 236; *see also* Brisbane
Queenstown (N.Z.), 285–86

Rabaul (New Guinea), 245, 258–59, 262
rabbits, 124, 293
racism: Aborigines, 74–75, 80, 83–85, 184, 327; Australia (White Australia policy), 29, 32, 34, 35, 44–47, 49–50, 98, 101, 173, 174, 208–09, 231, 327, 341, 342, 347, 348; Maori, 316, 317, 318; New Guinea, 46, 261, 275–76, 282, 327; New Zealand, 316, 317, 318, 327, 342
Radcliffe–Brown, A. R., 66
radio and television: Australia, 37, 43, 59–60, 63, 64, 123, 339; New Zealand, 331, 333
Rasp, Charles, 198
Reibey, Mary, 181–82
religion: Aborigines, 67–69, 75, 76, 77, 78, 82, 89; Aborigines, Christian missions, 66, 74, 85; Maori, 306, 308, 315, 319; New Guinea, 245, 246, 251–57 *passim*; New Guinea, Christian missions, 250, 256, 257, 259, 261, 267, 268, 276, 279; *see also* individual denominations
Rice, Walter, 153
Ridley, John, 190
Roberts, S. H., 27
Roberts, Tom, 54
Rodgers, Ian, 82
Roman Catholics, 66, 94, 96, 97, 185, 256, 257, 259
Roosevelt, Theodore, 293*n*
Rose, Lionel, 88
rugby, 51–52, 333
Ruhen, Olaf, 282
Russell, William, 47
Rutherford, Ernest, 331

Saarinen, Eero, 136–37
sailing, 62, 130, 131, 299
St. Denis, Ruth, 82
Saito, Shizuo, 341
Samoa, Western, 327, 338
Santamaria, B. A., 96, 97, 173–74, 185
Sawer, Geoffrey, 340
Scandinavian immigrants, 48
Scott, Ernest, 26
Scott, R. F., 296*n*
Scotter, Sheila, 37, 42
Scottish immigration, 28, 208, 294–95
sculpture and carving: Aborigines, 77, 82; Maori, 306; New Guinea, 245, 253
Sculthorpe, Peter, 59
SEATO, 340*n*, 348
Seddon, Richard John, 309–10, 320
Senbergs, Jan, 57
Sepik River and area (New Guinea), 244, 245, 252–53
Seventh-Day Adventists, 250
sexual customs, 42; Aborigines, 67, 68–69, 78, 84; New Guinea, 247, 251, 253, 257
Sharpe, Patrick, 57
Shaw, A. G. L., 21, 30, 44
Shaw, George Bernard, 289, 290
Shawn, Ted, 82
sheep raising: Australia, 1, 14, 24, 25, 27, 112, 119–21, 124, 126, 166, 167, 177, 187, 206, 230, 234, 336, 340, 342; New Zealand, 287, 293, 295, 300, 301, 303, 309, 310, 327–29, 330, 336, 337, 342, 349; shearers, 30, 119, 234
silver, 113, 178, 197, 198, 199, 230, 236
Simpson, George Gaylord, 8–9
Sinclair, Keith, 295
Singapore, 94, 335, 338–39, 340*n*, 343, 345
Skellerup, P. J., 304
skiing, 13, 285
Smith, Maria Ann, 177*n*
snakes and reptiles, 10–11, 181, 255, 291, 292
Snowy Mountains Scheme (Aus.), 13, 95, 143–45
soccer, 52

social welfare: Australia, 43, 75, 93, 98, 104, 107; New Zealand, 297, 302, 309, 311, 312–14, 331
Solomon Islands, 237, 264; *see also* Bougainville
Somare, Michael, 270
South American immigrants, 48
South Australia, 7, 25, 30, 186–91 *passim*, 194–202, 222; mineral resources and mining, 197–202; *see also* Adelaide
South Pacific Commission, 342
Spanish immigrants, 48
Spice Islands, 260
spiders, 11
sports, 34, 36, 51–53, 211, 303, 333; *see also* individual sports
steel industry *see* iron and steel
stock market (Aus.), 113, 118, 172, 206–07
Streeton, Arthur, 54
Sturt, Charles, 23–24, 188, 190, 197
Sturt, John McDouall, 24, 191
sugar, 230, 231, 237–38, 336
suicide rate (Aus.), 42
Sukarno, 280, 281, 338
Sunday Australian, 44, 107–08
surfing, 53, 132, 299
Sutherland, Joan, 59, 137
Swift, Jonathan, 19
swimming, 132–33
Swiss immigrants, 326
Sydney (Aus.), 3, 8, 16, 21–22, 25, 26, 28, 83, 127, 130–42, 145, 157, 158, 162, 164, 350; Art Gallery of New South Wales, 57, 139; Botany Bay, 20, 21, 132, 139; Government House, 139, 140; harbor and bridge, 21, 130–31; newspapers, 63, 64, 100; Opera House, 136–37, 168; University of Sydney, 27, 139

Tammur, Oscar, 269–70
Tasman, Abel, 19, 182, 288
Tasmania (Aus.), 3, 7, 16, 19, 23, 25, 29, 30, 115, 175–85; Aborigines, 73, 74, 183–84, 231, 307; convicts, 23, 176–77, 182, 183
Tasmanian devil, 180–81
Tasmanian wolf, 181
taxation: Australia, 91, 95, 101, 118, 125, 140, 191; New Zealand, 312, 313, 314, 334
tea, 252, 277
television *see* radio and television
tennis, 53
Teosin, John, 257–58
Te Rauparaha, 306–07
Terrill, Ross, 35
Thailand, 340*n*
theater, 58, 333
Tiabe, Handabe, 270
Timor, 94, 223
Tirikatene–Sullivan, Mrs., 317, 318
titanium, 112, 116, 206, 330
Tiwis, 77, 81–82
Todd, Sir Charles, 228
Tokelau Island, 287, 342
Torres, Luis Vaez de, 19
Townsville (Aus.), 237–38
trade: Australia, 1, 2, 27, 31, 39, 71, 93, 113, 114, 115, 121, 177, 178, 195, 199, 221, 236, 275, 335, 336, 337, 340–41, 342, 346–47; European Economic Community, 329–30, 336, 346, 347; Japan and U.S., 113, 341, 346; New Zealand, 2, 310, 311, 314, 323, 329–30, 331, 336, 337, 340, 341, 342, 346, 347, 349
transportation and travel (Aus.), 37, 42–43, 123–24; railroads, 15, 37, 123, 168, 175, 204, 219, 226; roads, 16, 37, 44, 167, 204, 240–41; shipping, 123; *see also* aviation
transportation and travel (N.Z.), 330, 335; *see also* aviation
trees *see* forestry and related industries
Trollope, Anthony, 161
Tucker, Albert, 56
Turkish immigrants, 48, 49, 209
Turnbull, Clive, 35–36
Twain, Mark, 1

Union of Soviet Socialist Republics, 7, 121, 174, 233, 344, 349
United Australia Party, 94
United Nations: China, seating of, 347–48; ECAFE, 340*n*; New Guinea as Trust Territory, 243, 245, 263, 265, 266, 271, 272*n*, 274, 275, 276, 282
United States, 20, 28, 30, 334, 340*n*, 348; and Antarctica, 7, 286, 287; and Guam, 282, 345; immigration to, 45*n*, 347; and Japan, 113, 341, 345, 346; and Korea, 345; SEATO, 340*n*, 348; South Pacific Commission, 342; Ter-

United States (*cont'd*)
ritory of the Pacific Islands, 265*n*, 282, 345; Vietnam war and Indochina, 100, 335, 337–38, 343; World War II, 94–95, 152, 162, 232–33, 245, 259, 262–63, 311, 335, 336
United States and Australia, 38, 101–02, 104, 152, 174, 335–36, 336–37, 338; American influence, 37, 38, 60, 91, 170–71; defense forces and treaties, 205, 229, 337, 340*n*, 343, 344, 345, 348; immigration, 1, 3, 28, 48, 49, 50, 161, 347; investment in business and industry, 2, 113, 114, 117, 122, 125, 126, 218, 219, 236, 341; land, ownership of, 88, 125, 212; trade, 121, 177, 199, 337, 341
United States and New Zealand, 336, 337, 338; defense forces and treaties, 337, 340*n*, 343, 345, 348; immigration, 288, 326; investment in business and industry, 337; trade, 330, 337
University of Melbourne, 170–71
University of Papua and New Guinea, 271–72
University of Perth, 210
University of Sydney, 27, 139
University of Tasmania, 176
uranium, 115, 225, 236
Utzon, Jørn, 137, 168

Van Diemen's Land, 23, 183; *see also* Tasmania
Victoria, Queen, 237
Victoria (Aus.), 7, 25, 28, 29–30, 44, 161, 162, 166–68, 171, 183, 198; *see also* Melbourne
Vietnam war, 100, 101, 107, 108, 152, 172, 324, 335, 337–38, 343, 345
volcanoes and earthquakes (N.Z.), 288, 289–90
voting and suffrage: Australia, 29, 30, 80, 92, 97*n*; New Guinea, 266; New Zealand, 310, 322

Wakefield, Edward Gibbon, 25, 187–88, 189, 294, 296, 297
Walker, Kath, 66, 88
wallabies, 1, 10, 244, 255
Ward, Russell, 31
Wardle, Sir Thomas, 213–14
water resources, 3–4, 13, 14, 16–17, 27, 95, 121, 143–45, 178, 210, 219, 240; hydroelectric power, 13, 95, 143–45, 178
Weipa (Aus.): mining, 113, 114–15, 116, 236
Wellington (N.Z.), 2, 284, 287, 294, 296–98
Welsh immigrants, 28, 208
Wentworth, W. C., 85–86
Wentworth, William Charles, 26, 28
West, John, 183
Westerman, Sir Alan, 126
Western Australia, 7, 25, 30, 125, 203–21; Aborigines, 66, 85, 208; mineral resources and mining, 30, 113, 114, 115, 116, 204–08 *passim*, 214–21 *passim; see also* Perth
West Irian, 243, 260, 278, 280–81, 283, 338; *see also* Dutch New Guinea
Wewak (New Guinea), 253, 259, 262
White, Harold L., 154
White, Patrick, 58, 61, 62
White Australia policy *see* racism
Whiteley, Brett, 57
Whitlam, Edward Gough, 108–09, 274
Whitmore, R. L., 125
Williams, Frederick, 55, 56
Williams, John, 62, 63
Wills, W. J., 24, 74
Wilson, Harold, 98
Wilson, Tom, 112
wine, 187, 190, 196–97, 211, 331
Withnell, Emma, 214
Withnell, Jimmy, 214
women, 38, 42, 123, 211; Aborigines, 67, 68, 69, 71, 72, 76, 78, 83, 84, 86–87; magazines 37, 42, 63; New Guinea, 247, 251, 252, 255, 262
wool *see* sheep raising
Woomera rocket range (Aus.), 85, 195
World War I, 35, 93–94, 261
World War II, 35, 89, 94–95, 152, 162, 174, 232–33, 243, 245, 256, 259, 260, 262–63, 311, 335, 336

Young, Archbishop Guilford, 185
Yugoslav immigrants, 1, 48, 52, 200, 209, 210, 220, 326
Yule, Charles, 260

zinc, 112, 113, 116, 178, 197, 198, 199, 230, 236

72 73 74 75 10 9 8 7 6 5 4 3 2 1

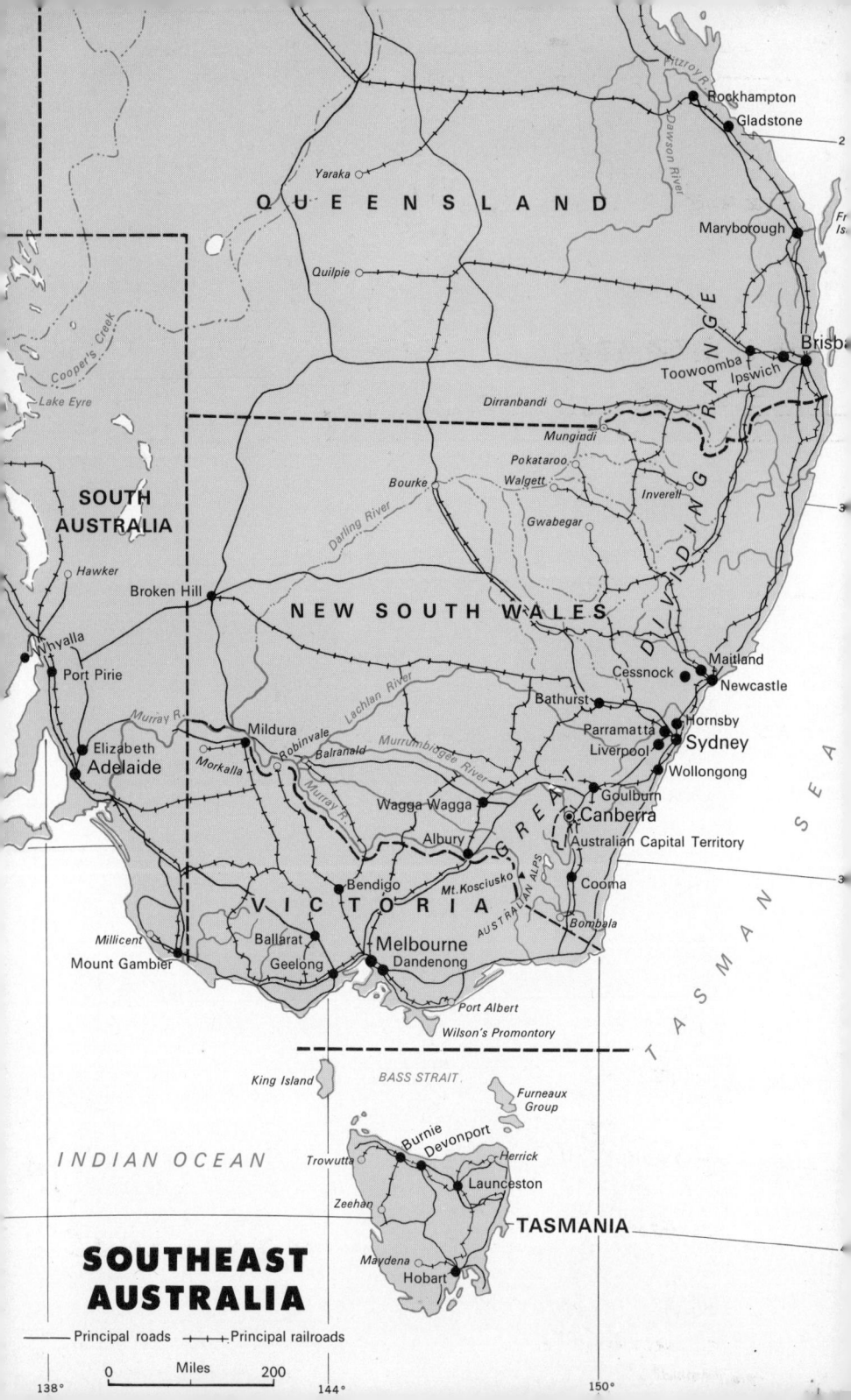
SOUTHEAST AUSTRALIA
QUEENSLAND
NEW SOUTH WALES
VICTORIA
SOUTH AUSTRALIA
TASMANIA
Rockhampton
Gladstone
Maryborough
Brisb
Toowoomba
Ipswich
Yaraka
Quilpie
Dirranbandi
Mungindi
Pokataroo
Walgett
Bourke
Inverell
Gwabegar
Darling River
Cooper's Creek
Lake Eyre
Hawker
Broken Hill
Whyalla
Port Pirie
Elizabeth
Adelaide
Mildura
Morkalla
Robinvale
Balranald
Murray R.
Lachlan River
Murrumbidgee River
Cessnock
Maitland
Newcastle
Bathurst
Parramatta
Hornsby
Liverpool
Sydney
Wollongong
Goulburn
Canberra
Australian Capital Territory
Wagga Wagga
Albury
Cooma
Bombala
Mt. Kosciusko
AUSTRALIAN ALPS
GREAT DIVIDING RANGE
Bendigo
Ballarat
Geelong
Melbourne
Dandenong
Millicent
Mount Gambier
Port Albert
Wilson's Promontory
TASMAN SEA
King Island
BASS STRAIT
Furneaux Group
INDIAN OCEAN
Burnie
Devonport
Trowutta
Herrick
Launceston
Zeehan
Maydena
Hobart
Principal roads
Principal railroads
0 Miles 200
138°
144°
150°